The
Unresolvable
Plot

The Unresolvable Plot

Reading
contemporary fiction

ELIZABETH DIPPLE

Routledge
New York and London

First published in 1988 by
Routledge, Chapman & Hall, Inc.
29 West 35th Street, New York NY 10001

Published in Great Britain by
Routledge
11 New Fetter Lane, London EC4P 4EE

© 1988 Elizabeth Dipple

Typeset by AKM Associates (UK) Ltd
Printed in Great Britain by
Richard Clay Ltd, Suffolk

Library of Congress Cataloging in Publication Data
Dipple, Elizabeth
The unresolvable plot: reading contemporary fiction / Elizabeth Dipple
p.   cm.
Bibliography: p.
Includes index.
ISBN 0-415-00661-9.
ISBN 0-415-00662-7 (pbk.)
1. Fiction——20th century——History and criticism.   I. Title.
PN3503.D54 1988
809.3′04——dc19   87-23080
CIP

British Library Cataloguing in Publication Data
Dipple, Elizabeth
The unresolvable plot: reading contemporary fiction
1. Fiction——20th century——History and criticism
I. Title
809.3′04   PN3503

ISBN 0-415-00661-9
ISBN 0-415-00662-7 Pbk

In Memoriam

———

Sybilla Schmidt
Fred Dipple

Contents

Acknowledgments

I wish to thank Janice Price of Methuen for her encouragement in this project, particularly at points when I felt that contemporary fiction was too big a wad to chew. There are also debts to be paid to friends who read parts of this book at various times during its composition, and reacted to them with lively interest: Sir Roger Walters, Dilys Carrington, Lynne Wilkins, Penny Hirsch, Albert Cirillo, Alfred Appel Jr, Len and Fran Schaefer. Martha Banta, Gerald Graff, and Samuel Hynes gave me unstinting support. Mary Kinzie's help was indispensable. I wish, too, to mention memorially Karin Strand, who was killed before the manuscript was quite finished.

I had extensive interviews with Russell Hoban and Umberto Eco, both of whom were notably open and candid in talking about their fiction, and I am very grateful to them.

Northwestern University gave me two terms of paid leave of absence to hasten the project, and the University of California at Los Angeles put their computers at my disposal in the final preparation of the manuscript.

PART I

Writing about contemporary fiction

MEMORY

Do not guard this as rich stuff without mark
Closed in a cedarn dark,
Nor lay it down with tragic masks and greaves,
Licked by the tongues of leaves.

Nor let it be as eggs under the wings
Of helpless, startled things,
Nor encompassed by song, nor any glory
Perverse and transitory.

Rather, like shards and straw upon coarse ground,
Of little worth when found, –
Rubble in gardens, it and stones alike,
That any spade may strike.

Louise Bogan

1

The unresolvable plot

Something in Shaker thought and theology . . . in its strange rituals and marvellously inventive practical life, in richly metaphorical language and imaginative use of dancing and music, has always seemed to me to adumbrate the relation of fiction to reality. We novelists also demand a far-fetched faith, quite often seemingly absurd in relation to normal reality; we too need a bewildering degree of metaphorical understanding from our readers before the truths behind our tropes can be convened, can "work".

John Fowles, *A Maggot* (1985)

Writing about contemporary fiction is a false game, not only because egregious choices must be made, but because the scene changes daily. When I began writing this book, I thought that Nabokov, who is indispensable in any study of postmodern work, would be my only dead author; in the process of its composition, Calvino died in 1985 at the age of 61, and Borges followed, full of years, in 1986. All humans are mortal, but perhaps fictions are too, and because of the unpredictable nature of art's longevity, a critic of the contemporary lives in the midst of staggering evanescence and blind gambles. Contemporary novels quickly become fictions of the past, and their questionable powers of survival are all too subject to canonical tastes and narrow academic decisions.

Critics of fiction, however, necessarily contribute to the story of story-telling – in fact theirs is the job of telling that story. This does not on the whole endear them to authors. The intemperate anti-academic American novelist, Gore Vidal, repeatedly claims that critics overstep their mark by presuming to judge when their qualifications for doing so are appallingly inadequate. Vidal is not alone in complaining of the arrogance and marked failures of imagination among critics, nor is the war between the artist and the critic particular to the present. Anthony Burgess argues that if literary critics had to write the books they so glibly dismiss they might learn charity; Doris Lessing is bewildered that critics can be so far from an imaginative middle ground in judgment; Iris

Murdoch says that criticism of her work is about as interesting to her as the rainfall in Patagonia; Nabokov's contempt became one of his themes. Saul Bellow's blunt indignation in an interview (1982) with *Esquire* magazine is richly expressive of authorial fury:

> As you grow older as a writer, you become more and more accustomed to talking to yourself. In what the punks like to call the literary milieu you'd think you'd find some *milieudniks* to talk to. You'd think there were heaps of people to attach yourself to. But you have to pick yourself through heaps of *no goodniks*, casts of thousands in the literary world who don't know what the hell I'm talking about.

Vidal is clear in his definition of the critic's job: (s)he should describe the work in question clearly and without prejudice, and then step aside and allow it to function. This is an admirable but impossible agenda.

Formal critical acts are powerful within the culture, and this is one reason they are resented. Aside from generating sales of books and contributing to the numbers game of popularity, the general reader in contrast has little to say in what persists. Moreover, as Charles Newman points out in *The Postmodern Aura: Fiction in an Age of Inflation*, the hyper-reactive energy of publishers and the pressures of media-oriented fashion are dangerous to residual ideas of value, because the standards involved in publishing any book and keeping it in print depend on the crassest terms of profitability. At the same time, the academic critic whose view is longer than that of publisher or journalist can also seem a frail vessel to bear the cargo of worthiness and uphold the reputation of the best works.

In the skeptical atmosphere of the late twentieth century, the security of Arnoldian touchstones or the power of authoritative voices from the Modern period – like T.S. Eliot or F.R. Leavis – are no longer available. In a relentless environment of canonical revision in literary studies within the universities, it is increasingly difficult to argue for the primacy or permanence of any text from the past, or from the traditional canons that most literary students believe represented the best that was known and thought. How much more difficult, then, to choose what is major or may become canonical in a present untested by time. It has, of course, always been hard to perceive one's own period justly, but in the midst of current publication practices and the quarrels endemic to media-incited tastes or academic circles, judgments are more capricious than ever.

In any given period, the best fiction matters, however, because – like all the other arts and sciences – it says something about our level of civilization. At the moment, while Franco-American and "cultural" academic critics denigrate the aesthetics of literature, fictionists continue to produce as though their activity counts. In any decade, the history of fiction is formed by the writers who are alive then – and the best work of the best among them becomes the history of that period. In writing about contemporary fiction, each decade is of vital importance, and the task is to decide *now* which are the writers whose work will form the collective canon that will later be called the history of fiction of the period.

In writing about contemporary fiction, the critic has two choices – either to gamble on the chances of the very young, or to go back a few decades in one's survey, and talk about those who began strongly, clearly influenced the present, and are still writing in their middle or late years. I've chosen the latter course, because the first few novels of a young writer are not reliably predictive, and because even when young novelists are interesting, their early work is too often merely promising and cannot accurately augur their ultimate significance or staying power. The youngest writers I write about, therefore – Umberto Eco and Cynthia Ozick – are in their 50s. The oldest are in their 80s. Three of them are dead. This is not a book about untried youth, but about writers of international dimension who form a base that can be examined as fundamental to the contemporary enterprise.

One of the difficulties in writing a limited history of or commentary on contemporary fiction is that, even if one chooses established writers – i.e. ones who have been around for more than a few minutes – there is no longstanding history of readership. One of the problems for the fictionist (and by indirect extension for the critic whose judgments are doomed to be dated) is the nervous question of whether the author will be included in an abiding history of readership. If (s)he is good – or lucky – enough, the future is assured, and sometimes, as in the case of Beckett or Borges, writers become legendary in their own lifetime. But legends fail, and the critic's responsibility in choosing among the writers of the present creates the need for criteria – which means we are immediately faced with the problems of theory at a subtle level. The changing lines of taste that dominate the success of any given type of fiction decade by decade are fuelled by theory to a degree alarming at the present moment, when academic literary studies are trying to rescue themselves from dullness by a philosophical–cultural stress that has almost caused the death of traditional literary studies as a subject.

The great critical temptation, therefore, is to adopt one or more of the many theoretical languages now dominant, and to make one's choices on that basis. There are two strong arguments against such an undertaking – first, the hostility most (but not all) writers feel toward *a priori* theories and, second, the absolute way in which such theories belie the reading experience. The simplest way to look at critical reception of contemporary literature is to emphasize the split between those readers and critics who firmly stick to convention, tradition, and the precepts of realism, and those who endorse the experimental. Quite a while ago – as literary criticism goes – Robert Alter in *Partial Magic* (1975) brilliantly described the line of anti-traditional experimentalism that goes from Cervantes through Sterne to the present, and there was no doubt that he endowed this mode with special value. Subsequently, as current critical schools eagerly break the stranglehold of mimesis, whole vocabularies are spawned in an attempt to escape conventional fiction. Some of these – like speech-act theory, semiotics, and reader-response theory – are useful in thinking not only about what might be happening now in fictional experimentation, but in dealing freshly with the past.

But the overall result of the upsurge of critical vocabularies has, unfortunately, been divisive, resulting frequently in a false valorization (Franco-American jargon word) of spurious fictions. Many enthusiastic readers, dedicated to ancient mimetic standards, have been alienated from new and interesting fictions by strident theoretical polemics, and as a result superb experimental fictions have too often become enemies of the reader rather than friends. Occasionally a good critic, essentially centered on texts, is capable of using dominant current theoretical vocabularies with enormous effect – like David Lodge or J. Hillis Miller – but most of them concentrate on narrow quasi-philosophical arguments that have very little to do with the persistence of fiction within the culture. In thinking about what writers to choose for a book on contemporary fiction and how to write about them, I found current theory an impediment in a way that rather surprised me. In the actual writing of this book, I used a limited number of ideas from the theories that now dominate the academy, but even so found myself likely to pervert the vocabulary deliberately in using it, and my tendency is always to drop the jargon and get back to the author's text. Many of my colleagues find this regressive on my part, but on the whole I think reading is more important than criticism.

Nevertheless, the theoretical basis leading to the choice of authors in a book like this is crucial. In this respect, the only current theories I found useful were the presentation of key vocabulary by Mikhail Bakhtin, a bit of Russian formalism, small parts of the work of speech-act theorists, and some of the semiotic theories of Umberto Eco. In this study, my major aim is to break the cliché that taste can go in only one direction, and that the reader must be dedicated to either conventional or experimental fiction. That distinction should by now be defunct, but it is not, mostly because of the split between authors who think about readers, and cultural critics who think about intellectual fashion. Theoretical critics tend not to be open to fiction that does not yield to their theories, and are culpable in their indifference to a broad spectrum of literary texts by their creative contemporaries. On the other hand, authors are often dull in their reliance on tradition, or acerbically unapproachable in their experimentalism.

The writers I have chosen are all fictionists for whom the act of fiction is vital, and whose allegiance to literature is not broken by external considerations. With the notable exception of Umberto Eco, who considers his fiction inferior to his theory, all write their novels under the aegis of literature as the highest value, dedicated simply to the principle that fiction functions as a significant ontology or mode of reality. Their work indicates a belief that fiction is necessary to the culture, and intrinsically – even compulsively – important as an activity. None is limited by grinding political axes, although most directly or indirectly reconcile aesthetic and social demands. They are interested in moral risks, spiritual obliquity, formal experimentation of some sort, and verbal play. All of them celebrate an open world, where the novel's major ontological task is to describe unfinished business.

*

This authorial sense of openness and unlimited possibilities helps to create the perverse sense of chaos that characterizes the current fictional scene and makes all decisions by both writer and reader transitory and subject to revision. It is therefore impossible to argue a thesis about contemporary fiction without excluding major kinds of works. In choosing writers to write about, even an unbiased critic as a matter of course excludes, but in any possible book about contemporary fiction, the authors chosen all represent something fundamentally characteristic of the present. I arbitrarily used three loose categories, from metafiction to versions of realism, fitting a middle range of quasi-experimentalism in between. I then chose three central writers for each category, reluctantly omitting other major novelists that I wished in one way or another to write about – John Barth, Stanley Elkin, John Fowles, and Michel Tournier, for example. I very much admire each of the writers I use, and in this respect this study discourages a doctrinal urging of one sort of fiction over another.

I am happier in the perverse chaos of many styles and intentions than in the futile defence of one *Gestalt*. As I worked on this book – and indeed as I read preparatory to writing it – I was delighted with the plenitude of the current fictional scene, and with its unresolvability. To talk about fiction from the 1960s to the 1980s is to have no boundaries except the historical ones. The most exciting factor is the persistence of fiction – decades after Ortega y Gasset announced the death of the novel. Not only has it persisted, but in some cultures – like eastern Europe and Latin America – it has leapt forward, not simply as an élite production but as an art for the people, for leftist ideologues, and for the bourgeoisie among whom the genre originated. The opposite is also true, for the coterie status of some types of novel has also strengthened, and there are many experimental novelists gambling dangerously on the ability and will of readers to perceive new formal possibilities within a dispersed culture. In every respect, however, fictionists are writing in more open and reader-gratifying ways than might, at a first hostile glance, seem to be the case.

Aside from questions of taste which are never resolvable, current fiction presents us with writers of high caliber for whom there are no holds barred and no doors closed. Although the quarrel between realism and experimentalism goes on, so many extraordinary things have happened within experimentalism that it ill behooves anyone to avert their eyes from it. Realism itself in its various versions has also produced enormous talents that must be dealt with in order to see the whole picture of our fortunate literary historical period. It is the purpose of this book to demonstrate a spectrum of possibilities now before us – and to urge openness toward it.

It is impossible to guess how the period from the 1960s to the present and beyond will ultimately be labeled. It certainly sees itself as separated from high Modernism, although the theorists who try to distinguish between the present and the earlier-twentieth-century past tend to be unconvincing. One particularly astute study, Alan Wilde's *Horizons of Assent* (1981), argues that there is a subtle difference between Modernism and Postmodernism in fiction that is evident in the kind of irony used. The contemporary novelist uses "suspensive" irony, which is ultimately connected to various versions of Postmodernism. Ihab Hassan in *The Postmodern Turn: Essays in Postmodern Theory and Culture* (1986) is fuller and more explicit in describing the current controversies surrounding the term "Postmodern," but it is still a hazardous enterprise to explain precisely how the parodic context of the present separates itself from the parataxis and equally ironic gestures of Modernism.

One of the problems lies in the present vocabulary – or lack of it. "Modern" is an old word that in the past always yielded to the passing of time and the coming of a new age. It is a peculiar quality of twentieth-century narcissism that Modernism in all the arts was perceived as final and absolute, with the result that it is now an established jargonistic period term for the first half of the twentieth century. In the late 1950s and early 1960s when the time came to rebel against the overlordship of Modernism, the hunger for the new was expressed by asserting Modernism's *passé* nature through a term that is combative and implies a surpassing of the recent past. And so Postmodernism was born. This is a troublesome state of affairs, in that the word "modern" still retains a conventional dictionary definition, and many readers – as opposed to cultural critics – feel that modern books are the ones that are being written now.

Similarly, Postmodernism is a falsely boastful word whose definition is uncertain at every level. A German sociophilosopher like Jürgen Habermas disputes its legitimacy in arguments against the French Jean-François Lyotard, who wrote *The Postmodern Condition: A Report on Knowledge* (1979). Literary critics and other users of the term within the arts cannot decide whether it should be employed historically to describe the period since Modernism, or as a weighted word indicating certain political, parodic, and stylistic tendencies. In literary studies, Charles Newman (1985) and Gerald Graff (1979) use it historically, whereas Ihab Hassan (1986), Linda Hutcheon (1984), and John Barth (1967) assume that it signifies styles and genres within the historical period following Modernism. In this book, I tend to use it in the latter sense, as a signal of specific modes or principles particular to our time. Although it is unavoidable in talking about contemporary fiction, I do not like the term, and prefer another rather new word, metafiction, to describe the issue at stake.

8

Metafiction became an established term to describe paratactic post-Joycean experimentation by the mid-1970s. In *Fabulation and Metafiction* (1979), Robert Scholes added his own tag, "fabulation," to certain kinds of ironic story-telling forms. Raymond Federman in 1975 (*Surfiction: Fiction Now and Tomorrow*) found his term "surfiction" more descriptive, but has no real quarrel with metafiction. By the time Linda Hutcheon wrote *Narcissistic Narrative* in 1984, the term was established as normative in describing contemporary experimentation – especially when that experimentation was brief, verbally paratactic or broken, multi-mediumistic, parodic, and significantly derailed from all previously accepted genres. Metafiction takes the reader's sophistication and complete absorption of genres from the past for granted, so that as a mode it builds ironically on top of the experienced literature of that past. It self-consciously seeks to play off against its antecedents, so that its breakages and gaps refer wittily to forms and genres well known to the reader. Its irony comes from the fact that it is referential to literature itself rather than to human experience: it is thus almost always anti-mimetic in the traditional sense, or contains ironic anti-representational elements. Many conventional readers find its verbal self-referentiality frivolous. Although some writers like Donald Barthelme are almost exclusively meta-fictional, many choose to use metafictional elements erratically in the service of larger and more complex structures.

Because metafiction resembles the post-structuralist stress on language theory (consider the famous alliance between Roland Barthes and Alain Robbe-Grillet), its vocabulary veers away from the old values of fiction. As a result, many metafictionists have argued against character, plot, content, and all the old standbys of the fictional act. Its absorbed attention to literature as a subject can be productive of major ontological breakthroughs, but it can also lead to an enlarged sense of gamesmanship that is less than worthy. In this respect, renovated ideas of parody are major in dealing not only with fiction that deliberately calls itself metafictional or Postmodern, but with almost all the novels of our period. Parody requires redefinition, because for many readers it still carries negative connotations indicating a degradation of a primary text by the wit of a destructively comic imitation. As metafictional norms proliferate, this standard but primitive definition is replaced by a more sophisticated idea of the positive effects of parody as a meditation on the literatures and texts of the past.

Jorge Luis Borges, writing Postmodern or metafictional texts long before such a genre existed, carefully reintroduced the old image of the mirror into the vocabulary of perception and literary structure. The French term *mise-en-abyme* – which stretches back to mirror-tricks in the painting of the Renaissance and to *trompe l'oeil* techniques – also indicates the compounded images of literary referentiality. The idea of infinitely mirrored repetitions (nested Chinese boxes is a comparable but less luminous image) is basic to *mise-en-abyme* as a descriptive term. As contemporary parody plays off new texts by mirroring them against their multiple antecedents, the effect aggrandizes the acts of literature through repetition, rather than belittling them. The parodies of Postmodernism are therefore potentially and felicitously productive of responses close to the marvelous. In the case of multi-talented writers like Borges and Calvino, for example, parodic effects help to build particular mentalist worlds where the backing of literary parodic allusion expands the possibilities of knowledge at a level both playful and profound.

Although parody is an extremely useful term in describing the interplay of past and present fictions, the idea of intertextuality is necessary as a complement to it. In semiotic theory (the study of signs and signifiers), where this term started out, the idea of the reader's active participation is major. (S)he contributes to the "polysemy" of a complex text – that is, to the production of readings or interpretations, which are all that count for the semiotician in thinking of a fiction. The existence of a text in itself is not an automatic condition for signification; the combination of reader and text, or even of text and anterior text(s), produces intertextuality – the complex interaction of minds and linguistic structures that produce interpretation. As intertextuality is currently seen in narratological studies, the pressure of anterior literature is always present in the act of reading – the experience of past books or cultural artifacts intrudes fruitfully on our reception of the present one.

When intertextuality is carried to a high level of self-consciousness as it is in our period, reading becomes a complexly generated experience. As a result, a study of the contemporary scene automatically becomes a more complicated undertaking than if intertextuality were quietly brushed aside as it is in the reception of simple genres like domestic fiction and romantic fantasy. The serious novel is now old enough to find its extended history unavoidable, and when erudite contemporary fictionists add the freight of their learning to the types within the genre, the possibilities become vertiginously productive of the unresolvable antinomies and splendid possibilities of the present.

In the transitory nature of things, however, the rise of the erudite or even mandarin novel may be just a periodic aberration. It is certainly true that in surveying the contemporary state of affairs, the ascendancy of the learned novel is definite – whether its learning comes from complex allusion within traditional allusive frames, or from its authorially determined intertextuality. As a result, the task of reading many current novels has become a serious academic exercise, challenging in a way that the more placid early history of response to the genre would not have assumed. It is transparently clear that Modernism in all its phases started this movement toward an academic complexity, with Joyce no doubt dominating the paratactic complication of the novel. This reliance on Modernism necessarily blurs the issue for the contemporary reader, and the difference between Modernism and Postmodernism remains obscurely difficult to talk about. It is nevertheless clear that contemporary writers on the whole have a more self-consciously available narrational vocabulary with which to conjure than did their Modern masters.

The question of audience response to complex experimentation and intertextual demands is an interesting one. The risky business of a novel's heavy demand on a reader has only occasionally been a deterrent: one thinks, for example, of the enormous popularity of Nabokov's *Lolita* in the 1960s, of Pynchon's difficult novels in the 1970s, or of Eco's *The Name of the Rose* in the 1980s. But there are persistent problems, particularly among American writers, where recent reception has generally been poor and quality nervously irregular. The most damaging factor has been the burgeoning of creative writing programs in American universities, where most fictionists now try to earn their living. The claustrophobia of the creative writing seminar, where writers write for themselves and each other in a tight little coterie of mutual applause, no doubt created the group of experimental American writers that this study takes little account of – writers like John Barth, John Hawkes, Robert Coover, William Gass, Stanley Elkin, Ronald Sukenick, etc. When in 1971 Tony Tanner published *City of Words* – a study of contemporary American literature in the 1960s – the world of American experimentalism looked bright and promising. Subsequently, there has been a failure of quality, an inability to see new directions, stiff new competition from Latin Americans and Europeans, and an almost total failure of audience response.

This failure of complex experimental writers to win convinced American or international audiences inside or outside of the academy has been countered in more recent creative writing programs by a new explosion of neo-realistic minimalism – a dull mode starring writers like Anne Beattie, Frederick Barthelme, Bobbie Ann Mason, and Raymond Carver. Because of its barren anti-adjectival, anti-adverbial unwittiness, this style also fails to win audiences – but it is easy to teach in creative writing classes to a clientele with little literary background or allusive competence. At the moment, while Latin America literature continues to march forward, American fiction is becalmed. European literature, on the other hand, is also in a state of at least semi-transition, as simpler modes return to a significant degree. On the continent – particularly in France and Germany – expansive sentimentality has reappeared, and may take over for a while. The British novel, always beleaguered by the French who sneer at its Bloomsburian bourgeois aspects, continues to be fairly traditional – but with pockets of brilliance, and its practitioners claim audiences and attention that fictions in other countries cannot command. The contours of change in fiction in the next few years are completely unpredictable, but it is fairly certain that after the vertiginous pleasures and slithering possibilities of the last few decades, readers will not allow a complete plunge back into the starkly conventional or simple.

*

The pleasures of being a reader in the current milieu are created by the dedication and even ebullience of the novelists themselves. Italo Calvino, who pondered the nature and fate of the reader deeply, argues posthumously in an interesting essay, "Whom Do We Write For? or The Hypothetical Bookshelf" (in *The Uses of Literature*, 1986), that the reader should never be written down to. Instead of taking a paternalistic attitude toward possible cultural inequality between author and reader, he points out that to condescend is to deny the open possibilities of response:

> If we assume a reader less cultured than the writer and take a pedagogical, educational, and reassuring attitude toward him, we are simply underlining the disparity. Any attempt to sweeten the situation with palliatives such as a literature of the people is a step backward, not a step ahead. Literature is not school.

Calvino's life-long dedication to the difficult art of reading is reflected in elaborate detail in his novel, *If on a winter's night a traveler*, where readers are urged to develop a cosmic openness to the unwritten – that is, to something that waits to be written and whose agents all authors are.

Calvino urges the kind of indeterminacy and openness encouraged by current fictional diversity. In his view, as developed through the diary of Silas Flannery in *If on a winter's night*, all books by all authors are part of a universal book with a unifying truth – a truth that comprises the written and the unwritten. All books should be read in order to enlarge the pictures of cultural possibility envisaged by all authors. True endings are found not in stolid or determinate formal conclusions to novels but in the infinite process of reading. Calvino believes in the endless dedication of readers who through the act of reading help authors to unlock the world of ontological possibility, thus rendering literary activity culturally as well as metaphysically major.

At a time when literary criticism is at its most anti-authorial, novelists themselves are committed to the value and achievement of fiction. Although aware of the illusionist quality of their work, many argue for a special realm of truth unavailable by any other means. The Peruvian Mario Vargas Llosa presented his case practically in *The New York Times*:

> the truth of the novel doesn't depend on facts . . . [but] on its own persuasive powers, on the sheer communicative strength of its fantasy, on the skill of its magic. Every good novel tells the truth and every bad novel lies. For a novel to "tell the truth" means to make the reader experience an illusion, and "to lie" means to be unable to accomplish the trickery. The novel, thus, is an amoral genre, or rather, its ethic is sui generis, one in which truth and falsehood are exclusively esthetic concepts. . . . Every novel, aside from being amoral, harbors at its core a certain skepticism. When religious culture enters into crisis, life seems divested of any binding schemes, dogma and precepts and turns into chaos. That is the optimum moment for fiction. Its artificial orders offer refuge, security and the free release of those appetites and fears that real life incites and cannot gratify or exorcise. Fiction is a temporary substitute for life. The return to reality is almost a brutal impoverishment, corroboration that we are less than we dreamed.

Which means that fiction, by spurring the imagination, both temporarily assuages human dissatisfaction and simultaneously incites it.

(trans. Toby Talbot)

The writer, knowing (s)he is in the position of manipulator, waits for moments when aesthetic truth will replace religious commitment of one sort or another. The high aesthetics of contemporary fiction are obviously skeptical substitutes, but Vargas Llosa sees that the illusionist trick of art is also intellectually and politically dangerous. It is interesting, in fact, to note the number of contemporary writers who not only see their art as a religious surrogate but also incorporate religious statement into their fiction as part of its function within the possible realms of meaning.

Julio Cortázar, the Argentinian writer who died in 1984, goes much further into a sort of mysticism about fiction than Vargas Llosa. In an essay in *Around the Day in Eighty Worlds* (1986), he urges readers to distinguish between fictional works of mere *métier* - technical competence - and those that come from an almost hallucinatory realm or trancelike compositional condition, called a "second state" by the Modernist, Robert Musil. Like Russell Hoban and even Doris Lessing, Cortázar sees the author as only instrumental:

> The truth is that my stories do not possess the slightest *literary* merit, the slightest effort. If some of them last, it will be because I received and transmitted what was latent in the depths of my psyche without losing too much, which comes from a certain experience in not falsifying the mysterious, keeping it as true as possible to its source, with its original tremor, its archetypal stammer ... the genesis of the story and the poem is the same: they are born of a sudden estrangement, of a *displacement* that alters the "normal" pattern of consciousness; in a time when modes and genres have given way to a noisy critical bankruptcy, there is some point to insisting on this affinity, which many will consider preposterous.

Although the existential idea of autobiographical content persists in fiction, larger cultural and spiritual concepts like those quoted above are very strong, and some writers - like Doris Lessing and recently John Fowles - balance diverse contents very carefully. Whereas the 1960s appeared to promise a long period of fictions of the displaced self, the anti-fiction of Sartre's egocentric world has not been sustained. The increasing urge toward objectivity, toward the transparence of the author and the open participation of the reader, alters the writer-reader bond. When authors now impose on their readers - and some compulsively do - rebellion occurs. No longer do we require anything like the magisterial prefaces of Henry James to mediate between the text and the act of reading, and indeed as prefatory material we are more likely to get curt, intrusive instructions or authorial interference at a limiting interpretational level. More than ever before in the history of fictional reception, the reader independently takes on the text - and the author eyes that reader with a new intensity. The result of the stress on this relationship can be readerly

13

estrangement or authorial displacement, but in spite of a bracing nervousness, this problem leads directly to new fictional potentialities.

In a mood of great ebullience, Cortázar claimed that there are no known limits to creative innovation in fiction as it is now practiced and received. In choosing a wide variety of types of writers, I hope that this book will demonstrate the overwhelming sense of unlimited possibilities open to us in our fortunate present. But the very aspect of limitlessness that makes contemporary fiction so full and open also prevents a chartable thesis or resolvable plot for the current fictional milieu. The constantly shifting boundaries, the exploitation of all perceived potentialities, the open new forms that predict a lively future, and the abiding sense of contingencies from the past all indicate that to look at the present is to see writers determined to produce the broadest range of fiction they are able collectively and individually to imagine.

Deciding to write a book that ranges along a loose organizational pattern in order to represent an unresolvable situation in the stylistics and thematics of contemporary fiction was a difficult idea to get used to. I precede the three main sections of this study with an essay on Graham Greene and Gabriel García Márquez, because their different but equal excellences can encourage the reader toward a breadth of acceptability within styles. The perversity of juxtaposing these two writers mirrors the perverse coexistence and impressive strengths of unlike types current in our period. From here I go on to metafiction – not because I value it above other genres, but because it is fundamental to all experimentation in our period. All readers know about realism, but many still shy away from the experimental, and it behooves us to start at a point where our period is particularly impressive. In writing about metafiction, I felt it necessary to go back to the old masters, and I have done so – concentrating on Borges and Nabokov over Beckett because Beckett has been over-studied elsewhere. Part III, on experiment and authorial imposition of meaning, is meant to be transitional to the final part, which is a presentation of writers who ironically exploit both the negative and positive connotations of realism.

The point of this study is to persuade fellow readers toward openness to all major contemporary fictional possibilities. The most objective way I could find of achieving this is through discrete essays on writers who are representative of fundamental ideas in contemporary fiction. The problem is to demonstrate what has been done and at the same time to keep the individuation within the work of each writer intact. By writing separate accounts of each writer, I hope there will be a cumulative demonstration of the achievement of our contemporaries. I do not aim at completeness in each essay, but at a way of making descriptive statements about the work at the same time as I spend a large amount of space on close reading and individual textual analysis. The act of reading in all its particular detail is the only means by which fiction persists, and I try at every turn to get as close to the texts as a reader can expressively do through an act of criticism. Aside from that, all I advise is that whoever reads this book should go back and reread the fictions themselves. That's where the life and action are.

2

The structures of solitude:
Graham Greene and
Gabriel García Márquez

Well over twenty-five years ago, the American novelist John Hawkes published one of his most interesting novels, *The Lime Twig* (1961) – an imaginative parody of Graham Greene's *Brighton Rock* (1938), and to a lesser degree of Eric Ambler's *Background to Danger* (1937). Twenty-three or -four years separated the two original books from this ingeniously parodic production – enough to distance Hawkes's novel from them in order to achieve at least one of his intentions, the creation of a newly resonant structure within a tediously established genre, the thriller. Hawkes's basic attempt was to loosen the bonds of genre, by emphasizing both its fluidity and the possibilities of its renovation. Although he succeeded within the atmosphere of genre debate, *The Lime Twig* had a limited life, and existed only within the ideologies of an American university coterie.

Meanwhile, the conventional Graham Greene, many decades after *Brighton Rock* and long after *The Lime Twig*, persists as a power in the field of contemporary fiction, continuing his subtle renovations in novels that demonstrate his evolving technical expertise and reworked forays into the themes of faith and doubt, fear and feeling. The thriller remains with him, altered significantly, in novels like *The Honorary Consul* (1973), *The Human Factor* (1978), and even *Doctor Fischer of Geneva* (1980), but he has also added elements of the old romance tradition to the latter, and introduced them as the novelistic base in *Monsignor Quixote* (1982).

Greene numbers among the great old men of fiction – like Borges, Nabokov, and Beckett – who did major work during the Modernist period, and survived into a reconstructive–deconstructive boom in fiction that has lasted right up to the present moment. Unlike these three who are partial molders of that boom, Greene has kept himself within boundaries that would remain recognizable to his British Modernist friend, Evelyn Waugh, who died in 1966. Much of his attention is fixed on technique – on that tradition of fine writing that British reviewers and readers continue to value in spite of the incursions of rougher styles and the intrusive sloppiness of American panache. In Greene, as in Waugh, the minimalist tautness of the style is endemic, and Greene has honed his technique unwearyingly through the decades that have been allotted to him. As he circles back to old themes, retaining his bleak male authorial failed hero, he seems an eternal presence, a writer spanning the century without a moment of temptation toward the innovations of writers like Borges, or García Márquez – for whom he has expressed admiration.

Gabriel García Márquez also respects Greene, and describes his limited debt to him. Two writers more divergent in subject matter and stylistic expertise would be hard to conjure up, and García Márquez in an interview with Plineo Apuleyo Mendoza acknowledges only a small technical influence:

> Graham Greene taught me how to decipher the tropics, no less. To separate out the essential elements of a poetic synthesis from an environment that you know all too well is extremely difficult. It's all so familiar you don't know where to start and yet you have so much to say that you end by understanding nothing. That was my problem with the tropics. I'd read Christopher Columbus, Pigafetta and the other chroniclers of the Indies with great interest, appreciating their original vision. I'd also read Salgari and Conrad and the early twentieth century Latin American "tropicalists" who saw everything through Modernist spectacles, and many others, but always found an enormous dichotomy between their versions and the real thing. Some of them fell into the trap of listing things and, paradoxically, the longer the list the more limited their vision seemed. Others, as we know, have succumbed to rhetorical excess. Graham Greene solved this literary problem in a very precise way – with a few disparate elements connected by an inner coherence both subtle and real. Using this method you can reduce the whole enigma of the tropics to the fragrance of a rotten guava.
>
> (*The Fragrance of Guava*, 1983, p. 32)

García Márquez, however, fastidiously removes himself from other aspects of Greene's style, the entire subject matter, and the themes of Greene's work. Each novelist reveals his own separate sources and influences in various places, but especially in Greene's *A Sort of Life* and García Márquez's interview with Apuleyo Mendoza entitled *The Fragrance of Guava*. Large contrasts between the two writers are defined by these influences, which are not simply historical or generational in their emphases. The early impact of Faulkner on García Márquez is too notorious, although it was dominant in *Leaf Storm* and powerful in a limited geographical way in *One Hundred Years of Solitude*; he has now almost completely overcome it. Similarly, Greene's skewing under the tutelage of Conrad and Henry James took some undoing and he has never claimed to be free of either.

The less spectacular influences for both writers are, however, more telling. Greene, born in the insular England of the late British Empire in 1904, read and bears the imprint of writers like Robert Louis Stevenson, Rider Haggard, John Buchan, James Elroy Flecker, Stanley Weyman, Captain Gilson, Rudyard Kipling, Lord Dunsany, G.K. Chesterton, Oscar Wilde, Walter Scott, Charles

Dickens; his poets range from Browning and Swinburne to the verse plays of Christopher Fry. The reading tastes that drove him are like those of the Anglophile Borges, but the latter was not afflicted by British imperial ideology as Greene was, nor did a national culture close off his childhood world. García Márquez, unlike Greene, began with Latin American and Spanish Golden Age poetry, and exploded into the life of prose through his reading of Kafka's *Metamorphosis* and small sections of Virginia Woolf's *Mrs Dalloway*. Then there were lessons (again technical) from Hemingway, the plays of Sophocles (particularly *Oedipus Rex*), Burrough's *Tarzan of the Apes*, Saint-Exupéry, and again Conrad. Above all, the international literature in which he soaked himself – including an intensive study of the European novel – guided his sophisticated development of technique. García Márquez also kept reading and rereading the Latin American poets, whose works he entwines inter-textually through *The Autumn of the Patriarch*.

The frequent ebullience of García Márquez's fiction is at odds with the taut severity of Greene's. Whereas Greene always strives to demonstrate the bleakly, corruptly political, García Márquez often fumbles his political statements and buries them in tall-tale metaphors to the point of hilarity – with the result that their impact is doubled. Many of the tendencies of these two authors can be traced to views of literature they gained from their original sources, and were impelled to pervert through their story-telling instincts and life experiences. Early driven to a pitch of imperial heroism by his late Victorian masters, Greene is goaded by a subjective sense of realism stemming from emotionally exaggerated memories of childhood miseries and the residual impact of his early Freudian psychoanalysis. The result is a dour reversal of the legendary imperial romantic literature that he and the modern world have necessarily betrayed. There are no more Prester Johns in Britain or the colonies – now reperceived in his novels as places that still excite adventures, but where the hero is characterized by failure and manifold inadequacies.

García Márquez, in contrast, appears to have no romanticized heroic model to subdue. Politically he – not to mention older writers like Augusto Roa Bastos and Alejo Carpentier – is fascinated by the semi-lunatic phenomenon of the Latin American despot, but he is even more driven by his Kafkaesque sense that a good novel is a highly imagined poetic transposition of reality. To label this process as "magical realism" and associate it with the entire Latin American group of writers in "El Boom" which began in the 1960s does a disservice to the particular quality of García Márquez's achievement. As he tries to describe his sense of how serious novels function, García Márquez says to Apuleyo Mendoza:

> a novel is reality represented through a secret code, a kind of conundrum about the world. The reality you are dealing with in a novel is different from real life, although it is rooted in it. The same thing is true of dreams.

In his own emotionally parsimonious way, Greene can have no argument with García Márquez's terms in this statement, for no code has been more secret than his. Greene creates large, mysterious spaces around his male protagonists, and titillates his readers by a tight withholding of substance. Like García Márquez, he saturates his fiction with dream material, always controlled to the point of evanescence. Both men see fiction as a reworking of life in order to refresh perception in imaginatively or poetically compelling ways. The mood, the forms, and the degrees of metaphoric allowance are in every way different, but the sense of deep encodement and conundrum is not.

Greene waspishly disagrees with any identification of his world as other than realistic, and particularly dislikes the term "Greeneland" to describe his tonal setting. Critics like John Spurling (1983) and Richard Hoggart (1970) persist in arguing that Greene's world is both negatively traceable and parodyable in ways that border on caricature, whereas Greene insists in *A Sort of Life* – one of his two narrow collections of autobiographical essays – that his reportage is precise rather than idiosyncratic:

> "This is Indo-China," I want to exclaim, "this is Mexico, this is Sierra Leone carefully and accurately described. I have been a newspaper correspondent as well as a novelist. I assure you that the dead child lay in the ditch in just that attitude. In the canal of Phat Diem the bodies stuck out of the water."

No doubt his readers believe him at this level of his defense. But the most trenchant withholdings in Greene's work are always ignored in his self-justifications – and he is very given to the *apologia*. A substantial denial of the real questions asked is typical of Greene, who seems not to realize that his withholdings are not as important to the texture of his fiction at the level of accurate reportage as they are in narrative tone and character transmission. His presentation of a world of excision and limited description is deeply characteristic of his voice as a writer. Whereas Saul Bellow glories in forging a strident, wittily achieved American voice, Greene wishes paradoxically and against all odds to be voiceless, to write perfectly so that simultaneously everyone will recognize him and no one will know him. In an odd way, he has succeeded.

For the stringent subject matters chosen by Greene, his parsimony is particularly apt, and does not require defense. All his books are set in political and religious contexts with literal historical co-ordinates. They are all contemporary to the time of writing, and therefore Greene in no way tries to recover or rewrite an historical past like Sir Walter Scott; many of them, like *The Quiet American, A Burnt Out Case*, and *Our Man in Havana*, are uncannily predictive of the future. For both Greene and García Márquez – and especially for the vast majority of specifically political writers in Latin America – the historico-political task of the novelist is the base on which other fictional concerns can be set. In *The Political Unconscious* (1981), Fredric Jameson describes this process within the history of the international novel as "history retextualized as fiction," and then proceeds to analyze the methodologies of Marxism under such an aegis.

A useful text in considering Greene's retextualizing of present history is Georg Lukàcs's analysis of Sir Walter Scott in *The Historical Novel* (1983). For Lukàcs Scott is representative of the English historical novel and his characters demonstrate the Lukàcsian standard of "typicality." The English novel is particularly prone to the vicissitudes of class struggle, but in spite of particularized demonstrations of violence, Scott and his countrymen always indulge in what Lukàcs calls the famous British compromise. This compromise boils down depressingly to the consolation of a world becalmed in a "glorious middle way," so that the rewriting of history is comforting rather than radically progressive. The British Empire's world of boys' adventure stories and imperial myth uneasily inherited by Greene participates in this Scottian compromise and is indeed artificially heightened by its adventure plots and by a less austere apprehension of class issues and polemical internationalism than Scott undertook. In order to become an honest writer – and indeed to achieve the fame he so early received – Greene had to retextualize the history of his present both in Britain and in Third-World countries (Africa, Indo-China, Latin America, etc.). In doing so, he had to reperceive the world, and to find a way of breaking away from the typicalities of character in the historical fictions that preceded him.

García Márquez is also a retextualizer of Latin American history, and as such shows imaginative energy equalled only by the most recent work of Mario Vargas Llosa. In the context of Central and South American literature, this is saying a great deal, particularly when one thinks of other major writers like Julio Cortázar, José Donoso, and Carlos Fuentes – and I mention only my favorites. In terms of that retextualizing, the fame of *One Hundred Years of Solitude* has been an impediment to García Márquez, in that its phenomenal reception has crowded out his other work. He himself considers *The Autumn of the Patriarch* the book by which he should be remembered – it is a book of careful research, tightly allusive writing, brilliant temporal experimentation, and poetic intertextuality. In spite of Gregory Rabassa's best efforts as translator, this novel unfortunately is inadequately open to a reader not totally immersed in the Spanish American world – to the point of knowing the slang of Colombian taxi-drivers.

García Márquez earnestly considers one of his most important tasks as a writer to be a poetic representation of the primary political problem in Latin America – the long existence of almost inevitably crazy dictators who derail the minds of nations. The levels of internal and external metaphors for politico-psychic determination in *The Autumn of the Patriarch* float and intertwine, as the rich, baffling contexts drift with pyrotechnical temporal tricks through images of beauty, bleakness, comedy, fantasy, political grotesquerie, and, above all, death.

The contrast between Greene's and García Márquez's retextualizing could not be more extreme, nor could such a comparison be more evidently wanting in decorum. Greene belongs to another world and another generation, but he is a Modernist persisting into the present, a writer who continues writing into old age, who befriends new authors with a committed generosity, who admires García Márquez and considers the innovations of Borges superior to the dull conventions of earlier Spanish American writing. Greene's positive criticism of the formal experiments of other writers began with his openness during his early career as a film reviewer, and indeed filmic techniques are part of his own technical development. The fact that he prefers to polish and ruminate over his original style and themes, although he is quite aware of other experimental directions in writers of his own generation as well as relative youngsters like García Márquez, shows one of the possible choices persisting within contemporary fiction. Juxtaposing these two superb writers can cogently demonstrate the unresolvable plot of contemporary fiction, and the reader's role in allowing fair space to both.

*

In spite of their distance from each other, García Márquez and Greene share extensive journalistic activity, unappeasable anti-Americanism, a taste for "good" Latin American dictators, a strong story-telling bent, an emotionally intent but controlled love for their characters, and a boundless commitment to the aesthetics of literature. They are also writers whose major theme is solitude, a theme with diverse connotations encompassing the differences between their worlds and their fictions. García Márquez was of course identified with solitude from the explosive moment of his first fame with *One Hundred Years of Solitude* (1967), and most of the critical work done on him concentrates on that subject and his exploitation of temporal history and narrativity. Greene, on the other hand, is typically seen as an occluded creator of alienated (even romantically so) characters in bitter worlds. Both these identifications are correct, and overworked. I will summarize the problematics of solitude briefly, and examine how these two writers wrested their extensive but unlike technical achievements from this partially shared, well-constructed ideological base.

The idea of solitude, so important to Latin American life in fiction and politics alike, has its expressive origin in Cervantes' *Don Quixote* – a book to which both García Márquez and especially Greene give allegiance. Don Quixote finally sees that he has throughout been caught between illusion and reality, in a fatal subjective space where his lonely poetic transformations of empirical experience lead to comedy and death. His splendid illusions, fed by Renaissance chivalric romances, show his vertiginous distance both from the unrealistic ideals deceptively created by literature and from the unbearable violence of quotidian experience in Renaissance Spain. His famous, hilarious, solitary imaginative acts lead him to an exposure of the lies of past literature and to a heightened need for imagination to create its own place – in

21

an austere and moribund spiritual world as large and flat as his own Manchegan plain.

Don Quixote is one of the most open and connotative of literary texts for contemporary writers, in that it has manifold uses politically, nationalistically, narratologically, and symbolically, and as such it is – together with the cosmic antics of *Alice's Adventures in Wonderland* – most frequently evoked by Postmodernists from historical and theoretical points of view. The Don's complete internal solitude as he lies dying at the end of Part II of his novel is a kind of self-creation; his death speeches and the composition of his legal will show that his deeply learned interiority can only find escape through the final transformation of death:

> "Let us go gently, gentlemen," said Don Quixote, "for there are no birds this year in last year's nests. I was mad, but I am sane now. I was Don Quixote de la Mancha, but to-day, as I have said, I am Alonso Quixano the Good. May my sincere repentance restore your former esteem for me."
>
> (trans. J.M. Cohen)

In the final solitude of his dying, where no one around his bedside can understand his internal text, Don Quixote apologizes to the writer of his fictional adventures. In an aura of anti-illusionist self-assertion, this character whose exit necessarily ends Cervantes's lengthy book, tries to break down the false co-biographical bond between character and author. Both Don Quixote and Cervantes live only through the fiction, on which they depend for whatever continuing reality they might have. Their lives of illusion and the ultimate exit of both at the end of the novel show that the creation of fictional myths necessarily asserts the deep solitude of thought – i.e. of the internal mental constructions of fiction that belong to the reader, the character, and the author alike. Fiction, in other words, creates solitude – not solidarity – for all participants.

The deep solitude of Don Quixote's imagination is essential to the existence of Cervantes's novel. It has never ceased to fascinate the European imagination, and is assimilated by Latin American ideology. The Mexican writer, Octavio Paz, succeeded in bringing the issue of solitude as a cultural phenomenon to the attention of North Americans and Europeans with his book, *The Labyrinth of Solitude* (1950). In the original text, Paz was particularly interested in identifying a context for Mexican culture specifically for Mexicans. As a result, the book is in various aspects vague and free-floating for those suffering from the rationalist emphases of the Euro-American mind. García Márquez, in a typically Latin American way, frequently criticizes North American cultural narrowness, with its emphasis on logical structures and its inability to drift with the kind of intuitive freedom that characterizes Latin American literature and thought in general.

The peculiar construction of Latin American solitude which is Paz's subject

has enormous political, psychological, developmental, and literary overtones
that are almost impenetrable to the rationalist western mind. When Paz writes,
for example, about secret language in the following terms, he distinguishes a
complexly emotional culture unshared by Anglo-Americans:

> In our daily language there is a group of words that are prohibited, secret,
> without clear meanings. We confide the expression of our most brutal or subtle
> emotions and reactions to their magical ambiguities. They are evil words, and we
> utter them in a loud voice only when we are not in control of ourselves. In a
> confused way they reflect our intimacy: the explosions of our vitality light them
> up and the depressions of our spirit darken them. They constitute a sacred
> language like those of children, poetry and sects. Each letter and syllable has a
> double life, at once luminous and obscure, that reveals and hides us.
>
> (trans. Lysander Kemp)

Spanish political theorists have put Cervantes' novel to use through the
centuries, but Don Quixote, with his borrowed language from the literary
past, does not predict this Latin American tendency to create dark, shared
verbal forms reflecting the sociopolitical quality of Spanish American life. To
put it another way, the Quixotic origin of solitude is here significantly
transgressed.

García Márquez told Apuleyo Mendoza in interview that he believes the
Latin American adage that the other side of solitude is solidarity. For him, the
concept of solitude, replete with political overtones and invaded by cultural
feeling, is equivalent to irremediable failures of human love and connectedness.
This is doubtless the easiest starting point for the Anglo-American mind, in
that it reduces the resonance and depth of the term "solitude," and particularly
renders his most famous book, *One Hundred Years of Solitude*, more accessible.
García Márquez also goes on to say that he believes that every writer essentially
writes only one book, and that his is the Book of Solitude – which is the theme
of all his writing. This is in fact not as easy or welcome a reduction of his work
as it at first appears to be. It is certainly true that vast, psychically lonely spaces
are enclosed within his characteristic plot structures, and his character
ensembles – whether family members, lovers, friends, political or martial
colleagues – are crushed and cut off by an ideological non-communality. But
his tales' metaphoric and mental separation from easy ontological interpretation is tied to styles and tones that encourage a depth of sensibility from
the reader to match the emotional power of the author.

In other words, solitude as a theme evokes García Márquez's stylistic
brilliance, producing a continuous experimentation with the possibilities of
his fiction. At the same time, it works towards a loving amelioration or even
transformation of a society dedicated to its own outcast status. In each book he
publishes, García Márquez re-evaluates his technical possibilities so that his
thematic adumbration will be more effective. Technically, he seems to have no
limit, but because learning to read *One Hundred Years of Solitude* was difficult

for his Anglo-American audience, the range of his technical experimentation elsewhere is often seriously played down. Tracing him backwards to the early stories and *Leaf Storm* is easy, because he incorporates a few of those tales into *One Hundred Years*, and because that novel floated around his work segmentally for years before its publication. When one looks at the major subsequent novels, however, the most obvious issue is that they bear no stylistic relationship to each other or to their famous forebear.

García Márquez claims to be outraged at the enormous success of *One Hundred Years of Solitude*, and in *The Fragrance of Guava* he goes so far as to say that technically the novel is not that good. Part of his objection comes from its continuing power to overshadow everything else he does, and the complaint is appropriate when one considers the poetic strain of *The Autumn of the Patriarch* (1975), the beautifully bare precision of *Chronicle of a Death Foretold* (1981), and the large sentimental power of *Love in the Times of Cholera* (1985) with its gorgeous, extended simplicity. But *One Hundred Years of Solitude* has survived two decades of undiminished popularity, and deserves its status. In spite of the limited but real international recognition of Cortázar or Carpentier, this book was singular in pushing aside the provincial reputation of Latin American literature. Borges's internationalism was famous, but for the writers of "El Boom" – the fomenting literary movement of Latin America in the 1960s – a newer thematic strain bearing little relationship to the European novel was required.

Major novels with certain thematic and compositional effects in common were around for García Márquez to consider – like José Donoso's *The Obscene Bird of Night* or Mario Vargos Llosa's *The Green House*. But *One Hundred Years of Solitude* particularized García Márquez as a voice in ways that neither Donoso nor Vargos Llosa with their comparable thematics of the house and civilization quite managed. Much of García Márquez's original success comes from the grace and fluidity of his style – his principal English translator, Gregory Rabassa, claims that he writes the most natural Spanish prose since Cervantes. But when one even begins to list the non-Borgesian names of that period in the 1960s – Asturias, Carpentier, Cortázar, Fuentes, Donoso, Vargas Llosa, Cabrera Infante – and considers how they continue to be unstoppable by anything except death, the intense nature of the competition is clear.

At the time of the publication of *One Hundred Years of Solitude* (1967), the Peruvian novelist Mario Vargas Llosa was in a mood to theorize about what he called the "total novel," and García Márquez became his subject in a study he entitled "García Márquez: History of a Deicide." In spite of the fact that in 1975 Vargas Llosa also wrote a study of another totalizing author, published in English as *The Perpetual Orgy: Flaubert and Madame Bovary*, the argument has not been lasting in terms of Latin American fiction, partly because his theory of deicide was rather muddled, and partly because the civilizational presentation of totality was too broad for coherence in hands other than those of García Márquez. Vargas Llosa had himself narrowly failed to write a really good book with *The Green House*, where his time frames, geographical intertwinings, and overlapping points of view are played in the high experimental form. But neither his style nor his narrative control was up to the task, and his recent work has shown a tendency to try to control fiction through a proto-narrative exemplification of history – an experiment that has made him into a better and more successful writer.

José Donoso, especially with *The Obscene Bird of Night* and more recently with *A House in the Country*, seems closer to García Márquez, especially to *The Autumn of the Patriarch* where the kaleidoscopic metaphors build with oneiric force. Nevertheless, although García Márquez has always expressed his recognition of his contemporaries, it never feels entirely right to bundle the members of "El Boom" together into the packet of "magical realism," especially as they have altered and reworked their subject matter so thoroughly since the 1960s. Nor does it make sense in the 1980s to condescend to these writers as merely exemplars of a tiresome style, as the English novelist, Julian Barnes, arrogantly does in his novel, *Flaubert's Parrot*. "Magical realism" was a self-induced tag, however, and García Márquez early encouraged its use.

In both journalistic essays and his interview with Apuleyo Mendoza, he stresses the unspeakable impact of the Amazonian basin on its inhabitants, and contrasts the Caribbean and the Andean climates and populations of his native Colombia. The excessive natural effects within Latin American countries combine with bewildering racial and religious mixtures to produce irrational, uncontained, and unrestrainable methods of perceiving the world. As a result, García Márquez can take things from both his Colombian cultural experience and his literary apprenticeship, and combine them in a way that transforms reality without belying it. Thus he entwines with equal stress accounts that are like Kafka's oneiric nightmares, and an apparently literal acceptance of the interpenetration of the worlds of the living and the dead; into what claims to be straightforward family and political life he inserts miraculous transformations of the ordinary, and bluffly uses bizarre tall-tales – like the miraculous transportation of Remedios the Beauty in *One Hundred Years* to heaven through the agency of bedsheets on a windy day. García Márquez says he learned this type of story-telling naturally through his grandmother's spontaneous use of what she considered true tales to explicate the world:

> As I've already said, my grandmother's stories probably gave me the first clues. The myths, legends and beliefs of the people in her town were, in a very natural way, all part of her everyday life. With her in mind, I suddenly realized that I wasn't inventing anything at all but simply capturing and recounting the world of omens, premonitions, cures and superstitions that is authentically ours, truly Latin American . . . . I was able to write *One Hundred Years of Solitude* simply by looking at reality, our reality, without the limitations which rationalists and

Stalinists through the ages have tried to impose on it to make it easier for them to understand . . . . [D]isproportion is part of our reality too. Our reality is in itself out of all proportion. This often presents serious problems for writers who can't find words to describe it.

(*The Fragrance of Guava*)

García Márquez also points out that each of his works demands its own style, and he is not dominated stylistically by the rich language of *One Hundred Years*:

I think the theme of the book determines the choice of technique and language. The language I use in *Nobody Writes to the Colonel, In Evil Hour* and in *Big Mama's Funeral* is concise, restrained and governed by a journalistic concern for efficiency. In *One Hundred Years of Solitude* I needed a richer language to introduce this other reality which we've agreed to call mythical or magical . . . . [In *The Autumn of the Patriarch*] I needed to find yet another language and extricate myself from the one I used in *One Hundred Years of Solitude*.

His finding of a language for *One Hundred Years* is a phenomenal success, and it is this inventive trueness of technique that thrust the novel to the forefront not only of the foment within Latin American literature but of the larger world of fictional possibilities. Coming within decades after Faulkner's phenomenal success in creating a language and a complex form for a geographical culture, it opened the doors to a literature of emergent civilization of the sort quickly caught up by, for example, Salman Rushdie in Britain. Its participation in Faulknerian and other late Modernist, post-Einsteinian experiments in time-scrambling gives it the kind of institutional cachet required for entry into the international canon.

Although García Márquez talks about the rich style required for *One Hundred Years*, he contradictorily argues its ordinariness, saying that "It's everybody's life story. Also, it's written in a simple, flowing, linear and I'd even say (I've said it before) superficial way." Given García Márquez's typical supple prose, this claim has its truths, and one can indeed say that his style is never baroque or mannerist, even in the midst of the ambitious poetic prose of *The Autumn of the Patriarch*. But there can be no doubt that all the technical devices of *One Hundred Years* are rich in the extreme, with surprises and special effects illuminating the text. A critic is always tempted to perform literary exercises out of reverence for the novel – to work on its epic frame, to interpret its cyclical view of time or history, to work on the house as a symbol, and to organize the generational flow around the almost everlasting character of Úrsula. None of this is entirely appropriate, however, and García Márquez says that his best reader is not one who adds to the critical detritus, but an old lady who laboriously rewrites his very words:

A Russian friend met a lady, a very old lady, who was copying the whole book out by hand, right to the last line. My friend asked her why she was doing it and the lady replied, "Because I want to find out who is really mad, the author or me, and the only way to find that out is to re-write the book." I find it hard to imagine a better reader than that lady.

(*The Fragrance of Guava*)

García Márquez implies in this passage that most critical tasks are secondary, whereas reading, rereading, and even being so textual as to copy out the novel to induce increased absorption are primary. In Italo Calvino's *If on a winter's night a traveler*, a best-selling novelist with a writer's block theorizes at length in a diary. As he tries to create the very essence of fiction at an almost idealistic level, he stops theorizing and begins to copy out the opening of *Crime and Punishment*. This act is both participatory and readerly: the primacy of a great novel can be responded to only through its own words.

And so I will copy out the first sentence of *One Hundred Years of Solitude*, as translated by Gregory Rabassa:

> Many years later, as he faced the firing squad, Colonel Aureliano Buendía was to remember that distant afternoon when his father took him to discover ice.

Although I cannot strain the patience of my publishers by writing out the rest of the book, let me quote too the last sentences of the ending, where in a paragraph lasting for two long pages, García Márquez blows the whole civilization of Macondo and the Buendías away through the dusts of time:

> Macondo was already a fearful whirlwind of dust and rubble being spun about by the wrath of the biblical hurricane when Aureliano skipped eleven pages so as not to lose time with facts he knew only too well, and he began to decipher the instant that he was living, deciphering it as he lived it, prophesying himself in the act of deciphering the last page of the parchments, as if he were looking into a speaking mirror. Then he skipped again to anticipate the predictions and ascertain the date and circumstances of his death. Before reaching the final line, however, he had already understood that he would never leave that room, for it was foreseen that the city of mirrors (or mirages) would be wiped out by the wind and exiled from the memory of men at the precise moment when Aureliano Babilonia would finish deciphering the parchments, and that everything written on them was unrepeatable since time immemorial and forever more, because races condemned to one hundred years of solitude did not have a second opportunity on earth.

The distance from the deceptive simplicity of the opening sentences to the complexity and time-erupting excitement of the novel's conclusion is great, but the reader is swept along from beginning to end by a maelstrom of devices, all loosely bound together by fascinating acts of solitude through generations of the Buendía family. In the process, García Márquez subtly and craftily prepares his receptor for the grand trick of the climactic last few pages. These pages – or this enormous paragraph (I have quoted only a small part of it above) – constitute a literary explicative game designed to teach something entirely new about narratology and the place of both the author and the reader within the act of fiction.

García Márquez's thematics in *One Hundred Years of Solitude* range from family to politics to a subtle study of narratology. In talking about the political, he tends to compartmentalize, saying that whereas *The Autumn of the Patriarch* is about the solitude of power, *One Hundred Years* is about the solitude of the family. But this novel also subverts heroic political myths through the character of the first Aureliano Buendía, who became a liberal radical, named himself a colonel, fought thirty-two wars, lost them all, and died in old age and solitude. His comrade-in-arms, Colonel Gerineldeo Márquez, recognizes the emptiness of the wars and their perversion of Aureliano through pride and the lust for power, but the fact that Aureliano loses all his battles is adequate to keep him from becoming the political patriarch of the next novel.

Nevertheless, the military-political Colonel Aureliano Buendía opens the novel by his presence in a sentence that rivals any great beginning or *incipit* in the history of fiction. The sentence is built to deceive in terms of readerly expectation, and to dislocate time. "Many years later" than what, one asks, since the story ranges from the founding of Macondo to its growth into a town as well as a civilization and a state of mind. The heroic centrality of Aureliano that the reader immediately expects is shortly to be disappointed. Given the finality of most firing squads, the assumption is that Aureliano as hero will die at the climax or end of the book, in a situation common to the Latin American military hero. And what does it mean to *discover* ice, even in a tropical setting?

Less than a hundred pages later – but not until then – we are told that Colonel Aureliano Buendía escapes the firing squad and that destinies in Macondo are always open-ended. Moreover, in this novel death does not obliterate a character should (s)he wish to remain spectrally within the world of the living, and the living may and frequently do wish to enter death-in-life. Whatever seems explicit or factual to the rationalist mind in this book is quickly released into a category that is mentalist rather than fantastic – that is, into a state that García Márquez always refers to as "real," and perhaps Nabokov is right when he says that "reality" should always have quotation marks around it:

> Over the years . . . I discovered that you can't invent or imagine just whatever you fancy because then you risk not telling the truth and lies are more serious in literature than in real life. Even the most seemingly arbitrary creation has its rules. You can throw away the fig leaf of rationalism only if you don't then descend into total chaos and irrationality . . . . [I loathe fantasy] because I believe the imagination is just an instrument for producing reality and that the source of creation is always, in the last instance, reality . . . . The difference between [imagination and fantasy] is the same as between a human being and a ventriloquist's dummy.
>
> (*The Fragrance of Guava*)

By the time the reader learns that his/her expectations of Colonel Aureliano Buendía's execution are broken, however, the amazing and often comic impact of García Márquez's narrativity is already absorbed. The first trick in reading this novel is to trust in disbelief. Transformations are constant, effects are unpredictable, and the inferences of exaggerated tall tales and folk mythologies seem to spring from neither author nor reader, but from the experience of the characters enacting them. The tremendous popularity of this novel within Latin America comes precisely from the fact that García Márquez's ethnic audience believes in the worlds that the characters invent; as narrator he himself is throughout most of the book a completely transparent presence.

The novel is organized around the image of the house, which is also the signifier of Macondo, the town whose founding, structure, and end miniaturize Latin American civilization. The unifying presence of the matriarchal Úrsula controls much of the novel's frame, but other women – like the equally matriarchal whore Pilar Ternera, the shadowy drudge Santa Sofia de la Piedad, the Andean Catholic Calvinist Fernanda del Carpo, the passionately neurotic Amaranta, and the last woman of the family, Amaranta Úrsula – crowd Úrsula in her structural task. When García Márquez finally allows Úrsula to die, curled up and helpless at the age of 125 or so, the book alters its structure – or rather slides into another frame almost unobtrusively in preparation for its windswept conclusion.

García Márquez says that the model for the shifting boundaries of the Buendía house was his grandparents' house in Aracataca, where he spent the early years of his life. The fictional Macondo is modeled on this village until the time of the last adult Buendía – Aureliano Babilonia, the decoder of Melquíades's parchments. When this Aureliano reaches his fictional ascendancy, the village retains the name of Macondo but takes on the essence of Barranquilla, the town where García Márquez spent his youthful poetry-reading journalistic days. In this very last section of *One Hundred Years*, the unified circular modality of the novel has changed so much that García Márquez is free to introduce four young literary men – the four "arguers" – clustered around the figure of a Spanish bookseller, the "wise Catalonian." One of these is Gabriel, whose girlfriend Mercedes works in the local drugstore. Gabriel is García Márquez's young Baranquillan self; Mercedes his wife of many years. This palpable intrusion of the author into the text goes beyond compulsive narratorial take-over; it is García Márquez's way of beginning to set up his ending where the sources of fiction will be displayed as clearly as possible.

Centered though this novel is on Macondo and the Buendías as a model of Latin American civilization, its structure indicates its devotion to an idea about literature. For García Márquez, the point is to urge fiction's connexion to a tall-tale version of meta-history and its transmission. Above all, he uses *One Hundred Years of Solitude* as a pattern for the acts and functions of the imagination, which he considers to be the central factor in literature. His "realism" is original in its sustained contemplation of how history is encoded into literature in the Latin American circumstance. This means, of course, that time and responses to it are major issues, but so too is the mind of the recorder and of his decoder. As the story of Macondo unfolds, the reader gradually receives "history" through authorial acts of memorial enlacement and encoding. The first occasion suggesting that history might collapse into immemorial night without words or meaning occurs with Macondo's insomnia plague. This obscure tropical disease wears down memory through sleepless months until all verbal ties with the outside world are lost. Recognizing their march toward the utter solitude of wordlessness, the Buendías label their most obvious possessions, writing notes to themselves to remind them that, for example, cows must be milked. But their minds slip so badly that even these verbal messages begin to lose their meanings, and they move toward silence and death.

The gypsy Melquíades intervenes with a magical potion to cure the Macondans of the insomnia plague just in time, thus restoring them to memory, history, and a continuing life within the realm of relative meaning. Melquíades is a magical manipulator in the novel, who from the beginning brings scientific devices that gradually take José Arcadio, the patriarch, through scientific history from magnets to alchemy and beyond. In other words, he presents the learning of civilization to a society with neither books nor a bookish tradition. As a mediator between learning and ignorance, Melquíades is a necessary visitor if civilization is to occur, and he early takes up the task of historian of the past and architect of the future. His visits are frequent but irregular; he dies several times, but manages either resurrections or spectral returns, so that his presence spans the generations of Macondo's symbolic one hundred years.

His most important task, however, is that of writer. With his obscure, almost supernatural gypsy background, he takes on cosmic qualities. As a writer-historian he inscribes the history of Macondo from beginning to inevitable end in Sanskrit – a language that needs scholarship in decoding, and that represents the Indo-European basis of western civilization. Locked in his secret room, he is visited by and instructs at least one melancholic, alienated Buendía per generation; as the generations pass, the scholarly Buendía of each period becomes more and more adept at decoding. Finally an Aureliano is able to read the history written by the magical Melquíades, thus bringing Macondo to its last moment, with the winds rising around the act of decoding to blow the whole novel away.

One Hundred Years of Solitude thus has three characters active in its verbal structure – in its presence as a narrative. First, Melquíades writes the parchments of its history with an epigraph that makes no sense until the end of the action: "*The first of the line is tied to a tree and the last is being eaten by the ants.*" As the last Buendía scholar finally reads the parchments, the pig's-tail baby is devoured by the ants; the simultaneity of the baby's death and his great-great-

great-grandfather's spectral presence tied to the tree breaks down the limits of time, at the same time as these two events define the symbolic boundaries of Macondo's history. Decoding can occur only when history - eternally present - is enacted and understood. In decoding, then, the last surviving Aureliano is also the active producer of the text, which can exist only through his act of comprehension. The third authorial presence is Gabriel - one of the four scholarly young "arguers" inserted into the end of the novel so that García Márquez can make his own authorial presence known after a long novel of transparent narrative where his voice has hitherto been unheard.

As a character at the end of the novel, Gabriel is important in that he is the only person in the latter days of Macondo who believes in its past history. As the novel's author and friend of the scholar–decoder Aureliano, he alone believes in the "truth" of historical Macondan events like the banana massacre or even the existence of Colonel Aureliano Buendía, now long dead. As an outsider-turned-insider, his task is to write the novel that the reader is undergoing, and he and Aureliano are both crucial in García Márquez's narratological strategy. Gabriel as García Márquez must write the book, but the quasi-historical novel cannot be completed unless the magical foundation - Melquíades' historical and prophetic parchments - is understood/decoded by a character within the text.

There is a trinity of compositional strategy here - from Melquíades who writes the quasi-historical text, to Aureliano who is part of that text, to Gabriel who is the literal writer. The reader is parallel to Aureliano as decoder, but without his actual narrative participation. The Macondo that is blown away at the end of the book signals closure. When the writer has finished his task and presented the text, when the reader has finished his/her task and read to the last page, Macondo is gone, the book is closed, the story of Macondo is over. The remaining character who existed in order to stress the idea of decoding is blown away with the town, and the closed book sets the reader back again into his/her private universe.

The genesis and production of fiction - from magical originator to a self-conscious decoding character, to the author who presents himself by name in the Proustian fashion, to the reader who reads and closes the book - are cunningly presented here, so that any reader is automatically exposed to García Márquez's perception of the fictional act. This strategy produces another chapter in the history of self-conscious fiction. Its originality, however, comes from the fact that the novel has not from the beginning, or through its extended middle, functioned according to the widely accepted agendas of narcissistic literature - nor does such an enslavement to typicality occur at any time in García Márquez's work. This is non-élitist fiction of great transparency - a sort of universal people's fiction that can be drifted through happily and episodically. Even the blowing away of Macondo at the end can be seen by innocent readers as another episode - like the levitation of the priest or

Mauricio Babilonia's butterflies. The ability to write a fiction of such sophistication with unpretentious ease is García Márquez's greatest gift.

In *One Hundred Years of Solitude*, the characters not only suffer various solitudes and show their basic inability to love, but the fiction itself comes from the solitude of Melquíades, and of the various Buendías who attempt scholarly preparations for the decoding of his parchments. The thematic stress of solitude is therefore both negative and positive, in that it isolates characters, but at the same time produces creative acts necessary for the fiction. In *Chronicle of a Death Foretold*, on the other hand, the author as decoder tries to piece together the congeries of mistiming and stupidity in the events that led to the murder of Santiago Nasar; he does so by trying vainly, in almost journalistic style, to pierce the solitude of characters who can be talked to twenty-three years after the murder. This flawlessly constructed novella is in its tightness the opposite of *One Hundred Years*, or indeed of the lengthy near-sentimentalism of *Love in the Times of Cholera*.

Although *Chronicle of a Death Foretold* is short, with its events timed to the minute and covering only a few hours on one early morning in the town of Riohacha, the narrator develops tone, facts, and characters with extraordinary economy. The techniques of compression were learned from García Márquez's long apprenticeship in short stories – a genre which he is unusually good at writing. As in the case of the suggestively haunting and technically brilliant story, "No One Writes to the Colonel," this novella pares down its verbal structures so that the technical demand on the author is enormous. Like Nabokov in *Lolita*, García Márquez is under great aesthetic pressure here, but he never miswrites a word – and Gregory Rabassa's translation into English manages to convey the precision of the original Spanish. Unlike the overflowing energy of *One Hundred Years*, the briskness of the tale shows another facet of the solitude of non-communication that is so important in García Márquez's thematics.

If *One Hundred Years* is about the solitude of the family and *The Autumn of the Patriarch* about the solitude of power, as García Márquez claims, then *Chronicle of a Death Foretold* is about the solitude within community. Riohacha acts like a comfortably unified place – everyone knows everyone else, and indeed most of the inhabitants are friends interrelated by blood ties. García Márquez shows how the very existence of machismo automatically combines with chance timing and the total inability of a society to accept the relatedness or responsibility that would prevent the twins, Pedro and Pablo Vicario, from killing their victim. So remote are the participants (they include the whole town, even Santiago Nasar's mother who accidentally bars the front door just as her son attempts to escape his death by running through it) from each other that they fail to take simple steps to stop the ritual butchery. Young men, women, friends, aunts, barmen, shopowners, the priest, the mayor – all are given ample chance to intervene, but no intervention occurs, and well before Santiago Nasar is actually slaughtered rumors circulate that he is already dead.

García Márquez's dramatic point is an indictment of a society where nothing connects. Long after Santiago's murder, the townsfolk still excuse themselves even though their guilt is obvious:

> But most of those who could have done something to prevent the crime and still didn't do it consoled themselves with the pretext that affairs of honor are sacred monopolies with access only for those who are part of the drama. "Honor is love," I heard my mother say. Hortensia Baute, whose only participation was having seen two bloody knives that weren't bloody yet, felt so affected by the hallucination that she fell into a penitential crisis and one day, unable to take it any longer, she ran out naked into the street. Flora Miguel, Santiago Nasar's fiancée, ran away out of spite with a lieutenant of the border patrol, who prostituted her among the rubber workers on the Vichada. Aura Villeros, the midwife who had helped bring three generations into the world, suffered a spasm of the bladder when she heard the news and to the day of her death had to use a catheter in order to urinate. Don Rogelio de la Flor, Clotilde Armenta's good husband, who was a marvel of vitality at the age of eighty-six, got up for the last time to see how they had hewn Santiago Nasar to bits against the locked door of his own house, and he didn't survive the shock. Placida Linero had locked that door at the last moment, but with the passage of time she freed herself from blame. "I locked it because Divina Flor had sworn to me that she'd seen my son come in," she told me, "and it wasn't true."

The two murderers, bound by a macho code of honor to revenge the supposed deflowering of their sister, tell everyone of their intention in a vain but desperate attempt to be stopped by familial, legal, or ecclesiastical authorities. García Márquez makes it clear that the failure of an entire community comes from a brooding inwardness and solitary unconnectedness that afflict each person to the point of paralysis.

Again, García Márquez's structural achievements carry the novella, which dodges from the present of the murder, to the past circumstances that cause it, to a future in which the narrator tries to reconstruct it. This temporal interweaving in *Chronicle of a Death Foretold* is accomplished again by the presence of the Gabriel García Márquez persona in the text – as though he were an investigative newspaper reporter trying to work out the truth of the tale. In a small way, since there is an historical basis to the story, this book is a hyper-literary and ironically mimetic analogue to his much earlier *Story of a Shipwrecked Sailor*, in which he gives the account of a Colombian sailor who drifted without food and water for ten days, returned home to a hero's welcome, and then was politically demoted to obscurity. But by the time García Márquez wrote *Chronicle of a Death Foretold*, his narrational techniques are developed to a much subtler degree, and he strongly exploits the possibilities in fiction for a nearly total transformation of reality.

García Márquez is part of the action in this fiction, but he is more apparently

33

present than in *One Hundred Years of Solitude*. Here, he is the first-person narrator, and his family – including García Márquez's mother, his sister Margot, his sister who is a nun, and his wife Mercedes – are all referred to. The deflowered woman is presented as his cousin, as are the two murderers; although the reader knows the nature of the fictional representation taking place here, the mesmerizing sense of reality is overwhelming. The narrator says he was among the group of young men at the huge wedding feast of the murderers' sister, who is returned dishonorably to her family late that night because her bridegroom has discovered that she isn't a virgin. But he also points out that "I had a very confused memory of the festival before I decided to rescue it piece by piece from the memory of others." The García Márquez narrator–persona says that in the process of investigation he discovered marginal pieces of information, a few of which he recounts, and which help in the piecemeal building of the edifice of the book.

Indeed, the major achievement of *Chronicle of a Death Foretold* is its presentation of pieces of information and blocks of time – each discrete and illustrative of the solitary separation that exists in this society. From these bits and pieces, the construction of a seamless tale that builds great suspense and anguish – even though the reader knows from the first page that the victim will be killed – is one of the best hat-tricks of fiction in a long time. When Santiago Nasar, brutally hacked and with his hands full of his intestines, topples dead in his mother's kitchen in the last few lines of the tale, the affect is deep, and the reader afflicted by an almost surprisingly inconceivable horror.

Out of separation and solitude, out of disparate pieces of cultural trivia, García Márquez at every turn in his career is able to build novels of unequaled power and imagination. His ability to patch up and piece together the materials of his society's imagination into large cultural frames is as important as his need to force the experimental boundaries of literature, and in both he has no peer.

*

In *Ways of Escape*, the second of Graham Greene's slim collections of autobiographical essays, he says that he consciously entered the Quixotic world in about 1961:

> At the end of a long journey, without knowing myself the course which I had been taking, I found myself, in "A Visit to Morin" and *A Burnt-Out Case*, in that tragi-comic region of La Mancha where I expect to stay.

He was still there, in 1982, publishing a slight and rather tender novel entitled *Monsignor Quixote*. In a writer as occluded as Greene, it is difficult to tell what resonances something like the Manchegan plain might call up, and it is impossible to know whether he perceives the tragi-comedy of La Mancha as connected to his own particular uses of solitude. As a European, Greene's cultural connexions are in some ways closer to *Don Quixote* than those of Latin

American writers whose culture is overlaid with so many other factors, as García Márquez is always eager to point out.

Greene has certainly played on the idea of solitude for a very long time indeed, and on the Quixotic distance between illusion and reality as well. His heroes usually try to close that gap and to discover reality through characterological means – that is, by using their bleak sense of failure and emotional withholding to keep the illusionistic or fantastic from breaking in. But Greene in interviews with Marie-Françoise Allain argues that:

> I started writing – at fourteen or even earlier – very young, anyway. I produced bad fantasies, fables of a sort. This propensity toward the fantastic, towards fantasy has remained a subdued undercurrent in my work. You'll find it in *Under the Garden* [an early work], in the short stories entitled *A Sense of Reality*, and of course in my last novel, *Doctor Fischer of Geneva*.
>
> (*The Other Man: Conversations with Graham Greene*, 1983)

The impression given by Greene's work, however, is that in general honest survival can occur only if fantasy is kept at bay – and the illusions of Don Quixote are not really confronted until *Monsignor Quixote*.

It is nevertheless true that Greene allows fantastic elements to leak fastidiously into his novels from time to time before this, occasionally in infelicitous ways that touch on the sentimental and weaken certain novels – as, for example, through the fantastic indications of canonization of the whisky priest after his execution in *The Power and the Glory*. But Greene's own interpretation of the primary Quixotic elements appears to center on the tragicomedy inherent in Cervantes. Before the publication of *Monsignor Quixote* in 1982, he kept himself under tighter controls, although it is true that the novels since the early 1960s have had a stronger eruptive comic impulse than some of the earlier ones.

Greene has, of course, been turning out novels (he used to call the early thrillers "entertainments," but gave that up decades ago) since the 1930s. As I try to place him in the context of contemporary fiction, it is, however, appropriate to stick to an historically Postmodern context. I will therefore concern myself only with *The Honorary Consul* (1973), *The Human Factor* (1978), *Doctor Fischer of Geneva or The Bomb Party* (1980), and *Monsignor Quixote*. Greene's early popularity and his quick mastery of a style, a voice, and the techniques of structuring fiction brought him early fame, and critical studies of him have been going on for a long time. These studies work out his theological position (perhaps, justly speaking, they recount his heresies), or describe and populate Greeneland. As time goes on, arranging Greene according to theme and taxonomic periodizations of the work becomes more tempting. Like Saul Bellow, he is out of academic favor at the moment because of his refusal to alter his commitment to realism, but his popularity among readers is unabated.

One of the results of his long productivity is that a vocabulary for talking about Greene was established a long time ago, and to write yet again about his religious commitment to doubt, his emphasis on failure and on divided loyalties, his bleak landscapes of the mind, and his eclectic political interests would sound like essays from the 1960s. It is possible to say that he simply keeps on going in the same way, but he also keeps writing new things on into the 1970s and 1980s that bear an imprint of contemporaneity in an interesting way. The four novels in question are all significant in different degrees; all except *Monsignor Quixote* to an extent echo vintage Greene. But one of them, *The Honorary Consul*, is arguably his best book; *The Human Factor* is a flawlessly conceived spy tale that quashes Le Carré's attempt to denigrate Greene's insistence that the worldwide ideological battle is between Communism and Catholicism; *Doctor Fischer of Geneva* is a negative fairytale in which the dragon is the cold greed of capitalism; *Monsignor Quixote* is an oddity.

In these novels, the idea of solitude is of structural significance to Greene as it is to García Márquez, and Greene's particular thematics of solitude continue to produce a kind of fiction welcome to the contemporary mind. Recently he has taken on the literary scene in ways that he did not do earlier. For years his heroes have read the English classics in odd political corners of the Third World, and the gap between the security of the English literary tradition and the grimly demented politics of the mid- to late twentieth century has been a useful device for him. But with his self-conscious movement toward La Mancha and his increasing interest in the desire-torn illusionistic mind of Don Quixote, Greene's current stance is more distinctly bookish than before.

In *The Honorary Consul* – the earliest of the four books under discussion – the literary content is unusually extensive, and much of that content serves as a direct commentary on the Latin American novel. Doctor Eduardo Plarr, Greene's typically solitary hero trying always to face the irremediable world, is the only resident in the godforsaken town on the Paraguayan border who reads books. With a touch of provincialism, Greene associates this habit with Plarr's English father, and there is no doubt that his judgments are to be seen as exemplary. As he reads, a contrast is set up between the *Ficciones* of Borges and the typical Latin American novels of machismo written by another character in the novel, Jorge Julio Saavedra. Note how Greene briefly but elegantly estimates Borges:

> He chose a collection of stories by Jorge Luis Borges. Borges shared the tastes he had himself inherited from his father – Conan Doyle, Stevenson, Chesterton. *Ficciones* would prove a welcome change from Doctor Saavedra's last novel which he had not been able to finish. He was tired of South American heroics. Now Doctor Plarr, sitting under the statue of an heroic sergeant – *machismo* again – who had saved the life of San Martin – was it a hundred and fifty years ago? – read with a sense of immense relaxation of the Countess of Bagno Regio, of Pittsburgh and Monaco. After a time he grew thirsty. To appreciate Borges properly he had to be taken, like a cheese biscuit, with an apéritif.

Plarr particularly admires Borges's precision – a stylistic factor that Greene cultivates unceasingly – as opposed to the fulsome clichés of the kind of old-fashioned Latin American novel written by Saavedra. By naming this character after the matronym of Cervantes whose full name is Miguel de Cervantes Saavedra, Greene implies that the flip side of the coin from the ironic and tragicomic world of Don Quixote is the overblown weight of clichéd romantic machismo that dominated the Latin American novel before El Boom. It is clear in *The Honorary Consul* that Saavedra is already out of step and has outlived his genre, even though he continues doggedly to write still another bad novel. He is deeply excited about his first "political" novel, starring a one-legged girl who symbolizes "this poor crippled country." Failing to see the inherent comedy, he explains his romanticism to a bored Plarr:

> "A poet – the true novelist must always be in his way a poet – a poet deals in absolutes. Shakespeare avoided the politics of his time, the minutiae of politics. He wasn't concerned with Philip of Spain, with pirates like Drake. He used the history of the past to express what I call the abstraction of politics. A novelist today who wants to represent tyranny should not describe the activities of General Stroessner in Paraguay – that is journalism not literature."

For Greene, the real novelist does not indulge in silly symbolism but describes the real General Stroessner in Paraguay, and his bored Plarr shows what Greene thinks of the tradition of romanticizing the nature of the artist. When the honorary consul's life is seriously threatened, the foolishness of Saavedra's conception of the sacred novelist is made fully dramatic. Plarr believes that founding an Anglo-Argentinian Club of the three Anglophiles in the town and writing an appeal to the London *Times* (Greene's life is full of letters to *The Times*) might move the Argentine government to action and thus save Fortnum. Saavedra, brought up on the macho overblown Argentine epic poem *Martín Fierro*, baulks at the prose: "To sign a piece of prose like that? It would be much easier to give my life." He then offers himself publicly as a substitute for Fortnum, but so low has his reputation become as new concepts of fiction rush forward that he is ignored.

The subtheme of the nature of fiction is strong in *The Honorary Consul*, but Greene humanizes it, admiring the fortitude and lonely persistence of poor Saavedra. When he sees the poverty that the dapper old writer tries hard to cover, Plarr is both appalled and impressed:

> He felt a new respect for Doctor Saavedra. His obsession with literature was not absurd whatever the quality of his books. He was willing to suffer poverty for its sake, and a disguised poverty was far worse to endure than an open one. The effort needed to polish his shoes, to press the suit.... He couldn't, like the young, let things go. Even his hair must be cut regularly. A missing button would reveal too much. Perhaps he would be remembered in the history of Argentine literature only in a footnote, but he would have deserved his footnote. The bareness of the room could be compared to the inextinguishable hunger of his literary obsession.

37

This literary obsession and the hard-earned footnote are more than Plarr has or achieves in the world, and the carefully constructed contrast between this old failed writer and the young successful doctor whose death ends the novel helps to give Greene's thematic point major emphasis.

As a typically Greeneian protagonist, Plarr lives in a solitude created by his own withholding of himself. He has a successful medical practice, has successful sexual affairs with married women, and is currently under what he is convinced must be a temporary enchantment with Clara, Charley Fortnum's young wife, on whom he has fathered a child that Fortnum believes to be his own. Plarr's emotional parsimony, which he believes to be a stern expression of reality, is imposed on Clara who is obviously in love with him, so that, following his insistence, she forces herself to suppress her natural sexual expressiveness. The last question she asks him, which he does not answer and later while awaiting his death in the hut in the *barrio* neurotically cannot remember, is, "Eduardo, will you always be angry if I love you?" By evoking Freudian oppositions, Greene shows how deep and humanly destructive Plarr's suppressions are.

In *The Honorary Consul*, the major characters are fully developed with an ease and sureness beyond even the best earlier books. Plarr is the only one in the novel who tries to live without passion and connectedness, and he is thus contrasted not only with the literary Saavedra, but also with the passionately committed revolutionaries, León Rivas and Aquino, with the astute and determined police chief, Colonel Perez, with Charley Fortnum who loves drink and tenderly loves Clara, and with Clara herself whom he forces into emotional suppression. This novel is dramatically about love and about its protagonist's failure to enact it. Unlike the novels of García Márquez where failures of love are endemic, this book celebrates loving connection and ends in desperately effective tragicomedy. Plarr dies through the stupidity of others and his own duplicity, but the weak, loving Fortnum survives to look after and understand Clara and to help her acknowledge her love of Plarr. In the hands of a less controlled writer, this ending would doubtless fall into sentimentality – something that occasionally almost happened in early Greene. But here the drama of solitude is perfectly sustained, and the corruption of the innocent in webs of politics and personal incapacities is flawlessly limned out.

Energizing *The Honorary Consul* is a sense of stupidity and crossed destinies in which the presentation of individual details is extremely important. Among the *données* of the book, the idea of naivety on the part of the functioning revolutionaries, León Rivas (an ex-priest, former believer and theologian, and schoolfriend of Plarr) and Aquino (a poet with theories about how literature is altered by political experience), is major. In obviously parodic style, they are given orders by their anonymous Paraguayan anti-Stroessner leader, known only as "El Tigre," who hatched the plan of kidnapping the American ambassador to Argentina. The fact that they get poor old Charley Fortnum who is British and only an honorary consul with no diplomatic status whatever, shows the level of innocence and stupidity at which they operate. Essentially Doctor Plarr is sentenced to death because of their incompetence, and because drunken Charley recognizes him when he comes to the *barrio* at León's request to give him medical aid. The elements of chance are huge, comical, and fatal.

The mistaken identity, leading to the revolutionaries' amateurish capture of Fortnum instead of the American ambassador, is in a way akin to a hilarious Latin American fictional incident. In Julio Cortázar's *A Manual for Manuel*, terrorists kidnap a penguin - and given Charley Fortnum's unimportance, they have the better deal. On the other hand, the entrapment of Plarr is connected not only to Fortnum and his attempt to be decent to the man he has cuckolded, but also to the fact that his father, who had abandoned him and his mother for political reasons when Plarr was 14, is believed to be in a Paraguayan prison. This political connexion makes Plarr suspect to Colonel Perez, and helps seal his fate. The buried psychic effect of his father's abandonment of him when he was an adolescent clearly shapes much of his withdrawn, withheld personality, and there is some sort of grand poetic assonance in the fact that he is told by León shortly before his own death that his father is dead - shot in the head while he was lying down. At the end of his life, Plarr too lies down, hoping to escape, but Colonel Perez's officers shoot him, also in the head, bringing him to the identical end. Fatherhood is the central theme of this book, as Clara's pregnancy and Plarr's neurosis indicate, and Greene ties all parts of action and imagery into this design.

If *The Human Factor* had been written thirty years before it was, Greene would no doubt have called it an "entertainment." It is a spy story written on a high level, enlaced with the conflicting ideas of solitude and connexion, and very much part of Greene's late thematic interests. Its protagonist, Maurice Castle, is a double agent out of gratitude for the love of his black South African wife and her young son, Sam. His limited political commitment is to certain aspects of the west rather than to Russia, but he is forced into a final betrayal and a quickly engineered escape to Russia because of a joint British-German-American-South African plan called Uncle Remus, which involves the nuclear bombing of certain homelands in order to control revolution within South Africa. Ironically Castle's help was not needed, but his steps are irreversible. The impact of the novel lies in its potentially predictive qualities (nuclear bombing in South Africa is a possibility), as well as its ironic depiction of love imperfectly shared because of the self-imposed solitude of Castle, the spy. He finally recovers love perfectly with his wife for a few hours by confessing his double agency, but loses it when he enters a permanent Russian solitude where his wife cannot join him because of the sheer chance that, at the propitious time, her son Sam is ill. Their separation is mediated by the fact that their love persists, but with no hope of reunion.

Greene's grimness in this thriller is directed less at politics than at his titular idea – human factors that should be positive in fact drive a life in impossible directions and shut off access to contentment. In 1936 Greene wrote an essay entitled, "Henry James: the private universe," in which he criticizes James's magnificent prefaces,

> where he describes the geneses of his stories, where they were written, the method he adopted, the problems he faced: he seems, like the conjurer with rolled sleeves, to show everything. But you have to go further back than the anecdote at the dinner-table to trace the origin of such urgent fantasies. In this exploration his prefaces, even his autobiographies, offer very little help.

Later in the same essay, he interprets James's working materials thus:

> They were materialists, his characters, but you cannot read far in Henry James's novels without realizing that their creator was not a materialist. If ever a man's imagination was clouded by the Pit, it was James's. When he touches this nerve, the fear of spiritual evil, he treats the reader with less than his usual frankness.

Greene has always acknowledged a debt to James, and like him took on the job of writing prefaces to his novels in the Heinemann/Bodley Head Collected Edition. These prefaces are not terribly useful, and as in the case of James, the reader has to go further back. Similarly Greene's autobiographies – *A Sort of Life* and *Ways of Escape* – do not illuminate very much. They are repetitive, and in a parsimonious way almost melodramatic in their reiterated accounts of his suicidal wishes, his games with Russian roulette, his adolescent psychoanalysis, and his other rather glamorous adventures. It is as though Greene decided to set limits on what he would give out, and Julian Symons, in an interesting review article on *Monsignor Quixote* in *The Times Literary Supplement*, argues that there is a fair amount of inconsistency and disingenuous fabrication in what he does tell. According to Symons, Greene is always interested in ambiguity rather than accuracy, and one could go so far as to say that Greene is a Henry James redivivus, who has been run through the heroics of the British empire and the corruption of the political present. Greene is particularly interested in the sense of evil, betrayal, and treachery in James, and his own view of human relations is aligned to these subjects as well.

The human factor as a longed-for base leading to a love that will inevitably be disconnected by events, chance, and our own characters is major in Greene's definition of solitude. When solitude is broken by love, as it is in *The Human Factor*, Greene automatically causes its return, and the rhythm of solitude–love–solitude is held steadily through these last books. In *Doctor Fischer of Geneva or the Bomb Party*, the protagonist – a middle-aged Englishman with only one hand (one is reminded of the one-legged girl in Saavedra's novel in *The Honorary Consul*), who works as a poorly paid translator in a chocolate factory in Switzerland – is suddenly, miraculously loved by the beautiful, lonely daughter of the richest and most cynical capitalist in Geneva. They marry and live happily, but this fairytale idyll is quickly broken by her death in a pointless skiing accident, and Jones is once more returned to solitude – but a solitude eaten at by the cynical corruption of his father-in-law's sadistic parties aimed at revealing the bottomless greed of the rich.

In a way, *Doctor Fischer of Geneva* is a chilling bagatelle – a means of releasing fantasy and then returning it to reality with a harshness reminiscent of the death of the original Don Quixote. In this novel Greene is briefer than usual, more romantic, allowing more childish hope, and crushing it with a harsh hand. Thematically and tonally, he is also not all that far from the next novel, which is the most atypical in his *oeuvre, Monsignor Quixote*. Here Greene retains his mixture of theological interest and political stress, but the novel is so allegorical, and played so tightly to the orchestration of *Don Quixote*, that it bears no extended resemblance to his previous novels. Picking up an allegorical form in which his two main characters are not only modern Spanish parodies of Don Quixote and Sancho Panza but representatives of mystical, doubting Catholicism and idealistic Marxism takes him out of the immediate ideologies of Cervantes's novel and into his own political thematics.

Like his "ancestor's," Monsignor Quixote's books cause him trouble: they are the great texts of western Christendom – Saint John of the Cross, Saint Teresa, Saint Augustine, Saint Francis de Sales, and the Gospels. These are opposed by Church orthodoxy which especially highlights the arid moral theology of Father Heribert Jone. Monsignor Quixote's behavior is perceived as mad when it is only innocent – indeed some of Greene's would-be comic descriptions of his holy innocence are the weakest parts of the novel. To the degree that he resembles his literary forebear, the Monsignor exists in the truth of doubt; his illusion at the end of the novel that the host of the Eucharist is present when there is nothing there connects to visionary mystical experience, and Greene clearly means the reader to see him as a gentle paragon of Christian behavior.

Monsignor Quixote has great charm, and is the warmest of Greene's novels. It is also the one that is closest to the intertextuality – the dependence on and inter-quotation among former texts – so celebrated in contemporary fiction. But aside from touching passages, it sits barrenly against its great Renaissance Spanish avatar, rather like John Hawkes's sterile *The Lime Twig* against Greene's own *Brighton Rock*. Perhaps a comment on the devices and tricks of the genre-wrenching quasi-imitative form of parody is made by these examples. On occasion, a great novel can be set in the arm of a previous great novel, but not often, and the device is dangerous and difficult to perform. Nevertheless, Greene's willingness to break pattern and go beyond a honing of his distinctive style shows his continuous tendency to remain a presence within the world of literature as long as he lives.

In these two master stylists, Gabriel García Márquez and Graham Greene, the paradox of contemporary literature is significantly played out. Both are widely read, immensely popular, infinitely accomplished. Neither is part of a small and self-consciously experimental coterie; both are accessible. Above all, both live and write and publish now, and they represent a part of that puzzling labyrinth that is contemporary fiction.

PART II

The masters of metafiction

3

Borges: the old master

Many of Jorge Luis Borges's readers – especially those interested in critical theory – see his prose works as self-conscious allegories commenting discreetly on the ontological status of fiction itself. This is an élitist way of fitting him into present fashions, but it is just to go along with those admirers who call Borges – the great reader who by his driftingly ingenious fictions teaches others to read – the old master of several sorts of literary Postmodernism. He is equally master of the art of writing a densely allusive and formidable new genre which, with typical humility, he continued to call the short story until the end of his life. Like Nabokov and Beckett, his early career is firmly fixed in high Modernism; unlike them he did not continuously advance to newer styles, but remained with his best work – the style of fiction, poetry, and meditation he established in the 1940s and 1950s, when his greatest work occurred. Borges's case, more than that of any other writer, indicates the problem of trying to distinguish between Modernism and Postmodernism in a historical way, and a textual study of his fictions takes the reader toward an exemplary rather than a theoretical view of what literary Postmodernism might actually be.

His competitor in both experimental categories – Postmodernism and brief fiction – is, of course, Samuel Beckett, whose recent return to the briefest of prose fictions – or dramas, or whatever they are – is characterized by increasing linguistic complications. On the one hand Beckett's late work expands the possibilities of language, and on the other it reasserts the Pirandelloesque desire of the author to evanesce, to use language forms endlessly and strangely in order to join finally the great silence toward which all of Beckett's protagonists yearn. Beckett stands alone and lonely at the end of the great Modernist-Kafkaesque-Joycean voice, refracting where Joyce and Kafka had joined, and grimly using literature's terminality in a way that paradoxically refreshes the idea of fiction as a free and licit genre-less mode.

Borges, on the other hand, took on a significantly different task in his fertile use of the bookish past to reopen a consciously literary world of readerly possibility. Beckett's work at the end of his career may be more in keeping with some types of Postmodernism, defined for literature by such critics as John Barth or Ihab Hassan and, in a culturally broader way, Jean-François Lyotard. His final breaking of conventional ideas like verbal expressiveness, form, content, intention, and meaning – all of the concepts, that is, that have to do with residual semantics as opposed to linguistic play and its immediate referents – accord with Postmodernism's longing to smash the pieties of literary history. Although Beckett may seem to have the edge in the experimental linguistic realm as well as in the philosophical skepticism essential to Postmodernism, the proliferating definitions of Postmodernism – at least those concerned with language and literature – accommodate Borges's fictions gracefully and eagerly. His work also gives practical and concrete evidence of the semantic richness possible within the inexhaustibility of any fiction, including and perhaps especially the metafictions of Postmodernism.

Of these two major writers who in 1961 shared the International Publishers' Prize, Borges is the one whose recent influence has shone more brightly for writers who succeeded him – including Calvino, whose theories about the task of fiction are, as I argue in a later section, more closely aligned with Beckett's. When the American John Barth first chose to define Postmodernism as a literary idea in 1967 in his seminal essay, "The literature of exhaustion," Borges's techniques and Barth's private interpretation of them allowed that essay to set a standard for other authors whom Barth wished to place within his perception of the Postmodernist mode. Barth's idea that the genres of literature are exhausted and must be played against parodically by any genuinely original contemporary writer was extrapolated directly from Borges's endless reflections on his own literary masters, and the subsequent creative parodic play that arose from these reflections.

Before Barth's use of Borges in this essay, the Argentinian's reputation was established beyond Latin America, and has steadily increased as contemporary critical schools of narratology belatedly stress what his fictions had already elegantly explored during the waning of the Modernist period. More significant than Borges's placement in the Postmodernist canon, perhaps, is the fact that his international reputation, dormant for too long, grew with astonishing rapidity and continues unabated. It is not simply that he is the writer most indisputably present on all reading lists of contemporary literature, but his impact is notably visible over a wide spectrum: on Latin American writers (even those who disagree with and often disapprove of him), on the French *nouveaux romanciers*, on American experimentalism, on Italian writers like Italo Calvino and Umberto Eco.

The case of Umberto Eco is of particular interest when discussing both Borges and the term Postmodernism, because in his *Postscript to The Name of the Rose* Eco indicates the confusion inherent in the inappropriate and inaccurate use of the term itself:

Actually, I believe that postmodernism is not a trend to be chronologically defined, but, rather, an ideal category – or, better still, a *Kunstwollen*, a way of operating. We could say that every period has its own postmodernism, just as every period has its own mannerism (and, in fact, I wonder if postmodernism is not the modern name for mannerism as a metahistorical category). I believe that in every period there are moments of crisis like those described by Nietzsche in his *Thoughts Out of Season*, in which he wrote about the harm done by historical studies. The past conditions us, harries us, blackmails us. The historic avant-garde . . . tries to settle scores with the past.

In architecture and the arts, Postmodernism began as a rather poor historical term for aggressive artistic production that attempted to assert the end of and freedom from the great period of Modernism that dominated the first half of the twentieth century. Quickly seeing its own disjunctive world-weariness, it connects with the proliferation of a series of comparable new *fin-de-siècle* jargon words with metahistorical overtones – post-nuclear, post-Freudian, post-humanist, post-cultural, etc. As a term, Postmodernism keeps trying to settle scores with the past; it tries with predestined futility to separate itself definitively from Modernism, to become something like a new Romantic movement with its own discrete types of irony and renewed parataxis. Fumbling as it must over the creation of new forms, Postmodernism now embraces all writers whose self-conscious structures can be defined as narcissistic narratives (see Linda Hutcheon's *Narcissistic Narrative*), that is, narratives that are endlessly self-reflexive in particular parodic modes not quite shared by Modernism.

Eco is also interesting in any discussion of Borges in that he deliberately invokes and parodies Borges in the novel, *The Name of the Rose*. The issues here are not simple, because the parody exists at several levels, from simple naming – his villain is the blind old would-be librarian, Jorge of Burgos – to the most complex reflections of images and narrative stratagems used by the Argentinian writer. The verbal similarity between the names Jorge Luis Borges and Jorge of Burgos constitutes a sort of game. Because the reader of *The Name of the Rose* knows that Borges was blind, infinitely bookish, and a jealous guard of the idea of labyrinths, mirrors, and libraries, Eco cleverly invokes his benign and admirable image as a red herring that will distract the imprecise reader from unravelling the detective plot with undue haste.

In a book of such strong intertextual stress, moreover, the evocation of Borges reminds the reader that *The Name of the Rose* is not merely a quasi-medieval fiction. It exists significantly in a post-Borgesian world, where the pressure is from the far past but also from the very near past – indeed from a writer alive and revered when *The Name of the Rose* was written and published. Eco, when asked as he frequently is why he evokes Borges negatively, simply says that certain debts must be paid. Many readers of Eco over-read those debts as, for example, Walter E. Stephens (1983) does when he posits Borges's fictions as the primary "anterior text" for Eco's novel. This partial view must be countered by saying that Borges's works are not singularly primary for Eco, or they are so only in ways that stress the medieval roots of both Borges and Postmodernism, a point that Eco is eager to make.

Like Borges (and indeed, like many formalist critics including Todorov) Eco sees the detective novel as a dominant metaphysical mode, the unraveling of which leads to major epistemological illustrations through which the author can impose his/her will, or at least demonstrate it to the reader. As metafiction has developed since the 1960s, this aspect of detective plot – of narrative within solvable mazes – has been major, and Borges's *modus operandi* a dominant influence. And like Borges, Eco contrasts the readable, solvable labyrinth with the endless mazes that are not made by humans but imposed by the mysteries of the universe. For Borges, however, the term "divine" is ironic, but not as alien as it is for Eco, whose essential scientism makes the world more readable (in spite of its infinite maze-like openness) than it is for Borges; similarly, "infinite" for Borges indicates a vast idealist slippage of time and space in a way that the Peircean Eco does not envisage.

When we come to the shared images of the two writers – the labyrinth, the library, the mirror – we cannot claim any particular influence of the older on the younger, but rather a commonality of response to literatures and cultures for these two writers who extend their reading far back into the lettered world of books where these ancient metaphors were endlessly repeated. No doubt the evocation of Borges is also interesting to Eco because of the tendency in contemporary studies to abjure obligations to the Christian past and its images, to refuse to pay debts or to recognize the richness present in the history of an idea. In the symbolic person of Borges, the most mandarin of contemporary writers, Eco finds a touchstone of cultural bookishness.

Bookish as he is, Borges writes amazingly short pieces, and in the process of doing so has been instrumental in legitimizing and defining a new genre within metafiction; indeed he has almost created the standard or background for the category of metafiction as it has been so eagerly seized by French and Italian theorist-writers, and more boisterously by American experimentalists from John Barth and Donald Barthelme to Steve Katz and Ronald Sukenick. The anomaly here is, of course, that Borges does not boast of himself as an innovator within genre, but rather as a perpetuator of the short story. Influenced though he is by the power of Kafka's oneiric vision, Borges criticizes all long novels – including Kafka's and Henry James's with their strong internal power – as tediously drawn out and unreadable. For Borges, the whole point or metaphor of each of Kafka's long books can instantly be perceived as inevitable. Borges expressed the problem of Kafka's entrapment in the mechanical in an interview with Fernando Sorrentino in 1972, translated by Clark M. Zlotchew:

I think Kafka, like Henry James, more than anything else felt perplexity, felt that we're living in an inexplicable world. Then too, I think Kafka became tired of the mechanical element in his novels. That is, of the fact that from the very beginning we know that the surveyor won't ever get inside the castle, that the man will be convicted by those inexplicable judges. And the fact that he didn't want to have those books published is proof of this. Besides, Kafka told Max Brod that he hoped to write happier books . . . . Of course I think Henry James is a much better writer than Kafka because his books aren't written mechanically like those of Kafka. That is, there isn't a plot that develops according to a system that the reader can figure out.

Kafka's weariness with the mechanical task of expansion from short idea into long novel is to one degree or another repeated in Borges's estimation of all novelists – indeed he has even claimed (no doubt falsely) that he himself never finished reading a novel except for the adventure stories of Robert Louis Stevenson. Certainly his own fictions – and in giving us the name *Ficciones* as the title of one of the collections he has named the genre of which he is master – are sparse in the extreme, tightly written with a high level of resonance at the adverbial and adjectival level, and slightly baroque in their architectonic frame. Each one is endlessly evocative, presenting a kind of whispered outline that the active mind of the reader must fill in. The suggestiveness of language, idea, and image demands its expansion through the perceptivity of the reader's mind. Unlike the narrowly confined traditional short story, these fictions are large, amenable to the most capacious and creative readerly imagination, and infinitely, vertiginously (to use some of Borges's favorite words) mysterious. His imitators can only parody him, and that at a fairly low level; ironically, some of the detractors of the aged Borges claim that in old age even he himself could only weakly parody what he achieved so brilliantly in middle age.

Be that as it may, Borges comes before us as the librarian who reads – believing this to be the first of all literary acts – and, in doing so, he finds inevitably ancient words and images, adventures and ideas. Through these he is driven to write, to create an endless sequence of repetition and intertwining between the two apparently dissimilar acts of writing and reading. He writes out of his reading (of books more frequently than of the world), as he believes all writers must, in order in turn to be read so that another rewriting will necessarily take place. He thus presents his own prose and poetry as part of the long string of inevitable verbal formations from Homer through the history of literature to Borges himself, and hence onward to his heirs. By this process, the concept of literature creating literature – one of the definitions of intertextuality – is automatic and irreversible for him.

Demonstrations of this compulsive unitary theory that joins reading to writing, through quasi-logical necessity, are ubiquitous in Borges's work, but are clearest in his story, "The Immortal," now published in *Labyrinths*, and his parable entitled "The Maker" in *Dreamtigers*. It is significant that this parable

49

was important enough to Borges that he used it as the title of the collection of fiction and poetry published in Buenos Aires in 1960 as *El Hacedor*. The decision to retitle it *Dreamtigers* in English moves attention from Borges's stress on the unitary identity of all "makers" – both writers and readers – to his habit of concentrating on one of his handful of resonant images, in this case the tiger of creation and perception.

In "The Immortal," Homer is the immortal immured in time and deformed by the architecturally maddening city of literature. He is now a barbaric, exhausted figure who long ago abandoned the edifices of words and lives primitively, wordlessly, and intemporally. In a subhuman state, Homer cannot die, but lives wilfully separated from illusioned, hopeful mortals who falsely believe in their active lives because they are unaware of the death-in-life that comes with the infinite repetitions built into all literature. As Borges's narrator grimly tells us:

> Death (or its allusion) makes men precious and pathetic. They are moving because of their phantom condition; every act they execute may be their last; there is not a face that is not on the verge of dissolving like a face in a dream. Everything among the mortals has the value of the irretrievable and the perilous. Among the Immortals, on the other hand, every act (and every thought) is the echo of others that preceded it in the past, with no visible beginning, or the faithful presage of others that in the future will repeat it to a vertiginous degree. There is nothing that is not as if lost in a maze of indefatigable mirrors. Nothing can happen only once, nothing is preciously precarious. The elegiacal, the serious, the ceremonial, do not hold for the Immortals. Homer and I separated at the gates of Tangier; I think we did not even say goodbye.
>
> (trans. James E. Irby)

According to Homer's vision, all serious readers and writers know that every human gesture or image is repeated again and again until through its eternal repetition it loses its force and ultimately becomes a merely tedious device of human sensibility. In writing such a passage, Borges argues that the bookish, literate mind must accept its own anonymity or non-subjectivity. This is rendered inevitable because of the history of literature, which is also the continuous reiteration of an eternal return. Not only does Borges claim several times that any person reading a line of Shakespeare becomes Shakespeare at that moment, but he repeatedly evokes Valéry to prove the unity of the Word under whose aegis all men are one, and all authors, especially Borges, are only readers. This ontological assumption of an eternal present imposed upon readers and writers undoes both history and fiction, at the same time as it wearily celebrates their compulsive permanence.

*

In *A Universal History of Infamy* (1972) Borges ranks reading and writing thus:

> Sometimes I suspect that good readers are even blacker and rarer swans than good writers. Will anyone deny that the pieces attributed by Valéry to his

pluperfect Edmond Teste are, on the whole, less admirable than those of Teste's wife and friends? Reading, obviously, is an activity which comes after that of writing; it is more modest, more unobtrusive, more intellectual.

(trans. Norman Thomas di Giovanni)

Borges's humility is central whenever he discusses the task of the writer, and the relative paucity of his production, the brevity of his fictions, the repetitions of themes and images, and the habit of republishing key stories in several collections all contribute to the impression of a small career aggrandized by genius. The result of his repetitions has been confusing or misleading for his readers on many levels. At the simple level of editions and published collections, readers find major fictions repeated in *Ficciones* (1962), *Labyrinths* and *Dreamtigers* (1964), *A Personal Anthology* (1967), and *The Aleph* (1970). Yet each collection is replete with new material, so that the dedicated reader must go through all the volumes Borges allowed to be published by various editors and translators (the situation of repetition is not notably different in the Spanish editions), with the result that (s)he is perforce again and again confronted insistently by the major works. Borges had several editors, and was always easily manipulated by them – although it is also clear that he tried to get his favorite fictions published often.

Critically speaking, this repetition of fictions in collection after collection leads to the ineluctable, probably just, conclusion that the central impact of Borges's fictional work depends on a few dozen stories, mostly dating from the late 1930s to the mid-1950s. Another ironic by-product of this repetition in publication is that the reader feels rather melancholy in picking up collections of later writing like *In Praise of Darkness* (1974) or *The Book of Sand* (1977) where the old favorites, by now engraved on the memory, are omitted, making some critics feel, in a way that would have delighted Borges, as though the old Borges were an imposter trading on the famous name of a Borges rendered familiar by reiteration.

The superficial peculiarities of repetition of the major fictions in the published collections are not, of course, commensurate with the deeper levels of repetition within the corpus and texture of Borges's work. In a famous little essay entitled "Pascal's sphere," he claims that "[p]erhaps universal history is the history of the diverse intonation of a few metaphors," and Borges has elsewhere frequently been willing to catalog his own repeated metaphors from his past in reading and writing: the mirror, the labyrinth, the library, the book, the tiger, the Minotaur, the knife. Their recurrence needs no comment, nor does their ancient history-of-ideas familiarity as literary and philosophical symbols. But Borges finds other sorts of metaphors elsewhere, and indeed symbolic objects for him are merely devices on which larger metaphors can be hung as a fiction progresses. From a thematic–metaphoric point of view, a more arrogant persona than any he projected could lay claim to being considered a philosophical writer. But such a false pretence is alien to Borges, and the reader is accurately told that the reiterated sallies into the nature of time and reality are merely playful exercises in the nature of metaphor, the major device of human perception within an unstable mental world. Repeatedly, Borges makes it clear that it is his task as a writer to examine and re-examine that instability. It is also, as he sees it, the task of literature itself.

He begins cunningly with the best metaphor of all – versions of himself, and indeed his work everywhere shows that the idea of the self of the fictionist can be partially identified with the status of fiction at a larger level. At every point, he demonstrates the slippery incoherence of any sort of existential identification of the self, and moves rapidly from there to the instability of "reality" and to possible–impossible refutations of time. Because the ironies of self-identification are central, many of the fictions play with the idea of the *Doppelgänger*, and Borges's thematic borrowings from Conrad, Stevenson, and Dostoevsky do not pass unacknowledged. The idea of the duality of the self, of its unstable partition in terms of both sensibility and history, is frequently applied to a character named Borges, whom the reader has the illusion of knowing.

The narrating persona of the fictions is thus often both a supposedly autobiographical self and an elaborately created persona indistinguishable from that self. The reader is left to ponder the question of whether (s)he is dealing with a standard fictional device or with the metaphysical problem of the existence and nature of the "real" Borges. The easy way out is to claim that Borges is always and only writing about the ontological nature of fiction – but this is not the best way. A partial clue is given in the story, "The Aleph," where a text-note by "Borges" claims the tale to be an outrageous amalgam of historical facts and parodic elements, all liberally laced with fictional creation. Since the idea of a mystical, total, world-spatial spot like the aleph would be possible for the skeptical Borges only as a metaphysical metaphor, the degree to which anything else in the story, including the character called Borges, can be trusted is open to question.

In many other stories where first-person narrators are identified as Borges, the same rich ambiguity pertains, and creates a semi-provable counterbalance to the negative judgment some critics have made of him as a coldly aloof, totally intellectualized writer. For the interesting thing about Borges as persona in all of his writing – stories, poems, and essays – is the projected warmth and sense of tragic presence. This very presence may be a contrived fiction, and particularly so in the light of Borges's repeated statements of human nonreality and instability. More than any other contemporary writer, Borges has rendered himself a creature of the page. Even when he appeared in the last years of his life on American campuses, in his frailty, blindness, and peculiar eagerness to answer the silliest of undergraduate questions about his life and times, the most justly conceived impression of him was that of an animated book. He sat on the stage, quoting long and eloquently from the poems of his masters as frequently as from his own work. The cultural implication of a mind made of literature is one that all his writing imposes on the reader: if Borges exists, he is literature; if we read, we are literature too, just as we are all Shakespeare when we read a Shakespearean line.

At the same time as Borges can be seen as a metaphor for literature itself, he remains a human being anchored by an oppressive sense of reality and historical time. At the end of his most important quasi-philosophical essay, "A new refutation of time," where only the fleetingly instantaneous present as opposed to past or future is perceived as real, he expresses the temporal and existential paradox:

> *And yet, and yet* . . . Denying temporal succession, denying the self, denying the astronomical universe, are apparent desperations and secret consolations. Our destiny (as contrasted with the hell of Swedenborg and the hell of Tibetan mythology) is not frightful by being unreal; it is frightful because it is irreversible and iron-clad. Time is the substance I am made of. Time is a river which sweeps me along, but I am the river; it is a tiger which destroys me, but I am the tiger; it is a fire which consumes me, but I am the fire. The world, unfortunately, is real; I, unfortunately, am Borges.
>
> (trans. James E. Irby)

To be Borges is more than to be a writer trapped by a stylized literary persona, and an Argentinian placed in history, and in no way can Borges see himself or his work as singular. In a little one-page parable entitled "Borges and I," the persona refers to "the other one, the one called Borges" to whom things happen. This alter ego who is a famous writer pre-empts all of Borges's tastes and characteristics, "but in a vain way that turns them all into the attributes of an actor"; the historically "real" Borges who walks the streets of Buenos Aires says, "I live, let myself go on living, so that Borges may contrive his literature, and this literature justifies me." But this other person, this writer who skews and renders vain the life, pleasures, and tastes of the real man, is only a part of literary history and only a part of the historical Borges:

> It is no effort for me to confess that he has achieved some valid pages, but those pages cannot save me, perhaps because what is good belongs to no one, not even to him, but rather to the language and the tradition. Besides, I am destined to perish, definitively, and only some instant of myself can survive in him.
>
> (all quotations from this parable trans. James E. Irby)

Borges is aware, however, that the division between himself as a world-historical being on the one hand and a writer on the other cannot be made distinct even by the sleight-of-hand that is this parable's method. At the end of the page the wistful words, "I do not know which of us has written this page," indicate the unwelcome unity of the plural self, as well as the fragility of the idea of authorship and the very being or authenticity of life or literature.

In *The Book of Sand*, Borges includes a late fiction entitled "The Other" which the narrating persona places in Cambridge, Massachusetts, in 1969. The basic image of the story is the old one of life as a dream, much used by Borges and his earlier avatars. In an aura of oneiric unreality the 70-year-old Borges is forced to share a park bench on the bank of the Charles River with a hostile and alien 19-year-old youth, who believes he is in Geneva, as the young Borges indeed was in 1918. (An elegant Borgesian footnote to this tale is that the old Borges returned to Geneva to die in 1986.) With considerable repugnance, the elderly Borges recognizes this other being as another sort of double – the self he was over fifty years ago. The two talk about shared childhood experiences that they interpret in radically different ways, with the older man disapproving of the tastes and airs of his previous self and the younger incapable of believing that this old stranger could be an image of his own future. The fantastic time-travel involved is in a sense memory-based for the old Borges (although he is in no way a celebrant of memory, and points out that he had forgotten how irritating and limited he was as a young man). But for the young man the situation is impossible, involving the creation of an inconceivable self in an inconceivable future. The fact that every person is many people as time refracts itself into the evanescent instances of many, many presents is central to Borges's conception of the self and a constantly repeated metaphor within his work.

But the multiplicity and ambiguity of the self depend primarily on the idea or shifting metaphor of time, and indeed it is justified to claim that all Borges's work includes in one way or another an ingeniously repeated refutation of time as the reigning tyrant it has been in western civilization. Subservient to this concentration on the subject of time and concurrent with it in all his writing is a critique of reality from the idealist point of view. When he argues in "Time and J.W. Dunne" against Dunne's system in which the future is seen through dream experience to co-exist simultaneously with the present and hence the past, Borges dodges the indelible attraction that seminal but peculiar book (*An Experiment With Time* – first published in 1927) exerted on the Modernist mind, influencing writers as disparate as Yeats, T.S. Eliot, Joyce, and Graham Greene. He disagrees with Dunne's ease in conflating time and reducing its mysteries, and he is delightedly skeptical about the unitive aspect of the eternal that such a system imposes:

> Dunne assures us that in death we shall learn how to handle eternity successfully. We shall recover all the moments of our lives and we shall combine them as we please. God and our friends and Shakespeare will collaborate with us.
> With such a splendid thesis as that, any fallacy committed by the author becomes insignificant.
>
> (trans. Ruth L.C. Simms)

Time is mysterious rather than real for Borges, because of his toying with idealist tendencies, first taken skeptically from the eighteenth-century Bishop Berkeley and then modified by Schopenhauer. Among Borges's repetitions are his frequent references to these two philosophers, who together with Josiah Royce focus his sense of how the mind exists in a real world. In Borges's paradox, the real world is undoubtedly out there, but it is only partially perceived as a product of the subjective mind. Knowledge for Borges is thus an accumulated set of extrapolations from the way in which experience is read and assembled by the individual perceiving consciousness. As a result, many of his fictions fruitfully demonstrate how the pressures of subjective interpretations can alter the feeling of reality or ontological interpretation of the world. In this respect, two of his fictions, "Tlön, Uqbar, Orbis Tertius" and "Funes the Memorious," are of particular importance – the first because it describes the permutations and combinations of an idealist universe which is the joint project of many subjective demiurgic minds, the second because it shows how a compulsive, even physical mental narrowness of perception can pervert all acceptable standards of how to live in the world.

In his essay, "Partial magic in the Quixote," Borges presents his central claim that "Every novel is an ideal plane inserted into the realm of reality," and through this definition he implies that the "realism" of nineteenth- and early-twentieth-century polemics is chimerical. In elaboration of this point, he elsewhere presents a parable entitled "A Yellow Rose." In this brief exercise, the mannerist poet Marino on his deathbed suddenly sees the terrifying gap between his overwrought description of a flower and its utterly real existence "as Adam might have seen it in Paradise." This essay is the ultimate denial of realism in literature, as Marino's vision demonstrates:

> And he sensed that [the rose] existed in its eternity and not in his words, and that we may make mention or allusion of a thing but never express it at all; and that the tall proud tomes that cast a golden penumbra in an angle of the drawing room were not – as he had dreamed in his vanity – a mirror of the world, but *simply one more thing added to the universe.*
>
> (italics added; trans. Anthony Kerrigan)

When the narrator adds the words, "this illumination came to Marino on the eve of his death, and, perhaps, it had come to Homer and Dante too," Borges implies that when literature and its progenitors are cured of the worldly vanity of realism, then even the greatest writers must in honesty realize that mimesis is impossible. They cannot imitate accurately, but simply add something else to the world; through their art, they insert a subjective or ideal plane into the realm of reality. The value of this depends on the quality of the author's vision, as well as his/her architectonics.

This insertion of an ideal plane is precisely the operative process of the difficult, comical, detail-ridden story, "Tlön, Uqbar, Orbis Tertius." This longest and, for some readers, most important of Borges's fictions begins typically in the mirror-and-book-haunted realms of reality, in a country house visited by him and his long-time collaborator, Bioy Casares. Throughout his life a fan of encyclopedias, particularly the *Britannica*, Borges with his friend turns to a volume of the *Anglo-American Encyclopedia* to look up a country called Uqbar to which Bioy Casares has just made reference. No entry can be found in spite of Bioy Casares's firm memory of having read about it in this encyclopedia. But a few days later in Buenos Aires, it magically turns up in four added pages in another copy of the same encyclopedia. In the heavily deterministic fictive world of the story, this is the beginning of a series of apparently chance happenings, all concerning books and sections of books that describe a vague, unreal, but thoroughly articulated place.

Like the Zembla of Nabokov's *Pale Fire*, it is possible to locate Uqbar somewhere in a quasi-geographical place (in the Near East in Borges's case, in north-western Russia in Nabokov's), but it is somehow not there, and not accessible to experiential reality. The librarian-as-detective is dominant in the tale, as Borges – always fascinated by occult ideas and mystical systems like the Jewish Kabbalah and the doctrines of the Rosicrucians – hunts down the nature and origins of this place, country, or imaginary planet that goes under any one of the triple names – Tlön, Uqbar, Orbis Tertius, almost as though this were its address instead of the fiction's title. The gradual shaping of this new world creates a second reality which it is the tale's task to adumbrate.

Various acquaintances in the tale progressively provide the sleuth character, "Borges," with the hidden encyclopedias and secret books describing this mythical place (it is notably not a utopia or "nowhere," however, because the force of its mental reality finally renders it tangible). It becomes obvious that this created world is the predetermined product of a quasi-occult group of scholars from many fields. In demiurgic fashion, they construct a world of slithering idealism where all language, thought, science, and material elements are the largely whimsical or wish-fulfilling subjective projections of the collective minds of their makers. On the one hand a deeply comic world fulsomely satisfying idealist dreams and playing hilariously with philosophical speculations, Tlön also projects material objects which grotesquely mirror and parody those of the primary reality in which human beings on earth believe they dwell. All the devices used by people in speculative ontological considerations are touched upon, and all "real" objects – from pencils and coins to the Realist notion of God – are given new material being. In fact, material manifestations are constantly altered and multiplied as people through their subjective idealism multiply the need for such controlled materials. Thus there are objects called "hrönir" that proliferate when the quantity of material objects expands according to the mentalist needs of individual people: a single lost pencil, for example, will be found by many people in many forms, each corresponding to the ideal pencil of each of the finders.

But Borges is not interested in merely amusing his readers with the comic creation of an *orbis tertius* with extended schizophrenic overtones. His sense of the alteration and corruption of the world by subjective thought is foremost here and, as he explores it, this fiction comes as close to bitter political statement as anything Borges, generally literarily apolitical in spite of his troubles with the Perón government, has ever written. At the end of the fiction,

Borges's narrating persona sits alone in a world taken over by Tlön's power, working on an unpublishable translation of Sir Thomas Browne's *Urn Buriall* – a book of ashes and history that links to the futility a writer like Borges must have felt at the outset of World War II, when history fell apart.

All fictions create secondary worlds, and Borges self-reflexively parodies such compulsive secondary creations. But if, as this tale argues, perception of and activity in the world are altered by human minds, it then behooves us to see the results parodically presented as they are here. As the bibliographical sleuthing activity of the Borges character progresses (there is absolutely no plot beyond this), strange material intrusions from the imagined realm into our world begin. We are told that the fantastic objects in Tlön have been so thoroughly imagined, projected, and accepted by their creators that they gradually appear in the daily world of ordinary experience. The first thing to materialize is a quivering compass packed in a French princess's silverware; one object, a small cone of bright metal and unbelievable weight actually finds its way to the narrator who recognizes its mysterious aspect: "These small, very heavy cones (made from a metal which is not of this world) are images of the divinity in certain regions in Tlön." These incarnations are followed by the total possession of the real world by this created fantasy world, so that even as the tale is being told, the "real" world is perverted and changed into Tlön, through Borges's ironically conceived brainwashing.

The idea that whatever genuine reality the inhabitants of the world can perceive might be lost by mentalist constructions and idealist theories is put in fantastic terms in this tale of takeover. But Borges as narrator is quick to point out that it is no more fantastic to believe in the mad subjective world of Tlön than to observe the rate at which equally mad political and social theories have been absorbed and believed in during the twentieth century:

> Almost immediately, reality yielded on more than one account. The truth is that it longed to yield. Ten years ago any symmetry with a semblance of order – dialectical materialism, anti-Semitism, Nazism – was sufficient to entrance the minds of men. How could one do other than submit to Tlön, to the minute and vast evidence of an orderly planet?
>
> (trans. James E. Irby)

According to the implications of this fiction, the human mind is debased by its complete dedication to system and order, and the false imposition of any orderly theory is always powerful enough to convert the world. This is one way of accounting for the political outrages of the century, and Borges does not hesitate in making the connection. At the same time, he uses this desperate slavery of human minds to systematic order to demonstrate human terror when confronted by the actual world – that is, by the unsettled and vertiginously labyrinthine ways of genuine experience. The world we inhabit – and Borges's fiction is essentially devoted to versions of and commentary on this world – is infinite, unknowable, and frightening. If all forms and theories illustrate our search for order, they must be overcome by further thought, and by a real entrance into and surrender to the inhuman, terrifying maze of reality, where the truth, whatever it is, can barely be perceived and certainly not understood:

> It is useless to answer that reality is also orderly. Perhaps it is, but in accordance with divine laws – I translate: inhuman laws – which we never quite grasp. Tlön is surely a labyrinth, but it is a labyrinth destined to be deciphered by men.
>
> The contact and the habit of Tlön have disintegrated this world. Enchanted by its rigor, humanity forgets over and again that it is a rigor of chess masters, not of angels.

Although the courage to enter the unknown realm of "angels" is asked for, Borges is obviously not optimistic about humankind's bravery.

The mind's capacities to enter Borges's vertiginous world of the "divine" (which is not to be interpreted as the religious, but as the empirically real) are limited by its passion for order, and in Borges's fiction there are many admonishing *exempla* against too much order. The artificial mentalist world of "Tlön, Uqbar, Orbis Tertius" has a recognizable rational base, but like the universe perceived and infinitely remembered by the tragicomic figure of Funes in "Funes the Memorious," it is perverted by mental excess. Unlike the creation of Tlön, Funes cannot conceive of or make an idealist world, because his mind – partly as the result of an accidental fall from a horse – is perversely limited as an infinite taxonomic storehouse of memory. His incalculable capacity to perceive differentiations means that he cannot simply remember a particular dog, for example, but must remember every hair and angle, and distinguish between the dog at 3:14 seen from the side and the dog at 3:15 seen from the front. The generic idea of dog is impossible for Funes, and indeed he is discontented with an inaccurate language system that does not have a separate name for every leaf and every tree.

The weight of the knowledge given to Funes by indefatigable memory makes conceptual thought impossible, as all mental functions are crowded out by the task of distinguishing endlessly among the leaves on a grapevine, or the multiple perceptions of every moment of time. In "Funes the Memorious" Borges again presents a comically inappropriate world vision, one dominated by a traditionally admired part of human consciousness – memory – and shows how an extended, absurdly precise application of it can lead to an impossible sense of the world. Because Borges is always somehow talking about the nature of fiction, the intolerable predicament of "Funes the Memorious" can also be seen as an allegorical representation of Borges's rejection of literary realism according to the demands of the nineteenth-century empiricist style, and there is considerable urgency in his use of a short story to reject the dolors of the 800-page book that extended empirical realism produced over a longish period of literary history.

*

Nevertheless, the quarrel with empiricism - and hence realism - remains central. In one of his late Minotaur fictions entitled "There Are More Things," Borges's narrator says:

> To see a thing one has to comprehend it. An armchair presupposes the human body, its joints and limbs; a pair of scissors, the act of cutting. What can be said of a lamp or a car? The savage cannot comprehend the missionary's Bible; the passenger does not see the same rigging as the sailors. If we really saw the world, maybe we would understand it.
>
> (trans. Norman Thomas di Giovanni)

For Borges, understanding the world maze is beyond human reach, because any perception of an object or event is partial and subjective. Taking this circumstance as a *donnée*, Borges urges on his readers the humble knowledge that we must live in perplexity. This does not preclude the need to interpret, however, and most of Borges's fictions and essays are ironic forays into hermeneutics. As his narrators present their materials and spurious conclusions, the reader is left with a haunting sense that nothing has been answered - that, in fact, the point of the whole exercise is unanswerability. All remains in the realm of the infinite or perhaps the divine, a term that Borges always uses with cool respect tempered by adamant skepticism. At one point in "The Congress" Borges asks whether there is anything holy on earth, or anything that is not, and this double attitude defines his approach to something like a skewed religious response. Any statement apparently connected to belief is immediately countered or its impact withheld by contextual skepticism. But it is nevertheless true that Borges equates the real, the vertiginous, the mysterious, the infinite, the unnameable and the unknowable with the divine; he also indicates that he does not know what this equation might mean.

If knowledge of the world must be partial even for the most ingenious, (Borges amuses us with his fiction, "Averroës' Search," where the medieval Arab genius, translating Aristotle, is unable to discover the meaning of the culturally alien Greek concepts of tragedy and comedy), then any reading of a circumstance, event, object, or text is only one of many possible interpretations. Hence the false certainties locked within the form of detective fiction are automatically destroyed. Both detective stories and adventure tales - Borges's two favorite modes - therefore lose their simplicity and certitude; they are, rather, placed in the position of having to be infinitely reworked in order to present the *mise-en-abyme* series of endless mirrorings and alternatives necessary in reading a text or reacting to a situation.

This impossible struggle with the paradoxes of accuracy and completeness dominates Borges's imagination throughout his career, as he presents images of infinity within enclosed form. Like all his dominant subjects, it is imaged repeatedly - from the concept of the novel as maze in the early tale, "The Garden of Forking Paths," to the idea of the endless book in the late fiction, "The Book of Sand." A particularly clear manifestation of struggle and repetition occurs in the parodic murder mystery, "Death and the Compass." Here the detective novel is reduced to its classic features, with a brilliant sleuth and an equally brilliant criminal; the clues demand a scholarly grasp of the Kabbalah and especially the four letters of the unspeakable name of God – the Tetragrammaton.

The detective, Erik Lönnrot, is modeled on Poe's Auguste Dupin and is secretly opposed by the gunman Red Scharlach (Sherlock?), whose name is planted at the beginning of the tale, but whose provenance does not in any obvious way connect him with the Kabbalist reading Lönnrot imposes on the murders. Lönnrot's *a priori* system of reading the clues can be compared to William of Baskerville's error in *The Name of the Rose*; in Borges's case the criminal ingeniously sets a plot to entice Lönnrot to the deserted villa, Triste-le-Roy, where he is killed in vengeance for the earlier imprisonment of Scharlach's brother. The first murder, from which Lönnrot much too cleverly and wrongly extrapolates the Kabbalistic key, in fact had nothing to do with Scharlach, but the latter reads his adversary well and knows that he will continue to impose this wrong pattern on all future events. With this knowledge as Scharlach's starting point, it is simply a case of entrapping Lönnrot in the maze of his own hyperactive ingenuity.

The fiction ends ironically with the murderer/non-murderer outwitting the detective, but Borges adds his own particular modification or twist, thus taking the thrust of the story out of the realm of detective plots almost completely. Whereas murder mysteries typically depend on their own narrowly formal closure, Borges turns this tale quickly into an unending *mise-en-abyme* situation acquiesced to by both antagonists. Theirs is not a unique story, but a repetition; another version of their combat will inevitably be played in another life or realm. It is understood that the combat has little to do with detectives, murderers, or revengers, but rather gives aesthetic form to competing attempts to reach a perfect, indeed the ultimate and infinite labyrinth. Before Scharlach shoots him, the defeated Lönnrot insists that although he failed to recognize the rectilinear labyrinth, it remains too simple, and he demands the Eleatic labyrinth of Achilles and the tortoise, of which Borges has written often:

> "In your labyrinth there are three lines too many," he said at last. "I know of one Greek labyrinth which is a single straight line. Along that line so many philosophers have lost themselves that a mere detective might well do so, too. Scharlach, when in some other incarnation you hunt me, pretend to commit (or do commit) a crime at A, then a second crime at B, eight kilometers from A, then a third crime at C, four kilometers from A and B, half-way between the two. Wait for me afterwards at D, two kilometers from A and C, again halfway between both. Kill me at D, as you are now going to kill me at Triste-le-Roy."
>
> "The next time I kill you," replied Scharlach, "I promise you that labyrinth, consisting of a single line which is invisible and unceasing."
>
> (trans. Donald A. Yates)

The idea of return, repetition, and alternative plots that haunts Borges's work at every level has both an aesthetic design and a heuristic function. If all stories must be retold, all lives relived, and all books reinterpreted again and again, the reader must be aware of his/her partial aspect within a vast cosmogony of understanding. The dominant sense in Borges's essays, poems, and fictions is that the human mind is only at the beginning of things, that the structures of the world and of literature are not exhausted, but are mis-interpreted through an arrogance imposed by logically rationalist and/or idealistically fantastic centuries. But Borges is no problem-solver, and his consistently ironic skepticism, directed at all orderly theories, indicates that there is no proper way to think in order to straighten the contorted roads of human experience.

*

The resonant symbols and catchphrases most often employed by Borges are rooted partly in Argentinian and world history (including Christian, Hebrew, Islamic, and Chinese), but most frequently come from written images of the far past. As in the case of Eco, Borges's erudition – his life as a reader – makes systems of thought from that past available to him, and gives him the devices with which he can fashion a new mode of literature. In "Pascal's sphere," published in his essay collection, *Other Inquisitions, 1937-1952*, Borges takes up Pascal's deformation of the idea of the divine as spherical. He particularly stresses the medieval pseudo-hermetic quotation picked up by Alanus de Insulis in the twelfth century: "God is a sphere whose centre is everywhere and whose circumference is nowhere."

This essay is only one of several adumbrations of this idea in Borges's work; in tracing the history of the idea in this essay, he shows how the certainties of the Middle Ages with their Realist God could render the phrase harmless. But for Pascal in the lonely insecurity of the Renaissance – the historical period that laid the bases of skepticism for the modern mind – its infinitude has become "*effroyable*." Borges's conclusion both explains his theory of repetition and indicates his commitment to a quasi-historical task: "Perhaps universal history is the history of the diverse intonation of a few metaphors." Every writer – like Pascal in this case – picks up the old metaphors anew, and his/her originality consists in what the Renaissance called "invention" – the new combinational aspects and specific genius that lead a literature forward.

Even more telling than the uncertainty of the centre and circumference of God asserted in this medieval quotation is Borges's frequent evocation of a major statement from St Paul (I Corinthians 13:12). In his essay "The mirror of the enigmas" in *Other Inquisitions*, Borges turns pointedly to Paul's mystical statement about seeing only partially while in the world. The phrase in question, as translated into Latin by St Jerome, is "*per speculum in aenigmate*" (the King James Bible translates it as "through a glass darkly" – modern translations of it are unspeakable); the words can be taken as an overarching description of the work and sensibility of Borges. The importance of mirrors as imaging, multiplying, and refracting is central for Borges, who adumbrates the curious phrase "in aenigmate" by turning subtly to two sources he quotes often – the *Autobiography* of Thomas de Quincey and the fragmentary works of Leon Bloy. As a reading of Borges would lead one to expect, the key to interpretation is the uncertainty felt throughout the centuries by Paul and the other great heresiarchs with whom Borges identifies – Blake, Swedenborg, de Quincey, Bloy. The word "enigma" signals the nature of all perception, and reminds us that literature's task is not to deliver medieval certainties but to ponder the mystery.

In an essay in *Prose for Borges* (1972), Emir Rodriguez Monegal painstakingly traces Borges's career as a reader, indicating how his writerly qualities modified that process. He uses collaborative evidence from Borges's mother to fortify his theory that a head injury suffered by the writer during Christmas 1938 and followed by a delirious high fever led Borges to begin writing a new sort of fantasy fiction in which the vertiginous was central. The theory of brain-fever can be bolstered by a strong Freudian response to his father's recent death. Whatever the actual circumstances, however, there is no doubt that from 1939 onwards Borges's writing took on the utter originality that formed reputation. Although he presents himself always as a reader as well as a writer, he bases both tasks on a radical, imaginative, skeptical questioning. The fundamental fascination of Borges's essays and stories always begins in his capacity to see oddness everywhere. As a reader, he stresses as does Nabokov the physical pleasure of reading, and as a writer he attempts to convey it by concealing mechanical aspects and playing as many variations as possible. As he puts it in the Preface to *Obra Poetica*:

> This preface might be termed the aesthetics of Berkeley ... because it applies to literature the same argument Berkeley applied to the outer world. The taste of the apple (states Berkeley) lies in the contact of the fruit with the palate, not in the fruit itself; in a similar way (I would say), poetry lies in the meeting of poem and reader, not in the lines of symbols printed on the pages of a book. What is essential is the aesthetic act, the thrill, the almost physical emotion that comes with each reading .... Literature's magic is worked on us by various artifices, but once the reader finds them out they wear off. Out of this comes the continual need for greater or lesser variations, which may recover a past or prefigure a future.
>
> (trans. Norman Thomas di Giovanni)

Although Borges is talking about poetry here, the essential statement holds also for his prose. The reader's necessary response to his language, as well as to his somersaulting plot turns, creates this excitement, although it is in crucial ways hard to locate Borges's conception of a reader other than himself. This difficulty in locating another reader does not mean that Borges in a disheartened way feels that an ideal reader cannot exist, but rather that (s)he is a shifting consciousness altered by time and history; like the great Averroës who cannot conceive of comedy and tragedy, all readers are locked within their culture and moment.

In a famous story that ironically parables his historical point of view, "Pierre Menard, Author of the Quixote," Borges makes his much quoted remark about enriching "the halting and rudimentary art of reading." Most of his critics take for granted that Borges, not his parodic Menard, has indeed pointed the way to enriching this "rudimentary art." Unless one wishes to accuse him of being mechanically baroque (as he himself claimed his early fictions are) or decadent (in the Tolstoyan sense of playing games until the reader sees through them and tires of them), there seems to be little doubt that the estimation of him as an enricher is true and enormously justifies his career. Yet it is strange praise for a writer who, in Mikhail Bakhtin's terminology, is distinctly monologic (a negative aesthetic term redeemed in Borges's case by irony) rather than dialogic.

For Borges, all readers as well as all writers are subject to their historical period as well as to their own consciousness. Thus Pierre Menard can write words in the twentieth century that are identical to Cervantes' words in the seventeenth, but the resulting passage is completely transformed by history and literary tradition into another sort of fiction. Borges as reader can only read according to his temporal constraints, and by implication all other readers must see themselves constantly in a new and unique situation where their experience is fresh and unrepeatable. Nevertheless, history both interferes with texts and undoes itself as it melts away before the primacy of a verbal construct. Paradoxically, every repetition of identical words is a change; every reader is both part of a timeless eternal return and adamantly not so because of the trap of history and time-bound sensibility.

It has become a commonplace to refer to Borges as the most learned of contemporary writers, and John Barth, for example, argues that the former librarian had read everything. This myth overestimates Borges in the wrong way, and in fact draws attention away from certain sorts of repetition that are central to understanding his role as a reader as well as a writer. Borges is often a rather shaky scholar, and lapses into errors such as attributing ideas to Francis Bacon or another Renaissance writer like Sir Thomas Browne, for example, rather than to their proper medieval sources. Because this is combined with his wry habit of creating sources and fulsome bibliographical references in the fictions, the reader must learn a firm distrust of Borges's scholarly references.

But his inaccuracies are irrelevant: for him the library is not a scholarly taskmaster, but a serendipitous quotidian experience that sets his mind and art in motion, and he should be judged as an artist rather than a scholar. His reiterated dependence on a small group of writers and thinkers reveals the degree to which he studied a limited number of masters – Cervantes, Quevedo, León Bloy, Carlyle, Schopenhauer, Berkeley, Josiah Royce, De Quincey,

Stevenson, Whitman, Novalis, Chesterton, and all sorts of books on the occult. This list is not meant to be exhaustive, inasmuch as Borges has read and written essays, poems, and fictions on many others, but it is important to mention the writers to whom he most frequently returns as touchstones for his work. This tendency to magnify a narrow nucleus of sources is related to his own thematic repetitions and indeed to his writerly instinct for combining new defeats with old misreadings. It is a notable characteristic of Borges's stories that their major impact has to do with defeats that are based on various false kinds of knowledge or misapprehensions. The fictions are interesting because their protagonists are irremediably wrong, or mad, or deluded, and by analogy the reader sees him/herself caught up in comparable misreadings of the world.

In recent years, however, Borges half-playfully described his work as monotonous, and in 1962 characterized his early, famous fictions as baroque and vain. In the Preface to *Doctor Brodie's Report*, he says:

> The same few plots, I am sorry to say, have pursued me down through the years; I am decidedly monotonous.... I have given up the surprises inherent in a baroque style as well as the surprises that lead to an unforeseen ending.
>
> (trans. Norman Thomas di Giovanni)

The mellowing of the late fictions, to which Borges says he has added the themes of old age and morality, indeed reduces their impact, although there is no change in the skepticism, images, and mystery that were there from the beginning. It is possible to divide his career into three phases: youthful, undeveloped writing to 1938, the great period from 1938 to 1953 or so, and a subsequent decline, and certainly there is no doubt that the writing of his middle period has a breathtaking excitement of formal aesthetic achievement and originality that has not been repeated. But there is also an unusual thematic and perceptual consistency in all his work that Borges never violated.

Norman Thomas di Giovanni, who worked in close rapport with Borges in Buenos Aires for ten years while translating the works into English, reports the author's excitement upon having his story, "The Circular Ruins," reread to him late in life, and his regret that he could no longer write at that level of genius. Because some of Borges's readers have been dismissive of his work for its mandarin aspect and accuse him of remoteness, it is best to recall the manic, restless excitement with which Borges himself claimed to compose that tale. In *Around the Day in Eighty Worlds* (1986), Cortázar – also an Argentinian – describes the passion of a writer of successful fantastic stories:

> It may be exaggerating to say that all completely successful short stories, especially fantastic stories, are products of neurosis, nightmares or hallucinations neutralized through objectification and translated to a medium outside the neurotic terrain. This polarization can be found in any memorable short story, as if the author, wanting to rid himself of his creature as soon and as absolutely as possible, exorcizes it the only way he can: by writing it.... [F]or his part, a good

reader will always distinguish those that come from an ominous undefinable territory from those that are the product of a mere *métier*.

Borges's readers acknowledge this "ominous undefinable territory" in the fictions, and "The Circular Ruins," one of his most resonant fantasies, succeeded in impressing even its humble author. If there is an archetypal Borges fiction, this is it, and to write about it is merely to travel a route repeatedly traversed by the best readers and critics of this phenomenal writer.

Every major Borgesian idea is present in "The Circular Ruins," whether by direct reference or shadowy allusion. In an essay on Bernard Shaw in *Other Inquisitions*, Borges says of good literature:

> Literature is not exhaustible, for the sufficient and simple reason that a single book is not. A book is not an isolated entity: it is a narration, an axis of innumerable narrations. One literature differs from another, either before or after it, not so much because of the text as for the manner in which it is read. If I were able to read any contemporary page - this one, for example - as it would be read in the year 2000, I would know what literature would be like in the year 2000.

The inexhaustible aesthetic resonance of this story is complemented by the fact that it is also about the infinite repetitions of creation throughout history. As a narration, it is "an axis of innumerable narrations" that must be read variously according to temporal constraints. "The Circular Ruins" has the aura of an ancient, even primitive tale focused on an imaginary present. A purposive creator arrives by boat at a mythic, archetypal spot marked by circular ruins beside a long, strong river. His task has been imposed by an unidentified agent; because the creator is a man in need of physical sustenance, necessities are automatically given by unimportant, uncharacterized peasants. Essentially he like Borges is alone in his universe. The history and provenance of the circular ruins, including the fire god that once governed them, are not given. The work of creating a human being - a sort of golem or homunculus - by dreaming it and then inserting this dream into the reality of the world, is parallel to the task of a demiurge, a god - or a novelist. Like many artists, this dreamer is inept in his first attempts, because he begins with an *a priori* notion of where and how a human being can be imagined. He wrongly looks for a student by dreaming an illusory college, and concentrates on a young man who turns out to be inadequate. Having erred, the dreamer–creator faces the most difficult recognition an artist must face:

> He comprehended that the effort to mold the incoherent and vertiginous matter dreams are made of was the most arduous task a man could undertake, though he might penetrate all the enigmas of the upper and lower orders: much more arduous than weaving a rope of sand or coining the faceless wind. He comprehended that an initial failure was inevitable. He swore he would forget the enormous hallucination which had misled him at first, and he sought another method.
>
> (trans. James E. Irby)

The new creative method demands that sympathetic and absolute attention be paid, and slowly his oneiric imagination articulates the heart, the limbs, and, most touching and difficult of all, the innumerable hairs on the man's head. This time the dreamer is successful, as the realistic novelist is when (s)he concentrates utterly and selflessly on his/her creation and nurses it into life. Like Cervantes or Marino in the essays discussed above, the author/creator succeeds in inserting this dreamed, idealist being into the plane of reality. Proud of his "son," the dreamer trains him in his task – which is identical to his own – and sends him down the endless river to the next set of circular ruins where this golem will repeat the steps of his creator's creation. But until the dramatic end of the tale, the creator, like all human beings, fails to see himself also as unreal, as a dream dreamt by a dreamer who in his turn was dreamt by a dreamer, and so on throughout history and prehistory to eternity. Only when he is forced to walk through fire and is not burned does he realize that he, like his created son, is unreal; similarly this son will believe in his own reality until it is denied him, in an endless cycle of repetition from the past into the future.

Like Kafka who felt the pressure of the oneiric, Borges presents a subtle argument about the artificial unreality of reality in this fiction, and through it argues that like Hamlet, like Alice in *Through the Looking Glass*, from whom the epigraph is taken, like Scheharazade, we may be fictions ourselves. The very basis of our lives in reality – whatever that is – may be merely imagined by a dreamer prior to ourselves as in "The Circular Ruins." But under any circumstances, it is largely unknowable. This oneiric unreality at one level comes simply from philosophical idealist thought, but it also has specific application to the ancient idea of artistic creation as a microcosm of divine creation. All works of art are imagined, dreamt at a deep level of concentration, but they are artificial; "realism" is therefore always a vain and impossible undertaking. One of Borges's favorite terms or ideas is that of the heresiarch – the arch heretic who questions all before him, and particularly all forms of established dogma. For Borges, the artist and writer (who is far from the abstract and frivolous game-player he has occasionally been accused of being), reality itself is an infinite *mise-en-abyme* that cannot be traced to any secure source and requires a brilliant heresiarch to demonstrate its infinite resonances. The reader who learns something of this has been taught by a Postmodern master, by the Borges whose bookish life has been dedicated to this elaboration.

4

Nabokov's ardors and pale fires

Vladimir Nabokov was born in the same year as Borges, 1899; literary tradition quickly linked them with each other and assigned Calvino to them as their younger brother. The three are thematically, tonally, and formally unlike, but they share an intellectualization of affect, a distaste for the pretensions of conventional realism, and an allusive habit that places high demands on the competence of the reader. In each case, the relationship of the text to the reader under the aegis of vast learning, ironic games, and experimental techniques is a central factor and, of the three, Nabokov is the most notably competitive and even hostile. Placing him in a proper context in contemporary fiction is a subtle task, and one that requires a just hand and an allowance for aesthetic arguments unlike those of any major writer in the mid to late twentieth century.

With Nabokov's death in 1977, the Anglo-American world lost its pre-eminent practitioner of literary gamesmanship and a writer of endlessly varied innovative techniques. Because of his twenty-year stay in the United States, Nabokov enjoyed being referred to as an American writer; his real homeland, however, is not the US, a lost Russia, pre-war Berlin and France, or cosy Switzerland, but international literature. His startling originality expresses itself in this spontaneous internationalism and keeps him from alignment with any past or present tradition: tagging him as a Postmodernist or experimentalist or even a Russian dependent is, like most tagging, a reductively culpable step that underestimates his specific free-floating originality.

As absolutely bookish as Borges, Eco, or Calvino, Nabokov adheres to a myth of experience through which coherent plot action is made to renovate the images and parody the forms of the rich literary past of the western world. His characters appear to participate in "reality" – a term Nabokov says should always be put in quotation marks – and many critics have fallen into the trap of trying to subject them to conventional methods of literary analysis. Nabokov's readers always perforce read more than the text they are given: if they fail to apprehend the allusive density of the stories or novels – which goes beyond referential name-dropping – they miss the larger possibilities of his work and deserve the contempt he never failed to heap on the literary critic at every turn. Nabokov expected a great deal from his readers, but also operated under intense pressure to write not like but at the level of his great masters from the past. These masters were his beloved Russians – especially Gogol, Pushkin, and Lermontov – and the European writers he lectured on lovingly first at Wellesley College and later, until the profitable success of *Lolita* (1958), at Cornell University. They also included Shakespeare, the history of poetry, and the long accumulated achievements of literature as an aesthetic world demanding total study, attention, and allegiance.

Although Nabokov finally belongs to no tradition or country, his memory is rooted in his beloved pre-revolutionary Russia, and the adult experiences he describes are foreign, alien, and exilic. To what degree the circumstances that befell him shaped his thematics must be open to conjecture; in a significant, almost alienated way Nabokov is the least personal of writers except in his first novel, *Mary* (written in Russian in 1926), and his book of autobiographical sketches, *Speak, Memory*, where he elegantly describes set scenes of his childhood and youth in Russia, Berlin, and France. But the characters and narrators in all his books are fueled by memory, not only by reminiscences of experience, person, and place, but also by their close alignment to the literary past. For Nabokov, a present and future exist only self-reflectively as the text or persona ponders its antecedents; the abysses of pre-birth and death structurally balance the space of consciousness between, as he writes in *Speak, Memory*:

> The cradle rocks above an abyss, and common sense tells us that our existence is but a brief crack of light between two eternities of darkness.... Nature expects a full-grown man to accept the two black voids, fore and aft, as stolidly as he accepts the extraordinary visions in between.... I rebel against this state of affairs. I feel the urge to take my rebellion outside and picket nature. Over and over again, my mind has made colossal efforts to distinguish the faintest of personal glimmers in the impersonal darkness on both sides of my life. That this darkness is caused merely by the walls of time separating me and my bruised fists from the free world of timelessness is a belief I gladly share with the most gaudily painted savage.

The task of the artist and of art is to supply and illustrate this interim, which uses experiential memory as a preparation for death. Comic and ingeniously parodic, all of Nabokov's fictions are obsessed with death and refer to the non-experiential other side of things, unreachable by any human means. Nabokov claims that in rebellious despair he early "groped for some secret outlet only to discover that the prison of time is spherical and without exits." What a writer must therefore work with is the *minutiae* of temporal existence, seen under the necessity of death.

In a preface to the posthumous collected poems, *Stikhi* (1979), Nabokov's widow, Véra, to whom all his books are dedicated, announced that his "chief theme" was *Potustornnost*, which means the other world, the beyond, or the hereafter. In 1981 this was inevitably taken up critically and rather overdone by W.W. Rowe, in *Nabokov's Spectral Dimension*, but it is true that all his fictions knock at the doors of timelessness. Nabokov shrugged off any sort of anthropomorphic survival, and his precise method of making *Potustornnost* a theme seems best explained not by forays into the supernatural but by an eloquent passage at the beginning of his penultimate novel, *Transparent Things* (1973):

> When *we* concentrate on a material object, whatever its situation, the very act of attention may lead to our involuntarily sinking into the history of that object. Novices must learn to skim over matter if they want matter to stay at the exact level of the moment. Transparent things, through which the past shines!
>
> Man-made objects, or natural ones, inert in themselves but much used by careless life (you are thinking, and quite rightly so, of a hillside stone over which a multitude of small animals have scurried in the course of incalculable seasons) are particularly difficult to keep in surface focus: novices fall through the surface, humming happily to themselves, and are soon reveling with childish abandon in the story of this stone, of that heath. I shall explain. A thin veneer of immediate reality is spread over natural and artificial matter, and whoever wishes to remain in the now, with the now, on the now, should please not break its tension film. Otherwise the inexperienced miracle-worker will find himself no longer walking on water but descending upright among staring fish. More in a moment.

The idea that only a "thin veneer of immediate reality is spread over natural and artificial matter," together with the beautiful apostrophe, "Transparent things, through which the past shines!" presents us with a primary way of seeing how Nabokov's texts function, and how his narrators perceive the intrusion of history, via memory, on their perception of the world. When the idea of the transparency of things is combined with a death-obsession, Nabokov's thematics become deeper than the parodic playfulness of the texts might indicate to the first "skimming" glance of the reader. His near contempt for the inevitably gross "misreadings" of critics shows Nabokov's wish that his readers fall through the surface of things to become teachable novices or real readers.

When John Shade, the "great American poet" in Nabokov's earlier novel, *Pale Fire* (1962), searches for and finds his title, he evokes the same image of transparency in trying to define his last poem: "But *this* transparent thingum does require / Some moondrop title. Help me, Will!" Shade's homely, memory-laden poem humbly places itself against the fire of the sun – that of Shakespeare as the greatest of poets – and stresses its distance from that sun as well as its stolen flame. The root passage is from *Timon of Athens*, IV. iii: "the moon's an arrant thief, / And her pale fire she snatches from the sun." The "moondrop title," the idea of a "pale fire," the poem as a "transparent thingum" all contribute to the idea of silvery remoteness from a brilliant source that characterizes Nabokov's best work. In actual terms, Nabokov is not making a negative judgment of his own fiction as late-born, but teaching us how to read it, how to use its pale, moondrop transparency to trace backwards through literature, to slip through the surface of artificial and material things into the vertiginous world he is dedicated to presenting.

Nabokov as a writer cleaves to no formal theory or literary type, and although some good work has been done on his frequent parodic modeling on Tolstoy and the other great Russians - see John Bayley's essay "Under cover of decadence: Nabokov as evangelist and guide to the Russian classics" (1979) as well as G.M. Hyde's *Vladimir Nabokov: America's Russian Novelist* - it is wrong to attribute influence in the old-fashioned comparative literature sense to either the Russians or any other of his myriad "sources." If John Barth's theory is true - that Postmodernism faces the exhaustion of genre and must now function ironically within a literature of *passé* forms - Nabokov is indeed Postmodern. But then, as Umberto Eco has pointed out, so are all mannered writers stretching back to Homer. Nabokov certainly feels that slavish adherence to genre or established past modes is a deadening thing, and a serious impediment to a writer. In his essay, "The tragedy of tragedy" (1984), he says:

> Consider the following curious position... a written tragedy belongs to creative literature, although at the same time it clings to old rules, to dead traditions that other forms of literature enjoy breaking, finding in this process perfect liberty, a liberty without which no art can thrive .... The highest achievements in poetry, prose, painting, and showmanship are characterized by the irrational and the illogical, by that spirit of free will that snaps its rainbow fingers in the face of smug causality.

In his fiction, Nabokov frees his work - and his readers - from the shackles of convention, and in doing so he works hard to introduce the idea of chance, or the oneiric, or an indeterminate fate into the sequence of events. In his last interview, with Robert Robinson of the BBC, he talked about the pursuit of butterflies, and thus unwittingly described the reader in pursuit of the Nabokovian text:

> As for pursuit, it is, of course, ecstasy to follow an undescribed beauty, skimming over the rocks of its habitat, but it is also great fun to locate a new species among the broken insects in an old biscuit tin sent over by a sailor from some remote island.

The remote island of the past, as well as the broken insects of genre through which we can pick to find the new species Nabokov presents, is a way of imagining how his passionate love of butterflies - natural aesthetic objects - parallels his sense of what, in describing *Lolita*, he called "aesthetic bliss" in literature.

Although Nabokov is not obsessed by his audience as Calvino and John Fowles are, he is nevertheless anxious that the works impose upon the reader that transparency of effect that is major in his aesthetics. In the interview quoted above, he talked about his task in an author-centered way:

> This writer's task is the purely subjective one of reproducing as closely as possible the image of the book he has in his mind. The reader need not know, or, indeed, cannot know, what the image is, and so cannot tell how closely the book has conformed to its image in the author's mind. In other words, the reader has no business bothering about the author's intentions, nor has the author any business trying to learn whether the consumer likes what he consumes.

Nabokov's autocratic sense of the limitations necessarily forced on the reader is further demonstrated in the volumes of his lectures, edited by Fredson Bowers. So far there is a volume of lectures on each of Russian literature, European literature, and *Don Quixote*. As a university lecturer Nabokov prepared carefully and lectured superbly, reading verbatim (with even the puns and jokes self-consciously put in and carefully timed) from note-cards. Each lecture is an essay of appreciative judgment or attack, in which he looks at the aesthetic and stylistic *minutiae* of the writer in question. His stress on detail places him in opposition to a comprehensive or ideological estimation of any novelist, and Nabokov is as impatient with such criticism as he is with ideological writers. Looking at these lectures gives us an extended demonstration of what precisely he meant by his use of the term "aesthetic bliss" to describe the affective power of good literature on the reader. He also very specifically tells how a reader should read:

> I use the word *reader* very loosely. Curiously enough, one cannot *read* a book; one can only reread it. A good reader, a major reader, an active and creative reader is a rereader . . . . When we read a book for the first time the very process of laboriously moving our eyes from left to right, line after line, page after page, this complicated physical work upon the book, the very process of learning in terms of space and time what the book is about, this stands between us and artistic appreciation. When we look at a painting we do not have to move our eyes in a special way even if, as in a book, we must have time to acquaint ourselves with it. We have no physical organ (as we have the eye in regard to a painting) that takes in the whole picture and then can enjoy its details. But at a second, or third, or fourth reading we do, in a sense, behave towards a book as we do towards a painting. However, let us not confuse the physical eye, that monstrous masterpiece of evolution, with the mind, an even more monstrous achievement. A book, no matter what it is – a work of fiction or a work of science (the boundary line between the two is not as clear as is generally believed) – a book of fiction appeals first of all to the mind. The mind, the brain, the top of the tingling spine is, or should be, the only instrument used upon a book.
>
> (*Lectures on Literature*, 1980)

Two things stand out here: first, Nabokov assumes absolutely that the first reading of a book barely counts, because the serious reader automatically rereads not just once but many times; secondly, "the tingling spine" is associated with the brain at an intellectual rather than an emotional level. For most readers and critics, this second point with its stress on the brain and mind would put the idea of response in the realm of hermeneutic analysis rather than "aesthetic bliss," but Nabokov does not allow this, arguing instead that the good reader is paying *particular* attention to the accreted impact of small details.

In the lectures themselves, Nabokov stresses the aesthetic brilliance of detail, the poetry of an author's distinctive language, the delicacy and accuracy of perception, and the innovative subtlety through which small, rich impressions are achieved. Similarly, in the essay "On a book entitled *Lolita*" which now accompanies all editions of that novel and where the phrase "aesthetic bliss" occurs, Nabokov argues for a proper reading of *Lolita* – one that, like his own memories of the book, would keep large interpretations, particularly moral ones, at bay:

> There are gentle souls who would pronounce *Lolita* meaningless because it does not teach them anything. I am neither a reader nor a writer of didactic fiction, and, despite John Ray's assertion, *Lolita* has no moral in tow. *For me a work of fiction exists only insofar as it affords me what I shall bluntly call aesthetic bliss, that is a sense of being somehow, somewhere, connected with other states of being where art (curiosity, tenderness, kindness, ecstasy) is the norm.*
>
> (italics added)

Nabokov contrasts these "states" with the Literature of Ideas, "which very often is topical trash coming in huge blocks of plaster that are carefully transmitted from age to age." His major enemy contemporary to him is Thomas Mann, and certainly Nabokov never wishes to send his readers even the smallest fraction of serious messages present in any Mann novel.

Almost all critical statements except aesthetic ones must therefore in a way be contrary to the wishes of Nabokov, and he strongly wills obedient readers to follow his mandate:

> And when I thus think of *Lolita*, I seem always to pick out for special delectation such images as Mr. Taxovich, or that class list of Ramsdale School, or Charlotte saying "waterproof," or Lolita in slow motion advancing toward Humbert's gifts, or the pictures decorating the stylized garret of Gaston Godin, or the Kasbeam barber (who cost me a month of work), or Lolita playing tennis, or the hospital at Elphinstone, or pale, pregnant, beloved, irretrievable Dolly Schiller dying in Gray Star (the capital town of the book), or the tinkling sounds of the valley town coming up the mountain trail (on which I caught the first known female of *Lycaeides sublivens* Nabokov). These are the nerves of the novel. These are the secret points, the subliminal co-ordinates by means of which the book is plotted.

Nabokov's essay on *Lolita* is, however, angry and disdainful, as were all his comments on the shortcomings of his critics. Many of his comments are basically wrong – not in any final way, but in the fact that his anger leads him to overstate his quarrels and make points quite different from the ones his novels dazzlingly illustrate. Irritated by the reception of *Lolita* as pornographic by its first American readers, Nabokov exaggerates his anti-moral line; bewildered by the success of Mann in America in the 1940s and 1950s, he vengefully puts him and all ideological novels into the realms of anti-literature. If Henry James was right in judging between narrative styles, saying that the novelist should show rather than tell, then the difference between Nabokov and Mann is that Nabokov follows the Jamesian prescription and shows us pictorially what he wishes us to *see*, whereas Mann tells us doggedly (in superbly wrought, Germanic high cultural prose – I refuse to acquiesce to N's attack) what he wishes us to *think*.

*

Nabokov's insistence that he has no moral in tow raises a serious question about *Lolita*, his greatest book and most enduring success. As part of the frame of the novel, Nabokov creates a primitively moral psychoanalytical literary critic, John Ray Jr, as a satirical example of the shortcomings of his genre. In Ray's *Foreword* to the first-person book written by the imprisoned Humbert Humbert, he parodies the foolishness of the sociological–critical–psycho-analytic–ethical–literary (remember Polonius) mind that only foggily perceives the nature of a literary text:

> This commentator may be excused for repeating what he has frequently stressed in his own books and lectures, namely that "offensive" is frequently but a synonym for "unusual"; and a great work of art is of course always original, and thus by its very nature should come as a more or less shocking surprise. I have no intention to glorify "H.H." No doubt, he is horrible, he is abject, he is a shining example of moral leprosy, a mixture of ferocity and jocularity that betrays supreme misery perhaps, but is not conducive to attractiveness. He is ponderously capricious. Many of his casual opinions on the people and scenery of this country are ludicrous. A desperate honesty that throbs through his confession does not absolve him from sins of diabolical cunning. He is abnormal. He is not a gentleman. But how magically his singing violin can conjure up a tendresse, a compassion for Lolita that makes us entranced with the book while abhorring its author!

Ray possesses the marginal quantity of aesthetic sense Nabokov is willing to allow to the critic/psychoanalyst, enough to know that the "tendresse" of a writer's "singing violin" can keep the reader entranced. But Ray's aesthetics are fogged over by moral intrusion, by his next statement that *Lolita* will be fascinating for psychoanalysts, and by an earlier claim in the *Foreword* that the book is "the development of a tragic tale tending unswervingly to nothing less than a moral apotheosis." In fact, the satire against the moralistic reader/critic that Nabokov believed would be obvious and amusing has been a marring problem for many readers, and one to which attention must be paid.

There are two reasons for this momentarily crippling moral difficulty: first is the response of ethical readers who at first gasp cannot perceive the ascendancy of the literary aestheticism that *Lolita* dominantly embodies. Second is what must be called Nabokov's naivety in assuming riskily that no large moral anger would be called forth by the particular sexual tastes of his anti-hero, Humbert Humbert; indeed his cavalier callousness about sexual practices is seen too in another way in his belittling attack on homosexuality in *Pale Fire*. Although all his fiction shows a notable interest in eroticism, Nabokov seems to under-estimate the sexual abuse of children, or rather his interest in literary possibility is so large that he fails to perceive another dimension. In the late 1980s when the misuse of children is so much before us, the plot of *Lolita* causes uneasiness and many readers stubbornly deny its higher forum of aesthetic excellence. In other words, Nabokov *should* perhaps, at least on one level, have a more exacting moral in tow.

On the other hand, and for dramatically important reasons, he cannot. I can think of no fictional text in which major incontrovertible forces battle each other more troublingly than in *Lolita*, but I must also agree with the aesthetic-narcissist school (see for example Genet and the late pornographic works of Robbe-Grillet) that unmonitored sexuality has vital uses within the aesthetic program of literature. But John Ray Jr is, from the point of view of most readers, right in saying that *Lolita* builds to a moral apotheosis, and indeed it is the apparent ethical reversal of Humbert Humbert's solipsism that forms the secondary theme of this great novel, making it not merely a product of narrow aestheticism but one of the more profound literary achievements of our century. Nabokov may be serious in claiming that a moral reading injures the text: certainly it separates a few scenes near the end of the book from the relatively unbroken parodic play of the work as a whole. On the other hand, the affective power in these scenes is stronger than the coolness required of parody.

Nabokov clearly has a program for the novel, and although he feels it is not the reader's business to intrude with an interpretation of its larger intentions, readers are instantly forced to see more than such elegant details as the splendid prose snapshot of Lolita playing tennis or one of the dozens of colors in Nabokov's sunsets. Beyond aestheticism, the reader's first large apprehension of *Lolita* must be that it is a celebration and continuation of the western literary tradition of love poetry. As such, it is played off parodically against a long string of antecedents that established the trope of the immortality of the beloved through the literary genius of the lover. The tradition echoes through century after century to what has seemed a dull terminus, so that finally in the twentieth century it has become apparently impossible for a Postmodern Catullus to sing to his Lesbia. Umberto Eco puts it nicely in *Postscript to the Name of the Rose*:

> But the moment comes when the avant-garde (the modern) can go no further, because it has produced a metalanguage that speaks of its impossible texts (conceptual art). The postmodern reply to the modern consists of recognizing that the past, since it cannot really be destroyed, because its destruction leads to silence, must be revisited: but with irony, not innocently. I think of the postmodern attitude as that of a man who loves a very cultivated woman and

74

knows he cannot say to her, "I love you madly," because he knows that she knows (and that she knows that he knows) that these words have already been written by Barbara Cartland. Still, there is a solution. He can say, "As Barbara Cartland would put it, I love you madly." At this point, having avoided false innocence, having said clearly that it is no longer possible to speak innocently, he will nevertheless have said what he wanted to say to the woman: that he loves her, but he loves her in an age of lost innocence.

In Eco's passage irony serves personal sincerity, which Nabokov replaces in *Lolita* with a pointed attack on the problematic solipsism that haunts twentieth-century literature.

Nabokov would agree with Eco that the innocence of any word-user's power of expression has been lost by our consciousness of the overwhelming pressure of antecedent literature, and by the fact that the intertextuality of all texts – the dependence of any fiction on the fictions of the past – challenges any artist's creativity to an extraordinary degree. But the antecedent literature that Nabokov the mandarin deals with is not Barbara Cartland or the American slang (and popular culture) with which he infuses *Lolita*, but the power of the great or canonical writers of the past. Writing before Harold Bloom came up with the phrase, "the anxiety of influence," Nabokov fails to feel it and instead celebrates the fact that originality emerges freely, not anxiously, from a stylization of the past, from a critique of and reference to predecessors.

Because he was writing *Lolita* in the early 1950s when he felt he was establishing himself as an American writer, it makes sense that Nabokov would first look backward to the most aesthetic American non-Puritanical writer to immortalize young girls – Edgar Allan Poe. Poe's incantatory poem, "Annabel Lee," presents Nabokov with an appropriately skewed image of the traditional beloved lady from American literature, and Nabokov can endow his "character" Humbert Humbert with a "real" passion for this girl as a first love and permanent obsession. HH meets and loses this newly re-personified fetish, memorially named Annabel Leigh, before either is yet 13, and therefore on a "realistic" characterological level, HH's sexual malady can be psychoanalytically justified. HH, however, is not so much a character in this novel as an ironic double or shadow of Nabokov's aesthetic ideas. It is therefore true, in the author's sophisticated lexicon, that HH is obsessed not for easy sexual or psychological reasons, but because celebrating love for a woman is the traditional path to poetic immortality (for the poet, for Nabokov), and because, as Petrarch knew with his *lauro-Laura* pun, successful literature crowns the writer.

Nabokov's controversial choices as an artist can be most clearly perceived in the light of this tradition. If one is possessed by literary idealism as Nabokov and his shadow Humbert Humbert are, nothing can look more irrelevant than psychoanalysis or the sociological–political ideologies that characterize cultural studies in the late twentieth century. As a result, Nabokov's attacks on ideologues are a severe criticism of what he considers an intrusion of the wrong sort of cultural data into the literary act. Although Nabokov was not at all patient with political ideologues, and although his work deliberately lacks political bite, he disdainfully contended that he, who had survived the revolution of the century and whose liberal Russian *émigré* father had been gunned down in Berlin when Nabokov was 22, did not lack political awareness – as a reading of the subtle novel of war-alienation and execution, *Invitation to a Beheading*, illustrates. This novel, as Nabokov reported to Alfred Appel, was written in 1934–5, largely during a fortnight of inspiration in Berlin. While Nabokov was writing, the Berlin sky was illuminated by searchlights from Nazi fêtes, and Hitler's terrifying, mesmerizing voice boomed from loudspeakers throughout the city.

But Nabokov seldom allows the aesthetic act to be broken in his fiction, and *Lolita* is an unpolitical novel. Poe-infested Humbert Humbert limns out his life within careful boundaries, wasting his pre-Lolita time on a misguided marriage, idle philological pursuits, phony scientific research, nervous break-downs, and deceiving his psychiatrists. Adamantly indifferent to politics, HH serves only his sexual need, which is a metaphor for the novel's literary obsession. This endlessly referential obsession joyfully, comically, and ardently brings before the reader the contrast and ironic interplay between the gorgeously literary (which is the novel's style) and the drably quotidian (HH's first wife Valeria and her taxi-driver, the grossly perceived Dietrichesque Charlotte Haze, the dolors of suburban life, the tedium of the European and American bourgeoisie, the perpetual comedy of low taste in American popular culture in the late 1940s). For many of the first American readers of *Lolita* this contrast was negatively seen as between the *haute culture* of Europe and the low culture of America. Nabokov took pains to avoid a condescending contrast by the initial references to Poe, and he spoke sorrowfully about it in his "On a book entitled *Lolita*":

> Another charge which some readers have made is that *Lolita* is anti-American. This is something that pains me considerably more than the idiotic accusation of immorality . . . . I needed a certain exhilarating milieu. Nothing is more exhilarating than philistine vulgarity. But in regard to philistine vulgarity there is no intrinsic difference between Palearctic manners and Nearctic manners. Any proletarian from Chicago can be as bourgeois (in the Flaubertian sense) as a duke. I chose American motels instead of Swiss hotels or English inns only because I am trying to be an American writer and claim only the same rights other American writers enjoy. On the other hand, my creature Humbert is a foreigner and an anarchist, and there are many things, besides nymphets, in which I disagree with him. And all my Russian readers know that my old worlds – Russian, British, German, French – are just as fantastic and personal as my new one is.

There is no doubt that this world of *Lolita* is fantastic and personal, at the same time as it is an uncannily evocative preservation of the way America looked after World War II. It recalls that period so accurately that its two primary juggling pins - aesthetic games and realistic accuracy - can indeed become confused in the eye of the beholder, and it is only by discriminating attention that the reader can distinguish between them. In *Lolita*, the literary world of the past exists as an ardent flame against which the American world is the pale fire and transparent thing of Nabokov's novel. The novel's deepest interest lies in its ability to rub against and reflect that remarkably complex literary past. Although references to Poe's Annabel Lee begin the novel, Poe is not its major allusive agent. Manic Humbert Humbert fulsomely evokes the young beloved girls who fused the western tradition in literature - from Catullus through Dante, Petrarch, Shakespeare, the Marquis de Sade, Lewis Carroll, Poe, to the comic figure of American radio's Fanny Brice - salaciously pointing out the prepubescence of the girls (but failing to conjecture on the age of Shakespeare's young boyfriend). Although the gothic and sepulchral charm of Poe's Annabel Lee was a useful inspiration for Nabokov as an aspiring American writer, she represents only the American part of a tradition extending far backward and whose most appealing figure for Nabokov as twentieth-century parodist is Lewis Carroll's nineteenth-century Alice.

No more convenient figure could exist for Nabokov's shadowy, doubled parodic purposes than Charles Dodgson/Lewis Carroll, whose whimsical comic tales told to Alice Liddell and other little girls have enflamed the Postmodern literary imagination. In every way, Carroll mirrors Nabokov's inventive bent. His use of games, both euchre and chess, as frames for *Alice's Adventures in Wonderland* and *Through the Looking-Glass*, are precursors of Nabokov's chess references in *The Defense, Lolita*, and elsewhere, as well as for the elaborate card-games in *Ada*. Carroll's self-conscious and magical illusionist shifting of the data and techniques of well-known Victorian tales and poems to confuse Alice as reader/receptor parallels Nabokov's dizzying attempt to keep his reader in a referential tumult. Finally, Carroll's creation of a non-realist world that arrogantly but playfully parades itself as natural and verisimilar - Alice's "Wonderland" - is a forerunner of HH's solipsistic and imprisoning universe, the latter laced with sex and pop culture vulgarity:

> She had entered my world, umber and black Humberland, with rash curiosity; she surveyed it with a shrug of amused distaste; and it seemed to me now that she was ready to turn away from it with something akin to plain repulsion. Never did she vibrate under my touch, and a strident "what d'you think you are doing?" was all I got for my pains. To the wonderland I had to offer, my fool preferred the corniest movies, the most cloying fudge. To think that between a Hamburger and a Humburger, she would - invariably, with icy precision - plump for the former. There is nothing more atrociously cruel than an adored child. Did I mention the name of that milk bar I visited a moment ago? It was, of all things, The Frigid Queen. Smiling a little sadly, I dubbed her My Frigid Princess. She did not see the wistful joke.

The "umber and black Humberland," bleakly opposed to the wonderland charms into which Victorian Lewis Carroll could invite a child, has a broader program of reference than merely the solipsism of HH. Nabokov has pondered literary history and its contemporary possibilities, and it is clear that *Lolita* is also a commentary on the taste and literary directions of the current century. An implied purpose of the novel's referential frame is to summon past tradition to illustrate anew the degree of original inventiveness necessary for individual poets/writers in period after period as the task of newness is perpetually intensified.

For Shakespeare, for example, writing his post-Petrarchan sonnets when the sonneteering movement was listless and worn out, the only paths of poetic originality lay in the celebration of shockingly new types – a young man, a sexually corrupt dark lady – in an ethical vocabulary alien to both the religious and secular sources of the tradition. In the nineteenth century, someone like Lewis Carroll was also stunningly new, although he was barely aware that he was in this tradition at all, or that his Alice belongs with the icons of the poetic past. Although his commemoration of Alice is of a dazzling inventiveness that reaffirms explosive possibilities within genres and forms, Dodgson and his narrator Carroll are unself-conscious and unreflective. Indeed, so hidden was everything from Charles Dodgson – even the basis of his sexuality as well as literary tradition – that neither he nor his friends, the children's parents, appear to have recognized abnormal urges in his desire to photograph nude little girls or to have a chaste cup of tea whenever he could with prepubescent maidens. For Postmodern, self-conscious Nabokov, such innocence is impossible, and the pressure toward newness is as obvious as it was for Shakespeare. An aesthetically original product was demanded.

Nabokov's contemplation of the tradition of love celebration in the middle of the twentieth century is bizarre, original, and daring. Having studied the past, he sees that the central and centrally ironic issue in love poetry – indeed the fissure through which a deconstruction of the tradition can occur – is the celebration of the very young. In the Middle Ages and Renaissance this produced first a religious ideal and then, by way of Petrarch, a progressively secularized theory of individual creativity. By the nineteenth century this literary genre's most original continuations involved innocently idealized fantasy or, in the case of Poe, a gradual inclination toward sexual stress and decadence. In the twentieth century with its sexual "enlightenment," Nabokov picks up the salient erotic feature from the past, invents the 9- to 14-year-old nymphet, and creates a heavily infatuated, solipsistic sophisticate – Humbert Humbert – to present a deeply ironic poetic game illustrative of the state of the art.

Looked at thus, the allegorical nature of *Lolita* comes strongly to the fore, and if Fredric Jameson (following Walter Benjamin) is right in arguing that Postmodernism is characterized by allegorical tendencies, *Lolita* proves very strongly *not* to be a book with a moral in tow, but a meditation on the nature of literature or genre within a self-generating narcissistic culture.

To the degree that *Lolita* is concerned with the history of a genre within a longstanding and abiding culture, it recognizes the turns and developments that culture has taken and continues to take. Even as this novel exquisitely celebrates a hyper-erotic and decadent sexuality, it comments on the unstable nature of genre itself. *Lolita* not only continues a poetic tradition, but also illustrates how poetry has been replaced by prose fiction in the nineteenth and twentieth centuries. The dominant form for extended audience reception of a major theme is no longer poetry, although prosodic elements are strongly present in prose as pressured and connotative as Nabokov's. His Humbert Humbert's prose also shows how generically extensive the novel form can be, and how, unlike the genre-obsessed poetry of the past, it can stretch itself into larger frames where genre ceases to be tyrannous.

In *Lolita*, Nabokov telescopes genres so that elements of poetic tradition coexist with the idea of the novel as romance and, even more pertinently, as detective fiction. Readers of *Lolita* quickly become enchanted hunters, pursuing not only the cruel doldrums of HH's affair with his nymphet but also the identity of the eerily cognizant man in the Aztec red car who invades the text during the first trans-American trip, pursuing the guilty pair and then being pursued himself as the guilty kidnapper of Lolita. Hunt and pursuit are major signifiers of the plot and the reader's primary point of participation, but every percipient identification the reader may wish to make is foreseen and punned upon by the narrator amid a density of clues that become evident only on rereading.

The reader quickly perceives that (s)he is forestalled, defeated by the author in a competitive game mirrored and manically extended by Humbert Humbert's pursuit of the guilty abductor, Quilty. The pun on the name (Clare Quilty = Clearly Guilty) is dyslexic – the misuse of q for g that characterizes a minor dysfunction, instantly recognizable by anyone who marks student papers. The elaborate literary game played across the motel-laden chessboard of America between HH and his Quilty–guilty double is allusive and connotative in the extreme; it is also a parodic representation of how the would-be mandarin reader tries not only to guess the villain but also to catch the references the competitive author has planted in order to win. And winning for Nabokov does not simply mean out-guessing, but establishing a supremacy of gamesmanship in which the author keeps the reader in his/her strenuous but humble place.

The idea of winning is endemic to the function of detective fiction, and indeed readers of murder mysteries reckon that if the Gordian knot of the mystery is easily untied the work has failed. The pitting of author against reader is thus an established convention, but in the case of *Lolita* its ramifications are lordly and extreme. Although Nabokov establishes an identifiable, graded series of doubles for HH – including Quilty, the Swiss detective Gustave Trapp, and the fraudulent foreign teacher and chess player Gaston Godin – the workings of *Lolita* as a detective novel are shadowed by ambiguity and symbolically psychodramatic gradations. Here, more clearly than in most Nabokov novels, the reader has the impression that the subject is always singular, that at one graded level of being everything shadows or multiplies the central consciousness that projects the fiction. As in an allegorical medieval psychomachia, all the male characters work their way back to parodic shadings of the original authorial mind, and *Lolita* should doubtless be seen as a burgeoning allegory of creativity contemplating its materials.

Nabokov is much more interested in this central consciousness than he is in the laggard reader who uses all his/her ammunition to keep up with the mandarin author. The game is lots of fun – infinitely absorbing, in fact – even though Nabokov always wins. The maintenance of a high level of authorial performance – the linguistic and referential ardor that is energetically poured into the novel's substance – is almost perfect, as Nabokov pushes himself word by word, phrase by phrase, sentence by sentence, to a stylistic standard that surges electrically through the text. *Lolita* is that rarest of literary artifacts – a text that one can pick up pleasurably over the years and read piecemeal or in small bits, so crafted and animated is every sentence, paragraph, and section. Meanwhile, all the dizzying games are completely functional in *Lolita*, unlike the excesses of *Ada*, where Nabokov's celebration of tradition, language, and self-reference must be seen finally as an illustration of what happens when the ambitions of an ingenious writer fail to balance his verbal self-indulgences in a sufficiently interesting way.

An allusive novel like *Lolita* invites work of the sort that Alfred Appel Jr's much admired *The Annotated Lolita* (1970) delivers, nor is there any question that the idea of hermeneutical commentary fascinated Nabokov not only as a writer but as a university lecturer. At the same time, Nabokov remained nervous about criticism, and stressed the likelihood of its incompetence. Because *Lolita* is generically complex, it is, like most books that parodically follow the outlines of genre, easily misread. When the tradition of detective fiction is so obviously evoked, the reading habits attendant on that genre are almost bound to ensue, and an eager clue-gatherer in the realm of genre logic will quickly apply rules of causality both to the solving of the mystery of Lolita's disappearance and to the sources of the allusions. But Nabokov everywhere makes it clear that the dull standard of causality (of the sort that would see HH not as a literary persona but a pathological case, or assume Aristotelian logic as central to an unraveling) is antithetical to the aesthetic irony of the games he plays. Instead, he presents a slithering, twisting, elaborately worked out and highly patterned dénouement that depends on irrational and illogical surprises, as well as on a new literary ensemble of parodic games and aesthetic gestures. Thus, in the book's twists and turns, a freakish fate (stressed through personification as Aubrey McFate, a boy on Lolita's class list) deliberately increases the instability of the novel and conceals much of its finely crafted, orderly impulse.

Because of Nabokov's emphasis on this irrational element, the moral apotheosis of *Lolita* becomes particularly interesting and contradictory. In Nabokov's aesthetic world where causality is perceived with distaste, ethical norms become an impossibility. The Modernist program from Gide's first breakthroughs has taken for granted that in the aesthetic realm the only ethical imperative comes from the artist's disciplined and pure allegiance to his/her art. Yet the "moral apotheosis" in *Lolita* provides the novel with an edge of seriousness that does not degrade but coolly co-operates with its elaborate aestheticism, and, in spite of Nabokov's protests, infuses a distinct moral power into all its gamesome devices. The most obvious area of ethical force is in the transformation of the narrator, a persona whose manically persuasive mask has from the first page been in contradiction with its apparent intention. Self-defensive in the extreme, Humbert Humbert nevertheless surreptitiously intrudes a vocabulary of moral self-loathing, and on two notable occasions, set in dominant moments of the narrative, sheds the mask completely. HH's elaborate self-defenses during Part I are abruptly ended in section 33, where his craven guilt and buying of Lolita's dependency are dramatically evident:

> In the gay town of Lepingville I bought her four books of comics, a box of candy, a box of sanitary pads, two cokes, a manicure set, a travel clock with a luminous dial, a ring with a real topaz, a tennis racket, roller skates with white high shoes, field glasses, a portable radio set, chewing gum, a transparent raincoat, sunglasses, some more garments – swooners, shorts, all kinds of summer frocks. At the hotel we had separate rooms, but in the middle of the night she came sobbing into mine, and we made it up very gently. You see, she had absolutely nowhere else to go.

Similarly, at the end of Lolita and HH's first trans-American journey, Humbert Humbert's narration slips into an abject acknowledgment of his solipsistic devastation of both America and Lolita:

> And so we rolled East, I more devastated than braced with the satisfaction of my passion, and she glowing with health, her bi-iliac garland still as brief as a lad's, although she had added two inches to her stature and eight pounds to her weight. We had been everywhere. We had really seen nothing. And I catch myself thinking today that our long journey had only defiled with a sinuous trail of slime the lovely, trustful, dreamy, enormous country that by then, in retrospect, was no more to us than a collection of dog-eared maps, ruined tour books, old tires, and her sobs in the night – every night, every night – the moment I feigned sleep.

Written ostensibly as an appeal to the "ladies and gentlemen of the jury" by a convicted murderer, *Lolita* with playful desperation presents itself as a carefully formulated document whose narrative consistency constantly lapses. Because the text openly concludes with the murder of the HH's alter ego, the guilty

Quilty, and Humbert Humbert's subsequent arrest, the defense it presents becomes increasingly tenuous and legally pointless. The "ladies and gentlemen of the jury" are those readers of the novel capable of judging. As the logic of the legal appeal fades, the strength of the novel's real theme - an expression and celebration of human love - grows. In HH's final meeting with Lolita, who at the ripe age of 17 is no longer a nymphet, his narrow sexual obsession is entirely replaced by a genuine love and moral apprehension of the person in front of him. This new Lolita, now transformed through poverty, marriage, and pregnancy into a sexless creature named Dolly Schiller, calls forth the detailed loving attention HH owed her from the beginning:

> You may jeer at me, and threaten to clear the court, but until I am gagged and half-throttled, I will shout my poor truth. I insist the world know how much I loved my Lolita, *this* Lolita, pale and polluted, and big with another's child, but still gray-eyed, still sooty-lashed, still auburn and almond, still Carmencita, still mine.

The selfish pleasure of possession is still with Humbert Humbert at this point, however, and in order to complete the moral apotheosis Nabokov takes one more step. After the dreadfully, complexly comic execution of Quilty, HH drives off the road to await his arrest; as he waits, he recalls with regret an incident that occurred as he searched for the abducted Lolita. Near a small town, he heard the sounds that come from a "normal" world where mothers and children are daily left while fathers go off to work:

> Reader! What I heard was but the melody of children at play, nothing but that, and so limpid was the air that within this vapor of blended voices, majestic and minute, remote and magically near, frank and divinely enigmatic - one could hear now and then, as if released, an almost articulate spurt of vivid laughter, or the crack of a bat, or the clatter of a toy wagon, but it was all really too far for the eye to distinguish any movement in the lightly etched streets. I stood listening to that musical vibration from my lofty slope, to those flashes of separate cries with a kind of demure murmur for background, and then I knew that the hopelessly poignant thing was not Lolita's absence from my side, but the absence of her voice from that concord.

This final admission that HH had been guilty of a larger crime than the literary murder of his Quilty–Guilty alter ego necessarily moves the novel into a higher ethical category. Through the terrible realistic act of absenting Lolita's voice from the concord of childhood, with or without her complicity, HH criminally indulged in the irradicable selfishness that this "documentary" account, this fifty-six-day writing spree, is dedicated to expiating. In a very real way, the killing of his guilty Quilty opens Humbert Humbert to a relinquishment of solipsism, and to a selfless poetic act - the immortalizing of a girl who, like him, like Nabokov, like all readers caught in the mesh of time, is subject to death. Nabokov makes it clear in the last paragraph of *Lolita* that his theme is the tragic placement of art with its potential immortality against the fragility of both the artist and his subject:

> And do not pity C.Q. One had to choose between him and H.H., and one wanted H.H. to exist at least a couple of months longer, so as to have him make you live in the mind of later generations. I am thinking of aurochs and angels, the secret of durable pigments, prophetic sonnets, the refuge of art. And this is the only immortality you and I may share, my Lolita.

Lolita reeks of death; within the confines of Humbert Humbert's request to the editor, it cannot be published until both he and Lolita are dead – but so is everyone else: Charlotte Haze, Jean Farlow, Quilty, even poor Charlie Holmes, despoiler of Lolita's purity, who has been killed in the Korean War and whose death constitutes the only historical–political identification in the entire novel. The particular pain of human fragility in the face of inexorable death is countered in the preceding quotation by the endurance of art from the primeval time of the aurochs to the highly self-conscious present – or from blind pre-consciousness to ironic self-consciousness. This sense of aesthetic continuity with its brave statement of artistic persistence is the most convincing – as well as the most splendidly idealistic – demonstration Nabokov makes in his fiction, which is elsewhere entirely ironic on the subject of the creative act.

Lolita is also Nabokov's only foray into an ethical mode, and it is arguably possible to say that the unfading success of the novel over the decades is connected to this factor. Certainly Nabokov's other novels and short stories are characterized by moral distancing, and the frequently erotic quality of their action projects both coolness and cruelty – and often despair. Thus from early novels like *King, Queen, Knave*, through *Laughter in the Dark* and *Transparent Things*, the dominant mood is one of brittle misuse and deprivation. Given its moral power, it is fitting to ask where Nabokov as a writer could go after the brilliant achievement of *Lolita*, but his work did not lose its consistency or falter in spite of some subsequent unevenness. In fact, occupied with translations from his earlier Russian novels as well as with new fiction, Nabokov kept himself visible and his audience impressed up to his death in 1977. There are significant lapses – notably the tediously self-referential indulgences of *Ada, or Ardor: A Family Chronicle* (1969), and the less than exciting final complete novel, *Look at the Harlequins!* (1975). But two post-*Lolita* works – *Pale Fire* (1962) and *Transparent Things* (1972) – add notably to Nabokov's reputation and increase the reader's apprehension of the thematic breadth of this major novelist whose work has left an ineradicable imprint on the methods of the Postmodern imagination.

*

Nabokov's instinct toward ardor, energy, and the imprint of newness is his most salient mark as a writer. The publication of *Pale Fire* in 1962 – shortly after *Lolita* and the touching, cruel, unstably narrated *Pnin* – ringingly proclaims his capacity to present a fiction whose originality of conception and structure has no real analogue. Totally unlike anything he had done previously, this novel is Nabokov's most extended and successful foray into comedy, under whose aegis he performs the other tasks that *Pale Fire* is dedicated to carrying out. Like *Lolita*, *Pale Fire* is a literary product to the core, but whereas the earlier novel examines the abiding nature of an ancient genre, the latter is a sort of spoof – an ostensible attack on the self-absorbed vagaries of criticism, and a study of the solipsistic mind's inability to concentrate on an external object.

The epigraph of *Pale Fire* places the novel in its tradition, as Boswell's Dr Johnson loses the drift of his subject and goes from the madness of a young nobleman to irrelevant private concern for his own cat:

> This reminds me of the ludicrous account he gave Mr Langston, of the despicable state of a young gentleman of good family. "Sir, when I heard of him last, he was running about town shooting cats." And then in a sort of kindly reverie, he bethought himself of his own favorite cat, and said, "But Hodge shan't be shot: no, no, Hodge shall not be shot."

If Johnson's wonderful conversation is taken as a primary text, then Boswell's reportage and commentary are comparable to the task of a serious critic exercising his powers upon it. Johnson, as author of the primary text, has shown his inability to keep his mind in tidy order as he allows himself to angle away from the subject at hand. As Nabokov takes up this theme of mental vagary, the drifter is not the author freely ranging from his subject, but the critic whose allegiance to the text is partial and oblique. Thus the text of the poem, *Pale Fire* by John Shade, is only a minor pretext for the passionately egotistical quasi-historical structure of his commentator, Charles Kinbote. Kinbote's madly solipsistic critical commentary is a comic *tour de force*, presenting a secondary text in a way that heralds the current deconstructive tendency to see the critic's commentary as equally strong textually as the work of art from which it derives its primary energy. In 1962, Kinbote's wild solipsism looked mad; in the late 1980s, it has become the norm in many critical circles.

Nabokov certainly meant his satire to bite hard; in creating Kinbote, however, he not only turned his shaft against the professional university critic, but also wistfully implanted the pathetic, tragicomic idea of the Russian *émigré* intellectual whose life is bounded by memory, pretension, and fraudulence. Like Pnin (who reappears in *Pale Fire* doing quite nicely) or Gaston Godin in *Lolita*, Charles Kinbote is locked in his mad memories and totally alien to the comfortable American academic community in which he and the "great" poet, John Shade, coexist. While John Shade writes a sturdy American auto-biographical poem in traditional, neo-Popian couplets – fueled by memory and thematized by a mediocre marriage, an ugly daughter's suicide, and his oneiric apprehensions of death – Kinbote re-creates this American domestic fiction as an occult reference to his lost Zembla – a land of dreams and paranoia where he may have ruled in irresponsible bliss.

The idea that a critic brings only private structures and eccentric peculiarities to the text is now a commonplace; when Nabokov was writing *Pale Fire*, the idea of hermeneutic accuracy was not yet a lost cause. Kinbote's basic exercise as editor of the 999-line poem, *Pale Fire*, appears from the beginning entirely straightforward, and one of the most methodical tasks a philological scholar can take on. He begins with a description of the text's provenance and holographic state; but on the first page he intrudes *in propria persona* with his own tic: "There is a very loud amusement park right in front of my present lodgings." Unable to keep his mind on his basic taxonomic task, Kinbote rapidly shows the pathological nature of his solipsistic energy, blaming the poet's widow, Sybil, and aggressively berating her chosen editors. His comic ingenuity in getting his hands on the manuscript, and his determination to transform the poem into a private historical document, both make nonsense of the scholarly task he has taken on. When the novel's reader has read through the poem itself, (s)he is quickly thrown into the maelstrom of Kinbote's mad psychology.

At the basis of the novel is the large question of an author's access to an audience. Nabokov does not give easy allegiance to the idea that the reader is dominantly creative; in fact, the whole thrust of *Pale Fire* is to show that the reader's madness intervenes to pervert a text that is in itself a declarative speech act or performative utterance. Shade's poem has its own integrity, but it is interesting that the novel's critics have not at all agreed on this primary issue. At once touching in a homely way and profound in its meditation on death, the 999-line poem is a major example of Nabokov's almost *sub rosa* attempt to talk about the eternal, the *Potustornnost* that his wife Véra claims to be his central theme.

Nevertheless, in spite of its incontrovertible edge of seriousness, Shade's poem is also parodic in a negative way – it suggests the lumbering aspects of American literature where the dullness of a fairly happy bourgeois marriage and the suicide of a fat, plain daughter show themselves to be inferior to the great realist themes of the nineteenth-century European novel. In the text of the poem, metaphysical Emersonian shadings also are presented in a bitter parodic mode, and it is clear that Nabokov can never force himself to take on the earnestness of American metaphysics. Nevertheless, John Shade contemplates the post-mortal fountain of Dante (taken up through a typo – f instead of m – by a stupid American woman who dreams of a mountain and fails to see the resonance of image and symbol) or the *grand peut-être* (the "grand potato" in Nabokov's irresistible punning) of Rabelais's conjectures about God, without allowing himself an ultimately serious engagement with the spiritual ideas that hover at the edge of the poem's discourse.

But in spite of its workaday themes, its artificiality of wit, and its stringency of form, the poem has an emotional as well as poetic impact that even a naive reader picks up on. Opposed to its almost apologetic integrity is the wildly irrelevant, disjunctive nature of the footnotes and commentary supplied by the critic, Kinbote. Kinbote's mournful exilic quality survives Nabokov's potent comic blows, for as he attempts to write about the poem he presents a novel that is a history of himself – and Nabokov always in his fiction makes it clear that the history we make is the subjective servant of memory. Kinbote says in one of his over-long footnotes, "I have no desire to twist and batter an unambiguous *apparatus criticus* into the monstrous semblance of a novel," but that is precisely what he succeeds in doing. Indirectly, Nabokov makes a point about the provenance of fiction in general, for it feeds on poetry, on academic tasks, on history, on the past, and on neurosis, and from this congeries comes an accomplished text. In the process of making this text are many twistings and perversions of other texts, and just as Shade's poem is perverted to create Kinbote's story, so Nabokov suggests all readings of any text will be. To be a critic is to pervert; to be an artist is to excel at perversion.

From the time of his exile, Nabokov was extremely interested in the art and hopelessness of translation; not only did he write about the theory of translation, but he also translated some of his own early works, works by Lermontov and Tyutchev, and most notably Pushkin's *Eugene Onegin* into English. His principle of translation involved direct transliteration, and he disliked any fanciful or poetic intrusion which would alter the verbal quality of the original text. Translation and criticism are parallel for him, and both tend toward inaccuracy; in *Pale Fire* he pokes fun at the dreadful awkwardness and errors in the inferior, wooden, Zemblan translation of Shakespeare's *Timon of Athens*, from which the novel's title is derived. *Pale Fire* can be seen as a comic statement of outrage against the hopeless range of mad inaccuracy that troubles the whole project of literature and literary transmission.

Although poor John Shade tries to transmit the felt quality of an ordinary life in his valedictory poem, it is picked up by Kinbote as a deeply encoded account of his own lost kingdom of Zembla – "a distant northern land" whose unreality is not quite provable. Kinbote's mythical Zembla is haunted by late Shakespearean texts, notably *Timon of Athens* and *Coriolanus*, but drably and inaccurately; it is nevertheless true that Shakespeare's rage in these two bitter plays parallels the anger exiled Nabokov only partially conceals through comedy. In *Pale Fire*, every referential text is suspect and inaccurately presented; by logical extension, both Shade's poem and Kinbote's commentary are implied to be false. Shade's former secretary even suggests that he reports incorrectly on the fate of his daughter, and an academic cocktail party conversation indicates that Kinbote's memories of himself as King Charles of Zembla are part of a neurotic and desperate self-aggrandizing dream.

Nabokov nevertheless attaches the fictions of *Pale Fire* to "reality" in a notable way, and, in the reality shared by both author and reader, exilic obsession and loneliness are effectively portrayed. At one point in his wonderfully mad commentary, Kinbote remarks that "bearded Zemblans resemble one another – and that, in fact, the name Zembla is a corruption not of the Russian *zemlya*, but of Semblerland, a land of reflections, of 'resemblers.' " All of Nabokov's fictional places are lands of reflections, rendered the more bizarre in this case by the fact that Nabokov's lost Russia cannot be recovered accurately or unironically; it can only be reproduced parodically by a frankly crazy commentator, whose heart's desire lies in a totally irrecoverable Zembla-semblance.

Like all Nabokov's fiction, *Pale Fire* takes as its main themes time and death, and the violence that they impose. Sweet, elderly John Shade is murdered, apparently by an escapee from a mental hospital; for Kinbote, however, there is, as usual, another text. For him, the murder is part of a shadowy conspiracy, in which the political past pursues him through the symbolically named person, Gradus. This assassin's dogged determination overbalances his comic ineptitude and makes him into a steadily approaching image of the Zemblan past. His target is, of course, Kinbote but, having incompetently missed him, Shade is good enough. Images of shadows, shades, and gradations of reality dominate this book – which is, like most of Nabokov's last fictions – above all about the solipsistic obsession of its central protagonist. Although Gradus is the shadow that kills, Shade is an earnest figure in a world of inaccuracy and literary impossibility. In a discussion with Kinbote, Shade talks about the function of moral men, but he does so in weary terms that dodge Kinbote's tedious Augustinian metaphysics: "All the seven deadly sins are peccadilloes but without three of them, Pride, Lust and Sloth, poetry might never have been born. . . . [The password is] pity." What emerges from this comically enacted novel of human foolishness and solipsism is pity, a sense that the poverty of the human spirit is metaphysically, laughably, sadly there, but not to be judged in grandiose terms. Similarly, Kinbote's wild misreadings are often treated with a pity that Nabokov himself only rarely submitted to.

*

The most metaphysical of Nabokov's fictions is the chilly novel, *Transparent Things* (1972). It is also the most alien and brutal since *Laughter in the Dark*, but it ingeniously covers itself with a surface patina of ordinary plotting and studied frigidity. Never in warm collusion with his reader, Nabokov here presents a cool study of a contemporary Euro-American world where the co-ordinates of the traditional novel – notably the love of hero and heroine – are shattered and perverted. The literary background of the fiction dates from Mlle de Scudéry's *Clélie* (1660), where the idea of a mapped *carte du tendre* projects the *préciosité* of platonic love; in literary history, this kind of source ultimately led to the heart-warming genre of domestic fiction. The pseudo-everyman of *Transparent Things*, Hugh (You) Person, yearningly says that he lives in a world in which the *amitié tendre* of the past has no avenue of expression – in fact, his relationship with his Belgian/Russian/Swiss wife, Armande, is described as the perversion of a *carte du tendre* into a "Chart of Torture." This miserable metamorphosis can and should be taken as Nabokov's description of the Postmodern state.

Hugh Person (you the persona) is a nervous hanger-on in the world – both the real world of America and the artificial world of literary production. A reader to whom Nabokov gives an unusual cachet in that he is not a critic but an efficient editor, Person is ill at ease in his body, his family, his marriage, his job, the world. The ostensible function of this novel is to remove him from his dis-ease in space and time to another realm of being signaled by death. He is an American, whose four trips to Europe lead him to adulthood, to marriage, to confrontation with a writer, and finally to a violent death. Europe – specifically the punning town of Witt in Switzerland – thus becomes for him a background against which he sets his memories, trying vainly and hopelessly to retrieve a lost past through a final visit. It is important in locating the literary co-ordinates of this novel to note that Proust was his high Modernist antecedent as a visitor to the past. Person's failure is specifically a Postmodern one, set coldly against the greatness of Modernism:

> What had you expected of your pilgrimage, Person? A mere mirror rerun of hoary torments? Sympathy from an old stone? Enforced re-creation of irrecoverable trivia? A search for lost time in an utterly distinct sense from Goodgrief's dreadful "*Je me souviens, je me souviens de la maison où je suis né*," or, indeed, Proust's quest? He had never experienced here (save once at the end of his last ascent) anything but boredom and bitterness.

Person's dreams of his dead wife Armande are always connected with Witt (like Zembla a metaphoric name) and Switzerland; in this Europe of his past, Person seeks a "spectral visitation" that might be accurate. His pilgrimage fails to comfort him through the recovery of a transparent past, but it gives him his death – carefully prepared for him from the beginning of the book. Fire and flames dominate this slender, restrained novel, and when they lick elegantly at Person's hotel door on the last page, his death metamorphosis into the other state of being is accomplished. Only at this point does a spectral voice finally intervene – probably that of the novelist-within-the novel, R, claiming that it's easy:

> Rings of blurred colors circled around him, reminding him briefly of a childhood picture in a frightening book about triumphant vegetables whirling faster and faster around a nightshirted boy trying desperately to awake from the iridescent dizziness of dream life. Its ultimate vision was the incandescence of a book or a box grown completely transparent and hollow. This is, I believe, *it*: not the crude anguish of physical death *but the incomparable pangs of the mysterious mental maneuver needed to pass from one state of being to another*.
> Easy, you know, does it, son.   (italics added)

The grimness of Person's life-long human misery – begun in his wretched childhood and continued through the unsatisfactory marriage – manifests itself in nocturnal violence through nightmares. These culminate in his oneiric strangulation of his wife, Armande, while he dreams that he's saving another woman, Julia, from death by fire. His dreams have always produced images of violence as the subconscious data from which the ghostly plot action of this novel springs. Through the taut, restrained prose of *Transparent Things*, Nabokov attempts to elucidate the subtle relationship between thing and image or dream; in this process, Person's unintentional act of violence joins the other metaphoric acts in the novel. Essentially Nabokov uses the image of dream madness as a spectral metaphor for the idea of metaphor itself.

The centrality of metaphors and their off-center equivalence to transparent "things" suspended in history are emphasized in the novel by the device of sardonically introducing R, a "major" writer whose books Person edits, into the fiction. R insists on calling his last book *Tralatitions* – which he says is a perfectly respectable pun defining metaphor – and in doing so he clarifies the pivotal act of metaphoric transmutation or metamorphosis. The transference of objective action or thing into the subjective aesthetics of metaphor central to all fiction is equivalent to the "mysterious mental maneuver needed to pass from one state of being to another." But Nabokov tries to guard the autonomy of this aesthetic function of metaphor by making it clear that the "realist" metaphor of Hugh's dream violence does not have a direct cause and effect relationship. Like the translation of Person from life to death, metaphor is entirely dependent on haphazard chance or the combinative genius of the writer – a thematic idea repeated throughout Nabokov's fiction. As in the case of the narrator's early definition of transparency, quoted at the beginning of this essay, *Transparent Things* as a novel almost casually inserts its metaphysical signposts. Thus the reader is told how chancy, chimerical, and irrelevant past, present, and future events are:

> Direct interference in a person's life does not enter our scope of activity, nor, on the other, tralititiously speaking, hand, is his destiny a chain of predeterminate links: some "future" events may be likelier than others, O.K., but all are chimeric, and every cause-and-effect sequence is always a hit-and-miss affair, even if the lunette has actually closed around your neck, and the cretinous crowd holds its breath . . . . Human life can be compared to a person dancing in a variety of forms around his own self . . . their spinning *ronde* going faster and faster and gradually forming a transparent ring of banded colors around a dead person or planet.

Transparent Things as a novel is contained in this spinning dance – in the coldness and misery of the plot, and in the sense of a bleakly violent metamorphosis into another state of being. Metaphor is the major narrative device through which this can be accomplished; the end is a bleak aesthetic pleasure derived from death itself. In this major sense, the actions and metaphysical import of this novel project a basic symbolic way of looking at Nabokov's work, composed as it is at some vertiginous point between the chanciness of life and the genius of art.

It should not take a reader long to notice the vast and intelligent obliquity of Nabokov's fiction, as well as its serious thematics. Although *Lolita* reeks of death, its essential gaiety masks its misery; within the frenetic comedy of *Pale Fire*, Kinbote lives for alternate states, claiming that Shade's whole being – and certainly his own – is a mask; in *Transparent Things* the austerity of unappeasable desire translates not into "aesthetic bliss" but into a transmutation that deprives Person of satisfying memories and demands that the destructive fires of the world remove him to another realm of being. As a reader looks backward on Nabokov's career, it is clear that under his apparently endless games lies an appalling metaphysical seriousness – a sense that there is another absolute mode of being which literature serves – whereas the inhabitant of our world, Nabokov himself, as Humbert Humbert says in *Lolita*, has "only words to play with."

5

Calvino, Beckett, and the cosmicomical reader

In dealing with these two writers whose kinship is only obliquely evident, it is best to begin with Beckett, who exerted real but subtle influence on Calvino, and whose dark nihilism contrasts with the sunny face Calvino consistently turns to an unconquerable, incomprehensible world. Both writers stress comedy as a primary mode; in Beckett's earliest collection of stories, *More Pricks Than Kicks* (1934), the Dantesque character Belacqua queries, "Was it to be laughter or tears? ... It came to the same thing in the end." Beckett has kept his audience laughing desperately for many years now, and as he enters his ninth decade the dire laughter is rapidly losing ground to linguistic meditation touched by pity.

As the master of deprivation and nihilism, Beckett continuously experiments with form, altering his methods of presenting narrative voices, while his thematics remain consistent. As a result, any assessment of his fiction must ally itself to all the voices presented, including those of his justly famous dramas. In the slow process of learning how to read Beckett, the reader studies initial steps in order to put them aside and move on to the next. Responding to Beckett involves three distinctly graduated tasks, of which the last is doubtless the one into which the author has most pointedly put his complex and original energy. Thus his creative process from the early stages of his career consisted of first imagining a scenario, then compiling its precise philosophical content, and finally, and most significantly, setting about the difficult task of finding styles and forms to contain it.

First, therefore, the reader absorbs the Beckettian scenario, which consists of a cosmos whittled down to chaotic emptiness where bleak comfortless houses or muck, garbage cans, cylinders, etc. constitute the living-quarters for the human sufferer(s). This wretched space is inhabited by one or more usually old and often ill characters who have only bizarre objects to comfort them (sucking stones, a sack of canned tunny, bananas, boots, a tomb), and every text is dominated by someone's – not always these character(s)' – relentless need to talk, to keep going on, even though, as Beckett put it early in his career, there is "nothing to express, nothing with which to express, nothing from which to express, no power to express, no desire to express, together with the obligation to express."

Having accepted this scenario as the principal *donnée* (although Beckett would object to such a literary cliché), the reader must secondly go on to the philosophical underpinnings of the work – a task "literary" readers like Alvarez and Federman have found repugnant, but without which Beckett's career is underestimated. His philosophical stance, like his basic scenario, remains remarkably stable, as Eugene Webb (1970) has pointed out. Afflicted by an inescapable Cartesian duality, Beckett has fruitlessly tapped and rejected the tough consolations of Heideggerian and Sartrian existentialism; although he bluntly claims that he is no philosopher, his Nietzschian point of view – that we necessarily, hopelessly, lovelessly live in chaos, that there is no way of understanding the world and no access to knowledge or reality – is almost made to the measure of French anti-semantic philosophers (Barthes, Derrida, and their followers) now fashionable on the literary scene. Unlike other writers whose theme is despair and death, however, Beckett has clearly earned his nihilistic credentials through close philosophical study as well as nameless suffering – and many critics, including most recently Lance St John Butler (1984), have been careful to alert us to this fact.

The duality that marks and distinguishes Beckett's work extends through all its facets. Thus his compulsive urge and obligation to write is countered by a conviction that silence is necessary; his characters live in chaos and long for order, even as they live in hopelessness but cannot, even with vast ironic resources, quell hope; as dull despair settles in, language paradoxically gains strength and energy; death is contradicted by the endless animation to keep going on; in the midst of consistent nihilist belief life doggedly persists, and the once radical young Beckett himself ages like Tithonus. As he carries on and on, this remarkable writer continues to move through stages and changes in form, to the dismay of some of his critics who moan with every new publication that surely this is the last one. Nevertheless, the unending creativity of new linguistic forms remains his most abidingly interesting achievement.

Beckett early made it clear that the fragility and expressiveness of form challenge him bitterly, and indeed it seemed that after the completion of the trilogy (*Molloy, Malone Dies, The Unnamable*) in the 1950s Beckett was stalled. With no new thematic material and the danger of fruitless repetition cramping his advancement as a writer, he felt stymied after writing *L'Innomable* with its "complete disintegration. No 'I', no 'have', no 'being'. No nominative, no accusative, no verb. There's no way to go on," as he said in a 1956 interview with Israel Shenker. "For me it gets more and more difficult. For me the area of possibilities gets smaller and smaller." But like his characters, Beckett lives in the dual position of being unable to go on and the ironically compulsive need, as one of the trilogy voices puts it, to "keep going, going on. Call that going? Call that on?" In a 1961 interview with Tom Driver, Beckett stresses his and all writers' necessary contemporary commitment to form in a world governed by chaos or "the mess":

> What I am saying does not mean that there will henceforth be no form in art. It only means that there will be new form, and that this form will be of such a type that it admits the chaos and does not try to say that the chaos is really something else. The form and the chaos remain separate. The latter is not reduced to the former. That is why the form itself becomes a preoccupation, because it exists as a problem separate from the material it accommodates. *To find a form that accommodates the mess, that is the task of the artist now.*

(italics added)

Beckett's search for a form characterizes his work from the beginning, and although it reduces his fiction quantitatively after the trilogy, producing shorter and fewer pieces, there is no diminution of energy and of straining to fulfill the task of the artist as he described it over twenty-five years ago. Perhaps the most exciting thing that Beckett tried was his switch in the mid-1940s from English to French for reasons that are largely inscrutable. At one point he said that it was easier to write in French without style, but there is no doubt that his innovative French stylistics have influenced contemporary French literature. In becoming a French writer, Beckett did not abandon English, and translated his work into his native tongue with contradictory results that make it essential for the Beckettian to read the works in both languages. Beckett claims to hate translating, but his quirky care in doing so is evident.

The analogue or perhaps contrast of bilingualism here is with Nabokov who also, often in partnership with his son Dmitri, translated his early Russian works into English with varying degrees of suppleness. In doing so, he lamented the loss of his versatile Russian tongue; although Nabokov wanted the novels translated in order to allow them an audience denied by the Russian regime, he pushed himself less in the task of translating them than he did in writing his English-language novels, where he achieved a total personal replacement of the Russian language through awesome pyrotechnical stylistics in English. I cannot read Russian and can only repeat the conjectures of others who indicate that when Nabokov was very active in the translation of the early works – as in *Invitation to a Beheading* or *King, Queen, Knave* – the English is more pliant and expressive, and less literally dependent on the Russian original. In Beckett's case, it is interesting to note that the translations from French to English vary in technique and perhaps even in intention. They are sometimes literal, but frequently not: often the French achieves more, but sometimes the English does; on frequent occasions the connotative structure of sentences and phrases in the two languages produces different effects and unlike meanings. A few decades ago it was suggested that Beckett through years in France was losing his grip on English, but that idle theory has been thoroughly discredited by linguistic critics, and more directly and dramatically by his vital translations of such recent pieces as *Mal vu mal dit* into *Ill Seen Ill Said* (1982).

Evidently Beckett feels that in some oblique way two languages are required for every text, and his delivery of both languages is only one of his dualisms and one of the ways by which he tries to find forms "to accommodate the mess." His stance from the beginning has been a post-Mallarméan belief that literature must operate out of silence rather than tradition, an aesthetic that works well with his skepticism to destroy reliance on the literary history of a fictional past. His voices are nevertheless often aware of their stylistic excellence and ironically declare that some expression of hopelessness is nicely put. Their parodic sense of themselves as echoing only literature projects them into the parodic Postmodernist idea of historical belatedness – an idea, I might add, that Beckett did not emulate from current theorists, although he might have helped to invent it. Beckett operates from the position that the fictional forms of the past are completely gone and that new forms are required. Although his first novel, *Murphy* (1938), has a traditional plot and setting, he quickly turned from that form, and when later characters like Molloy try to write themselves, they express the silly lying incompetence – as well as the comedy – of fictional tradition: "Then I went back into the house and wrote, It is midnight. The rain is beating on the windows. It was not midnight. It was not raining."

Beckett's dramatic step in the early development of his career was to clear away the detritus of the past in fiction. It is hard to know precisely when this decision occurred, but it is best to start with one of the few autobiographical facts Beckett gives us in veiled form and through oblique references. Although not formally sharing Joyce's style or urge toward unity, Beckett also experienced his own version of a sacramental artistic moment or epiphany, as Joyce called it. In 1945 during a visit to his mother's house, Beckett had a moment of what he calls, with some embarrassment, revelation or vision, which inaugurated a new period of writing he refers to as "the siege in the room," lasting until the end of the trilogy. This revelation told him that his thematics must henceforth come "from the dark he had struggled to keep under," and from this point on the access to joy, comfort, and sexuality is cut off. The nexus in Beckett's work that describes this revelation is a brief, elliptical section in the play, *Krapp's Last Tape* (1958). Banana-eating old Krapp listens restlessly to tapes made by his pretentious young self long ago, including a statement reflective of Beckett's 1945 visionary experience:

> Spiritually a year of profound gloom and indigence until that memorable night in March, at the end of the jetty, in the howling wind, never to be forgotten, when suddenly I saw the whole thing. The vision at last. This I fancy is what I have chiefly to record this evening, against the day when my work will be done and perhaps no place left in my memory, warm or cold, for the miracle … [*hesitates*] … for the fire that set it alight. What I suddenly saw then was this, that the belief I had been going on all my life, namely …. [*Krapp curses, switches off, winds tape*

forward, switches on again] – great granite rocks the foam flying up in the light of
the lighthouse and the wind-gauge spinning like a propeller, clear to me at last
that the dark I have always struggled to keep under is in reality my most – [*Krapp
curses, switches off, winds tape forward, switches on again*] – unshatterable association
until my dissolution of storm and night with the light of understanding and the
fire – [*Krapp curses louder*, etc.]

Impatient constipated Krapp busily tries to force the tape on to the following
description of sexual pleasure he knows is on it, but the voice of his younger
self talks instead of the revelation of a creative fire that produced an
"unshatterable association" that is indeed Beckett's.

Once the thematics of desolation thus became clear to Beckett in a
metaphysical sense, it followed that fictional forms must be altered radically to
conform to this desolation. Above all, the interference that false consolations
of descriptive and emotional plenitude in traditional fiction had temporarily
lent to the world of literature must be denied. From this point on, various
linguistic and logical experiments became primary in Beckett's attempt to
convey his basic human–inhuman scenario. As a result, Beckett's fiction is
definable through its semantic loss and syntactic gain. Hugh Kenner in *The
Mechanic Muse* describes how Cartesian dualism combines in Beckett with the
binary logic that has now produced the mechanical intelligence of computers.
This led to the maddening logic of passages in early novels like *Watt*, where
every possible permutation and combination of events are presented in order to
give the former sloppy plenitude of the novelistic genre a more strictly logical
structure. The parodic effects thus produced are funny and entirely anti-
novelistic, heralding a destruction of the old form and the need for something
else.

Concurrent with his experiments in fictional form is Beckett's work in the
theatre, where the use of distinctive dramatic voices infuses the brilliant
savagery of his comedy with the linguistic stress that all his work exhibits.
Although he frequently writes for particular actors – one thinks immediately of
the splendid actress Billie Whitelaw among others – Beckett is canny enough to
know that dramas, like novelistic texts, will survive most powerfully as written
verbal forms where even punctuation and stage directions are more important
than any single live dramatic enactment. At the same time, his various styles
demand – or at least come across better through – spoken presentation. But
because the texts are so succinct, grammatically particularized, innovative, and
precise, the silent reading process is forcibly slowed down and one of the major
novel-reading problems thus necessarily eradicated. Speed, carelessness about
detail, and subsequent indifference have unfortunately become intrinsic to the
idea of novel reading, but since Beckett's early use of logical and syntactic
games, no reader's comprehension can keep up to a brisk reading of his prose.
The more dense and opaque the fiction and dramatic pieces, the harder it is for
the lone silent reader to follow them quickly.

On the one hand it is clear that Beckett candidly tries to brake the speed-through indifference that afflicts careless readers; on the other hand, the prose is constructed with such swift energy that when spoken properly – and very fast – by a well-rehearsed performer, the intrinsic speed projected by the human voice is part of the act of comprehending the text. The idea that outside vocal help is required by a text is as old as the ancient rhapsodes, but it is new to the late-twentieth-century idea of the novel which, at this point in our culture, is not perceived as a genre to be read aloud. Beckett's use of actors, tapes, musical evocations, and electronic devices has inspired a vast and generally failed array of experimentation by writers who call themselves metafictionists. Experiment with the design of the page and the use of other arts to give new form to the fictional act range from John Barth's electronic play in *Lost in the Funhouse* to the writers presenting themselves in Raymond Federman's collection of work entitled *Surfiction*, and there can be little doubt that Calvino's *The Castle of Crossed Destinies* is indebted in some way to this Beckettian movement.

Beckett's major contribution, like Shakespeare's, is verbal, however, and its primary location will remain the page, with its punctuation and print. In his prose piece, *Ill Seen Ill Said*, the scene itself is set like print in black and white – the blackness of the old woman's garb, of the night, of the absence of light, as opposed to the whiteness of her hair, her face, the stones of the pasture through which she passes to visit the tomb. This is a print-oriented fiction, in which "under the hovering eye" the consciousness of the narrator and hence of the reader is fed bleakly by the scene that (s)he reads pictorially through the black-and-white of the text Beckett has provided.

*

At this point Calvino must break in – and not only because he is a profoundly print-oriented writer constantly provoking the reader to syntactic considerations of the authorial act of writing. His last book, translated by William Weaver as *Mr Palomar* (1985), is, like Beckett's *Ill Seen Ill Said*, a study of thought, perception, observation, and the power of prose to render what the "hovering eye" can and cannot see. The idea of the seeing eye is central to Modern and contemporary fiction, but it is fraught with ambiguity and a delicate sense of its own frailty. In *Ada*, Nabokov's Van Veen defines the artist as "an underground observatory," a terminology that heavily recalls a certain realm of realism as opposed to Nabokov's punning, parodic word-play in this novel. Beckett implies by his title and the shifting strains of expressiveness in *Ill Seen Ill Said* that the disciplined eye of not one watcher but twelve fails to get far enough in either perception or expression as it watches the grim accumulation of bleak time sloping toward death's dateless night. In *Mr Palomar*, the lens of the great Californian observatory is called on to parallel the eye of one man as he contemplates his closely perceived and meditated bourgeois world.

For Beckett, the "hovering eye" is always the eye of the mind that attempts to align human pain and the endurance of life with the expletives of longing darkness that compose his last works. Beckett's first novelistic character, Murphy, dwells in a buoyantly comic fiction that looks at a moribund "nothing new"; forty-five years later in *Worstward Ho* (1983), the last phrases evoke only the negatives of Beckett's career:

> Enough. Sudden enough. Sudden all far. No move and sudden all far. All least. Three pins. One pinhole. In dimmost dim. Vasts apart. At bounds of boundless void. Whence no farther. Best worse no farther. Nohow less. Nohow worse. Nohow naught. Nohow on.
>   Said nohow on.

The repetitive "nohow"s appear to deny the writing compulsion that has always driven Beckett; to push onward as he and his characters have always done is to go "worstward," driven by longing in a Beckettian landscape that has become unintelligible at the literal level and even in terms of its minimal scenario. The "ill seen ill said" world of the fiction that precedes this one by a year has grown worstward into a text of the "missaid" where expressiveness is past and what has been said or is being said can in no way lead the eye of the mind on. Nohow.

Calvino's eye through the agency of Mr Palomar in his last book is in deep contrast to Beckett's, although the parallels in their sense of literary problems are remarkable. In both cases the dominant perceiving eye is the author's, and the conventional discursive idea that fictions are only fictions is open to question. As Beckett's Unnamable says, "All those Murphys, Molloys and Malones do not fool me." Nevertheless, because Calvino died just as *Mr Palomar* appeared in English translation (in September 1985), his Anglophone audience sentimentally overstresses the connection between Palomar and his playful creator. The "novel" ends with a section entitled "Learning to be dead," and Palomar dies just as he understands how meditation on his own death brings about the ultimate paradox of human perception. The paradox is demonstrated when Palomar understands that, like all mankind, he is caught between his limitations and their ironic opposite – in other words, between his characterological inability to perceive and express enough, and the infinitude of descriptions potentially possible for each human being to articulate. Thus, in an essay written while *Mr Palomar* was in press in Italy, Calvino points out that he is essentially absent-minded: if he observes something interesting like an iguana in a zoo – as Mr Palomar does – he must consciously choose to compose a description of it, or he will forget and lose it forever. Human creative potentiality can be lost in a flash of laziness.

Calvino builds *Mr Palomar* subtly as an ascending scale of metaphysical consideration, beginning with physical observation and expanding modestly through the particulars of an ordinary bourgeois social life; the natural apex of the last moment in this fiction conjures up the metaphysical possibility of human readiness for death. The fluke in nature that ended Calvino's life at the precise moment of the reception of his most clearly metaphysical book by the significant English-speaking segment of his audience is a pathetic fallacy that would have amused this whimsical writer. It is, however, doubtful that Calvino did or would ever have wished to enter a metaphysical realm with the serious and even dreadful urgency of Beckett. His ironic laughter has always had its cosmic aspects, but whereas no one could accuse Beckett of frivolity, some critics have seen Calvino as merely a player of ingenious but pointless games. Although Beckett may have helped to invent the particular combination of ideas that contemporary critic–philosophers have made fashionable, Calvino has seemed to some readers only to embody in trendy form the fictional theories of the dominant French schools. Thus the work of the major post-structuralists – Emile Benvéniste, Roland Barthes, Jacques Derrida – can be applied closely and with a fair degree of accuracy to his work from the mid-1950s up to *If on a winter's night a traveler* (1979), and the influence of the French *nouveau roman* together with the *exercises de style* of the Tel Quel group can be seen as heavily significant. This reduction of Calvino's work has been perniciously tempting to academic critics – presumably of the sort that Gore Vidal once intemperately described in the *New York Review of Books* as "the hicks and hacks and hoods" of academe – and may have contributed to the extreme popularity of Calvino in university circles.

Gore Vidal himself, an American historical novelist of different talents than Calvino's, supports another reading of his admired Italian friend – one that is both more traditionally aesthetic and more metaphysical. In his elegiac description of Calvino's funeral, again in the *New York Review*, Vidal quotes an earlier account he wrote of Calvino's work, in which he claims that the latter's desire to achieve a coalescence of reader and writer succeeds automatically in the fiction: "Reading Calvino, I had the unnerving sense that I was also writing what he had written; thus does his art prove his case as writer and reader become one, or One." Calvino wrote back eloquently, affirming Vidal's estimation and indirectly denying accusations that would identify him as a mere mouthpiece of the theorists:

> I have always thought it would be difficult to extract a unifying theme from my books, each so different from the other. Now you – exploring my works as it should be done, that is, by going at it in an unsystematic way . . . have succeeded in giving a general sense to all I have written, almost a philosophy – "the whole and the many," etc. – and it makes me very happy when someone is able to find a philosophy from the productions of my mind which has little philosophy . . . . The ending of your essay contains an affirmation of what seems to me important in an absolute sense. I don't know if it really refers to me, but it is true of an ideal literature for each one of us: the end being that every one of us must be, that the writer and reader become one, or One. And to close all of my discourse and yours in a perfect circle, let us say that this One is All.

Far from perceiving his own work as a systematic expression of the theories of others, Calvino is a grazer in the pastures of ideology; an erudite man, he absorbs the trends of his period and uses them sporadically and unsystematically. At the same time, he understands the need some critics have of the security of system. In 1962, he wrote in his introduction to the English translation of *I Nostri Antenori* (*Our Ancestors*):

> I will give no more than these very general points [of interpretation] because the reader must interpret the stories as he will, or else not interpret them at all and read them simply for enjoyment – which would fully satisfy me as a writer. So I agree to the books being read as existential or as structural works, as Marxist or neo-Kantian, Freudianly or Jungianly; but above all I am glad when I see that no single key will turn all their locks.

Although some excellent studies on Calvino as novelist-cum-theorist have been done (the most useful is Jo Ann Cannon's *Italo Calvino: Writer and Critic* (1981). Calvino is indeed a writer for whom no single key will turn all the locks. Vidal's restatement for Calvino of the ancient paradox of the one and the many is no doubt the closest description that can be given of his work.

In the last years of his life, Calvino rose high in the estimation of the international literary establishment, and in doing so could have veered into arrogance. There is a perhaps apocryphal story told among academic Italianists to the effect that one Italian critic wrote a demeaning survey of Calvino's career, describing him as an almost perfect example of a merely minor writer. (I can't find this survey, and it may be part of another fiction.) As the story runs, Calvino, far from being offended, wrote an enthusiastic letter, thanking the condescending fellow for putting him in precisely the right category. Some critics who have wished to belittle him – the most notable in English being James Gardner – have gone beyond this to open attack, refusing to allow his work aesthetic achievement, intellectual originality, scientific play, or theoretical independence. I mention the demurrers specifically, because such grand statements against any writer are logically irrefutable; in these cases Calvino is the victim of an increasingly negative reception accorded to all "experimental" fictionists as a neo-realistic minimalism takes over in America, and the Europeans move toward sentimentality.

More than any other highly accomplished writer in the experimental mode – Barth, Barthelme, Robbe-Grillet, Nabokov, even Borges – Calvino's work raises the question of affect in fiction; those who dislike his work tend mistakenly to use the accusations of coldness that have characterized negative critics of this group of writers in general. It is certainly true that the quasi-philosophical theorists of literature in France and America have argued for the "death of the author" and the total impersonality of the unvalorized text. Yet Calvino infuses his fictions with a deeply personal sense of his manifold personae as a writer; frequently operating from a distanced and controlled theoretical stance, he has achieved a personalization and humanization of the text that few contemporary writers – including realists – have been able to project. In an essay entitled "Myth in the narrative," (Federman 1975) Calvino gives some idea of how this personal infusion in a fiction might occur for a writer like him:

> Literature is a combinational game which plays on the possibilities intrinsic to its own material, independently of the personality of the author. But it is also a game which at a certain stage is invested with an unexpected meaning, a meaning having no preference at the linguistic level on which the activity takes place, but which springs from another level and brings into play something on that other level that means a great deal to the author or to the society of which he is a member.

The successful raising of "an unexpected meaning" in Calvino's work springs from the parodic play and combinational games that characterize most definitions of Postmodern literature. But whereas many – even most – Postmodern writers would argue for (barren) aestheticism and impersonality, Calvino clings to semantics and to the idea of the sociopolitical function of literature. It has been evident since the mid-1950s when Calvino published his collection of Italian fairy and folk tales that he took to heart the interesting theories of the formalist Vladimir Propp, who in *Morphology of the Folktale* (1968) argued that storytelling could be reduced to thirty-one narrative functions. Without enslaving himself to this particular set of functions, Calvino always puts his work into formal taxonomic frames. Even his letters and essays tend toward the taxonomic, and he likes to number his points even when they don't function as points. If literature invites formalist analysis, he is always there giving us a clearly enunciated method for the framework that he has worked out. Thus, for example, the seventy-eight cards of the tarot deck control the form of *The Castle of Crossed Destinies; Invisible Cities* is divided into eleven groups of five cities each; and *Mr Palomar* is structured on nine triads of steadily increasing metaphysical value. The temptation to admire Calvino's fiction for the precision of the framework and its arithmetical taxonomy is great, and is unfortunately also partly responsible for the spate of arid academic articles explaining tediously how Calvino's innovative forms work.

But the compelling factor in his success as a fictionist comes from the "unexpected meaning" rather than the narrow "combinational game which plays on the possibilities intrinsic to its own material, independently of the personality of the author." When Nabokov talks about the snapping of the "rainbow fingers" of the creative artist in the face of form, convention, or genre, he gives a way of perceiving Calvino's lightning leap from formal taxonomy to brilliant infusions of individual genius, from the linguistic to the highest semantic levels. Because his formal play is so extensive, however, his ultimate seriousness can be underestimated, and the non-formal levels of significance that are brought into play are often subtly mysterious rather than openly allegorical. Calvino nevertheless wants his readers to respond at any level convenient to them – from simple enjoyment of his innovative playfulness to a metaphysical musing on the vast areas of human experience that ground his enterprise. In the process, he often in notes or interviews gives rough guidelines that will set the reader thinking beyond the surface of the text, as he does for example when he says that the trilogy that makes up *Our Ancestors* – *The Cloven Viscount, The Baron in the Trees*, and *The Non-Existent Knight* – can be looked at simply as "a case of moral themes suggested by the central image, and developed in the secondary stories." Never, however, does he violate or try to direct the responses of the reader in a pointed way.

Calvino's sense of the relationship between his fictions and the deeper problems of his own historical period is the major area to which attention can be paid. Having begun his career with short stories and a novel in the Italian Neo-Realist mode of the 1940s and 1950s (practiced notably by Calvino's first sponsors, Cesare Pavese and Elio Vittorino), he turned with the *Our Ancestors* trilogy of the mid-1950s to a different, fabulist style. His first novel, *The Path to the Nest of Spiders* (1947), was in deep contrast to the new style heralded by *Our Ancestors*. *The Path* is entirely neo-realist, with a vagabond boy, Pin, as its central character. Pin joins the anti-Fascist partisans, but lacks ideological commitment, and has only the poverty of his background and character with which to carry the plot. Calvino's talents at the age of 23 announce themselves firmly, and the novel characterizes the anti-Fascist post-World-War-II Neo-Realist style, in spite of the poetic evocation of its title and dominant image pattern. But Calvino's early short stories, also in the realist mode, better demonstrate his subtlety, and gradually led him toward a broader, apolitical range of writerly possibilities.

Through the subsequent decades, Calvino worked for the Einaudi publishing firm, and also wrote for a living as a journalist, critic, and semi-political commentator; at the same time he steadily produced fiction of many sorts. It is clear from comments he interspersed in his essays that he found the tapping of his own experience as a Ligurian partisan in *The Path to the Nest of Spiders* to be improperly and unproductively personal. His early short stories, many of which have been translated only recently in the collections entitled in English *Marcovaldo, Difficult Loves*, and *Adam, One Afternoon*, allowed him to use a whimsical undercutting of the currents of neo-realism to lighten and aestheticize that narrow political style. For some of his admirers, however, the later fabulist element in Calvino obviates all of this earlier work, and many are surprised to find the quantity of hackwork and politically leftist essays he produced. In fact, it behooves those who find him a frivolous and even uncommitted writer to look at the entire corpus, and to see the degree to which all his thinking has an acutely experienced political underpinning.

The absolute turning point in Calvino's career occurred while he was working on the collection of fables and fairy-tales he collated and retold from multiple versions throughout Italy; this book was published in 1956 as *Fabie Italiane*, but was not available in English until 1980 when his international reputation was well established. Not only was he fascinated by the vitality of the fables, but by the fact that each regional version transcended the stereotype of its folk-tale original. In talking about the Sicilian Giuseppe Pitré's pioneering work on local fables, for example, Calvino made this typical sort of discovery, mentioned in the introduction to the English translation of his own collection:

> The secret of Pitré's work is that it gets us away from the abstract notion of "people" talking; instead, we come into contact with narrators having distinct personalities, who are identified by name, age, occupation. This makes it possible to uncover through the strata of timeless and faceless stories and through crude stereotyped expressions, whose inner rhythm, passion, and hope are expressed through the tone of the narrator.
>
> (trans. George Martin)

A highly formalist view would retain the stereotype and spell the death of literary impact; Calvino discovered that fantastic literature with its set formulae can be manipulated by the imaginative narrator to take a step forward in literature:

> Those who know how rare it is in popular (and nonpopular) poetry to fashion a dream without resorting to escapism, will appreciate these instances of a self-awareness that does not deny the invention of a destiny, or the force of reality which bursts forth into fantasy. Folklore could teach us no better lesson, poetic or moral.

Always keyed to the demands of reality, Calvino discovered early that the necessary limitations of mimesis can be conquered ironically without under-cutting the seriousness of semantic intention. He therefore follows those enchanted routes that guided the quasi-fantastic literature of the past – whether he evokes a folkloric or a high artistic tale (like that of Ariosto or Shakespeare) in his own fictions. As Calvino increasingly set his work referentially or intertextually against that past, he became one of the most allusive and literary of writers, employing his own erudition in order to tease the reader into a vital reconsideration of how the fantasy of literature interacts with experienced human reality. Calvino's later work is thus literary in the extreme; he is a writer whose referent is always bookish, even while his subject is an attempt "to discover what we can actually do today." When asked shortly before his death by *The New York Times* (Mitgang 1985) what fictional character he would like to be, he responded tellingly:

> Mercutio. Among his virtues, I admire above all his lightness in a world of brutality, his dreaming imagination – as the poet of Queen Mab – and at the same time his wisdom, as the voice of reason amid the fanatical hatreds of Capulets and Montagus. He sticks to the old code of chivalry at the price of his life, perhaps just for the sake of style, and yet he is a modern man, skeptical and ironic – a Don

Quixote who knows very well what dreams are and what reality is, and he lives both with open eyes.

Like Mercutio who saw every experience, comic or tragic, as an occasion of inventive wit, Calvino never allows a felt despair at human incompetence to obscure the tonal quality of his work; untrammelled by a dreary conscience that would make every fiction into a political statement, he nevertheless nudges the reader toward social ideas as he pirouettes through his fancies.

From the time of the three novellas that constitute *Our Ancestors*, Calvino committed himself to the short, distinctive piece as the natural unit of his writing, and never again reverted to conventional genre as he did in *The Path to the Nest of Spiders*. Unlike most conventional fictionists who divide their production between the short story and the novel, Calvino in the major part of his career wrote tales and fantasies that he bound together in ingenious overarching forms, so that no later work, including his longest fiction, *If on a winter's night a traveler*, can be called a sustained novel in any generic way. The innovative idea of becoming a major fictionist by writing only short pieces may owe something to Borges's *ficciones*, but Borges miniaturizes and abhors the unity that Calvino seeks as he pulls many tales and ideas into a large controlled taxonomic structure. In Calvino the need to create many pieces in order to make one construction is a formal echo of his ideological desire to use literature ironically to describe the multiform, unconquerable structure of the twentieth-century world.

The most difficult task of Calvino's chosen method is that of transformation into the new. His compulsion toward new written forms, as he says in his 1983 essay "The written and the unwritten word," illustrates some of the ways in which the bewildering world of our experience is echoed and affected, but not mimetically reproduced, by the ordering power of literature. In describing his situation, Calvino sounds like Beckett, and it is interesting to contrast the two writers' formal solutions in their own writing to their identical perception of the need for new form. Whereas Beckett is impelled to excise the fantasies of the literary past, Calvino devours that past and attaches all his work to a rereading – even a calculated misreading – of it. Both writers are indebted to Kafka, as is Borges, and both are dedicated to the destruction of conventional mimetic illusions and the idea of necessarily new styles. Calvino asks:

> But is mimesis the right way? My starting point was the irreconcilable contrast between the written and unwritten world; if their two languages merge, my argument goes to pieces. The true challenge for a writer is to speak about the tangled mess of our century using a language so transparent that it reaches a hallucinatory level, as Kafka did.

Achieving the transparency of language demanded by newly expressive styles occasions a stripping of prose for Beckett, but an allusive increasing of its function for Calvino. Whereas Beckett batters strenuously against the barriers of an unimaginable truth, Calvino charmingly, even gaily, shows the impossibility of the writer's ultimate achievement. It is therefore possible for Calvino's reader to imagine, because of the cheerful format of his books, that this impossibility is not as major as the internal anxieties of the fictions imply.

The nineteenth-century polemics of realism made fiction appear to prove the positivistic and ameliorative nature of literature. As Calvino sees it, however, the twentieth century – affected first by Viennese and recently by French philosophy – has upset this placid state of affairs, and made the uneasy relationship between the word and the world it represents totally problematic. He is always aware of the difficulties intrinsic to language's inability to serve as a straightforward semiotic code; its subject is always simultaneously both the world and its own narratological function. That is to say, language is not merely representational but also part of the user's perception, which is automatically limited by the dualistic nature of the world, divided as it is into objective reality and subjective narratives made by language. In "The written and the unwritten word," Calvino points out that late-twentieth-century people have generically become *homo legens*; trapped by language, we are readers not only of the printed page, but of television, of the landscape, of the world as we see it, which we relate to our private schemes for order through conventional word usage.

He uses himself as an illustration of the difficulty that arises from a serious consideration of the difference between the outside world and the world of the printed page. Every written text is a machine whose fuel is the language that produces stories; the reader's activity is

> more than an optic exercise, [it] is a process of involving mind and eyes, a process of abstraction, or rather an extraction of concreteness from abstract operations, like recognizing distinctive marks, breaking down everything we see into minimal elements, assembling them in meaningful segments, discovering all around us regularities, differences, recurrences, exceptions, substitutions, redundancies.

Calvino, wearing his ingenuous hat, describes himself as a reader whose expertise in dealing with the printed page is complete, and "even if what I understand is only a small part of the whole, I can cherish the illusion that I am keeping everything under control." The sense of the reader as supreme and of the written text as something that can be mastered is an illusion, but it is one cherished by the print-oriented person who feels comforted and secure within the black-and-white page. As Calvino points out, however, the reader's security ends with the white borders of the text. When the book is left and the perceiver confronts the outside world, the chaos of dualism is complete, and (s)he must acknowledge that "we raise our eyes from the page to look into the darkness."

At no point does Calvino ever indicate that he or any other writer can illuminate the darkness of the chaotic mystery of the world. The quest of the writer in a world split between the written and the unwritten is nevertheless unitive: secure as (s)he might feel with the written world, the writer's task is to wrestle with the problem of what language can actually do, and Calvino's career can be described as an anxious pro-literary battle against chaos.

At the end of the tavern section of *The Castle of Crossed Destinies* (1973), Calvino's narrator eloquently expresses the difficulties the writer must confront. Caught between the combinational nature of literature and his sense that as the writer he has a metaphysical urge to express himself, this narrator tries to tell his own story in competition with the other tale-tellers who fight for and spread their tarot cards across the table. In this comically frustrating allegory of writing and reading, all the other would-be narrators are mute and can tell their stories only by lining up a series of tarot cards that crudely approximate their history, while the narrator alone is allowed to read and interpret. Collected in two parts – one set in the castle, the other in the tavern – the book's many narratives are limited by the pictorial language of two seventy-eight-card tarot decks – one deck from the fifteenth century, the other from the eighteenth. These old decks of cards are nevertheless touched with mystical significance, as are the tales they evoke – from Shakespeare, Ariosto, Boccaccio, the history of the novel, fairy- and folk-tales, etc. – which represent the whole history of western story-telling.

Although all the characters have been robbed of both spoken and written language, their desire to express themselves – to write their own story as it were – remains undiminished. As they scramble after tarot cards, they are hampered by the narrowness of their only expressive tools. The cards are limited in number and representational possibility – as words are – and require a sympathetic and insightful reader or interpreter. The narrator is both reader and writer, and the eloquent interpretative acts are entirely his. As he interprets each line of tarot cards as set out by an enthusiastic would-be story-teller, he allows his language to blossom and his conjectures to bear fruit. The results are imaginative, creative commentaries on the limited line of cards each story-teller can deploy – and it is clear that Calvino is using this means to illustrate how the reader, an alter ego for the narrator, authors every text.

In all of Calvino's fictions, the narrators are uneasy, aware that their semiotic use of word-narration – their tale-telling – is likely to fail to find a creative reader, or to be obliterated. In one of the best-known stories in *Cosmicomics* – a book comprising cosmic quasi-scientific tales told by Qfwfq, a character who has existed in many scientific incarnations from the moment of the big bang to futuristic suburban New Jersey – this multiform creature–narrator complains about his unsuccessful attempt to leave a personal sign in the universe. During one of the early 200-million-year revolutions of the sun through the galaxy, the curious palindromic Qfwfq made the first, virgin semiotic gesture by a conscious creature in the cosmos:

– once, as I went past, I drew a sign at a point in space, just so I could find it again two hundred million years later, when we went by the next time around. What

105

sort of sign? It's hard to explain because if I say sign to you, you immediately think of a something that can be distinguished from a something else, but nothing could be distinguished from anything there; you immediately think of a sign made with some implement or with your hands, and then when you take the implement or your hands away, the sign remains, but in those days there were no implements.

Qfwfq fails to make a personal imprint on the universe, however, because his unique sign is obliterated by the competitive sign-making of another creature. Through this charming little tale, Calvino evokes the insoluble problems of personal creativity and the author's private appeal to the reader. Calvino's dominant themes always relate to this subject, which he finds both troublesome and joyful. If literature is equated to sign-making, Qfwfq's sign shares with all literature the problem that there is no private, personal text. Any writer who looks forward or backward through the history of texts must find that (s)he is not unique, but compulsively connected to both past and future. Qfwfq's narrative voice during this tale is so early in the history of the galaxy that he has no sign-making antecedent and can only be enraged at his upstart follower, but all subsequent writers both mimic the past and affect the future.

As a manifestation of this kind of inescapable intertextual thinking, Calvino wrote his major texts - *The Castle of Crossed Destinies, Cosmicomics, t-zero, Invisible Cities, If on a winter's night a traveler* - all of which are dependent on prior texts. Although deeply and primarily literary, Calvino does not believe that the book of the world is readable through only one lexicon. Hence his referential frame taps the history of both science and literature, and his ironic awareness is such that he pretends no definitive interpretation of either mode. Although every tarot tale in *The Castle of Crossed Destinies* evokes and recasts a major literary piece from the past, Calvino assumes that his narrator - like every reader - can be allowed to retell or recast the thing at will and according to the conditions of the present. In *Cosmicomics* and *t-zero* the scientific models of the cosmos are accurate only in their presentation of a subjective reading of a particular moment in the history of science. The condition of being either a reader or a writer thus implies complete involvement in the allusive history of the written word or sign, and one of the pleasures of dealing with Calvino's fictions is this constant evocation of the complex tale-telling past.

Calvino creates his new styles through a surprising series of structural and fantastic literary revivals. Thus he both renovates the chivalric tales of the past and projects science-fantasy characters; he also claims that he forces himself with every new book to perform something that he as a writer feels he cannot do and has never done before. The result is that, with each text, the reader has a sense of never having read this writer before, of never being able to anticipate the formal or semantic features of the fiction. In the letter to Gore Vidal quoted above, Calvino expresses his admiration that Vidal was able to find a grounding pattern in fictions that try never to be predictable or centered in a narrow ideology or aesthetic. His literary aim is to keep the reader off balance in order to maintain the renovation of literature to which he dedicated his life. Such renovation cannot occur within the framework of the conventional, nor can it occur, in Calvino's opinion, through the agency of a writer who writes according to constantly reiterated formulae. Similarly, a reader who reduces texts to mechanical devices – like Lotaria with her computerized criticism in *If on a winter's night a traveler* – deadens literature and encourages a new illiteracy.

Calvino always praises impassioned but notably unsystematic reading of the sort practiced by Lotaria's sister, Ludmilla, whom he describes as the ideal reader. Behind the allegorical idea of Ludmilla in *If on a winter's night a traveler* lies Calvino's conviction that a perpetual renovation of literature through the passionate interaction of reader and writer is the primary means whereby fiction achieves both its affect and its *raison d'être*. Gore Vidal correctly identifies Calvino's goal as one of unity between reader and writer, and significantly links it to a metaphysical preoccupation with the One, as well as with an unspeakable or unsayable world toward which Calvino's apparently playful fiction reaches:

> In a certain way, I think we always write about something we don't know, we write to give the unwritten world a chance to express itself through us. Yet the moment my attention wanders from the settled order of the written lines to the movable complexity no sentence is able to hold entirely, I come close to understanding that on the other side of the words there is something words could mean.
>
> ("The written and the unwritten word")

In *If on a winter's night*, however, Calvino appears on the surface to be at his least metaphysical and most acutely gamesome; for contemporary readers interested in confronting the idea of metafiction at its highest level of accomplishment, this novel is surely the best example available. It is also a showpiece for the virtues of the very idea of metafiction, in that its readability and charm are in no way vitiated by the dominant aesthetic and parodic experimentation.

As in the case of Muriel Spark's *Loitering With Intent, If on a winter's night* is a virtuoso piece that uses fiction as an almost purely technical vehicle, whose primary purpose is to present the author's literary credo. The fact that it entertains on a high level in the process is its major immediate virtue. That credo, in Calvino's case, states the reliance of the writer's productive creativity on the parallel instantaneous creativity of the reader. The book's ingenious opening consists of a chatty apostrophe to the "reader" by a persona who tentatively claims to be Calvino himself. The putative reader is addressed in friendly fashion as "you," and this "you" almost instantly turns into a major character within the fiction. He is not you (and certainly not me), but a man who has just bought Calvino's new book entitled *If on a winter's night a traveler*, and who is eager to be enthralled by the authorial act of story-telling.

Although rather boastful about his work, Calvino as author-persona is in a nervous state of neediness - a state in which he must urgently persuade the reader to participate, to agree with his claims as author, to share with him an obsession about literature. There is, of course, an automatic contradiction built into Calvino's approach, in that the authorial act is of necessity domineering, and the "you" is allowed no free selfhood at all. In keeping with Calvino's theory that reader and writer should be one, this "you" character is both separated from, and a sort of alter ego for, the author. He is also a carefully created fiction whose readerly responses satisfy Calvino as a writer. Yet "he-you" is secondary as a receptor of the texts to another crafted character - Ludmilla, also called the Other Reader - with whom he and other people in the fiction fall in love.

Any actual reader of this curious novel will, from the beginning, have questions and demurrals; most notably, women readers object to the rapid identification of "you" - putatively the universal reader - as a man, an automatic excluding device for at least 50 per cent of the book's receptors. Equally jarring is the friendly but dictatorial hauteur the Calvino narrator employs in describing the process of reading at the beginning of the book. Instead of accepting Calvino's comically defined reader, most readers are alienated from the addressed "you" and very aware indeed that they have not entered a dialogue with the writer. They perceive, rather, that they are participating in a fiction that imposes itself ingratiatingly on them as readers.

A shadowy parallel to this imposition of the writer on the reader is the nervousness with which the major writer character of the book - Silas Flannery - attempts to approach the impassioned Ludmilla, both when she is depicted in her role as a woman reading in the sun in a state of complete absorption, and when she visits him and he attempts to achieve unity with her by jumping on her sexually. Flannery's journal, which is imbedded in the plot-line (such as it is) of the novel, ruminates on the task of the writer and his desperate need for response from the reader. In true allegiance to contemporary literary theory, the text itself and *a fortiori* the writer behind it have no reality without the response of the absorbed reader, who in a sense creates the work more profoundly than the writer, and on whose reactive grace the author anxiously depends. Flannery expresses the situation thus in his journal as he describes himself scrutinizing the reading Ludmilla through a spyglass:

> At times I am gripped by an absurd desire: that the sentence I am about to write be the one the woman is reading at that moment. The idea mesmerizes me so much that I convince myself it is true; I write the sentence hastily, get up, go to the window, train my spy-glass to check the effect of my sentence in her gaze, in the curl of her lips. . . . At times it seems to me that the distance between my writing and her reading is unbridgeable, that whatever I write bears the stamp of artifice and incongruity . . . . At times I convince myself that the woman is reading my *true* book, the one I should have written long ago, but will never succeed in

writing, that this book is there, word for word, that I can see it at the end of my spyglass but cannot read what is written in it, cannot know what was written by that me who I have not succeeded and will never succeed in being. It's no use my sitting down again at the desk, straining to guess, to copy that true book of mine she is reading: whatever I may write will be false, a fake, compared to my true book, which no one except her will ever read.

The paradox built into *If on a winter's night a traveler* dramatizes the unclosable distance between the writer and the reader, and makes all possible writers subject to unappeasable frustration. Underlying this theoretical novel therefore is considerably less cheer than its energetic playfulness indicates. Calvino is always ready to speak of an "ideal literature," and indeed sees every potential fiction as one in which the text will tease the reader into a magically complete unity with the creative moment of the author in the act of composing that fiction. The sorry reality of literary reception as depicted in this novel, however, reveals the impossibility of this ideal, as Calvino takes his text through all typical levels of reception, treatment, and handling of literature that can occur at both literal and fantastic levels.

The complex fiction-within-fiction or *mise-en-abyme* structures of *If on a winter's night* operate on many levels, all of them beamed at the potentially ideal reader whom the author tries to imagine in vividly diverse ways. The three major structuring principles can be seen on a gradient from the purely formal to the increasingly ideological:

1. The creation and maintenance of a structure aligning this novel with the history of the novel form. Thus there is a beginning, middle, and end, in accordance with the Aristotelian formula. As in the conventional novel, there is a hero and heroine who meet in the beginning, struggle through complex difficulties in the middle part, and finally marry so that they may read happily ever after. The male character is called "you" or "the reader"; the female is named Ludmilla, but she appears in many other fictional identities, and is known too as "the other reader," the ideal reader, and occasionally also "you." The reader (male) and the other reader (female) are seen in a traditionally sexual relationship, even though it is obvious that the male reader is in competition with the writer for the affection and absorbed attention of the woman – the ideal reader as well as the sexual object.

2. The technical virtuosity through which Calvino carries out his major experimental impossibility: i.e. the writing of a novel that consists of nothing but beginnings or "incipits," an idea that had long fascinated him. In certain aspects of this experiment, Calvino is palpably influenced by André Gide's *The Counterfeiters*, although his carrying through of the experiment is both more pointed and more accomplished than Gide's High Modernist novel. In order to make his point completely clear, Calvino resorts to the Gidean device of incorporating a diary by a writer into the text – in this case, the diary of Silas Flannery, a blocked Anglo-Irish popular writer who broods on the impossible

compulsive necessities of literature. Flannery wishes to erase himself from his writing, in order "to transmit the writable that waits to be written, the tellable that nobody tells." The problem of writing is symbolized by a butterfly that flutters between the ideal reader's eyes and the page; Silas as writer wishes to catch the airy but completely real essence of that symbol within the text. As he thinks about the nature of literature, he decides that the most exciting moment in a book – before its possible doldrums for the reader or the misery of blank pages waiting to be filled for the writer – is its beginning, the moment of transition from the unwritten world to a new world. Here Flannery – like Calvino in the ten *incipits* that constitute the extended middle section of this novel – prefers the conventional opening,

> an attack from which you can expect everything and nothing. . . . The facility of the entrance into another world is an illusion: you start writing in a rush, anticipating the happiness of a future reading, and the void yawns on the white page.

What Flannery says he would like to accomplish is the impossible thing that Calvino actually achieves in this novel: "I would like to be able to write a book that is only an *incipit*, that maintains for its whole duration the potentiality of the beginning, the expectation still not focused on an object."

3. A well-articulated survey of the fate of literature in the real world, from its writer's failures, through the incompetence of publishers and production managers, to university professorial narrowness, critical misreadings, deadening mechanizations of the text by literary professionals, corruption of the langauge through translation, fantastic politicizing of the work, the mad desire of special interest groups to possess and pervert it, etc., etc. The fact that *If on a winter's night* remains buoyant and persistently comic in the face of this dreadful catalog of poor receptors is one of Calvino's great achievements. But the positive comic power – and the novel's quintessential seriousness as well – comes out of a deep cosmic commitment to a much more metaphysical element that Calvino obviously believes pertains to the situation of literature and ascertains its continuation. Silas Flannery's journal again carries the burden of Calvino's theme of human intelligence:

> There is thought in the universe – this is the constant from which we must set out every time . . . . Only when it will come natural to me to use the verb "write" in the impersonal form will I be able to hope that through me is expressed something less limited than the personality of an individual . . . . And for the verb "to read" . . . [i]f you think about it, reading is a necessarily individual act, far more than writing. If we assume that writing manages to go beyond the limitations of the author, it will continue to have a meaning only when it is read by a single person and passes through his mental circuits. Only the ability to be read by a given individual proves that what is written shares in the power of writing, a power based on something that goes beyond the individual. The universe will express itself as long as somebody will be able to say, "I read, therefore *it* writes."

Calvino's emphasis on the universal attaches itself particularly and pointedly to the writer, who struggles to abandon his ego in service to a higher task; but only in the reader can individual genius be seen, and this genius expresses itself above all in acquiescence to the act of reading. When reading stops, the fusion of the individual and the universal expressed in literature is destroyed. But it is everywhere clear that Calvino, who sees all humankind as readers of the world, the landscape, the object as well as the book, does not envisage the cessation of this activity or the end of the Word. It is useful at this point to compare Calvino with the less renowned Russell Hoban, in that the two writers both perceive the author as a servant of a cosmic thought system that the writer is obliged – indeed, driven – to transmit. Whereas Hoban is relatively indifferent to the reader, assuming that it is that reader's problem if (s)he fails to attune him/herself to the dancing allegories the disinterested author is instrumental in transmitting, Calvino stresses that only through the individual reader can the universal be realized – not by the author, not by the text, but by the reader's generous act of giving her/his intelligence and attention to the moment of textual reception.

This readerly acquiescence and power lays an intolerably heavy burden on both the natural and metaphysical resources of the reader. Any of us might question how to become adequate to the task, and despair at our limitations – as Silas Flannery despairs as a writer – in the face of such a demand. Calvino sets up an almost mystical definition of the nature of the reader – and when his interspersed comments on an ideal literature are combined with this, the reader of fiction might wish to resign and take another job. The history of fiction is in fact quite humble, however, and has always been characterized by the flimsy, the contingently realistic, and the frivolous. It is in no way part of Calvino's intention to deny this past history and suddenly to aggrandize fiction in a pretentiously unattainable way. Nor can his male character ("you") or his female reader (Ludmilla) be placed in the category of intellectual giants. Instead, Calvino makes it clear that the metaphysical magic of literature can be transmitted only when it is first grasped simply at the ancient levels of story-telling and of conventional narrative tricks involving the personality of the narrator, the charm of plot turns, the distinctive quality of character, and all the other tale-telling paraphernalia well known to the common reader. His presentation of the infinitely desirable Ludmilla – desired by the author as his ideal audience as well as by the male reader who wishes to emulate as well as possess her – is therefore less lofty and keenly designed than his ultimate ideology would indicate, and much of his strength as a writer depends on the simplicity of his patience and his desire to make his fiction attainable to any reader gracious enough to turn his/her attention to it.

Ludmilla is thus conceived of as a capriciously protean character, delighted by everything she reads – and at the same time dissatisfied with whatever genre is evoked. Having begun to read a new fiction, she quickly points out that she prefers its opposite, and like the restless pursuer of the ideal literature that she and all readers are, she always yearns insatiably for an unattainable form that would satisfy her metaphysical need to grasp the Ur-fiction that lies at the heart of the universe. She and the male reader ("you") meet in a bookstore because they have both bought Calvino's new book, only to find that the novel, some hypothetical version of *If on a winter's night a traveler*, has been misbound at the printers; as they try to find the continuation of this truncated story, they receive nine new *incipits*, each with a suggestive title making up part of a sentence that cannot be completed until the last of the ten beginnings has been presented.

In the course of the many beginnings that comprise the extended middle section of this "novel," Calvino manages in high ironic form to present self-consciously hilarious parodies of ten different types of fiction, including the spy novel, the eastern European political and domestic saga, the tough Franco-Italian crime novel, the South American Borgesian gaucho tale, Japanese floating-world pornography, the murder mystery, the mirrored *mise-en-abyme* trick, the world as the metaphysic of the page, etc. Each tale has to be capable of whetting the reader's interest, and each has to be broken into by an external publishing event, or an event peculiar to the job of finding, getting, and having copies of books or manuscripts. The breaking off of each *incipit* therefore fulfills Calvino's desire to write a book consisting entirely of beginnings. It is also part of his self-imposed task of driving the novel onward through its other two dominant structural intentions – to keep the plot flowing towards a conventional comedic closure through the marriage of the hero and heroine, and to compose it as a large, unitive, and even metaphysical demonstration.

Ludmilla's protean tastes do not alter a few crucial facts: first, that as ideal reader she makes everyone nervous – the author (indeed all the authors in the book), the primary male reader, and her mechanically dogged critic-sister Lotaria; second, that as a reader she is insatiably curious about all forms and possibilities in literature. Although she has no distinctive qualities of taste or accomplishment – as shown through her own haphazard book collection, chosen not for theme or type but only because of their newness and availability – her strength as an allegorical ideal lies precisely where Calvino wishes his readers to acquiesce. She represents an openness to all literature without prejudice or pretension, and she is never satisfied, never appeased, never finished. Like the members of the OuLiPo group of writers – a group of scientists, scholars, and writers who play with the possibilities of fiction, to which Calvino belonged, – Ludmilla longs insatiably for a *potential* literature, one that will never be attained but toward which metaphysical seekers, whose tools are the humble narratives of the universe, must constantly strive.

When all the *incipits* of *If on a winter's night a traveler* are finished, the reader ("you," masculine) finds himself in the library, that repository of books that plays a major symbolic role in contemporary fiction. But it too fails to deliver the full texts of the ten novels into the hands of the reader; although all the titles are in the card catalog, none is available, for the maddening circulational reasons that all library users experience daily. While he waits, "you" strikes up a conversation with seven unlike types of readers in the library, each stating his individual preference in ways that accumulate to make a statement about the ultimate unity and inexhaustible resonance of the reading experience. Each of the following seven sentences comes from a different reader in the library, and their totality sums up Calvino's sense of the reader's compulsions:

> "The stimulus of reading is indispensable to me ... even if, of every book, I manage to read no more than a few pages ... [which] enclose for me whole universes, which I can never exhaust."
>
> "Reading is a discontinuous and fragmentary operation ... this is why my reading has no end; I read and reread, each time seeking the confirmation of a new discovery among the folds of the sentences."
>
> "I, too, feel the need to reread the books I have already read ... but at every rereading I seem to be reading a new book, for the first time."
>
> "Every new book I read comes to be a part of that overall and unitary book that is the sum of my readings."
>
> "In my case, too, all the books I read are leading to a single book ... but it is a book remote in time, which barely surfaces from my memories ... a story that for me comes before all other stories and of which all the stories I read seem to carry an echo, immediately lost."
>
> "The moment that counts most for me is the one that precedes reading."
>
> "For me ... it is the end that counts ... but the true end, final, concealed in the darkness, the goal to which the book wants to carry you."

"You" the reader complains how everything has gone wrong for him in his conventional limiting desire to read steadily through a fiction from beginning to end, arriving at one interpretation, and controlling the boundaries of the text. The other library readers, freer in their tastes and compulsions, associate the Ur-text with the *Arabian Nights* and point out to "you" that the phrasal titles of his ten *incipits* form a sentence which is in itself a new *incipit* or beginning:

> "If on a winter's night a traveler, outside the town of Malbork, leaning from the steep slope without fear of wind or vertigo, looks down in the gathering shadows in a network of lines that enlace, in a network of lines that intersect, on the carpet of leaves illuminated by the moon around an empty grave – what story down there awaits its end? – he asks, anxious to hear the story."

This threading together of the ten titles of the tales, or reiteration of the fictions, once again begins the endless task of trying to write anew in the world of letters that outside world that longs insatiably for expression. The seventh library reader reminds the other readers that the "ultimate meaning to which all stories refer has two faces: the continuity of life, the inevitability of death." The Aristotelian idea of structure involving a beginning and an end must ultimately be fitted to this cosmic theme, as the seventh reader explains: "having passed all the tests, the hero and the heroine married, or else they died." Choosing

113

continuity and life, the character "you" determines to marry Ludmilla, with the result that Calvino's book satisfies standard and ancient story-telling structures, even as it opts for the continuity of fiction that will keep all contemporary Sheherazades perpetually in the business of writing in new and ever newer forms – as Calvino did – for the delight of the reader, until the darkness falls.

The primary demonstrations of *If on a winter's night a traveler* combine the delights of the traditional novel in its manifold generic representations with the highly experimental modes that govern the often bewildering structure of this self-consciously Postmodern novel. Calvino's double allegiance to the new (i.e. to the discoverable forms that suit contemporary experience) and to the tale-telling conventions of the past characterizes his work, and makes him a much more vital and serious writer than a narrow dedication to aesthetic metafictionalism would manage to do. Unlike Beckett who fights the forms of the past, Calvino plays with them, lovingly refitting them to a new cosmic dispensation in which ideas of unity, continuity, and the mysteriously metaphysical counter the darkness that contemporary people see all about them.

In his last book, *Mr Palomar*, Calvino went even further, in that he limited his interest in current narratological theory and returned to an early poetic compulsion in fiction – that of observation of the natural and social worlds, and a steady building of this observation toward metaphysical interpretation. Always interested in what the human being can do with words and how they can serve observation and experience, he carefully limits himself in *Mr Palomar* to the poetic capacities that occur between observation and thought, with the result that this book is less obviously ambitious than the fictions that immediately precede it in Calvino's *oeuvre*. This quirky quasi-novel reminds us of the quieter and humbler tasks of fiction – a worthy reminder by an unpretentious writer that as a genre experimental fiction can all too easily, in many senses, lose its way if it jettisons its adherence to the dramatic but simple excitements of the literary past and the experienced present. In even the most fantastic of his works, Calvino would bind reader and writer to these significant co-ordinates.

PART III

Experiment and the problems of meaning

6

A novel, which is a machine for generating interpretations: Umberto Eco and *The Name of the Rose*

When a theorist writes a novel, problematic issues are raised in the never stable relationship between text and reader, as the theories of the author are in a sense unavoidably imposed on the reader. We may actively rebel against the overlordship of the author at any time as, for example, so many receptors have to the strident narrative voices of John Fowles or Saul Bellow. But, in our acquiescence to the author's narrativity – that is, in the fact that we read the novel ardently enough to carry on with it – we succumb to being dominated at least temporarily by the impact of the theory in question. By 1980, at the age of 47, Umberto Eco had established an international scholarly reputation for his work in semiotics – the theory of signs and signifiers – with such books as *Opera Aperta* and *The Role of the Reader*. In that year the Italian edition of Eco's now famous novel, *The Name of the Rose* (*Il Nome della Rosa*) appeared under the imprint of Bompiani, the publishers of his scholarly work. The novel was quickly translated into many languages to wide and almost universal acclaim, with the English edition coming along rather belatedly in 1983, elegantly translated by the American expatriot, William Weaver. Its reception in the English-speaking world is a publishing phenomenon. Popular in Britain, the novel exploded on the American market, with something like 1,700,000 copies sold in the first two years of its life.

Given the problem of private coterie self-indulgence in much self-consciously Postmodernist contemporary fiction and the resulting dwindling of readership, the success story of this very good and intellectually ambitious novel presents an almost unanalyzable situation. It is not simply that the popularity and extravagant sales of *The Name of the Rose* throughout the western world – and the figures are astounding – indicate to many that the novel at hand should not be very good, or must at least be suspect for all serious novel readers. But ironically *The Name of the Rose* is a particularly demanding novel that not only asks its reader for impassioned attention to the intellectual milieu of the fourteenth century; it also taps Eco's Peircean theories of infinite semiosis and illustrates his idea of the "model reader" in a polysemous act of intertextuality. Such a dose of specialized vocabulary is dismaying when applied to a bestseller, but fortunately for the majority of non-academic readers, such technical terms never emerge from the smooth narrative drive of the text. For those who persist through the daunting first hundred pages (Eco says in *Postscript to* (or *Reflections on*) *The Name of the Rose* that "those first hundred pages are like penance or an initiation, and if someone does not like them, so much the worse for him. He can stay at the foot of the hill"), the book is superb entertainment and splendidly evocative at many levels. Even the inevitable negative backlash that follows such an unpredictable success is inadequate as a counter-force to the power of a work that persists in satisfying and exciting a wide range of readers.

One way of estimating the book's success is to stress its *jouissance*, to misuse Roland Barthes's term somewhat – its ideological celebration of human laughter against an Antichrist who would destroy it, as well as its demonstration of the joyous energy of its author. At various points in his works and interviews, Eco has said that what cannot be theorized about must be narrated, and certainly this text erupts with a clean energy that achieves much more for more sorts of thinkers than his theoretical work has been able to manage. Unfortunately this statement would be wounding to Eco, who has been irritated by the dominance granted this novel which he sees as a game, a minor exercise composed in the interstices of his serious – and to him much more important – semiotic–philosophical work. Unlike a writer like Iris Murdoch, who dislikes having her philosophical thought brought up in the context of her novels, Eco appears to assume that his reputation will rest on the semiotic work, and that the novel should be put into a minor context within that realm.

Nevertheless, Eco has been a constant popularizer, and if fiction is seen as an act of popularizing, it can be categorically stated that he has reached a wider audience and in many ways – when one includes the positive response of medievalists and historians – a more responsive one through *The Name of the Rose* than his structuralist semiotics could do. As in the case of Italo Calvino, the peculiar circumstances of Italian culture and its media dispensation have had much to do in molding a writer like Eco. Like the other handful of Italian cultural heroes, Eco has a longstanding journalistic career aside from his professorship at the University of Bologna and frequent lecture trips to Germany, France, and particularly America. As writer of a popular column in the magazine *L'Espresso*, he has had another means of reaching a larger audience than his technical books and essays; as a journalist his theme has been consistent with the thought promulgated in the more inaccessible texts. Basically he wishes for an open cosmos of understanding in which all of culture will be seen not as something frozen, closed, disciplined into a rigid myth, but reverberative, used as an infinite, polysemous, interlocking system of signs to lead the mind fluidly forward. The conventional enshrining and codification of cultural fact or artifact for him are systems generated by simple allegory and leading to tyranny, frozen logic, and the sort of rigid theocentric dogma that *The Name of the Rose* is dedicated to breaking.

The strength of Eco's ideological commitment can be frankly and directly expressed in journalism and especially in theoretical criticism. His theory of the tasks of narrative and of the occlusion of the author within the realms of fiction raises other problems, however, that challenge his consistency in talking about readers' reception of *The Name of the Rose*. As a literary critic he has always argued that no text can move into being by itself: the interpretative role of the reader is central, and indeed the polysemy of a work can only be achieved by the reader, whose productive reading of the text is what really counts. In semiotic theory in general, no text is in itself a condition for its own signification. It depends on the interaction of reader and text, or even text and other texts for its emergence. This reciprocal process produces the idea of intertextuality, which, through Eco's constant evocative, unfootnoted quotations from "anterior" texts, is the dominant stylistic mode of *The Name of the Rose*. This novel gives effective reinforcement to the idea of texts infinitely talking to and illuminating each other. Dominantly, however, there is the reader, whose mind is in constant activity as (s)he reads the authorially implanted signs through the lexicon of his/her own knowledge and necessity.

For Eco, the reader must be "free." Although the author implants the signs and imagines the possibilities that the "model reader" might pursue, the authorial task is essentially finished when the book is written. Eco, who in the wake of his novel's mammoth popularity was excessively present to his readers through media interference, has repeatedly said that the author must not interpret. Indeed his efforts not to do so have been both stalwart and ironically disingenuous. When asked for the ultimate code that would transform the philosophical metaphysic of the novel into a statement, Eco claims that he doesn't know what it is, or indeed what the novel is about, and he constantly throws the task of interpreting to the reader. Unfortunately, Eco quickly and it seems unconsciously broke his consistency with the rapid publication of a little explanatory book entitled *Postscript to* (in Britain, *Reflections on*) *The Name of the Rose* (it appeared in English, translated by William Weaver, in 1984, one year after the novel). The resulting contamination of the reader's freedom despite Eco's claims to the contrary cannot be underestimated, for almost every fact he gives us directs the reader in a predetermined way.

To begin with, in *Postscript to The Name of the Rose*, Eco describes and, in keeping with his critical bias, limits all novels as "machine[s] for generating interpretations." Surely only a literary critic could ever conceive of a novel in such a way. Even more surely, only a writer also paid an annual university salary would allow his view of the reader's response to art - what Nabokov tellingly described as "aesthetic bliss" - to be darkened by the professional aspects of interpretation that characterize so much of what Eco himself has subsequently said or written about his justly famous, tantalizingly entitled first novel. All his demurrals about authorial interference tend to disappear when the novel becomes a machine and its product nothing but interpretation. But Eco cares passionately about interpretation, about the sort of sign-reading advocated by the American philosopher C. S. Peirce that led to the field of semiotics, Eco's chosen academic specialty and passion, into which he has here poured his passion for the Middle Ages.

Perhaps the production of an adjunct text like *Postscript* seemed necessary for reasons having to do with Eco's urgent sense of the need for more elaborate interpretations from his readers. He himself describes it as a permissible text in which some of the primary ideas and genesis of the novel could be made visible without authorial interference. Indeed, the surprisingly low analytical level of most of the Anglophone reviews, even by major reviewers like Richard Ellmann, indicated that in fact many vague commentaries occurred, but few complex, interesting, or original interpretations were generated. Continental reviewers on the other hand were much more eager to interpret and particularly to impose contemporary political meanings on *The Name of the Rose*. Eco claims that *Postscript* had its origin during a period when he was doing a lecture tour in Germany after the novel's first success there; he was boringly asked the same questions over and over again until he and his translator began referring to the reiterated questions as # 1, # 5, etc. According to his account, *Postscript* was a published attempt to stave off the same questions.

Under any circumstances, anyone teaching the novel (and it seems made for the academy, so eagerly does it welcome a wide range of pedantic quirks in various academic minds) quickly discovers that for readers the reaction of marvel is much greater than that of interpretation. Partly because of problems with decoding, serious contemporary fiction has spoken to an increasingly narrow audience, with worrisome consequences such as the proliferation of coteries and a sad diminution of receptivity on the part of the well-educated average reader. Here, however, was a complex book that great numbers of people wanted to read for pleasure, and although one can perhaps argue that *The Name of the Rose* is the most unread bestseller in history, it aroused a variety of responses throughout Europe and America that unexpectedly cut across many boundaries of interest.

This is far from the first time an academic has turned his theories into fiction, but not since Sartre has the resulting ideological narrative so deeply seized the imagination of the reading public. It generated intellectual excitement in almost all quarters, and for once united the idea of a "university" or élitist novel with the ideal of a fiction for all readers. European reviewers saw it as political and topical; murder mystery fans were delighted; lovers of the historical novel were given their heart's desire; medievalists were generous in their admiration; learned readers celebrated its intertextuality – its apparently endless evocation, through direct quotation, of text after text from the past, from the Bible to Augustine to Wittgenstein, from Aristotle to St Hildegard of Bingen to

Borges. The busiest commentators of all were the academics, particularly in Europe but in America as well, and an Eco industry was begun, tracing down every allusion to Eco's extensive critical publications and to his semiotic theories, and identifying all of the often obscure literary, theological, and philosophical texts incorporated as *disiecta membra* into the deceptively "unified" surface of *The Name of the Rose*.

Indeed, interpretations show themselves to be uncommonly tightly controlled in advance by Eco's framework; paradoxically, this novel has turned out decidedly *not* to be in any straightforward way a free "machine for generating interpretations" as its author claimed in his *Postscript to the Name of the Rose*. Interesting interpretations on the whole have only recently begun to be generated, and perhaps a "free" interpretation is impossible. The first responses were off-center and useful only in small local terms – in the way, for example, that individual phrases, pages, and sections of the novel could be reacted to by the individual reader, or in the way that a critic and disciple like Teresa de Lauretis, for example, could slavishly connect to a theoretical context planned and planted by Eco. The problem lies partly in Eco's lexicon of critical theory, in the fact that the term "interpretation" means different things for the ordinary reader or critic than it does for the theoretical semiotician. Eco does not want his novel ruined by excessive concentration on theoretical concerns, but he is a fictionist whose double expertise, in a way imposed upon the reader, divides and obscures his intention, whatever it may be.

Most theorists believe that Eco's intention is the proving and illustration of his semiotic theories, and probably, teacher that he is, Eco began with this in mind. But he also obviously had a thoroughly good time in writing the novel, and it is to this and to its narrativity that most readers respond. John Freccero, in "The fig tree and the laurel," points out that St Augustine, as Eco well knows, talked about *uti* versus *frui* in respect to aesthetics, *uti* = use (the proper ethical or typological response) versus *frui* = enjoyment (an almost impious self-indulgence), and Eco merges the two in new and contemporary terms. What emerges from the well-earned success of this novel is a double argument or bifurcated response, in which theoreticians will choose the route of use and in doing so will be tightly controlled by Umberto Eco, the theorist. Readers of fiction, also but more subtly manipulated by the authorial voice, will go off in the other direction and receive the book with the pleasure the text generously delivers. But what does one do with this duplicity? Where and when ought the reader to feel that his/her job is to try to follow the hidden argument decodable primarily by the scholar or theorist, and when by contrast do more purely literary pleasures present us with a better or more authentic means of talking or writing about the text?

This nervous ambiguity about response was, but did not dramatically seem to be, a great problem when we had only *The Name of the Rose* itself – before, that is, Eco chose to interfere openly *in propria persona*. Like most successful authors unappeased by the enormous international critical and financial success of their novels, Umberto Eco also shows a negative side. He has seized every chance to rush through academic and popular high-priced international lecture circuits, and shows poor judgment in using the popularity of his novel to push into translation and print such early and meretricious books as his dated essay on James Joyce's aesthetics (*Aesthetics of Chaosmos*, originally published in Italian in 1966), as well as his 1952 dissertation on St Thomas Aquinas (recently issued by Harvard University Press) and glossy collections of his journalistic semiotic essays. At the same time he also continues to produce good scholarly work, including a rapid flow of books on semiotics – most recently, *Semiotics and the Philosophy of Language*. It remains clear at most levels that Eco sees his fiction as a tool for his theory, and that his desire is to be mammothly known in both realms simultaneously – as useful semiotician and theorist, and as famous novelist. This may be megalomania, but on the whole the case is more interesting than that, inasmuch as Eco, unlike most successful novelists, seems to consider the general public educable within his theoretical standards, and understands those standards as socially, politically, and culturally ameliorative.

It is troubling, however, to turn attentively to the tiny, expensively produced volume mentioned above, *Postscript to The Name of the Rose* (1984), an essay of considerable charm that denies one of its own central tenets – namely that the author should leave his original text alone. The form of publication itself presents a curious aspect, in that *Postscript* is published separately – and therefore not seen as integral – only in languages other than Italian. In Italy, Bompiani now binds it in one book with the novel as an adjunct to all editions, rather like Mann's afterword, *Die Entstehung* is now bound in most German editions of *Doktor Faustus*.

As it turns out, *Postscript* may be moderately useful to the relatively few non-Italian general readers who read it, but the condition of being pre-empted by the author, *hors de texte* so to speak, is interestingly reflective of a central problem in the reader's fate *vis-à-vis* contemporary fiction in general, where the author can be, and often is, competitively and noisily present. It is also a telling symptom of the nervous indeterminacy of the place of the novel in a reader's universe, or to reverse this into a more subtle issue, the reader's place in the writer's or novel's world. In spite of his theoretical statements to the contrary, Eco cannot limit his lexicon, let his reader go, or completely allow the text its own route.

Postscript raises problems on many levels, from the simplest to the most complex, and certainly is a unique moment in interpretative as well as in recent publishing history, a moment that goes beyond the standard interviews that most fictionists are willing to give to literary critics, journalists, and TV talk-show anchormen. Much more pointed than Mann's description of *Doktor Faustus* or Nabokov's short, ironic, question-begging essay ("On a book entitled *Lolita*") published regularly in all editions of *Lolita* since 1958, Eco's supposedly serendipitous *libellus* has some of the same intentions Mann's and Nabokov's essays had – such as clarifying the publishing history, accounting for backgrounds, providing information about genesis and process, and, most significantly, directing the reader whose perusal of the original text is not considered trustworthy. At the same time it is evident that the project of writing an afterword was for Eco an ineluctable part of either the ambiguous original intention or the popular post-publication result of *The Name of the Rose*. And whereas neither Mann nor Nabokov had demurrals about straightening out the reader, Eco has noisily proclaimed many, and continues to claim himself innocent of interference.

It seems to me programmatic that the novel needed something like the *Postscript*, in that the fiction itself imposes the following negative situations on the majority of the book's receptors: (1) this complex and scholarly book was not aimed at the general reader who only doubtfully knows why (s)he has been so absorbed by it; (2) the bookish non-scholar, or the reader not interested in current theoretical literary criticism such as Eco's own studies in semiotics, will automatically be bewildered and perhaps even feel resentment at the possibly excessive literary–textual aspects inherent in the putative murder-mystery's dénouement; (3) the extensive use of incompletely translated Latin throughout feels like a deliberate attempt to exclude all but certain kinds of readers – those whose knowledge of Latin is in good order, literary medievalists, and historians of the philosophical problem of the long Nominalist–Realist debate in the Middle Ages and how it might, through Peircean inversions, relate to current ideas of epistemology.

Since the scholarly-specialist group constitutes a fit audience though few, it apparently became obvious to Eco that more explanation could or should justifiably be forthcoming. The fact that he originally chose not to translate the last lines of the novel – the most telling Latin quotation in the book – makes it clear that from the beginning he intended secretiveness or refined decoding. The words "*Stat rosa pristina nomine, nomina nuda tenemus*" conclude the novel, and the intrinsic signs contained in these words are, in the book's original unpostscripted form, clear only to a mandarin few.

With scholarly problems lurking behind, but not in any way affecting, the popularity of *The Name of the Rose*, the question of authorial responsibility as opposed to the task of the reader/critic must be raised. Eco is fond of referring to Joyce's puzzles in *Finnegans Wake*, and reiterating that the ideal reader of Joyce – and he hopes of this novel too – is afflicted with an "ideal insomnia." But surely that insomnia is productive of decoding, of a thoroughly intelligent, participatory reading of Joyce's linguistic signs, of the reader's being, in short, the best of all possible semioticians. Although altogether too many critics have published "keys" to Joyce's work, the process of enjoyment so strongly celebrated in Eco's commentary on his own novel and in his references to Joyce comes not from such crutches, but from the ideal reader's doing his/her job well. To put it another way, Joyce certainly helped out his critics in the 1930s, but did we ever want or need Joyce as author to publish an oblique commentary, even on a book as endlessly allusive as *Finnegans Wake*? Inevitably we must also ask if we want Eco to have written his *Postscript*, and into what category he has put his readers as the result of it.

In *Postscript*, Eco says (I wish him health and long life), "The author should die once he has finished writing. So as not to trouble the path of the text." In our deconstructionist time, it is easy to see this simply as a straightforward death-of-the-author statement. The useful conversation produced by a novel is not a dialogue between author and reader, but between text and reader (the author being at least metaphorically dead), and the restless urgency many contemporary writers feel to explain their work to their public is, at least theoretically, deplored by Eco. But he also subtly modifies his position, calling on Edgar Allen Poe in his own defense: "The author must not interpret. But he may tell why and how he wrote the book." The area of the licit should be fairly clear through this constraint, but in effect the amount and kind of information Eco gives both contaminate interpretation and impose significant limits on it. Just as one can be irritated when Thomas Pynchon deliberately and ironically misreads his recently issued early short stories in his 1984 preface to *Slow Learner*, so the reader of *Postscript* cannot avoid observing the tyranny imposed by Eco in his graceful giving and withholding of crucial information in this quasi-explanatory, only putatively non-interpretative essay. An easy example of this tricky area of friendly tyranny lies in the fact that the Latin of the final quotation of *The Name of the Rose* is identified by Eco as coming from Bernard of Morlay and is then set in a vaguely broad rather than precise context. "*Stat rosa pristina nomine, nomina nuda tenemus*" literally means "the former rose remains through its name; we keep only pure names." But Eco tells us in *Postscript* that

> the verse is from *De contemptu mundi* by Bernard of Morlay, a twelfth-century Benedictine, whose poem is a variation on the *ubi sunt* theme (most familiar in Villon's later *Mais où sont les neiges d'autun*). But to the usual topos . . . Bernard adds that all these departed things leave (only, or at least) pure names behind them. I remember that Abelard used the example of the sentence *Nulla rosa est* to demonstrate how language can speak of both the nonexistent and the destroyed. And having said this, I leave the reader to arrive at his own conclusions.

No educated medievalist can think about the name of the rose without knowing that the evocation is Nominalist; Eco mentions Abelard, but in fact queers the direction of enquiry toward the more casual aspects of a *carpe diem* theme, which can indeed lead to a simple and comfortable reading for those who do not wish to enquire too far into the possible stretch and play of the text. But the mention of Abelard must indicate to the next level of reader that Abelard too should be checked out within an unweaving of the referential frame, and of course the educated medievalist will know that all roses in the Middle Ages were shadowed by Abelard's use of that example in laying the Nominalist groundwork. Just as the novel's hero, William of Baskerville, contrasts the religious and political comprehension available to the "simple" of his time to that practiced by the learned, Eco here firmly guides the two poles of his audience.

I would argue strongly that Eco does not leave the reader "to arrive at his own conclusions," but that in deciding how much information to give in the *Postscript* he engineers a simple reading for the simple and complex but precise work for the *cognoscenti*. He follows his controlled dispensing of limited information with the following statement:

> A narrator should not supply interpretations of his work; otherwise he would not have written a novel, which is a machine for generating interpretations. But one of the chief obstacles to his maintaining this virtuous principle is the fact that a novel must have a title.

If a novel is indeed a "machine for generating interpretations," then an authorially controlled range of possibilities should in honesty not be externally presented beyond the highly connotative title, simply because such an apparatus closes the possibilities of still further readings, and holds the reader in the author's interpretative grasp.

From his first book on semiotics and criticism, *Opera Aperta* (1962), Eco has been obsessed with the contrast between "open" and "closed" texts, and all his subsequent theoretical works have tried to explain the difference between the two. If a novel is "a machine for generating interpretations," some definition of an open text, requiring polysemous or infinite interpretation, is in order. In lectures, Eco delights in tracing the closed idea of allegory and contrasting it with the open system of symbol, proving the progression by working from Augustine to the pseudo-Dionysus and Giordano Bruno. His emphasis is theological, separating *allegoria in verbis* (rhetorical/grammatical criticism) from *allegoria in factis*, which deals with the increasing need in the Middle Ages and Renaissance to interpret Christ polysemously.

What precisely Eco means by terms like an open text or infinite semiosis remains rather obscure, however, and finally the exact nature of the contrast between open and closed texts is sharply modified by the fact that Eco tends to think like a hybrid cross between Thomas Aquinas and C. S. Peirce. In other words, his idea of infinite semiosis or interpretation cannot at all be generalized by the reader into an interpretational Abbaye de Thélème, where, to quote Eco's beloved Rabelais, *Faicts ce que Voudras* (interpretational chaos) is the order of the day. Eco argues that in any given text the symbol (the vehicle whereby we formulate an interpretation) is anchored to the terms of that text, and therefore infinite semiosis is possible only insofar as the text controls the terms of the interpretation the reader might make. To put it directly and rather negatively, there can be infinity only within prior constraints: any number of readings is possible except those that deny the text's basic mandate.

Let me modify this negative statement by putting it more exactly into the context of Eco's idea of infinite "interpretation": arguing from a predominantly historicist bias in his theoretical works, Eco claims that interpretation has always depended on the "encyclopedia" of knowledge within which the text was composed or is received. This encyclopedia of knowledge can be assumed to a degree within the text's milieu and immediate historical period, but in a changeable world, something automatically happens every day that over a period of time challenges our models and makes our interpretations shifting and ultimately unstable. The encyclopedia of assumed knowledge for reading a text is generally taken for granted by the author, but (s)he cannot assume its universality or persistence. Nevertheless, in positing the idea of a "model reader," the author can assume at least temporarily that (s)he and the reader exist within the same encyclopedic frame, and indeed that the author is godlike in positing a world/cosmos and educating the reader in its terminology. Thus Eco creates a model reader who will respond positively to the Middle Ages and the Nominalist–scientistic–progressive world he posits. Readings that belong in other free-floating categories are basically excluded.

In conjunction with this sort of thinking about the creation of the "model reader," Eco closes other doors without apparently noticing them. In all of his work including *Postscript*, and especially in *The Role of the Reader*, he presents the author's task in creating the *model reader* as a project that at first glance looks quite benign. The model reader is apparently one whose interpretative fluidity is such that the author can write for him/her, foreseeing and building into the text every possible reaction or reading conceivable. Under such subtly and fluidly predetermined circumstances, the Eco-esque reader is at the opposite extreme to the now fashionable Nietzschean idea that interpretation is not found within the autonomy of the text, but made by the creative reader. Eco cantankerously or paradoxically argues that the reader is free to make his/her own interpretation, but not creatively: (s)he is bound by the manipulation of the providential author. His is most decidedly not the line of the current catch-phrase of "creative reading," where the reader challenges the author as an equal maker of the text, although Eco does allow the reader small private originalities (what, for example, is the nature of William of Baskerville's pity, if he has any?). Observe the author as maker/creator of the model reader in *Postscript*:

> What model reader did I want as I was writing? An accomplice, to be sure, one who would play my game. I wanted to become completely medieval and live in the Middle Ages as if that were my own period (and vice versa). But at the same time, with all my might, I wanted to create a type of reader who, once the initiation was past, would become my prey – or, rather, the prey of the text – and would think he wanted nothing but what the text was offering him. A text is meant to be an

experience of transformation for its reader. You believe you want sex and a criminal plot where the guilty party is discovered at the end, and all with plenty of action, but at the same time you would be ashamed to accept old-fashioned rubbish made up of the living dead, nightmare abbeys, and black penitents. All right, then, I will give you Latin, practically no women, lots of theology, gallons of blood in Grand Guignol style, to make you say, "But all this is false; I refuse to accept it!" And at this point you will have to be mine, and feel the thrill of God's infinite omnipotence, which makes the world's order vain. And then, if you are good, you will realize how I lured you into this trap, because I was really telling you about it at every step, I was carefully warning you that I was dragging you to your damnation.

"God's infinite omnipotence," "I was dragging you to your damnation": surely this is the rhetoric of a medieval, theologized version of the very attractive nineteenth-century idea of the passive reader whose intelligence and sensibility are controlled by the writer–god into whose hands we submit ourselves with no deconstructionist intention. All is foreseen, all providential in a world where infinity and freedom in their usual definitions are disallowed. Only the plurality of worlds (historical periods, special interests, ideological preconceptions, etc.), productive of a plurality of encyclopedias, can open the text beyond the author's evocations as he designs the model reader.

*

The Name of the Rose, then, is a controlled book in spite of Eco's ambiguous protestations, didactic or perhaps even propagandistic in its design. The medieval idea of *sententia* or meaning contained in and even obscured by the husk of entertainment for the simple is paramount. Its agent is William of Baskerville, the Franciscan monk hero of *The Name of the Rose*, who talks and talks, consistently teaching the young Benedictine novice Adso who, in old age, becomes our narrator. Through a brilliant sequence of narrative ordering, these progressive verbal lessons become the novel's ideological vehicle, and as such subvert the text's ostensible task of solving the mystery of the increasing number of dead monks. William's conversations and explanations give us both historical and philosophical information, and once the original or primary pleasure of the novel, finding out whodunnit, has been served, it is with increasing care that the reader returns to the magisterial words of this unambiguous and utterly trustworthy secondary narrator. The book's real narrator – Adso of Melk in old age remembering and modifying the Adso he was in youth – is of course transparently untrustworthy, like Nellie Dean in *Wuthering Heights* or Serenus Zeitblom in Thomas Mann's *Doktor Faustus* (a source Eco mentions). But like other narrators in the venerable reportorial tradition, Adso renders the words of his subject faithfully, even while he undercuts him judgmentally.

An ambiguous thread in the labyrinth of William's pedagogy is the contrast between the simple and the learned. The beliefs of the simple spring from their unprescient desires to link the social miseries of their lives to the shifting theological fashions rising with unequal authority from the philosophical disputes of the learned. The contrast William's cogitations set up between the simple and the learned can ironically be applied to the two audiences Eco has succeeded in addressing, and indeed dualities and bifurcations are central to all the thinking that this rich novel gives rise to. Although the substance of this book firmly and aggressively addresses the learned, its saving strength and marvelous possession are its educational kindness to the simple, its sense of function within a novelistic rather than a purely semiotic–theoretical–philosophical frame.

In spite of Eco's theoretical leanings, the popularity of *The Name of the Rose* surely comes from its "husk" qualities rather than its *sententiae*, and the inevitable backlash against it has begun with naive practical (as opposed to theoretical) critics re-evaluating it and claiming crankily that it is contrived. All books within the detective-novel genre are, or else they would not be capable of being thus described by Eco: "And since I wanted you to feel as pleasurable the one thing that frightens us – namely, the metaphysical shudder – I had only to choose (from among the model plots) the most metaphysical and philosophical: the detective novel." When the American critic Edward Mendelson seriously but bizarrely states that *The Name of the Rose* is inferior because of its contrivance and shallowness to a small, contained novel like John Fuller's medieval-monastery metaphysical fantasy, *Flying to Nowhere*, he is obviously arguing from premises that are more innocently novelistic and less ambitiously ironic than Eco's. Given the aspirations and achievement of the two novels, he is comparing apples and oranges on the basis of the mere and barren facts that both texts are set in the Middle Ages and have a monk detective–hero. This desire to read the novel merely novelistically cannot, of course, be considered a fault, since the book is indeed a novel and the only, far from debased, means by which Eco's name and ideas could ever have come so dramatically to the forefront of international contemporary attention. It is nevertheless essential to a just reading of *The Name of the Rose*, to uncover some of its message to the *cognoscenti* before turning to the pleasures it also grants to the simple, to the ranks of eager and even naive readers of novels, among whom I count myself an enthusiastic member.

It would be monomania indeed if Umberto Eco's primary didactic attention in this novel were directed toward an exposition of an arid strip of semiotic theorizing. But his voracious appetite for the objects and ideas of culture – Aristotle, the Middle Ages, comic strips, current film, etc. – indicates that his theory is largely a means of making the history of human insight coherent and subject to analysis. In an important incident in *The Name of the Rose* the narrator Adso, caught by the hallucinatory drugs that protect the forbidden library of the Aedificium, is given a sudden, bookish illumination in the midst of the labyrinth, quite different from the illuminations of the gorgeous medieval texts on which he has been fixing his eyes:

My eye became lost, on the page, along gleaming paths, as my feet were becoming lost in the troublous succession of the rooms of the library, and seeing my own wandering depicted on those parchments filled me with uneasiness and convinced me that each of those books was telling, through mysterious cachinnations, my present story. "De te fabula narratur," I said to myself, and I wondered if those pages did not already contain the story of future events in store for me.

The idea that one is oneself the subject of all tales told – *de te fabula narratur* (the tale is told about *you*) – takes Baudelaire's *hypocrite lecteur - mon semblable, mon frère* back in history to the Middle Ages and stresses the book's – any book's – primary ability to cancel the boundaries of time. This medieval tale laced with the history of a period apparently so separated from ours enforces our identity with its world rather than our historical alienation. Italian reviewers were not wrong when they claimed that Eco's novel was politically apt to the late twentieth century; it is equally true that its intellectual directions are those that Eco sees as pertinent to and urges upon contemporary thinkers.

It is significant that whereas William thinks, Adso, his pupil-grown-old, writes, making a book that will be the only agent of communication. William's thought processes, ideas, conclusions, skills, and drive toward truth would be terminal without the existence of a book that talks of him and, even more crucially, of the other books through which he learned to make his mind function at its high level of achievement. The fiction that Adso innocently and ignorantly presents about his master is, like so much medieval fiction, an emplotment of larger, general truths that Eco wishes to communicate. The major point of the novel is that no book is an independent entity, and private existential self-referentiality is an impossibility. The degree to which the mind is formulated by written data and our perusal of them is immeasurable. As William explains it to Adso:

> "Often books speak of other books. Often a harmless book is like a seed that will blossom into a dangerous book, or it is the other way around: it is the sweet fruit of a bitter stem. In reading Albert, couldn't I learn what Thomas might have said? Or in reading Thomas, know what Averroës said?"
>
> "True," I said, amazed. Until then I had thought each book spoke of the things, human or divine, that lie outside books. Now I realized that not infrequently books speak of books: it is as if they spoke among themselves. In the light of this reflection, the library seemed all the more disturbing to me. It was then the place of a long, centuries-old murmuring, an imperceptible dialogue between one parchment and another, a living thing, a receptacle of powers not to be ruled by a human mind, a treasure of secrets emanated by many minds, surviving the death of those who had produced them or had been their conveyors.

This is certainly non-novelistic thinking, even in a period like our own where all sense of definition or genre as imposed by the nineteenth century was lost long ago in the rising mists of Modernism. The novel has always assumed that "each book spoke of the things, human or divine, that lie outside books."

Realism depended on mimetic correspondence, and even after Joyce's parataxis or fragmentation, some kind of correspondence theory has been essential. The post-structuralist argument that language is always the subject of language has created a plethora of fictive ironies, but the idea that books are always about books and not about knowledge of either human or divine things is even for the modern mind as unbalancing as Adso's perception of it. Even more significantly, the idea that all books narrate us (*de te fabula narratur*) pushes us into a non-existential area where we live only within the mythos of books and die in and by texts. *The Name of the Rose* is almost endlessly about books, that "treasure of secrets emanated by many minds, surviving the death of those who had produced them or had been their conveyors," in that it consists of an extended collection of quotations, and whispers at every point of the books our culture knows and which this text endows with extended resonance.

Near the end of *The Name of the Rose*, Adso tells us that he returned to the ruins of the monastery many years after its destruction by fire, wandering about picking up torn bits of surviving parchment that he carried back to Melk. These disordered, tragically partial shreds of the great library reflect the theme of *disiecta membra*, ill-assorted, cast-aside fragments of a once unified whole, that is so important to the ironies inherent in this novel. Adso's pitiable collection of verbal fragments cannot be pieced together into coherence, just as the monk Salvatore's language cannot become other than a nearly incomprehensible *macedonia* of the various languages and dialects – French, Provençal, Italian, and Latin – that he has picked up in a scrambling, politically wretched struggle from poverty into his present comfort as a permitted hanger-on in the abbey.

When the idea of the scattered fragments or *disiecta membra* is combined with the trope of the world-turned-upside-down (semiotic adynaton), it becomes clear why the particular form of *The Name of the Rose* is so useful as an ideological vehicle. Within the framework of Eco's thought, one might say that the text is an ingenious strategy to produce a model reader who will see the avenues through the labyrinth opened by the collection of quotations, which constitute the *disiecta membra* of the novel. Moreover, it is then the quest of the model reader to transform the metaphysical mysteries, as well as the real ones, into a tentative statement, and in this case the statement must irreducibly be one that asserts a disordered world of fragments in which system and thought are only intermittently successful. If there is any firm message in this novel, it is about the calamitous impossibility of statement or order in a chaotic, constantly shifting universe.

Of the many sub-genres of the novel genre from Victorian times to the present, none has been as pervasive among authors purporting to write beyond the merely popular than the idea of the detective novel. One thinks automatically of Dickens, Poe, Collins, and Conan Doyle in the nineteenth century and Nabokov, Spark, Murdoch, Calvino, and Greene in the twentieth. And of course it was the power of detective fiction that first began the deterioration of the rigid European-art separation between high and low culture. Part of the attraction came from the sheer perspicacity of Edgar Allen Poe's detective, C. Auguste Dupin, who was almost a fictional alter ego for the American philosopher C. S. Peirce, with his passion for empirical observation and the conclusions such sign-reading automatically lead to. Even more popular and attractive was the creation of Sir Arthur Conan Doyle's foolproof sleuth, Sherlock Holmes (a worthy successor to the English medieval cognitive empiricists, Roger Bacon and William of Occam, celebrated in *The Name of the Rose*), whose genius spawned whole collections of twentieth-century detective-heroes and -heroines. Eco of course invokes the shade of Conan Doyle's tale, "The Hound of the Baskervilles," when he names his sleuth William of Baskerville. Indeed the first episode of *The Name of the Rose*, in which William guesses that the abbot's horse is lost and locates it, is comically parodic of any Sherlock Holmes story. Eco, who is not above dallying with his readers' intelligence, thus falsely formulates in many readers from the beginning the expectation that this will be a tidy account of a solved murder mystery.

And things are duly unraveled, but almost by mistake, for this book turns the detective novel (and everything else) upside down by showing how fragile and chancy William's deductions are, and how skewed and almost defeated he is in following his bookish theories. Early in the novel, Adso gives us a clue to the strangeness of this novel's world when he stops the narrative to express in his own words and many borrowed from medieval sources his extended aesthetic delight at the sculpted stone doorway of the abbey church. The long, eloquent passage illustrates one of Eco's many successes in this fiction – his splendid ability to free medieval visual representation from mannered rigidity into vividly felt beauty of form – but it also shows how apt a vehicle for thematics such contemplation can be.

An apocalyptic vision of the Last Judgment, the stone sculpture (Eco's model is the entrance to the abbey church at Moissac in Gascony) reveals to the ecstatic Adso an anonymous image of ordered justice and cosmos. The judging figure is of course the Christ of the Apocalypse, but is identified neutrally as the "Seated One" and the figures of mankind, evangelists, prophets, etc., are torqued and twisted as they writhe inward toward the throne, the object of attention. The ornamentation surrounding the sculpture is of the grotesque world-turned-upside-down sort reminiscent of the Boschian bestiary that Adelmo, the monk–illustrator whose corpse begins the series, had typically painted in his manuscript illuminations. As Adso suddenly loses his capacity to name Christ and neutralizes him by calling him simply the Seated One, he inverts his elsewhere obvious, obedient, conventionally held faith, and the torque of the bodies of men and animals in the sculpture indicates an almost baroque twisting of order, a *discordia concors* or reversal of unified harmonic order.

Within the framework of this aesthetically enrapturing medieval sculpture, then, Adso perceives or constructs a partial semiotic adynaton or world reversal that illustrates the structure and intention of this novel. The naive reader, expert in the art and craft of reading murder-mysteries, will search in vain for the orderly world of well-contained cause and effect in *The Name of the Rose*, where the vagaries of fragmentation are triumphant, and where every object has to be looked at with an insight and vividness not typical of conventional perception. This need to look carefully is, of course, endemic to an alert reading of the detective novel in general and is characterized by this book's detective-hero, William. But William is in crucial ways a failed hero: he stumbles on his dénouement while his reasoning has demonstrated its limitations, and much of his intelligence is vainly deployed. Eco makes it clear in *Postscript* that he assumes a process of reader-transformation, that it is his will to alter the perceptions and expectations of those who are following the text, and obviously he wishes to alter and in certain ways enrich cant notions of hero and solutions:

> The reader was to be diverted, but not di-verted, distracted from problems. *Robinson Crusoe* is meant to divert its own model reader, telling him about the calculations and the daily actions of a sensible *homo oeconomicus* much like himself. But Robinson's *semblable*, after he has enjoyed reading about himself in the novel, should somehow have understood something more, become another person. In amusing himself, somehow, he has learned. The reader should learn something either about the world or about language: this difference distinguishes various narrative poetics, but the point remains the same.

Among the many things necessarily learned by a reader following Eco's signposts is that the closed, terminal logic of preconceived designs or theories impedes the ability of the observer to see what is actually in front of him. So William, like Borges's detective Eric Lönnrot in "Death and the Compass," is led astray for altogether too long by his bookish ingenuity – in this case his knowledge of the Book of Revelation and the fact that the monastery is famous for its quantity and quality of illuminated moralized Apocalypse manuscripts. A rigid pattern of killings reflecting the images of the seven trumpets of Revelation appears fascinating but is wrong. While he concentrates on such a preconceived set piece, William temporarily fails in other much more crucial tasks like solving the riddle to the opening of the *finis Africae* and locating the proper identification of the mysterious and lethal book. Eco's point here is transparently pedagogical and in keeping with his essential idea of open as opposed to closed texts. William, in assuming even temporarily that the solution to the murders might lie in the closed text of the Apocalypse, becomes a bad reader reliant on a limited anterior text rather than working under the aegis of infinite possibility. The interesting point is that William has been trained in openness and scientism, and his lapse into pattern or closedness gives a stern example of how treacherous the inaccurate use of signs is for even the best mind.

When Eco talks about openness, he implies that any response accurately reflective of the referential encyclopedia of both author and reader should be allowed equal freedom or primacy. For this reason, apparently, he claims that he as author does not and should not interpret. Hence those who wish to read the novel as detective fiction may do so without violating the boundaries or *a priori* function of the text; but in interview Eco claims that naive readers have carried this aspect too far, seeing *The Name of the Rose* only or primarily as a detective novel. The implication is that the integrity of the book has somehow become darkened in the process. At the same time, he acknowledges this novel as both detective and historical fiction, and much authorial energy is devoted to making it both. Nevertheless, the percipient reader of *The Name of the Rose* should find his/her way fairly quickly to another mode of reading that indicates the marginality of the novel's detective story cast. Put briefly, this latter aspect is primarily tonal and functional, associated with the semiotics of Peirce and Poe, as well as medieval empirical scientism in the English tradition of William of Occam and Roger Bacon. Once a sense of sign-reading is gained through William's complex example of success and failure, the reader can then work on the more pointed directions of the fiction.

Here there can be little doubt that, despite all of Eco's deflections of this subject, his real purpose is didactic to a quite extraordinary extent. He claims that in the written word there is only one authorial intention (*intentio auctoris*) which is the book itself, its textual existence being its only interpretational boundary. At the same time he argues that as author of *The Name of the Rose* he has permitted or guided the recipient toward a vast plurality of interests and interpretations pursuable by the reader who is free to choose any one possibility from the multitude presented. But in fact the various dominant subjects meet not in infinity but within the logical extensions of the text itself, and one can give fairly objective descriptions of the almost propagandistic thrust of the thematics of the novel.

If there is a thoroughly wrought and stable theme in our time it is that of indeterminacy as opposed to the tyranny of the absolute. In textual terms, this means that freedom of interpretation fights against the idea of an anterior, established truth, and Eco in this novel is one of its most adamant and interesting exponents. His passion for the Middle Ages allows him the presentation almost *sub rosa* (allow me the pun) of an intellectual situation very much analogous to our own, whether we think of ourselves as mere citizens or active critics of the present. Eco gives his motivating signal through the title of the novel with its Nominalist connotations, and there can be no doubt that the medieval Nominalists were the ancestors of our relativist world of whirling symbols and constantly realigned models. Nominalist thought automatically led to scientism in that Nominalism denies that abstract thought can be based on other than names (or models). These must be altered, decoded, rethought because empirical evidence and relentless Aristotelian logic, applied to both

133

abstract names and concrete experience, progressively render such rethinking necessary.

The enemies to the Nominalists, the Realists, bear no real resemblance to the novelistic or Auerbachian tradition of realism, but are in fact Platonist–Augustinian in impulse. The Realists are so named because their constant reference is to an anterior reality such as the world of forms or God – in Christian terminology, a Logos whose stability is eternal, unquestionable, and separated from the empirical experience of our world. Their automatic referent is the divine; their psychological frame that of *contemptus mundi*.

Eco's espousal of the Nominalist background is obvious from his title, but he allows his naive narrator, Adso, to open the novel with the evocation of the Logos from the Gospel according to St John: "In the beginning was the Word and the Word was with God, and the Word was God," thus beginning *The Name of the Rose* with a strong text for the Realists and closing the book with a strong text for the Nominalists. Adso sees himself as "the transparent witness of the happenings that took place in the abbey," but he does not perceive as an old man and only dimly as a youth the lessons his master tries to teach him through the events and conversations of the book. The detective–Nominalist William sets himself progressively against the set pieces of medieval doctrine, the idea of the comprehensibility of the Logos that makes God exist, and reliance on an anterior text like the Apocalypse. The idea of an absolute anterior text can give explanation and comforting coherence to a world-turned-upside-down, composed of *disiecta membra* or fragments that William's contemporaries too easily identify as signs of the devil in the world.

Adso as narrator assumes that eventually coherence in a world apparently ruled by evil will be revealed by or resolved in God, and that he, now an old moribund monk, will in death enter the world of mystic bliss so luminously expressed by fourteenth-century saints. His flight into the divine nothingness is an anti-interpretational escape from a largely meaningless, disjointed world imaged by his senseless parchment fragments collected from the ruins of the monastery. This disjointed world is, on the other hand, one that the hard empiricist mind – like William of Baskerville's – sees as necessary and something to be worked with. Adso's report of his fragmentary, meaningless parchment sheets is throughout the novel ironically paralleled by the intertextual congeries of quotation that comprises the fiction, and the idea of chaotic indeterminacy is textually reinforced. As Adso describes it and as readers accept it, the hopeless compulsion to work on the fragments and partial signs of the universe is illustrated by the, for Adso, incomprehensible text of the novel itself:

> The more I reread this list the more I am convinced it is the result of chance and contains no message. But these incomplete pages have accompanied me through all the life that has been left me to live since then; I have often consulted them like an oracle, and I have almost had the impression that what I have written on these

pages, which you will now read, unknown reader, is only a cento, a figured hymn, an immense acrostic that says and repeats nothing but what those fragments have suggested to me, nor do I know whether thus far I have been speaking of them or they have spoken through my mouth.

Had Adso followed William's teaching closely and precisely, he could have perceived the irony intrinsic to the human situation which William is at such pains to illustrate. As the monastery burns to the ground, the master and the novice, in the novel's most important conversation, discuss the errors of William's initial techniques:

"I have never doubted the truth of signs, Adso; they are the only things man has with which to orient himself in the world. What I did not understand was the relation among signs. I arrived at Jorge through an apocalyptic pattern that seemed to underlie all the crimes, and yet it was accidental. I arrived at Jorge seeking one criminal for all the crimes and we discovered that each crime was committed by a different person, or by no one. I arrived at Jorge pursuing the plan of a perverse and rational mind, and there was no plan, or, rather, Jorge himself was overcome by his own initial design and there began a sequence of causes, and concauses, and of causes contradicting one another, which proceeded on their own, creating relations that did not stem from any plan. Where is all my wisdom, then? *I behaved stubbornly, pursuing a semblance of order, when I should have known well that there is no order on the universe.* . . . The only truths that are useful are instruments to be thrown away. . . . It's hard to accept the idea that there cannot be an order in the universe because it would offend the free will of God and His omnipotence. So the freedom of God is our condemnation, or at least the condemnation of our pride."

(italics added)

This statement of semiotic necessity leads Adso to a desperately brief moment of insight that summarizes the torque of human existence in a medieval world in which the concept of God is demonstrated as impossible:

I dared, for the first and last time in my life, to express a theological conclusion: "But how can a necessary being exist totally polluted with the possible? What difference is there, then, between God and primogenial chaos? Isn't affirming God's absolute omnipotence and His absolute freedom with regard to His own choices *tantamount to demonstrating that God does not exist?*"

(italics added)

All of *The Name of the Rose* leads to this skeptical conclusion, a conclusion that Adso can speak momentarily, but then forgets forever. William answers the question by positing another sort of ironic necessity and Adso's final questions go unanswered except by inference:

William looked at me without betraying any feeling in his features, and he said, "How could a learned man go on communicating his learning if he answered yes to your question?" I did not understand the meaning of his words. "Do you mean," I asked, "that there would be no possible and communicable learning any more if the very criterion of truth were lacking, or do you mean you could no longer communicate what you know because others would not allow you to?"

This conversation implies Eco's situation as didactic writer and ironic apologist for a skewed, indeterminate, necessary world. The human mind has materials to work with, but through logical inference no God (i.e. absolute anterior text) and no perfect unraveling of reality. If reality is temporarily found in a small way – as, for example, Jorge is found at the base of most of the monastery murders – it happens partly by chance and partly by semiotic decoding. Human intelligence makes us sign-readers but does not guarantee our courage to be accurate or our consistency; this novel offers us a parody (and Eco is quite aware of the parasitic nature of parody) of the tightly contained structure of the murder mystery, and in doing so proves definitively that the very existence of the genre is a mental fiction, and an illustration in its own unrealistic way of an anterior idea whose dominant quality is easy certainty rather than the ambiguous, indeterminate world in which life is incomprehensibly led. This ultimate labyrinth of actual chaotic life is in deep contrast to the mannerist, decodable labyrinth of the monastery's library, and as Eco subtly shows, an orderly view of life is to reality what the tidy murder mystery is to this novel's detailed and extensive exploration of the indeterminacy of the world and the limited possibilities of the human mind.

*

There are other areas of ideology within *The Name of the Rose* that must not be overlooked in estimating its intellectually didactic nature. As an historical novel it involves the reader in some of the major disputes of the fourteenth century, notably the controversy about apostolic poverty and the quarrels about the laughter of Christ. At the same time, William's presence as imperial legate challenges the injustice of inquisitorial methods in the Church as practiced by men like Bernard Gui, and his position ultimately indicates the need to break the secular power of the papacy so misused by John XXII in Avignon.

The wealth of material about the "heretical" Fraticelli and Dolcinians, and parallel controversies within the Franciscan order, give a rich and firm texture to the irreducible political ramifications of the novel which are socialist and ameliorative in nature. In *Postscript*, Eco says that early in his thinking about the fiction he wanted to make his investigating hero a contemporary priest who read the left-wing Italian newspaper *Il Manifesto*, but there can be little doubt that this is another red herring thrown at the reader to divert him/her from the larger issues. Certainly a socialist inclination toward change in society is an automatic outgrowth of the novel's emphasis on seeing human beings as part of a mobile system in which empiricism must discover whatever routes there might be toward justice. And the dominant idea that dogmas represent closed, repressive texts automatically argues against both right-wing establishmentarianism and doctrinaire Marxism.

But *The Name of the Rose*, despite its historical strengths, never wanders very far from its bookish inclinations. Behind its structure is not only the necessary fourteenth-century opposition between medieval Realism and Nominalism, but also between Platonism as a fixed mode and Aristotelianism as a steady movement toward change and amelioration. Most of the deaths in the monastery occur because of the ideological duel being fought by William and his arch intellectual adversary Jorge of Burgos; the two adverse characters were obviously essentially created as allegorical representations of the two schools of thought that are thrown into absolute conflict in so many ways in this novel. Whereas William represents a manifold idea of openness, Jorge fights to the death against Aristotle's opening out of the Platonic system, and in a stroke of ingenious bookishness Eco builds his whole dénouement on the lost second part of Aristotle's *Poetics*, the book on comedy whose argument fits so well into the quarrel about the laughter of Christ.

Early in the novel, William makes it clear that the monkish love of books in this library world can lead to death, and petty quarrels arise about the nature of bookishness and its power. Indeed, the monks in the abbey are more likely to have a point of view about the knowledge obtained from the specific kinds of books that interest each of them than they are to have a character in any traditional novelistic sense. But in spite of its intertextuality and vast allusive frame, *The Name of the Rose* does not immediately impress on many of its readers the degree to which its task is the presentation of the primacy of books. Books and their denotation in the life of the mind, of the spirit, of society, and of the individual can actively lead to death which, in this novel, easily comes from ideological controversies and from pursuing the wrong text of forbidden knowledge. As a result, some readers have proclaimed their disappointment that the real culprit could be a blind, atavistic old man whose hatred of Aristotelian progressive thought could lead to moral destructiveness on a hugely impenitent scale. Some put it more bluntly, disliking the idea that all of the murders in the abbey could connect to nothing more "serious" than the lost book on comedy in Aristotle's *Poetics*.

But for Jorge the destruction of that book is major to the maintenance of Christian faith; for William its survival is equally important for its ironic potentiality and the connexion of that potentiality to ameliorative steps forward for the questing mind. As the two adversaries confront each other in the *finis Africae* of the library for their final "shoot-out," Jorge desperately explains why Aristotle's treatment of laughter – laughter that would overturn the world in a senseless anti-Logos or Anti-Christ – must destroy the eternal certainty of Christianity:

> "Because it [the treatise on comedy] was by the Philosopher. Every book by that man has destroyed a part of the learning that Christianity had accumulated over the centuries. The fathers had said everything that needed to be known about the power of the Word, but then Boethius had only to gloss the Philosopher and the

divine mystery of the Word was transformed into a human parody of categories and syllogism. . . . We knew everything about the divine names, and the Dominican buried by Abo [Thomas Aquinas] – renamed them, following the proud paths of natural reason. . . . Before, we used to look to heaven, deigning only a frowning glance at the mire of matter; now we look at the earth, and we believe in the heavens because of earthly testimony. Every word of the Philosopher, by whom now even saints and prophets swear, has overturned the image of the world. But he had not succeeded in overturning the image of God. If this book were to become . . . had become an object for open interpretation, we would have crossed the last boundary . . . from this book many corrupt minds like yours would draw the extreme syllogism, whereby laughter is man's end! Laughter, for a few moments, distracts the villein from fear. *But law is imposed by fear, whose true name is fear of God*. This book could strike the Luciferine spark that would set a new fire to the whole world . . . and from this book there could be born the new destructive aim to destroy death through redemption from fear . . . this book – considering comedy a wondrous medicine, with its satire and mime, which would produce the purification of the passions through the enactment of defect, fault, weakness – would induce false scholars to try to redeem the lofty with a diabolical reversal: through the acceptance of the base. This book could prompt the idea that man can wish to have on earth (as your Bacon suggested with regard to natural magic) the abundance of the land of Cockaigne. *But this is what we cannot and must not have*."

(italics added)

Jorge's frantic belief that the loss of the central, authoritative Logos must mean the loss of all knowledge and certainty is countered by William's optimistically progressive notion that "I would match my wit with the wit of others. It would be a better world than the one where the fire and red-hot iron of Bernard Gui humiliate the fire and red-hot iron of Dolcino."

But Jorge is adamant, and in his wonderfully mad bibliophagy as he tears the poisoned pages of the linen book and stuffs them into his mouth, Aristotle's text is lost – and so is the splendid library, in a holocaust or ecpyrosis that reflects a new sort of apocalypse, the end of a cosmos of books that in the fourteenth century still cannot be used as a vital source to forge an enlightened world.

It remains palpably true at the end of *The Name of the Rose*, however, that the stylized character of William of Baskerville has achieved success of a major sort. Eco is scrupulously accurate in creating this twentieth-century fourteenth-century man, giving him thoughts that could be historically possible in a world that had created cognitive scientists like Roger Bacon and philosophers like William of Occam. Yet William is of necessity defeated by history and by an overriding ideology whose adversaries were not yet ready to take the progressive steps necessary to create the empirical world already implied in Nominalism. At the same time, his triumph lies in self-analysis and in the fact that he has seen clearly and justly judged the whole episode. William of Baskerville passes the tests set by Peirce in talking about "the ideal inquirer."

He is not yet – nor are we – in an adequately advanced position to imagine what the philosopher Hilary Putnam might "idealize" as life at the end of enquiry, but he accomplishes the ameliorative aim of Eco's novel.

The reader of this carefully designed novel should, if (s)he follows the author's thorough instructions, be transformed into a being ready for the next steps necessary in a neo-enlightenment of contemporary man that is Umberto Eco's most aggressive and kindly task. Only a churlish reader would be unwilling to allow him his success at this point in his mission.

7

Muriel Spark and
the art of the exclusive

Occasionally in the British novel a voice occurs which predates what will, in literary historical terms, become an established subform within the genre. In the case of Muriel Spark, this forerunner aspect can be mistaken for a clever continuation of the past or a marvelous phenomenon in the present in which the new genre appears. It is perhaps necessary to argue that all art has its inescapable continuities, and that even Beckett, for all his bizarre novelty, continues in a unique conjunctive way the literary tasks of Kafka and Joyce. The innovative Muriel Spark, with her odd ellipses that fit so well in the metafictional scene of the last decade, has been part of the annals of contemporary British fiction since the 1950s. Although very much taken for granted by her compatriots, she is ranked highly for cruelly limited reasons that, at this point in the late twentieth century, seem slightly off-base, if not downright irrelevant, to many readers of her brief novels.

Evelyn Waugh's death in 1966 more or less marked the end of Modernism in English fiction, and since then Muriel Spark and Waugh's remarkable friend, Graham Greene – Spark's earliest patron – have often been lumped together in a stale way as old-fashioned Catholic novelists, to the detriment of their other strengths; like Saul Bellow who still groans under the appellation of "Jewish writer," both are diminished by the narrowness of such tags. Because of her early alignment with the British Catholic group, Spark, although popular, has been generally held in less esteem and seen as less original and quirky than a fair reading of her fictions allows. Her wit and comedic talents have always received full – even fulsome – credit, and in this respect she has often been compared favorably to Waugh himself. Like Waugh and Greene, Spark has an elegant, much celebrated prose style – one that is a bare and precise exercise in minimalist effect. But this effect goes beyond diction, which after all only serves the larger function of the novels, and Spark can be seen from the beginning as an expert in what the contemporary reader would classify as cool metafictional minimalism.

Spark's work can be estimated justly only when it is isolated from the nexus of British figures in which her reputation has falsely flowered – Waugh, Greene, the sparsely original Ivy Compton-Burnett, and even Iris Murdoch, who is often crazily compared with Spark only because both are women novelists of the same age and both have religious interests. When Spark is released from the burden of English context, it is startlingly evident not only that this is a completely original voice, but that she has been quietly, carefully building up an *oeuvre* of a highly experimental sort that looks absolutely at home in the thematics of the new that have become almost neurotically central to the last part of the twentieth century. For readers who might rebel against this extraction of Spark from her long established place, it is instructive to look not at her antecedents but at the present – at writers like the American parodist, Donald Barthelme, or at younger writers, slowly building notable reputations, who are consciously or unconsciously like her – particularly the greatly talented American, Renata Adler (*Speedboat* and *Pitch Dark*) or the English comedic genius, Alice Thomas Ellis. In both cases, these newer writers beg for comparison with Spark; indeed, reading her prepares us as readers for the elliptical style and restless irresolution of such novelists. It is in fact a side effect of the metafictional minimalism invented by Spark that the reader amid laughter and tautly concealed emotion often simply gives up on the project of understanding what is happening in the crafted fiction.

Having just waded through too many critical studies of Spark – most of them emphasizing the early work, since she is not fashionable in academic circles at the moment – I am struck by the confident, banal interpretations given to her complexly peculiar novels, whose slippery potentiality is always, probably through Spark's authorial intention, slightly beyond the reader's grasp. The simplicity of reducing her fiction to narrow dogmatic or theological stances is always tempting, because Spark herself often tediously invites it – particularly in early books such as *The Comforters*, where her heroine, Caroline Rose, will not sleep with her lover because she has become a Catholic, or *The Mandelbaum Gate*, where the converted heroine wishes not to marry her divorced fiancé without a proper annulment from Rome. Spark never openly moralizes, although she certainly dogmatizes. Even in her recent fictions, Spark often persists in the idea of Catholic conversion, but is increasingly lax on the ethical front, where she is puckishly preoccupied by an uncomfortable and sometimes frivolous obsession with lawlessness, violence, and terrorism. Nevertheless, reliable critics, including David Lodge with his Catholic tastes and Frank Kermode with his catholic ones, classify her as the best – or at least among the best – of fictionists in English. It behooves us to see where this judgment comes from, and how Spark's decisions about form and aesthetics work toward the originality of her achievement.

Spark has been helpful to her readers in presenting a novel, *Loitering With Intent* (1981), which is almost a handbook of the devices, theory, and points of

141

view that govern her career. This is the first time (I am not counting the short stories) since her second novel, *Robinson* (1958), that she has written in the first person, but her novels are all so univocal that this is hardly a major element. It nevertheless points to the nature of Spark's subjective and exclusive narrative voice, and hence to the area where she is most vulnerable to negative criticism. Like many metafictionists - American, Latin American, French, German, Italian - with whom she may or may not be acquainted, the dominant "affect" of her work is cool in the extreme, and indeed she is an exclusivist who, like many other contemporary novelists, seems convinced that there are few good readers.

In *Loitering With Intent*, the general reader is personified and parodied in her heroine Fleur Talbot's perfidious friend, Dottie. Identified as a detestably conventional "English rose" type, Dottie can be relied on to misunderstand both the author and the characters in the novel Fleur is writing, to impose false and rigid moral values, and to disapprove of the inhuman "coldness" of the author's point of view. The distinctive issue of coldness - the primary requirement of the detached metafictional style since the first manifestos by the French *nouveaux romanciers* - is celebrated and defended in Spark's novel, in semi-post-structural linguistic terms that deny the mimetic realism of fiction. This detached linguistic quality is illustrated when Dottie objects to one of the characters in Fleur's novel as evil and wanting in moral dimension, and Fleur responds dismissively:

> "Then Marjorie is evil." [says Dottie]
> "How can you say that? Marjorie is fiction, she doesn't exist."
> "Marjorie is a personification of evil."
> "What is a personification?" I said. "Marjorie is only words."
> "Readers like to know where they stand," Dottie said. "And in this novel they don't. Marjorie seems to me to be dancing on Warrender's grave."
> Dottie was no fool. I knew I wasn't helping the reader to know whose side they were supposed to be on. I simply felt compelled to go on with my story without indicating what the reader should think. . . .
> "You know," Dottie said, "there's something a bit harsh about you, Fleur. You're not really womanly, are you?"

This reduction of character to a crafted ensemble of words, on which no moral or semantic judgment can be pronounced, is paradoxically both dominant and regressive in Spark's work. The result can be the utter confusion of the reader who is trying to come to terms with the limited explanatory mode of the books: in other words, many serious readers have Dottie-like characteristics. While Fleur the novelist abandons the idea of realism in character presentation, arguing that her Marjorie exists only as words, the reader necessarily senses here, and throughout Spark's novels, that an extended sort of allegory is going on in a strange and perhaps barren way. This allegory refers in any given Spark tale to a subject matter of fragile comprehensibility.

I was, for example, unconvinced by Frank Kermode's review of *The Only Problem* (1984) where he argues that Spark's 1963 novella, *The Girls of Slender Means* is about holy poverty. This reading is a tenuous extrapolation of critical "meaning" from the last sentence of the novel, plus frequent narratorial utterances proclaiming how very nice people with no money were in the years just after World War II. A very different sort of reader, I had thought it was "about" loss and concomitant martyrdom; I equally thought it a slippery book that lived self-consciously on the edge of frivolity, teased by the dark shadows of death, and I have never felt secure in my admiration or grasp of it. It does not much matter whether Kermode or I can be counted as having an accurate line on *The Girls of Slender Means*; what matters is the sense the book imposes on the reader – its demand that explanatory allegorical identifications be made. The novel's tone and comic effect, however, appear to be doing the opposite, simultaneously overturning the reader's urge toward meaning and dismissing what Walter Benjamin described as the melancholy seriousness of allegorical meaning, in which the fictional world becomes an ideological thing.

When readers enter one of Spark's novels where the diegetic mode (i.e. the straightforward narration of events in story form) appears to be major, we in fact enter a no man's land where authorial decisions about the form and potential reception of the tale are as flimsy as the ambiguous and often sleazy main characters we confront. By narrative impact, Spark indicates that the development of her fictions is both artful and capricious, and in the above quotation from *Loitering With Intent*, her alter ego Fleur makes it clear that simple exposition of moral tone or of semantic intention for the sake of the reader is infinitely less important than getting on with her task in a state of creative absorption. The reader is indeed left free, asked to do her/his own work, and to intuit the various levels of meaning imposed by the authorial intelligence. Most readers will fail, as Dottie pre-eminently does, in this novel where Spark presents a comic outburst against the idea of the crass common reader. This negative reader wants things explained to her/him, but nevertheless persists in idly making ill-conceived negative judgments:

> I told him [Solly] that Dottie continued to complain about my *Warrender Chase* and consequently I was sorry I had ever started reading it to her.
>
> "You want your head examined," said Solly, limping along. He was a man of huge bulk with a great Semitic head, a sculptor's joy. He stopped to say, "You want your head examined to take notice of that silly bitch." Then he took his part of Edwina's pram-handle, and off we trundled again.
>
> I said, "Dottie's sort of the general reader in my mind."
>
> "Fuck the general reader," Solly said, "because in fact the general reader doesn't exist."
>
> "That's what I say," Edwina yelled. "Just fuck the general reader. No such person."
>
> I liked to be lucid. So long as Dottie took in what I wrote I didn't care whether she disapproved or not. She would pronounce all the English Rose verdicts, and

we often had rows, but of course she was a friend and always came back for more. I had been reading my book to Edwina and to Solly as well. "I remember," said Edwina in her cackling voice, "how I laughed and laughed over that scene of the memorial service for Warrender Chase that the Worshipful Company of Fishmongers put on for him."

As this quotation shows, *Loitering With Intent* divides the sheep from the goats with Spark's typically judgmental crispness. Since we don't have the text of Fleur's *Warrender Chase* before us, it is impossible to divine how evocative – or, given what we know of Fleur's ideas, how minimalist – the description of the Worshipful Company of Fishmongers' dinner might be. What we do know is that laughter is a more efficacious and correct response than earnest moralizing. This sounds right, and carries an appealing Horatian delight-and-instruct aura. But it is also clear that non-ideal readers of Fleur's shadowy novel are considered enemies, in this black-and-white allegory of aesthetic good and evil.

Nevertheless, the general reader whose very existence is denied by the author's loyal supporters, Solly and Edwina, must be authorially dealt with. Firmly personified in Dottie as the conventional English rose, this sort of reader is seen through a barrier of well-deserved condescension. Interestingly, the symbolic Dottie also remains a "friend" throughout, in spite of her unbounded defection, stupidity, and dishonesty. The would-be exclusive author, represented by Fleur, requires and serves readers like Dottie, who represents a wide and necessary public. But Fleur's heart is with the bizarre and grotesque – and with the reader whose finely honed sense of comedy, like the wild Edwina's, leads to endless laughter in the face of the high comedy of cool plotting. Fleur, the author–persona, has such marvelous self-confidence, however, that despite the comically narcissistic ironies she self-consciously works with, she is insidiously intimidating to the real reader, who knows that just as Dottie stupidly loses any argument, so must any objector to the Sparkian narrative ego.

When a strong authorial pseudo-religious judgment like Fleur's is made of the reader, we all wish to be on the side of the angels, and Spark has no demurrals about demanding that we stand up to be counted with the splendidly impious Solly and Edwina, rather than with the "good" Catholic, Dottie. Spark's moral intrusion, or her insistence that a good reader also be an interesting eccentric (as all of us wish to be), gives a buoyancy to the reading process that can be denied only retrospectively – if at all – when the critic looks at the whole *oeuvre* and contemplates its ethical and aesthetic ambiguities.

Spark's bag of tricks includes not only this constant demand for the perfect – as opposed to the trite general – reader, but also a curiously out-dated mystique about the nature of the artist – the kind of thing that occurred in Modernism with Joyce or Mann. Fleur celebrates this mystique in her novel, in high although ironic terms that free her from the conventional restraints of realism,

144

at the same time as she claims to display as much realism – or even hyper-realism – as she deems necessary. Some of her serious witticisms on the subject must be quoted from *Loitering With Intent* in order to demonstrate the intensity of her point and the seriousness of her belief in art as divinely joyous:

> I wasn't writing poetry and prose so that the reader should think me a nice person, but in order that my sets of words should convey ideas of truth and wonder, as indeed they did to myself as I was composing them. I see no reason to keep silent about my enjoyment of the sound of my own voice as I work. I am sparing no relevant facts.

> What is truth? I could have realized these people with my fun and games with their life-stories, while Sir Quentin was destroying them with his needling after frankness. When people say that nothing happens in their lives I believe them. But you must understand that everything happens to an artist; time is always redeemed, nothing is lost and wonders never cease.

> People often ask me where I get ideas for my novels; I can only say that my life is like that, it turns into some other experience of fiction, recognizable only to myself ... even if I had been moved to portray those poor people in fictional form, they would not have been recognizable, even to themselves – even in that case, there would have been no question of that. Such as I am, I'm an artist, not a reporter.

Spark begins with the assumption that the realistic raw materials of fiction require radical transformation, and that the transformational act can occur only through the magical agency of the artist. For that artist, events and characters are empirically rooted in reality, but often imagined prior to it:

> The process by which I created my characters was instinctive, the sum of my whole experience of others and of my own potential self; and so it has always been. Sometimes I don't actually meet a character I have created in the novel until some time after the novel has been written and published.

Arguing that she is "a magnet for experience," Fleur says that as an artist she "was aware of a *demon* inside me that rejoiced in seeing people as they were, and not only that, but more than ever as they were, and more, and more." This artistic intensification of the real, or ironic hyper-realism, is an artificial structure contrasting absolutely with the psychological, morally dangerous, and quasi-realistic "frankness" encouraged in the members of the Auto-biographical Society by Fleur's power-hungry enemy, Sir Quentin Oliver.

Perceived from the point of view of the soft world of the realistic novel, Spark's insistent argument about the special nature of the writer and her/his intensification of reality looks both odd and contradictory. In the coolness of Spark's post-structuralist mode, however, all mucking about with mere literal realism – and particularly with the idea of "frank" emotional or psychological "affect" – is frowned on for inviting sentimentality and its questionable, unattainable adjuncts of truth-telling and sincerity. Instead of such false realist baggage, Spark carefully posits "truth and wonder" - poetic and religious qualities that surpass simple observation or emotional "frankness," while they surge toward something "more, and more." Although repeatedly reminding the reader that her trade is only with words ("Warrender Chase never existed, he is only some hundreds of words, some punctuation, sentences, paragraphs, marks on the page. If I had conceived Warrender Chase's motives as a psychological study I would have said so. But I didn't go in for motives, I never have"), Spark through Fleur's agency keeps before the reader a mysterious sense of the artist's specialized achievement.

This unspeakable artistic *je-ne-sais-quoi* is partially described in *Loitering With Intent* through serious parodic reference to the sublime delight an historically remote artist felt in the world as he created his artifacts. Spark's spokesman here is the Renaissance Italian artist–craftsman, Benvenuto Cellini, who wrote a joyous, boisterously boastful account of his life as an artist. Fleur (Spark) particularly delights in Cellini's opening sentence:

> All men, whatever be their condition, who have done anything of merit, or which verily has a semblance of merit, if so be they are men of truth and good repute, should write the tale of their life with their own hand.

Cellini wrote at the age of 58, when his career was advanced; young Fleur, convinced of her potential power and importance as an artist, knows that in the future she will have done something of merit through her art and life. *Loitering With Intent* is the document she finally produces in middle age. Meanwhile, she knows that before autobiography is permissible to her, other tasks intervene: "One day, I thought, I'll write the tale of my life. But first I have to live." She also, like Cellini, must build up a stock of artifacts - novels that justify her "merit" and without which a responsible autobiographical act would be inappropriate.

In keeping with this necessity, she has given herself over to the writing and publication of her first novel, *Warrender Chase*, is working on her second, *All Soul's Day*, and planning her third, *The English Rose*. There is no hint here of anything like the blocked writer; instead, prolificacy is taken for granted in a joyous world where the artist's destiny is automatic, complete, uncomplicated, and infused with metaphysical joy. Cellini reiterates that everything in the blessed world conspires to allow him to "go on his way rejoicing," and Fleur - who as a religious Catholic is a specialist in strict adherence to role models - follows him, embracing the delights and vicissitudes of her own life. Even the miserable walk home from Kensington High Street tube station on a cold rainy night sends her on her way rejoicing.

Only the harshest of readers could fail to respond to the self-confident exuberance of Fleur as narrator and artist-persona. Irritating though Spark's archness often is, Fleur Talbot is one of her best realized and most charming characters. An interesting factor in considering Spark's career is that she has changed very little thematically or stylistically from the beginning. Although *Loitering With Intent* is fairly recent in Spark's well-sustained *oeuvre*, it is deeply related to her first published novel, *The Comforters* (1957). In that excellent novel, the thematics of the origin of artistic production and the presentation of the heroine, Caroline Rose, constitute inspired typological preparation for the achievement of *Loitering With Intent*. Like the much later Fleur Talbot, Caroline Rose is an artist figure, although her major creative effort at the moment involves writing a theoretical critical book to be entitled *Form in the Modern Novel*.

This signal of Spark's interest in formalism and theory at the moment she began her career should not be overlooked. It is, however, hard to tell whether Caroline is also writing a novel in which she is a character, or whether she is desperately trapped in a Borgesian world where she is only a progressive idea in the mind of an unknown author–creator who types out her thoughts and activities at the very moment they occur to her. The supernatural cognition of this alternative author haunts the book and almost drives Caroline mad, suggesting the *mise-en-abyme* thematics of Kafka, Borges, Calvino, and many other metafictionists. This Alice-in-Wonderland situation of unreality penetrates to the heart of the problem of fiction as a special ontological art form, a theme Spark explores in both early and late novels.

Above all, these works show Spark's obsessive but minimally expressed interest in the nature of fiction as it relates to the divine – a difficult subject on which to maintain the coolness she obviously values. It is ambiguously significant that *The Comforters* evokes the Book of Job, to which she has also returned fairly recently in *The Only Problem* (1984). Spark's dominant compulsion in these novels is to align the art of fiction with the burden and obligation of the religious life. In *The Comforters*, Catholic Caroline Rose tries to unite the two, and to go even further in ontological terms, as she describes her painfully haunting private revelation of the authorially controlled fiction she must unavoidably participate in in the early novel. For her, the idea that fictional characters suffer bewilderment at the hands of their creators parallels the suffering of humanity before an only partially perceived demiurgic God. Much later in Spark's career, Harvey Gotham in *The Only Problem* goes even further in the *mise-en-abyme* of creators, and distinguishes between a "real" God and "a fictional character in the *Book of Job*, called God." The first major Sparkian heroine, Caroline, nevertheless begins the questioning process that continues to be major in Spark's subsequent novels:

> "How can I answer these questions? I've only begun to ask them myself. The author obviously exists in a different dimension from ours. That will make the investigation difficult.... I have what ought to be called a delusion. In any normal opinion that's a fact.... The normal opinion is bound to distress me because it's a fact like the fact of the author and the facts of the Faith. They are all painful to me in different ways."

The peculiar way in which the three thematic issues of this first novel are paralleled raise questions that can also be seen elsewhere as Spark's major concerns: (1) normal opinion about human sanity (which the speaker has lost because of her abnormal experiences of hearing a supernatural typewriter); (2) the idea of godlike authorial control over characters; (3) the reality for Caroline of a theological universe. "Normal" opinion automatically aligns itself with that of the crude "general" reader, and Spark indicates that thoughtful self-consciousness separates serious readers and admirable characters from gross general commonplaces about normality. As Caroline sees it, she is either an authorially created character in a novel or a God-created person in the world: under any circumstances, her hallucinatory experiences separate her from simple normality. The moment this separation is recognized, she becomes a special case, a stranger in the normal world, and this aspect of deep alienation, imposed by fiction or religion, is the deepest grounding theme in Spark's work.

A more precise illustration of this point can be found in *The Prime of Miss Jean Brodie* (1961) where the tellingly named character, Sandy Stranger, admits her estrangement from the ordinary world by converting to Catholicism and entering a religious order under a new name, Sister Helena of the Trans-figuration. In doing so, she signals her cloistered separation not only from the ordinary grimness of working-class Edinburgh which appalls her, but from the fanciful fictional interpretations the zany schoolmistress, Miss Jean Brodie, irresponsibly put on everything when Sandy was a schoolgirl. As a nun, Sandy achieves fame as the author of an "odd psychological treatise on the nature of moral perception, called 'The Transfiguration of the Commonplace'." Like many of Spark's signs this treatise – not to mention Sandy's symbolic new name, Sister Helena of the Transfiguration – appears to transmit a simple message, but is in fact subtle to the point of impenetrability.

David Lodge aestheticizes the concept of transfiguration, seeing it as a way of talking about the particular quality of Spark's elliptical writing which, in accordance with Russian formalist theory, creates the world anew – and in a limited way this is correct. But Sandy's life – her *vita nuova* – is ambiguous in the extreme. Miss Jean Brodie's professional life ends in ignominious early retirement, because Sandy betrayed her teacher's Fascist, pro-Mussolini politics to the headmistress in a deliberate move to stop her pernicious influence over the "set" of schoolgirls in her charge. Yet this is not primarily a political book, and Miss Brodie's idle flirtation with Fascism in the 1930s does not fully account for Sandy's willfully destructive act.

Years later, as Sister Helena of the Transfiguration, Sandy explains, "It's only possible to betray where loyalty is due." As in most Spark novels, the larger issues of politics and morality are never central, whereas subtler aesthetic or spiritual reasons, sparingly limned out, are set shadowily at the hub. Sandy's estrangement from the world first manifests itself in the compulsive act of betrayal, through which Miss Brodie's radical fantasies – falsely transfiguring the ordinary quotidian world for the girls in her "set" – are halted. In spite of the expected transfigurations implicit in the spiritual world of grace, Sandy's academic theme and subsequent fame, however, are not religious, and her renowned treatise is specifically psychological. The implication is that Miss Brodie, to whom Sandy could not remain loyal, nevertheless once provided a vital although frivolous mode of transfiguration from which Sister Helena, despite her religious conversion, cannot absolutely separate herself.

In this respect, Miss Brodie can also be seen as a type of artist – but one whose fantasies are false and tainted, and to whom no loyalty is due. Sandy destroys the worldly transfigurations of this false fictionist and embraces a religious ideal, but her writing remains ambiguously in the realm of the secular – in a world where the most influential factor in her life was, as she says in the last sentence of the book, "a Miss Jean Brodie in her prime."

Seen in this way, this novel, like Jane Austen's *Mansfield Park*, becomes a morality tale in which a subtly ethical statement is made about the nature of fiction and the danger of false representations. Perhaps Spark's offhand way of talking about her work, echoed by Fleur Talbot's attitude in *Loitering With Intent*, springs from a source of the kind depicted in this reading of *The Prime of Miss Jean Brodie*. Like Sandy/Sister Helena, Fleur as a committed religious person who is also a writer can use her creativity primarily – perhaps only – in the secular world, and fiction is therefore necessarily her natural métier. At the same time, *Loitering* demonstrates that without denying the essential fantasy of literature, the worthy artist infuses her/his work with a reality, joy, and truth that are inseparable from religion and which, for Spark, define the aesthetic task of fiction.

Regardless of the potential or even evident frivolity of many of Spark's main characters, those most obviously to be admired are usually Catholics, and often converts. The reader is made aware of the quality of admiration required by means of the narrative voice, in combination with the thoughts and actions of the character in question. Much has been written about Spark's Catholic dogmatics, but the particulars of what she considers "proper" belief must inevitably be extrapolated – a factor that contributes to the secrecy of the novels, as well as to their dominant exclusivity. This exercise is sometimes very difficult, however, and must spring in large part from the tonal setting of the fiction. Typically, all spiritual quality – as opposed to dogmatic behavior – is tossed off as self-evident, or as something anyone of Spark's private coterie relationship with the better sort of reader would tacitly include. As Fleur Talbot explains in *Loitering With Intent*, she as artist knows enough about the travails of spirituality – as presumably the percipient reader does – and can concentrate more detailed energy on attacking the enemy and concentrating on her art:

> I too was a Catholic believer but not that sort, not that sort at all. And if it was
> true, as Dottie always said, that I was taking terrible risks with my immortal soul,
> I would have been incapable of caution on those grounds. I had an art to practise
> and a life to live, and faith abounding; and I simply didn't have the time or the
> mentality for guilds and indulgences, fasts and feasts and observances. I've never
> held it right to create more difficulties in matters of religion than already exist.

Concealed in the last sentence is all the spiritual difficulty that serious
Catholicism no doubt demands of its followers, but Fleur reveals her
spirituality only by connecting her brand of Catholicism to her Cellini-esque
task of joyous art. To have "an art to practise and a life to live, and faith
abounding" implies a high vocation, and Fleur, who reminds us "what a
wonderful thing it was to be a woman and an artist in the middle of the
twentieth century," assumes that her finger is on the pulse of being.

As a first-person narrator, Fleur is relatively rare in Spark's usually third-
person novels; tonally, however, she is typical, and turning attention to her
presents the case for or against the Sparkian narrator. The first obvious issue is
that of gender, in a circumstance where the feminine is always predominant; no
reader can be in doubt that Spark is a woman writer, even to the degree of
cashing in on the strengths (?) and weaknesses of clichés about "femininity."
Spark established her monolithic narrative persona in the 1950s, well before
the women's movement as such began in the 1960s, and her clichés are
therefore very much of the past – and doubtless more irritating for this reason.
The only other major British writer trapped (from the reader's point of view) in
a sexual persona to such a potentially negative degree is John Fowles, whose
self-glorying masculine aggression matches Spark's rather bitchy feminine
coyness. In both cases, readers have complained about the non-participatory
imposition of authorial will on the reader, who has no choice except
acquiescence or open rebellion. The subtlety of narration and persuasion
found in so much contemporary fiction is deliberately not present, and both
authors therefore open themselves riskily to the grace of their reader's
response.

In Spark's case, the narrator always assumes a flirtatious charm that relies on
its sexual impact. The saucily impertinent voice never considers neutrality
through the persuasion of either a reasoned argument or significant
demonstration (which since Henry James has been the preferred form).
Released from the burdens of both showing and telling, Spark thus, whether
she is writing in the first or the third person, can automatically allow herself the
ellipses for which she is famous, and from this freedom springs the distinctive
style.

Such an account makes Spark look too self-indulgent, however, and the
extension of Fleur's character in *Loitering With Intent* redeems her own
excesses as well as Spark's. The fictional Fleur frames her charming autobiographical account by beginning both the novel and the last chapter with an

account of a friendly policeman interrupting her poetry-writing in an old graveyard in Kensington. The two sentences are worth quoting: "One day in the middle of the twentieth century I sat in an old graveyard which had not yet been demolished, in the Kensington area of London, when a young policeman stepped off the path and came over to me" and "It was right in the middle of the twentieth century, the last day of June 1950, warm and sunny, a Friday, that I mark as the changing-point in my life." This firm setting of the novel in the middle of the century, as Fleur goes on her way rejoicing at being a woman and an artist, is a typical example of the quality of Spark's wit. This is a metafictional parody of the ancient idea of epic narrative begun *in medias res*; thus, through the idea of being in the middle of things historically and joyfully, Spark connects her heroine's artistic life with the tremendous fictional structures of the past. Thus she perfectly combines extensive symbolism with comic play – and the grand with the humble particularity of Fleur's quotidian life.

The policeman veers from his path to check unusual activity, sees that Fleur is safe and sane, and in conversation with her volunteers the information that among the offenses he thought she might have been guilty of in that lonely graveyard was that of loitering with intent. The book takes its theme and title from this moment, when the idea of the artist's aberration – of being potentially if not actually on the fringe of legal misconduct – is seen as symbolically useful. Although Fleur's aberrant activity in this episode – and by extension the artist's in general – may look suspicious, she actually wishes to befriend the law and share her cheer (and sandwich) with him. Similarly, she may appear to be loitering with intent – as she is certainly doing with the Autobiographical Association – but her loitering has to do with realist observation, and her intent with the licit transformations of art. For Spark, the artist is always off the path of the ordinary, somehow looking criminal, although in fact aiding rather than hindering society through her/his creative activity. Some such reasoning also, surely, accounts for Spark's constant flirtation with the unlawful in all her fiction – from diamond thieves in her first novel to terrorists in *The Only Problem* – and for her quirky partial sympathy with it.

It is fruitful also to think of Spark's narrator in terms of certain kinds of critical–cultural terms currently finding favor in the academic world. Again, Mikhail Bahktin's idea of the monologic as opposed to the dialogic is appropriate to this discussion, as are the Russian formalist terms, *fabula* and *szujet*. There is an element in contemporary metafiction that must properly be described as anti-fictional, and early in this century Bakhtin, in describing the excellence of good novels, isolated one element – the monologic – that causes fiction to turn against itself. He chose Dostoevsky as an example of supreme mastery over the preferred dialogic form, arguing that the multiple points of view and variety of voices in Dostoevsky enlarge and universalize the potentialities of literature, whereas in monologic fiction either the narrow boundaries of language or the ego of the author is forefronted with detrimental effect. The monologic chooses to be limited and barren and, in Bakhtin's view, can never be considered great literature. Frank Kermode attempts to redeem Spark from Bakhtin's monologic category by opening the one escape hatch Bakhtin built into his system. The monologic can be rescued through wit and irony, which can be seen to align Spark's work with carnival, another of Bakhtin's celebratory terms.

Attempting to defend Spark as a major writer in spite of her calculated separation from standards set up by such a critic dramatically shows how separated readers and theorists must ultimately be. Spark's monologic – indeed monolithic – narrative mode is undeniable and, unlike that of Borges or Calvino, it is also exclusively closed to emotional response. The carnival aspect of her puckish comedy is equally evident, but I would not categorize her as a broadly carnivalesque writer in a way that Fielding, Thackeray, Dickens, etc. certainly are. It's a stupid idea to second-guess the dead, but I doubt that Bakhtin could have admired Spark, and a defense of her must enter another sort of critical discourse.

The Russian formalist distinction between *fabula* and *szujet* – between a novel's undigested elements of narrative or allegorical freight and its plot or apparent subject – does indeed retain a strong hold on the reader's imagination. The idea of the encoded duality of narrative, where the plot (or discursive act of tale-telling) is almost a red herring whose techniques can be discussed separately from the pressure of thought and opaque intention that informs all literature, is attractive as a way of organizing one's response to Spark's work. It feels correct to say that she separates the two, and she certainly depends enormously on the reader's ability to leap from one of her short discursive descriptions to large, unstated premisses. Her mode of plot brevity is characteristic of all her novels and short stories, and an example of her conviction of its success as a method can be found in Fleur Talbot's description of her successful ellipses in *Loitering*:

> But I invented for my Warrender a war record, a distinguished one, in Burma, and managed to make it really credible even although I filled in the war bit with a very few strokes, knowing, in fact, so little about the war in Burma. It astonished me later to find how the readers found Warrender's war record so convincing and full when I had said so little – one real war veteran of Burma wrote to say how realistic he found it – but *since then I've come to learn for myself how little one needs, in the art of writing, to convey the lot, and how a lot of words, on the other hand, can convey so little.*

(italics added)

The persistent question in Spark's work is whether she is entirely right in arguing confidently for the spare style that is singularly hers and on which her reputation is built. As the coolness of affect that characterizes metafiction has become more acceptable to readers, Spark's hyper-modernity is as evident as her self-assured narrators claim. But with the rumbles of innocent neo-realist minimalism and the re-sentimentalization of narrative on the horizon in recent contemporary fiction, her negative critics might be gaining ground. As Oscar Wilde put it, "Nothing is so dangerous as being too modern, one is apt to grow old-fashioned quite suddenly." Nevertheless, Spark's reputation does not falter, even though some of the early novels have aged poorly. Of her two recent books, *Loitering With Intent* is probably her most brilliantly fused and successful novel. In *The Only Problem*, on the other hand, we see her operating at her most self-indulgently elliptical, with serious and problematic results.

One difficulty in reading Spark is the strong sense that one has been left out at both levels. At the level of plot or narrative discourse, only the bare bones – bolstered by amusing but capricious opinion – are presented; an even more serious omission of the reader occurs at the level of ideology, where Spark is always tantalizingly oblique – but the obliquity itself asserts each work's underlying complexity and demands readerly percipience. So skillful is Spark at presenting an indirect sense of the seriousness of her fiction and the almost statemental value of its underlying intention that the reader is left with an unappeased longing toward some sort of informational critical act. As a result, Spark's critics have generally been eager to explicate or to expose the hidden secret: the more Postmodern the work, it seems, the more old-fashioned the critical tools called into play. This compulsion has no doubt led to the quantity of theological explications the early books called forth, but the novels themselves remain elusively beyond such tasks.

Spark's plots are not on the whole strong or interesting. Oddly enough, the rather unsatisfactory short stories set in Africa, where she spent some years as a young woman, are the most potentially interesting, but she has never used African subject matter for the longer fiction – novellas and novels – on which her reputation rests. The strength of her imagination lies in the skillful projection of circumstances – many of them bizarre or supernatural – out of which springs the interaction of sketchily but pithily outlined characters. Spark's mischievous admiration for illegality in all its forms, from theft to murder, may be temperamental, but it also functions as a filler – or a means of plumping out the flatness of situations for subtly imagined ends. I said above that transformation, together with aberration, is her major subject – transformation that may be psychosocial in obvious ways, but is spiritual at root, and the stubborn irresolution of her novels certainly presents an attitude toward the vagaries, inconsistencies, and treacheries of spiritual life.

Spark's oblique, proudly occluded spirituality is firmly aligned with two subjects endemic to the dominant modes of fiction in the late twentieth century – purely self-conscious linguistic enactments, and a solipsistic existential concentration on the self as primary case. Kenneth Burke in *The Rhetoric of Religion* says that "What we say about *words*, in the empirical realm, will bear a notable likeness to what we say about *God*, in theology." Spark's statement

through Fleur that fictional characters have no reality and are only combinations of words on the page is paralleled later by Harvey Gotham's claim in
The Only Problem that God is merely a fictional character in the Book of Job. In
both cases, the slippery use of words and linguistic structures substitutes for
important subjects that can be evoked but not fully realized in a work of fiction.

In Spark's work, the brevity, the ellipses, the parsimony within the verbal
structures are all limited signs pointing to something else that has to do with
"reality," "truth," and "wonder." Similarly, the term "God" is only a semiotic
fictional device whereby an unspoken set of abstract ideas can be brought
before minds unable to perceive without concrete example. Spark assumes that
human beings work through fiction because spirituality is beyond their control
or understanding. Fiction is humble enough, but if handled freshly and
uncompromisingly it can successfully use the historical caprices of ordinary
existence as the primary letters through which the secret codes of divine
complexity are indirectly written. For a writer like Spark, it follows automatically that conventional judgments by the crass general reader are less important
to an incomprehensible spiritual circumstance than the sublimity of ironic
laughter.

Another aspect that Spark, like many contemporary writers, concentrates on
is the idea of fiction as a combinational game through which autobiographical
or even narcissistic material can profitably be threaded. In many ways, Spark's
work always in one way or another – through her personal invasion of the
narrator's voice or through the kinds of women characters envisaged – makes
her own self the centrepiece and object of celebration. Many of her women
characters are secular half-Jews (Spark had a Jewish father and an Anglican
mother) who convert to Roman Catholicism, and as so often in twentieth-
century fiction, the reader has the uncomfortable sense of knowing too much
indiscreet stuff about the author herself. In this respect, of course, Spark is
wildly outdone by such writers as John Fowles, Saul Bellow, Norman Mailer,
or Doris Lessing, all of whom shamelessly invite voyeurism by dropping
incidents from their own biography into their novels. But again, the strongest
explanatory novel in Spark's *oeuvre, Loitering With Intent*, indicates the degree
to which she is attracted by the fascinating issue of autobiography as the central
theme of fiction. For her, as this novel demonstrates, the artist must consider
her/himself as the possible subject of her/his art.

Spark always sets her novels against the background of literature, mostly
English – as when she has the Abbess of Crewe substitute Marvell's lyric poetry
for the august words of the liturgy, or has the doomed victim in *The Girls of
Slender Means* tape an elocutionary reading of Gerard Manley Hopkins's "The
Wreck of the Deutschland" before she dies in the fire. The literature evoked is
in each case appropriate to the biography of the woman that the fiction is
dedicated to presenting. Here in *Loitering With Intent*, the historical literature
Fleur calls on entirely reflects autobiography. The secular *Vita* of the artist

Benvenuto Cellini is balanced by and contrasted with the religious *Apologia Pro Vita Sua* of Cardinal Newman, whose life and letters had much to do with Spark's own conversion.

Spark's point about autobiography is so strong that, with the exception of Fleur's own novel, *Warrender Chase*, all the other literature – real or fictional – referred to in this novel is autobiographical. Not only are these two historical models evoked as central texts, but the novel itself is Fleur's narrative presentation of her own autobiography. To keep the subject absolutely at the forefront, moreover, her lover Leslie writes a novel about his bisexuality entitled *Two Ways*, and all the members of the bogus Autobiographical Association work on brief, dull accounts of their lives, which are heavily fictionalized blithely at first by Fleur and destructively later by the villainous Sir Quentin.

Contrasted to this autobiographical material is Fleur's actual first novel, *Warrender Chase*, whose fictional characters and action are eerily echoed by Sir Quentin's life and that of his weak, pitiable underlings in the Autobiographical Association. The parallel between Fleur's fiction, which precedes her connection with the Association, and the reality of that group is almost total, right up to the death of Sir Quentin in a car crash comparable to the one that Fleur had used as the opening scene of her *Warrender Chase*. This uncanny resemblance – in which life follows art and, through Sir Quentin's plagiarism, actually steals from it – shows the primacy of artistic creation, as well as the mystical prescience of the artist. For Fleur as artist, her predictive novel is an item in her autobiography – part of what she accumulates to make herself worthy of the autobiographical act, and hence in some way equal to Cellini in art and Newman in spirit.

As a novel, *Warrender Chase* also looks boring and uninventive in the extreme. Although we are told as an additional autobiographical fact that it became a bestseller and ensured Fleur's success and fame as a novelist thereafter, it is a far cry from the fascinating novel-within-a-novel that we see in self-conscious *mise-en-abyme* fiction like Gide's *Les Faux-Monnayeurs*. Spark's major problem is the need to plot or, in this case, plod through a shadowy story line that has no genuine interest except in its precognition of events and characters in the real world and its creator's biography. In other words, Spark suggests that *Warrender Chase* is a simple, straightforward story that could not possibly survive on its own, but must be fed by the metafictional paradoxes, devices, and occluded statements that make up not Fleur's novel but Spark's. It is not unusual for literary structures involving a tale within a tale or a play within a play to sacrifice the inner integument in order to cast luster on the dominant product (see *Hamlet, The Tempest, A Midsummer Night's Dream*, Murdoch's *The Black Prince*, Calvino's *If on a winter's night a traveler, inter alia*). But in Spark's case, this lowered vitality in the fictional fiction also reflects her own relative indifference to plot as a compelling aspect of literature.

Spark's task in *Loitering With Intent* is to present an argument about the nature of the artist's autobiography, relating it to the created works of art that are part of that autobiography. In Fleur's presentation of her relations with the other characters in her account of her life as she lived it *in medias res*, she conveys not only a conceptual idea of good versus bad readers, but a vision of the artist's subject matter – which is a vision of life or reality transformed by the imagination of the writer. We are told directly that both the reality and its artistic transformation present in *Warrender Chase* are so accurate that a reader who squirms under the impact of Fleur's manuscript – like Sir Quentin – can do little in his own life except to ape the artistic presentation, thus perverting the world and effecting his own power-centered transformations. But the real artist, Fleur, imagines and transforms in a separate sphere of the mind, without harmful reference to the living beings that surround her. Her act and art are therefore harmless, and ultimately ameliorative in their excellence.

Her positive and joyful innocence is in deep contrast to the malign power of Sir Quentin, who scorns her imaginative capacity and plagiarizes her characters (who bear an uncanny resemblance to individual members of the Autobiographical Association, just as her fated Warrender Chase resembles Sir Quentin himself), in order to destroy and morally undermine those in his power. In doing so, he imposes fictional lives stolen from Fleur's account on his victims, who are too weak to resist him. He does so not in the playful way that Fleur as his secretary rewrote the Association members' autobiographies in order to infuse life and fun into dull material, but perniciously. As a result, already fragile personalities are further diminished.

Unlike Fleur, who does not wish to impose on the lives of others but to exercise her detached imaginative capacities, Sir Quentin falsely urges "frankness," thereby signaling a version of conventional "realism" with its questionable "sincerity." As plagiarist and power figure, his demonic ends are effective, and indeed he succeeds in causing the suicide of one of the members. As artist, Fleur's purposive ends are somewhere between neutral and ameliorative, in that she is convinced that the very fact of art brings joy to life, even as it uses linguistic claims to avoid moral judgment. But she also has her victim. In playing out his parallelism to her novel, Sir Quentin eerily dies in a car crash reminiscent of that of Fleur's Warrender Chase – thus casting question on the nature of his doom and its relation to the "higher" precognitive power of Fleur's art.

In spite of the metaphysical implications, Spark's major point in dissecting the uses of autobiography is to prove it to be a primary device and plotting tool. This extends ideologically through all her work, and although she seldom employs the first person as she does in *Loitering With Intent*, her plot construction uses the straws and bricks of human biography and autobiography as its principal building materials. It is not simply that she infuses personal autobiographical material and experience, but that she believes the artist begins with it, and is constantly subject to the self-consciousness that individual life vividly supplies to all humankind – particularly to the artist or the religious person, both of whom have the power to transform or metamorphose their *données*.

The Only Problem (1984), the novel following *Loitering With Intent*, is equally interested in the placement of artistic biography against actual biography, or fiction against a currently lived life. Here again Spark goes referentially back to *The Comforters* for one of the original themes in her published work. The Book of Job gave her the title of that first novel, and implied the suffering of her heroine, Caroline Rose; *The Only Problem* also takes up the problems of the Book of Job, which is her fictional backdrop for the story of the rich Canadian, Harvey Gotham, and his terrorist wife, Effie.

Not only is Job a referent for *The Only Problem*, but its major characters all, because of Harvey's study of and obsession with Job, comment on and work out interpretations of the central ambiguities of the Book of Job. But the novel actually concerns itself with the ironic distance between that magnificent palimpsest of fiction and the currently progressing biography of Harvey Gotham. The name Gotham implies that he is a sort of fool whose real life is only a parody or soft imitation of the suffering and indignation of Job. As a casual theologian and student of the Book of Job, Harvey keeps going back to the history of Rabbinical and Christian commentary on the text. The interpretation that compels him most is pictorial – Georges de La Tour's painting of Job and his wife in the museum at Epinal; rich Harvey even buys a cottage and then a château in order to be near the picture, and visits it regularly. Again, as in *Loitering With Intent*, the events of art precede those of life, for Harvey sees a deep physical resemblance between Job's turbanned wife and his own beautiful, estranged wife, Effie.

Harvey is made to suffer at metaphysically indifferent hands as was Job (and indeed all of us are), and as he meditates on Effie's defection into terrorism he sees that de La Tour was presciently there as commentator, establishing an intuitive antecedent to Harvey's present life. De La Tour's dramatic representation of Job's turbanned wife reminds him of Effie, and the resemblance between life and art takes on uncanny intensity when Effie, shot dead and lying on a mortuary slab with a towel wrapped around her head, reminds Harvey of Job's elegantly dressed wife in the painting. Art's ability to predict and even shape the events of non-fictional characters' "real" life is stronger in this case than it is in the comparison between Job and Harvey, but the potential impact of each illustrative case is similar.

The Only Problem is also an economical illustration of Spark's belief in the strength of art and its parallel, the spiritual world, as opposed to the tawdriness of ordinary life or the quotidian. In Spark's eyes, art is our study and our guide. Harvey's real superiority over other characters in the book is that he has the moneyed privilege of concentrating on a supreme fiction (the Book of Job), against which he can measure the quality of human life. Through this there can be – and is in his case – some minor elevation of the moral sense. Harvey is aware that he is not Job's equal, but it is typical of Spark that she trivializes this gap between Harvey and Job in order to emphasize its extent.

Harvey knows that his life is relatively soft; he is also morally aware that he has "failed [Effie] in action," and is therefore not the blameless man Job was when God goaded Satan to get to work on him. Yet when he actually localizes the difference between himself and Job, Harvey frivolously says that the primary divergence is in the fact that he doesn't have Job's boils. Since no hand has been set on his body and since he believes that the blow that destroyed the fortitude of Job, setting him into argument against theodicy, was these boils, Harvey feels somehow theologically cheated. Certainly the reader is flummoxed by the essential non-comparison between Job and Harvey – the latter a petulant ordinary man whose love even for the baby Clara can be clouded over by the noise she makes, and whose sufferings are slight as he lives in moneyed comfort (which he doesn't lose) and arrogant selfishness. Like Job his tale has a melancholy "happy" ending after Effie's death, in that he is allowed to adopt Clara, Ruth is pregnant with his child, and he like Job feels doomed to a prosperous life. The loss of Effie and his incompetence before her criminality are coolly handled; if this small action parallels the high tragedy of Job and its deflating divine reward, it does so in a very minor way indeed.

Perhaps the tale of rich, comfortable Harvey Gotham is the best illustration of Spark's peculiar and contradictory powers. Separated from the splendor and pain of Job by his money (it is depressing to note how many of Spark's characters are decadently, shamelessly rich), selfishness, and frequent frivolity, Harvey enacts a life whose contingent content is the subject of Spark's archly witty book. But this life and novel remain at an unbridgeable remove from the higher regions where art and the spirit might be able to drive forward the questing human soul. In this novel, as in all Spark's attenuated fictions, are reflected the tawdry deprivations of the ordinary life, as well as the barren materialism of the world that this wry and often inspired writer wishes "joyfully" to transmit through the satiric agency of comedy.

Spark's occlusion and surely intended elimination of her audience's comprehension remain problematic and fail to balance the wit, satire, and parody with which she typically works. The scrambled ambiguity of even her best fictions fights against the luminosity her narrators seem to assume is automatically present in her art. The ellipses of her metafictional mode are nevertheless often stunningly effective. But all metafiction tends, as Nabokov argued without using this faddish term, to put everything that has to do with truth or reality in quotation marks, thus marginalizing and even destroying the concept of the real, and certainly ending conventional realism within the genre of the novel. But unlike most current metafictionists Spark has higher quasi-semantic ambitions, in that there is a shadowy religious thrust to the novels, which often creates a genuine affect and equally often falls flat. She also seems to believe that the novel as she practices it is elevated because it is to be conceived as a branch of poetry. As her Fleur Talbot says in *Loitering With Intent*, "In fact I've started a novel which requires a lot of poetic concentration because, you see, I perceive everything poetically." So be it. As readers, we are left to think what we can. On the whole, Spark's work is impressive indeed, but I do not believe it is the best fiction currently written in English, and I falter before its admirable but strangely conceived high-handedness.

8

Russell Hoban:
this place called time

The problems that occur in terms of audience response to American writers like John Barth, John Hawkes, Robert Coover, Ronald Sukenick – the list can and should go on in order to indicate the wide-ranging modes within a general category of experimentalism – spring at least partially from the fact that these "cool" and often violent metafictionists have their roots in the universities and have depended on a narrow coterie audience for much of their success. In this milieu, they are rapidly being replaced by neo-realist minimalists, but over the last fifteen or twenty years their reputations were made fairly secure. Nevertheless, their espousal and development of European (particularly French and Italian) experimentalist procedures with formalist, aesthetic, and/or anti-semantic stress has short-circuited for many readers outside of the American university creative writing programs which they and their friends dominated until recently.

Supplanted as they are now in the academy by the popularity of minimalist techniques, Barth and his experimentalist colleagues nevertheless suggest and guard a potent movement within American fiction. Originating with the ambiguous and multi-directed ambitions of, most notably, Coover, Donald Barthelme, and Barth himself twenty years ago, this movement's decline must be lamented. The cultural sophistication brought to the realm of fiction by such writers cannot be overstressed, and their ironic play against large allusive frames provides fiction with a largesse that makes minimalism look tiny indeed.

But, as the troubled case of Barth himself shows, readers are resistant to a cold fiction that overworks its Postmodernist irony and entirely repudiates the formulae of a reputedly *passé* genre which the audience persists in adhering to. One can go so far as to say that if the essential old categories of fiction like character and coherent meaning are annihilated, few readers can be expected. As American academic experimental fiction declines, most potential readers have found other kinds of books to satisfy their residual print-culture yearnings, or have found other cultural objects to contend with. From the point of view of audience, the ineluctable conclusion must be that textual self-consciousness as the primary *raison d'être* for fiction – unless skillfully done and subject to other semantic tasks – can only be a whimsical undertaking, as Barth himself illustrates in his *Chimera*. Whereas many writers have succeeded brilliantly within this range – Beckett, Nabokov, Borges, and Calvino, for example – American and French writers, with the exception of Pynchon and the early Robbe-Grillet, have notably failed to win audiences or to make an adequate international impression.

The telling factor governing success in experimentation is dramatically connected to the author's own sense of audience and her/his recognizably demonstrated commitment to a non-hermetic sense of literary function. The idea that fiction must in some way express a declarable function is, of course, subject to a quagmire of objections, including problems of ethical over-bearance. George Steiner, in an essay in *The Times Literary Supplement* in 1985, suggests a solution through a summoning up and defense of what he calls the Cartesian–Kantian "as if" wager – the assumption on the part of writers and readers alike that barren narcissism must be kept at bay by a sturdy although unprovable claim to the significance of the work. In other words, we should act in our judgments of fiction as if it were at least potentially a bearer of truth.

Only experimental metafictionists can satisfy contemporary critical schools of literary theory and cultural studies, with their radically skeptical bias and denial of ethical possibilities. Very few theorists are in fact interested readers of fiction, however, with the result that Steiner's "as if" wager appears to open the door once again for writers whose sense of fiction's luminous (or Leavisite) value is central. In the light of this sort of potentiality, I wish to discuss Russelll Hoban as a dramatic example of a novelist for whom character and plot are almost as secondary as they are for the metafictionalists, but who uses radical experimentalism and textual self-consciousness as tools to express both ideology and belief in a way that theorists must consider both old-fashioned and compromising.

Russelll Hoban writes from a strange area, and at every turn has had his reputation unintentionally diminished by two factors. First, his route has been unconventional: like Michel Tournier in France, he made his original impact on the world of fiction as an uncommonly successful writer of children's books, a point which unjustly impeded his subsequent acceptance as a serious broad-ranging fictionist. He thinks, like Tournier, that children's fiction can and should be connected to the deepest levels of thought, with the result that his recent style in children's books is perhaps too deeply aligned to the patterns of his adult books, with their subconscious subverbal levels. But Hoban has written dozens of effective and popular children's tales, including the classic *The Mouse and his Child* (which also qualifies as his first full-length novel), and the various adventures of Frances the badger among others; he also still occasionally throws out another no doubt necessary money-making charmer such as the comic quasi-science fiction, *They Came from Aargh!*, in which three space blokes come to earth to eat cheese omelettes and chocolate cake prepared by a mummosaurus.

The second, and more difficult, fact is that Hoban is an American, born in Pennsylvania in 1925, who has lived in Britain since 1969 and has, paradoxically and against all odds, become a specifically English novelist. In a study like this one, where nationality can be seen to have much to do with the trends, forms, and reputations of the writers in various contexts and countries, Hoban is in an outsider's position. American critics have largely ignored him; American readers see his frame of reference and vocabulary as irreversibly English, and although both *Riddley Walker* and *Pilgermann* were reviewed in appropriately fashionable American journals like *Time, The New York Times*, etc., Hoban is not anything like the visible writer in the United States that he is in Britain. Even in Britain there is trouble, for his indomitable reputation as a writer of children's books, and the near submersion of theoretical problems in his fiction under a religious apprehension of the world, has caused many of his readers - particularly those stressing *The Mouse and His Child* and *Riddley Walker* - to identify him somewhere on the lines of C.S. Lewis or J.R.R. Tolkien. Just as Lewis had trouble with his audience when he changed his style and enlarged his dimensions in his late book, *Till We Have Faces* (1956), so Hoban has not yet received the place he deserves within a serious account of fiction in Britain and the United States in our time.

To begin with, it should be obvious to the reader of any of Hoban's six (to date) "adult" novels, published between 1973 and 1987, that he has much more in common with an experimental–metaphysical writer like the early Samuel Beckett than with the Christian polemics of C.S. Lewis. He does, however, write with a peculiar, complicated generosity of reference that connects him with an easy directness to the fantastic, fabulous, and mythic. At the same time, his work is clearly akin to the philosophical problems intrinsic to the epistemology and ontology of Beckett and many other contemporary writers, like Italo Calvino, for example, whose cerebral and theoretical play is always more primary and less spiritually felt than Hoban's. Moreover, abstractionist though he is, Hoban is able to set a novel ironically but comfortably against his own sort of practical experience, and there is a homeliness in his work that his *semblables* lack.

Thus Neaera H., for example, one of the characters of *Turtle Diary* (1975), is, as Hoban was when he first arrived in London, an illustrator and writer of children's books. She exists in a context where both the finding of subjects and writing itself are seen as an ordinary job, subservient to a larger ironic rhythm of the intransigent difficulty of fitting post-industrial life within the now almost alien continuities of nature. Hoban has, moreover, never lost the sudden apprehension of the comic or the extended joys of verbal trickery that characterize the best of children's fiction and make it such a difficult genre to write well. This retention can also have its negative side, and on occasion, particularly in *Kleinzeit* (1974), *Pilgermann* (1983), and *The Medusa Frequency* (1987), an overly robust verbal play can vitiate the otherwise exemplary discipline of style and wit that Hoban frequently demonstrates.

Inevitably, Hoban's novels have progressively become more complex in both texture and impact. Although the dominant themes were present in the first fabulist novel, *The Lion of Boaz-Jachin and Jachin-Boaz* (1973), the next one, *Kleinzeit* with its setting in a hospital, in barren city rooms, and in the London Underground, expands and resonates with patterns reminiscent of Samuel Beckett's *Murphy* or even to a degree Iris Murdoch's *Under the Net* or Joseph Heller's *Catch-22*. A sketchily traced character, Kleinzeit contrasts inhuman post-industrial bleakness with comically personal run-ins with a once lovely but now ironically experienced and barely available past. This lost past is symbolized by specific objects or evocations – yellow paper demanding words, a Glockenspiel, the harmonic but tragic myth of Orpheus and Eurydice, God himself. The dichotomy between indifferent machines and once resonant cultural objects is well maintained, and held in careful relationship to the book's dominant subject.

Hoban's subject in *Kleinzeit* and throughout his work is the source and questionable power of the Word in all its ambiguity within the comic play of fiction. The symbolic action is metaphoric, abstract, and aesthetically based from the outset, when the anti-realist protagonist Kleinzeit, eternally a small-timer as his name indicates, is hospitalized for an incurable pain "along the hypotenuse from A to B." The palpably metaphoric reality–unreality of such a pain is combined with the personified presence of Death. In *Kleinzeit*, real and unreal are held in a magic circle where the personified image of Hospital and its power over disease and death artificially construct a background for the metaphysical anxiety of the writer who is also the experiencer, the quester, and the doomed.

Like all interpreters, including those who are or will be writers, Kleinzeit wants not only to learn the secret of the tyranny of paper and its necessary junction with the word, but also to command and control the very problem of interpretation itself. In the symbolic logic of the novel, the word keeps slipping theologically toward the Word, largely as a result of a mystically textual self-consciousness that is forced on Kleinzeit by the demands of blank yellow sheets of paper that are constantly thrust at him. As he begins to interpret himself as a creator, he longs to make a significant contribution, which he knows can come only by making something out of the apparently immutable disjunctions of the world as he perceives them. Technology, fiction, and the quasi-divine material that once had mythic status should therefore serve as a secure key to the secrets of life and its agent, literature.

During his quest for coherence, Kleinzeit desperately questions an absurdly suspect source, the personified Hospital (every object is rendered animate and given personhood in this novel) about the harmonic myth of Orpheus and Eurydice. This myth is central here as a key to comprehension, and has grown in Hoban's writing until extensions of it became the basis for his new novel, *The Medusa Frequency*. Kleinzeit certainly does not receive orthodoxy in response (Hoban's heroes never do), but the answer is nevertheless far from technologically slick. Hospital's partly flippant statement – one that Hoban obviously sees as having serious truth-claims – is that Eurydice in the Underworld can be read or interpreted as representing "the inside of things, the place under the places." Orpheus's need to live actively and progressively in the present world of time is in deep contrast to Eurydice's opposite anti-time complementarity:

> Orpheus cannot be content at the inside of things, at the place under the places, said Hospital. His harmony has brought him to the stillness and the calm at the centre and he cannot abide it. Nirvana is not his cup of tea. He wants to get back outside, wants that action with the rocks and trees again, wants to be seen with Eurydice at posh restaurants and all that. Naturally he loses her. She can't go outside any more than he can stay inside.

So Eurydice remains in and is symbolic of "the place under the places," while Orpheus's absolute need to live in the present of the world, to be fully human, takes him rapidly and perpetually to death – as Hospital says, "they tear him apart, and there's the head going down the river again, heading for Lesbos."

This turning of the myth yields a strong contemporary image of the Orphic artist and, by the direct and generous association Hoban automatically makes, of mankind in general living in a death-oriented present (which is seen as a place) on the outside of some profoundly beloved but impossible inside space. This apprehension is accompanied by an equally strong statement that puts all fictions and myths in a properly puzzling area of indeterminacy: "What does it all mean? said Kleinzeit. How can there be meaning? said Hospital. Meaning is a limit. There are no limits."

Kleinzeit's frightened and sentimental longing for limits and hence for closure is metaphysical. He wants a world where meaning is narratable and hence either clearly outlined within the fiction, or subsequently explainable through hermeneutic help from an authority. His desire can thus be extended to audience reception of literary texts, where it is symptomatic of that audience's lingering failure to accept the in-built despairs and illimitation that high Modernism in all its forms attempted to deliver. Now, in the late twentieth century, Modernism has long been intellectually and artistically grasped, and Postmodern thinkers decades ago replaced the epistemological processes of Modernism. Nevertheless many readers, and any Kleinzeit or small-timer whose longings for comfortable texts remain great and who unpretentiously wishes to write or read or just think about the problems of interpretation, have become uncomprehending observers for whom the idea that "there are no limits" remains alien and frighteningly unacceptable. A self-consciously symptomatic scene like this one demonstrates again how persistently many reader–interpreters reject Modern and Postmodern hermeneutic instability. It also shows the conflict between the almost *de rigueur* preoccupations inherent in most contemporary fiction and the recalcitrant stubbornness of a general reading public that longs incurably for the meaning-oriented consolations of older forms of writing, interpretation, and belief.

It is important to note, however, that the question posed to Hospital as authority and the answer Hospital declines to give refer as strongly to a metaphysically religious world as they do to a literary construct, and in this respect this moment in the text of *Kleinzeit* is representative of all Hoban's work. Seriously and riskily, Hoban typically enters a territory considered defunct or outrageous by most other writers whose literary–theoretical aims are as extensive as his. But in a primary way he is a writer demonstrating major theoretical positions, no matter how contradictory or confusing his stance might appear. On the one hand, his sense of the priority and limited signification of the word can align him to post-structuralist thought, and his insistence on the absolute, oblique deconstructibility of any construct makes him seem ultimately Derridean; on the other hand, the best way of reading his fiction from a theoretician's point of view is probably by exploiting a semantic line of consciousness that goes from Søren Kierkegaard to René Girard and Paul Ricoeur.

Without belaboring Hoban's potential ideological–fictional alliances, let me simply say that reading his fictions ineluctably awakens the reader's sense of contemporary literary theory in a way achieved by only a handful of Postmodernist fictionists such as Alain Robbe-Grillet, Umberto Eco, Italo Calvino, John Barth and John Fowles. Hoban is more difficult to categorize than any of these because his religious apprehension is as strong as his literary intention – which occurred without his studying the theorists. In other words, Hoban's approach is primarily to the spiritual world, and like Saul Bellow, he employs fiction with all its literary tools and anxieties as a primary means of working toward theological knowledge; the opposite is equally true for him, in that the paraphernalia of the spiritual past of the Jews and their offshoots – Christianity and Islam – can be read as mere devices to deepen the possibilities of fiction as a primary *literary* experience which hungrily uses everything in its ken.

Obsessed by form as most Postmodernist writers are, Hoban is unique in placing it and the human experience it serves spatially in a metaphorically extended place that is called time. But time as such for him is not significantly sequential or in other ways connected to temporal theories about the flow of form, and in this respect Hoban shows his separation from the total time-orientation of Modernism and indeed of fiction in general, as Paul Ricoeur has described it in *Time and Narrative* (1985). Hoban asserts that in his novels it is always the thing-oriented shape of a particular place that sets the idea spinning. In the acknowledgments in *Pilgermann*, he states his case most directly:

> *Riddley Walker* left me in a place where there was further action pending and this further action was waiting for the element that would precipitate it into the time and place of its own story. . . .
>
> The look of the stars burning and flickering over Montfort, those three stars between the Virgin and the Lion with their upward swing like the curve of a scythe, the stare into the darkness, the hooded eagleness of the stronghold high over the gorge, the paling into dawn of its gathered flaunt and power precipitated Pilgermann into his time and place and me into a place I hadn't even known was there.

From his early novel, *The Lion of Boaz-Jachin and Jachin-Boaz*, Hoban consistently shows that the first human breakthrough of his heroes must be the knowledge that the space any person inhabits is subjectively identical to time, but that time as spatial is neither linear nor circular: "Jachin-Boaz, naked in the dark, touched the map. 'There is only one place,' he said, 'that place is time, and that time is now. There is no other place.' " This recognition means that the clear, abstract, interpretative exploration of geographical space illustrated by the maps sold and made by Jachin-Boaz must also be replaced. The novel labors to illustrate that the primary external signposts that mark our whereabouts must give way to an intensive *haecceitas*, or intensely experienced thingness of the present world, as it touches all the powerful, substantial, often mystical structures of the restlessly perceiving mind.

And hence, if I read Hoban accurately enough, the plot flows. The genesis of *The Lion of Boaz-Jachin and Jachin-Boaz* is a particular place, King Ashurbanipal's North Palace with its lion friezes, now reconstructed in the British Museum. A middle-aged character, Jachin-Boaz, lives in a time period when lions are extinct and like dinosaurs remembered only through arts and science. Jachin-Boaz begins his adventures in the Middle East with his map shop, his son, and a specially drawn, exhaustive map he has made for that son. In this partial allegory of fathers and sons, the son rejects the tyranny of the map which is also the image of a tidy voyage through the highly plotted lifetime his father intends for him. He prefers an obscure quest for the surely irredeemable time when (which is equivalent to the place where) lions, long gone in Hoban's oddly mythical fictional construct, can be found, if only by the determined and magical imagination. After the son's pointed rebellion, the congeries of places, through plot time, moves the errant father and eventually the son too to a vaguely evoked London. Here the hero's mind utterly dislocates the historical time of his experienced present, and by collapsing time he creates a miracle. By intensive mental concentration on the ancient obsolete idea of a lion, remembered only through iconographical images, the middle-aged Jachin-Boaz improbably incarnates and experiences an apparent and realistically dangerous creature in the streets of London. This act magically demonstrates the individual mind's opening up of its own creative possibilities through idealist energy. The hero's peculiar ability to create this lion as an evidently real creature with appetite and all too damaging claws is not, however, his own singular achievement. Jachin-Boaz's son, whose name, Boaz-Jachin, indicates a circular and reciprocal relationship with him, is the motive force behind the quest, which originates in an archetypal father–son failure of understanding and the lion-like rage that accompanies it. The son rejects a future of semiotic mapmaking and signposting, demanding a heroic past in an unknowable, unseekable form: in short, he demands a place where the (in the fiction) now extinct lion species exists. This place is unmappable because its time is, according to reason or history, lost, but its memory remains and its reality for those who believe in either memory or eternity is therefore, perhaps, and perhaps madly, possible. As the father–hero gradually learns:

> Everything that is found is lost again, he thought for the first time. And yet nothing that is found is lost again. What is a map? There is only one place, and that place is time. I am in the time where a lion has been found.

The genesis of the lion in the novel can be seen as a psychiatric aberration, and indeed both Jachin-Boaz and his lover Gretel spend some time in a mental hospital as a result of his visionary–real encounters with this impossible, extinct creature stirred into existence by the *folie-à-deux* relationship between father and son. For it is significant to note that each man's mind is bounded by his own narrow destiny until set directly and indirectly into motion by the other. Jachin-Boaz has lived well enough although impotently with his middle-aged wife, resenting the narrow mapshop life imposed on him by his terror and failure in the face of the scientific career his own father had willed for him. Having assumed that his cowardly map-making life-choice will be repeated by his son, he is completely disoriented by a rebellion parallel to his own rejection of his father's plans for him. The further idea that a human mind may desire the lost past and be transformed by it sets him and later his son on an uncharted road with no end in sight.

Equally important in the subjective idealist or even schizophrenic world of this novel is the fact that the observation and production of purely visual images constitute a magical force that affects the lives of both men and forces them to action. In Hoban's world things themselves have a power-laden presence that lies waiting for human perception to co-operate with them. Thus the rebellious son, Boaz-Jachin, sets the story in motion when, at the moment of denial of his father, his eye by the sheerest chance picks out a lion-shaped iron doorstop in the shop; as a next step he compulsively contemplates the stone lion reliefs in the great hall of Ashurbanipal's palace not far from his town, which for him is the only reliable museum repository for the lion lore of a distant past.

Particularly attracted to one stone image of a lion stuck with arrows biting the wheel of the king's chariot that inexorably pulls it up to the king's spear and death, Boaz-Jachin recognizes the icon as a complete symbol for the wheel of life, death, destiny. The lion is the image of all creatures' potential bravery in the face of pain, despair, and death; the king is the untouched agent of mortal cruelty. The lion's courage in biting the wheel is splendid but fatal, bravely touching but futile. Boaz-Jachin next draws a series of sketches in which he makes time run backward by depicting a complete undoing of the imminent death of the lion: in five large consecutive redrawings of the scene, he gradually reaches the desired state of things: " 'The second spear, the last weapon, the spear of the king, lies under our feet,' said Boaz-Jachin. 'We rise up on the turning wheel, alive and strong, undying. There is nothing between us and the king.' "

As the fiction switches back and forth in omniscient third-person narration, describing the actions and reporting the words of father and son, it becomes clear that there is a specific magical connection between the power of mental projection in the father and the salvational lion drawings of the son. Meanwhile, like the lion in the stone relief, the father Jachin-Boaz is being drawn further and further up the wheel toward the moment when he will inevitably be killed: the destroyer – in this case the subjectively projected lion rather than a king – will not simply rake his arm with its claws, but claim him. No impassioned poetic human song addressed to this dream-lion by Jachin-Boaz can touch its absoluteness as it tracks its creator even in the mental hospital, where only the maddest and most schizoid of the patients can see it stalking the grounds and biding its time. In that hospital, one patient explains why not everyone can see the lion specter:

"But you've got to expect that sort of thing here. After all, why have they put us in the fun house? The straight people agree that some things are not allowed to be possible, and they govern their perceptions accordingly. Very strong, the straight people. We're not so strong as they. Things not allowed to be possible jump on us, beasts and demons, because we don't know how to keep them out.

"Others here can see my faces and they can see your lion, even though you may want to hug it to yourself like a teddy bear. If your lion weren't possible you'd be happy to share the impossibility. But people get very possessive about possibilities, even dangerous ones. Victims become proprietors. You may have to grow up a little. Perhaps you'll even have to let go of your lion one day."

Partly because of his own courage and acceptance of inevitable death, partly because of the unkilling of the lion depicted in his son's drawings, Jachin-Boaz, newly reunited with Boaz-Jachin on the embankment of the Thames, leaps forward into the jaws of the raging lion, thus bravely and metaphorically biting the wheel as the imaged lion had done in the stone relief centuries ago. Father and son find themselves not destroyed, but laughing wildly in each other's arms, their estrangement and death both removed from them, and the lion gone. As the madman had predicted, the terrifying subjective image is obliterated, given up by the newly matured mind. The two heroes, having learned their lessons in this surprisingly didactic novel, prepare to go forward into the indeterminate vitality of their de-mapped world.

The Lion of Boaz-Jachin and Jachin-Boaz is the most cheerful novel in Hoban's "adult" *oeuvre*, and is obviously redemptive in intention. In the next novel, *Kleinzeit*, the ending is conventional enough, with Kleinzeit temporarily avoiding death and heading off with his charming nurse into a shared future in accordance with the tradition of comic closure. But the place called time is more haunting here, and the presence of a jovial but muddled God can effect no large miracles and guarantees very little. In the meantime major meta-physical and ontological issues are raised, making the ending seriously parodic of convention in a way that cancels out any frivolous response to the comedy of an all's-well-that-ends-well affair:

> Not to worry, said God. You'll have luck. You're lucky.
> Do you mean that, said Sister. Am I really? It hasn't always seemed that way to me.
> Well of course it never does, said God. I don't say you're *especially* lucky. Just a good ordinary everyday sort of luck. That's as much as I've got myself, and I don't know anyone who's got more. Universe, History, Eternity, anybody you talk to these days, we're all in the same boat.

And of course the third novel, *Turtle Diary*, juxtaposes death – the suicide of one minor character and the corpse of an alley cat – with a newly found but complete self-reliance in its two major protagonists. *Turtle Diary*, recently made into a film with a bleak screenplay by Harold Pinter, is a subtle and touching book – an edifying read, but not as important as Hoban's other fiction. Nowhere in these three novels, however, can the reader find full preparation for *Riddley Walker*, the novel that built Hoban's reputation, and the one paired in his mind with *Pilgermann*.

*

"Our woal life is a idear we dint think of nor we dont know what it is. What a way to live."

Pairing *Riddley Walker* with *Pilgermann* has many justifications, not the least being the setting of *Riddley Walker* in a far distant post-nuclear-holocaust future, and *Pilgermann* in the far past, in the last few years of the eleventh Christian century when Pope Urban II had titillated the imagination of Europe by exhorting men to formulate the First Crusade. Both these (quasi-) historical periods are popular in the fiction of Modern and contemporary writers: Aldous Huxley's *Brave New World* and George Orwell's *1984* are almost obscured by the significant achievements of recent utopian and anti-utopian science fiction as a genre (see, as good examples, Doris Lessing's *Canopus in Argos* series, the works of Stanislaw Lem, or Denis Johnson's *Fiskadoro*); and several contemporary writers like Umberto Eco, Stanley Elkin, and John Fuller, to name only a few, have set some of their highly experimental fiction in the Middle Ages, the period increasingly seen as Postmodern mankind's starting point. Neither historical futuristic conjecture nor past reconstruction, however, is the major issue in Hoban's *Riddley Walker* and *Pilgermann*, riveting though each setting is. In both cases an ontologically real place is constructed by the narrator, and this necessity creates an enquiry into the nature and structure of narrative itself, as well as its relation to its sources.

The resulting stress on the nature of the narrating persona makes the two complementary novels pertinent to the central questions of narratology itself. But unlike Calvino or Fowles, Hoban handles the subject without palpable reference to the narratological or semiotic theories currently dominant in discussions of fiction. His narrators' self-consciousness is not pointedly subtended by contemporary theories and is entirely self-referential within the text; as a result of this, both novels are free to creep into the broad, suspect areas of metaphysics and belief so unpopular in an adamantly cerebral milieu. For example, at the end of the first chapter of *Pilgermann*, the disembodied narrator who survives only as consciousness unbounded by time, suddenly sounds like Saul Bellow's Artur Sammler at the end of *Mr Sammler's Planet* praying forth a definition of man's moral contract. Here is Pilgermann's version of it as he surveys history from Abraham to his obscure present:

> A covenant with God is made from between the pieces of oneself; it's the only place where a covenant can happen, no covenant is possible until one has divided the heifer, the she-goat, the ram of oneself.... If you measure with what is called time it's a long way from here back to Abram's pieces.... I am only the waves and particles of such as I was but I have a covenant with the Lord, the terms of it are simple: everything is required of me, for ever.

Kleinzeit had in a small way understood this absolute covenant as he tried to overcome pain and the fear of death, but Pilgermann is historically and epistemologically more sophisticated. Riddley Walker on the other hand lives in an anti-civilization that has, to quote Nabokov's sad *émigré* Pnin, "nofing left, nofing, nofing!" As poor Riddley puts it when he and Lissener stand before the ruins of the giant computers at Fork Stoan (Folkestone), "O what we ben! And what we come to!" He must deduce whatever covenant he might make from a few barren and ill-understood texts that require constant reinterpretation in an unstable world – not as entirely unlike our own as most of us would like to think – where hermeneutical exercises fail to enlighten, and generally yield a morass of foolish errors and dangerous arrogance.

Without in any way denigrating the impact and success of the imagined "historical" world of *Riddley Walker*, the reader must first take on a hermeneutical task – one that necessarily concentrates on the constant pressure of narrative experiments and possibilities this novel struggles with. More interesting than just a sympathetically imagined, primitive, and engaging character from the well-worn science fiction theme of the horrible residues of nuclear war, Riddley Walker's very name images his double function: the narrator as riddler, and the Beckettian necessity to keep going, to keep walking the road, through the space Hoban calls time. Inevitably, given Hoban's sensibility, language flounders in its inadequacy to express its own centrality. As the text toils to present its working materials – i.e. the ideas it tries to express – the reader joins Riddley in the task of putting together a coherent tale. Lissener, a major secondary narrator and maker of the fiction, describes the endless job that he, his fellow Eusa people, Riddley, and the reader must share:

> He said, "No when I talk in a fit or what Im saying now that dont mean nothing thats jus only the outers of it. It never comes the woal thing realy without the all of us gethering. Weare just like scattert peaces of a broakin pot them peaces wont hol water without theyre gethert nexy and glewt ferm in the shape of holding dont you see. I cant make the shape of holding oansome."

It is surely not coincidence, given Hoban's inclination toward religious reference, that this appears to evoke the Hebrew idea of the Shekinah; the sign of the presence of the one unitive God is frequently imaged as a pot, breakable but held together by that Shekinah. Riddley's is a world abandoned by the Shekinah, where only shards remain, and Lissener knows that both he and Riddley, indeed all who can understand the task at all, are under orders to put things together in an act that is both self-reliant and infinitely shared by all human sensibilities accessible from both the present and the past. As Lissener puts it within the private semiotic code of the novel:

> "I know I soun like Im trying to little you down but that aint what Im doing Im trying to bring on that seed of the red in you Im trying to strong it on Im trying to rise your hump. Dyou lissen me? Im trying to get you to be your oan black dog and your oan Ardship . . . . Becaws you wont all ways have me wil you."

Breaking this code is Riddley's undertaking as narrator and quester, and indirectly it is also ours as readers. Later in the narrative Riddley begins to understand the nature of Lissener's instruction, but within his growing comprehension there are serious gaps and broken intuitive distortions. Meanwhile, Lissener, a teaching character who has been trying to untie the knots of meaning, joins the Eusa people in Fork Stoan where, indulging in debased symposiums (some poasyum) with these malformed remnants of the computer élite (Puter Leat) from the far past, he is lost to communication and killed. As a result Riddley Walker is again left with only a few shards and pieces of the central knowledge Lissener in his limited way could still manage to tune into.

In creating a world utterly separated from ours and by coding or even encrypting its meaning, Hoban allows himself formidable access to ways of exploring the various geneses of fiction. From beginning to end of its experimental procedure, *Riddley Walker* questions the major issues of reality and knowledge within any civilization (text) as it gropes toward expression and/or meaning. In the first place, there is, of course, the problem of language. One might argue that *Riddley Walker* is part of a long line of novels heavily dependent on dialect, beginning in the nineteenth century (one thinks of Sir Walter Scott, Mark Twain, George MacDonald, even, alas, George Eliot) and continuing, in my opinion, for much too long. It is more accurate, however, to place it in another category – the creation of an absolutely consistent literary language ambitiously aimed at the projection of a secondary world, in the style of Edmund Spenser's *The Faerie Queene*. Hoban's verbal forms, although difficult at first, are much more readily comprehensible than the obscure "elven" linguistic experiments of J.R.R. Tolkien or the work of the Welsh poet David Jones in our century. Of the various languages spawned by recent science fiction, only the limited linguistic experiments of Denis Johnson in *Fiskadoro* are comparable. Certainly there is no sort of fairy world in *Riddley Walker*, where the language is simply the inevitably corrupt residue of a once coherent and expressive English, in a world where the books have been lost, the spelling destroyed, the words bastardized, and the concepts the words once adequately expressed endlessly muddled.

The only document remaining from the period before the leveling nuclear holocaust is, by the casual operations of chance, a brief pamphlet entitled *The Legend of St Eustace*. This gives, in cathedral-hand-out prose, an unimaginative description of the thing-oriented source of Hoban's novel – Dr E.W. Tristram's reconstruction of the fifteenth-century wall painting of the legend of St Eustace in Canterbury Cathedral. From this depressingly ordinary pamphlet has sprung the only text to be written after the nuclear holocaust, aside from Riddley's current ambitious project in trying to spell out "what the idear of us myt be." The Eustace-derived "sacred" scripture is called the *Eusa Story*, a divine text with thirty-three verses (old systems of numerology that enthrone long-forgotten Christian symbolism like the magic of the Trinity or Christ's age at the crucifixion are heeded in this superstitious society). As a work of biblical density and importance, it has been memorized and given catechismal and exegetical expansion, as has the minor cathedral pamphlet. These exegeses are given by the authoritarian character, Goodparley, and others of what must finally be called the priesthood of this dismal new and necessary world, a world that in almost 2,500 years has progressed nowhere compared to the twenty Christian centuries that preceded it.

Starting from total desolation, this society has been able to keep only bits and pieces of the past, a sort of florilegium, in which vague phrases from the once extensive and sophisticated technological sciences survive in debased ways. These are combined in primitive form with various confused readings of the St Eustace legend, with the result that religion and science mingle perfectly in a unity C.P. Snow and other exponents of the two cultures could never have imagined. Thus the image of the crucified Christ ("the Littl Shynin Man") that appeared to that hunter saint between the horns of a stag becomes hopelessly and comically confused with the splitting of the atom ("the Littl Man the Addom"). The resultant tales all incorporate two characters, one called Eusa who is obviously a version of Eustace as representative of religion, the other, looking like a medieval devil, is known as Mr Clevver, or Mr On the Levvil, or Drop John, the man on the back, the equivalent of scientific achievement.

This fictional world does not, however, separate the idea of a god from the idea of science, for Eusa is also a scientist and is reputed to have been ambiguously responsible for the dropping of the bombs. The initial source of the destructive bombing lies in a muddled way in various coalescences of the tale and of the two principal characters, Eusa and Mr Clevver, who enact it in its many fictional versions. But the texts cannot be unraveled or the truth known; this is a world where Riddley can at maximum learn the insoluble paradox that "the Spirit of God," a now incomprehensible term from *The Legend of St Eustace*, is both the "chemistry and fizzics and all its what the 1 Big 1 come out of," and some magical power at Cambry (Canterbury) that remains on the road with him. For him as tale-teller, and hence for the reader, there is no way toward a reliable single epistemological truth. The many accessible and bewilderingly contradictory fictions may help, but their ancient and present versions are as obscure as their interpretation. As the "tel woman," Lorna Elswint, puts it, "You hear diffrent things in all them way back storys but it dont make no diffrents. Mostly they aint strait storys any how. What they are is diffrent ways of telling what happent."

Hoban could have made this an easier book by dismissing "what happent" as straightforward nuclear destruction, but his major point has to do with verbal gnosis. Thus the human mind seizes on oral formulas, versions, or connexions of disparate tales, and persistent symbols become compounded means of trying to reconstruct the world and its history into unity. The fact that either the apparently good Eusa or the evil Mr Clevver might have been the primary guilty intelligence behind the bombing is confusing. But it is no more so than the fact that the dogpacks (mankillers of a most terrifying sort) can become not only "frendy" to Riddley but major magical factors in his slow retrieval of the necessary and mystical direction of the world.

When the "Eusa Story" describes the splitting of the atom as a Pandora's box instituting the "Master Chaynjis" of the two and the one, there is no doubt that a computer binary system is being evoked as surely as is the theological problem of the duality and the unity of the universe. It is also clear that the entire natural universe speaks to any "Lissener," so that Riddley or any acute person can actually take on a prophetic poetic mantle and create a unique fiction under the inspiration of the "Power" at Cambry. Thus, in spontaneously creating a highly imaginative parable about stones, Riddley becomes a spokesman and enactor of Hoban's theory of fictional inspiration: "This nex what Im writing down it aint no story tol to me nor it aint no dream. Its just some thing come in to my head wylst I ben on me knees there in that stoan wood in the woom of her that has her woom in Cambry. So I'm writing it down here."

In order to make a whole account of his civilization, Riddley as riddler and story-teller has to gather together the systems of telling that existed in the past, as well as those created or continuing in the present. His world is animistic and determined, and from the first combination of significant events – the death of the boar, the death of his father, the sacrificial suicide of an old dog on Riddley's spear, the stillborn child – to his strange escape and adoption by the black dog, leader of the Bernt Arse pack, there is no doubt that he has been singled out by something like the spirit of the universe for a special if occluded task. Humbly ignorant but constantly thoughtful, Riddley tries to read the signs presented to him, and in setting them before the reader, he makes us all sharers in an often comic, often desperate search for coherence.

His civilization, if such a term can be used, is one in which oral formulas are forced to function to the near exclusion of written ones, and indeed the culture educates its young exclusively in terms of ancient verse games whose meaning is unknown. The moment the character Lissener appears, it is made obvious that the verses chanted by the children have encrypted meaning, and Riddley, like the reader, is excited at the chance of working out the hidden material. Moreover, gnostic vibrations continue to extend from all Riddley's experience, most persistently from the puppet shows that are given by Goodparley and Orfing. These shows originate both from the political power center of "the Ram" (an island separated from the inland and obviously named after Ramsgate in this post-Kentish fantasy), and from some quasi-divine force reflected in the Eusa–Eustace story.

The performances begin with a "zanting," an oral formulaic chanting by the audience, and then are performed through spontaneous inspiration (it is pointedly stated several times that each show is new and different, reflecting not the whimsy of the puppeteer but of Eusa himself). The first performance in the novel is an allegorical enactment of Eusa's original construction of computers – memory banks formed to create good times for all people. In an archetypal display, Mr Clevver, obviously by his appearance an updating of the medieval devil, takes over the computer for the power of evil and makes it into an agent of bombs and death. As a way of telling what happened in the "Time befor Time," this is a skillfully constructed show starring Eusa as a benign and mystical god, in spite of the contradictory doctrine that he is also supposed to have made the 1 Big 1 and hence is directly responsible for the end of the former civilization.

But the singular power of the Eusa shows, with their quasi-divine, quasi-political force, is providentially broken by Riddley's magical finding, in the diggings at Widders Dump, of a blackened old hand puppet of the apparently immortal rascal, Punch. Goodparley, the puppeteer and master of whatever pathetic bits of history are known, then tells Riddley of an ancient puppet show starring this comic villain and his Pooty (Judy). Unlike the putative spontaneity of the Eusa performances, this show had its own determinate forms, so that no attempt to produce a drama with these characters can have other than set predetermined action. For Riddley, Punch immediately represents an expansion of possibility within the area of showing or enactment: because the Punch and Judy show exists, the Eusa shows are not the only symbolic showings. Once again the dominant idea of this book, that one will always become two, and vice versa, is enacted. *Riddley Walker* ends with its hero on the road, a writer and puppeteer, feeling himself to be metaphorically humped like the devil, like Punch, like Eusa who was made crooked after the bad times, with the creativity of Drop John, who represents the ultimate unity of all these characters, on his back continuing to seek, to tell, and never to know the truth.

The processes by which Riddley, led by strange and often magical forces, gradually and partially unravels the signs and signals that the universe lays in his hands, demonstrate Hoban's version of human creativity and its sources. Riddley is not entirely speaking for himself when he says, "Theres all ways a connexion aint there," nor is Lissener when he states, "you cant make up nothing in your head no moren you can make up what you see. You know what I mean may be what you see aint all ways there so you cud reach out and touch it but its there some kynd of way and it come from some where." At its most remote, this idea of creativity has mystical connotations of the subconscious, indicated by the "tel woman" Lorna Elswint's description of "some thing in us it dont have no name. . . . Its some kynd of thing it aint us but yet its in us. Its looking out thru our eye hoals . . . . Its afeart of being beartht." This thing is in a sense Riddley's inspiration: it represents the subconscious, and is also an updating of the idea of the Muse as well as the Spirit behind the Word.

However the inspiration works, the motivating point in the novel is the creation of a new anti-existential, anti-solipsistic narrating self. Riddley begins by being flummoxed and puzzled by the passive verbs in his life – by his being apparently chosen to kill the boar, the old dog, perhaps even his father, by his having had his life spared and then having been selected by the black dog leader of the pack. He knows that his finding of the ancient Punch puppet is not gratuitous, and he is even more impressed by the curious coalescence of already encountered symbols during his discovery of the real center of power at Canterbury. Suddenly a talismanic idea central to all the songs and "zantings" of his world, the wood in the heart of the stone, is dazzlingly imaged for him by the underground Gothic arches in the vaults of the ruins of the cathedral. He sees these arches as the shaping of "trees" in aesthetic proportions by human hands that understood the power of stone.

This insight is followed quickly by his being cunningly led to the "hidey-hoal" where he finds a wooden face with tendrils of leaves growing from its mouth. Its resemblance to the image of Eustace's original stag antlers and to Goodparley's face are all brought together in a marvelous display of the unity at the heart of all things. This *objet trouvé*, passed on to him magically by the knowledge of the black dog pack leader from the old pre-destruction days, miraculously actualizes a face he had once pictured to himself and named

"Greanvine." The indication is that his imagination is not his own, but part of a vast racial unconscious of the sort celebrated by C.G. Jung. Although Riddley has been able to compose his fanciful little fictional essay entitled "Stoan," he now realizes that his private creative power comes from a greater source, and that all the various egoistic powers fought for by such characters as Granser and Goodparley are chimerical and false.

This insight significantly precedes a circular re-enactment of history, as the first primitive steps in this lateborn society are once again taken toward the production of gunpowder. The necessary chemical combination of saltpeter, charcoal, and the much sought after yellow stones, sulphur, have mythical proportions through the plot's progress, but in a groping, inconclusive way. The discovery of all the ingredients of this primitive formula (primitive, that is, from the point of view of the technology of thorough warfare – the Eusa people are out for more advanced stuff) begins another phase of the Master Chaynjis, all of which must be danced or played out as inevitable steps toward recreating the first Pandoresque act of splitting the atom. For Riddley, however, the new road toward destructive warfare is a matter of indifference, knowing as he now does that spiritual knowledge also awaits, that "the worl is ful of things waiting to happen. . . . You put your self on any road and some thing wil show its self to you. Wanting to happen. Waiting to happen. You myt say, 'I dont want to know.' But 1ce its showt its self to you you *wil* know wont you. You cant not know no more."

Shortly after his major re-education by Lissener, Riddley learns that as a self he is neither singular nor special, although apparently chosen as a prophet and actor for his people. Although he begins his cogitations as a unique and "oansom" person, he quickly loses this habit of lonely thought and recognizes his connexions with everything present and past:

> Swaller me up or spit me out I dint care I dint have no 1 on my back only my self. Only my self! Looking at them words going down on this paper right this minim I know there aint no such thing there aint no only my self you all ways have every 1 and every thing on your back. Them as stood and them as run time back way back long long time they had me on ther back if they knowit or if they dint. I had Lissener on my back plus a woal lot moren him I cudnt even say what all it wer and mor and mor I wer afeart it wer coming to something I wernt going to be hevvy a nuff for.

Riddley's experience of the center of power at Canterbury when the dogs danced and he saw into the heart of things makes him realize that he is part of a thinking universal sensibility: "If you dont think then some thing else wil think your thots theywl get thunk any how." As a chosen transmitter, he has been shown special things, and the necessary conclusion has been his knowledge that:

> THE ONLYES POWER IS NO POWER. Well now I sust that wernt qwite it. It aint that its *no* Power. Its the not sturgling for Power thats where the Power is. Its

176

in jus letting your self be where it is. Its tuning in to the worl its leaving your self behynt and letting your self be where it says in *Eusa 5*: ... in tu the hart uv the stoan hart uv the dans. Evere thing blippin & bleapin & movin in the shiftin uv thay Nos. Sum tyms bytin sum tyms bit.

This anti-solipsistic sense of an impersonal power that guides the world is subtly bolstered throughout the novel by an even more highly deterministic demonstration of compulsive narrative power. In his first interpretative "connexion" after a zany trinitarian initiation rite, Riddley spontaneously blurts out what Lorna describes as a "trants reveal": "EUSA'S HEAD IS DREAMING US." The oneiric quality of this revelation is of course reminiscent of Lewis Carroll's Alice who is told by Tweedledum in a passage resonant with meaning for many contemporary fictionists that the sleeping king is dreaming her and that if he were to awake she would cease to exist. It is also connected to a frightening insight Riddley briefly confronts much later in the tale: "What if its you whats making all this happen? What if every thing you think of happens?" The terror of this question lies in the idea of the world as the subjective dream of each perceiving being, and indeed Hoban often asserts the power and reality of the individual mind's imaginings. But these oneiric, idealist theories are altered and assuaged by the deterministic necessity that increasingly lies behind Hoban's fictions – the idea that the details of the plot have been worked out by an Other (Eusa, or whomever), and the human agent is merely its transmitter, the one who has listened to, noticed, fallen on the perceptions essential for the necessary transmission to take place.

Throughout *Riddley Walker* one sees the building up of an elaborate mythology, based on ill-understood, mostly oral formulaic texts; gradually this mythology, compelled by outside forces, leans toward the riddling and oblique written word that it is Riddley's task to produce as a necessary next step forward in the magical historical process of the "Master Chaynjis." In this process, everything he discovers is connected to a past set of ill-understood but supremely insistent mythologies; it is Riddley's job to interpret these, while he compulsively builds up new ones for transmission. Like many major fictions, *Riddley Walker* may be said to have as its subject the production and exploration of mythology which comes both from the tales and icons of the past, and from the present where the fiction is lived. As Borges says in describing Don Quixote's peculiar role in the transformation of human sensibility: "For in the beginning of literature is the myth, and in the end as well."

*

Although *Riddley Walker* presents many versions of fiction, many sorts of story-telling, and an absorbing array of symbols, it nevertheless holds together in significant conventional ways. The sturdy honesty and hence the reliability of Riddley as narrator give the reader a sense of conventionally solid first-person narration, and the narrative techniques as a whole follow the basic novelistic rules involving the alternation of summary and scene set down by Gérard

Genette (1980). The fiction is thus rendered secure and, despite all its fascinating vagaries of process, is seen by its readers as comprehensibly conceived. Like the three adult novels that preceded it in Hoban's *oeuvre*, *Riddley Walker* is ingeniously constructed, but the sense of authorial control is absolute. Hoban's next novel *Pilgermann* presents another case entirely.

Here the narrator is a disembodied consciousness, a being able to pass at will through various historical periods, and one who chooses to appear in the phenomenological world of his readers as an owl, if at all. The owl was a major figure in one of the stories-within-the-story of *Riddley Walker*, but here it is more pointedly connected to the ancient idea of Wisdom, one of the symbolic centers of *Pilgermann*, as it is in the novels of Michel Tournier. Hoban's new and bewildering narrative voice learned Wisdom from various sources – from the bewitching Sophia of the adulterous affair leading to his castration when he was a Jewish man in the eleventh century, from another much more vulgar Sophia he meets on his travels, from the idea of the church of Santa Sophia in Constantinople, and finally from the accumulated but nevertheless limited wisdom he has encountered during the timeless centuries since his death. Now, long after his death in 1099 during the First Crusade, he is merely "waves and particles":

> I don't know what I am now. A whispering of the dust. Dried blood on a sword and the sword has crumbled into rust and the wind has blown the rust away but still I am, still I am of the world, still I have something to say, how could it be otherwise, nothing comes to an end, the action never stops, it only changes, the ringing of the steel is sun in the stillness of the stone.

Reading Hoban's work produces a nexus of often repeated images – the owl, the crow, the lion, castration, ruins, the wheel, stones, to mention only a few – combined with well-limned religious invocations that help in the production of a world recognizably his. Nevertheless, the existence of the narrator of *Pilgermann* in a hidden corner of consciousness identified only as "this place called time" removes this book from the adherence Hoban's other novels had to the past of conventional fiction. Indeed, in this novel the reader feels specifically that (s)he is toying not with a reconstruction of the medieval past but with another sort of invocation. Whereas *Riddley Walker* opened itself out to interpretation, or rather to the indeterminate nature of hermeneutics, *Pilgermann* is more like an unperformable research project. Hoban anticipates the reader's need and supplies brief footnotes naming texts that have been significant to him; he also indicates his sources – unconventional and unpopular translations of the Bible, together with Jewish midrashes and Islamic ideas.

The peculiarities of language in this novel spring from these translations and sources, as well as from the necessity of the historical material. In using these materials and forcing them frequently toward a lofty rhetoric of traditional prayer, Hoban takes on another linguistic quest. I must with reluctance say that I find the resulting style rather precious and purple-patched. In all his novels, Hoban is a consistent and verbally impressive stylist, and *Pilgermann* combines a highly descriptive poetic power with artificial word inversions and attempts at a religious ritualization of language that probably tries more than it can achieve in our expressively mean-spirited time. The result is that the reader is constantly forced to confront invocations that almost manage to pull off a vast rhetorical feat; the effect succeeds in evoking a linguistic past even though it may fail on occasion to create the tonal emphasis required.

As a novel, *Pilgermann* risks a great deal in terms of both language and formal coherence. The now disembodied persona of the medieval pilgrim–Jew is composed of the waves and particles of consciousness, and is amazingly like a computer in its access to connexions: it describes its narrative power as that of "a microscopic chip in that vast circuitry in which are recorded all of the variations and permutations so far." Although lacking Riddley's freshness of tonal control, directness, and naivety, this quest toward the heart of the matter is no less riveting.

Pilgermann is a formidable novel, and its evocations more extensive than those of its predecessor. It is freed from the clichés of post-nuclear-holocaust science fiction that *Riddley Walker* must deal with and which, in a sense, belittle even that marvelously original novel. The theme of the anti-solipsistic narrator is so far advanced by this time that Hoban does not even endow his persona with personhood. The eleventh-century incarnation whose tale this is is seen from the standpoint of long past history. Pilgermann's insights and quest for knowledge are all modified and even rendered bitterly comic by his current position; his pilgrimage and travels on the eleventh-century road are part of a fiction long ago enacted but not ended with his death during the siege of Antioch. In this novel, the idea of God as a specific entity is much more important than anywhere in Hoban's earlier work. But this God is specifically mediated by a stern unyielding Jesus who serves as the interpreter and only available representative of a God who is only and appallingly "an impossible requirement." Job-like, the narrator asks question after unanswered question, partly to build up a theology of an unanswerable God, but also to posit the primary condition of fiction, the indefinable congeries of uncertainty that constitutes the creative act. In many ways, *Pilgermann* is the nexus from which all of Hoban's fiction can be read:

> As I have said before, a story is what remains when you leave out most of the action .... Who is this Pilgermann, this drifting wave-and-particle vestige of a castrated Jew, who is this Pilgermann to have an opinion on the matter? From where I am now I see the universe isotropically receding in all directions. I am, equally with all other waves and particles, its centre. From that centre I speak as I find, and I find that I have questions for which neither the Gospels nor the Holy Scriptures offer answers. Theologians and fathers of the Church cannot confound me, they have no firmer ground on which to stand than I.

Why, asks Pilgermann, recalling the stone images of the life of Christ in Naumburg Cathedral, must Judas enact his role before Christ? Why, to put it into more secular terms, must all mankind remain pilgrims, forever on the road to an unredeemed dualistic future?

> Do it that the cosmos may uncoil its onward energy, that the wheel may go on turning: night and day, plus and minus, eden and gehinnom, matter and anti-matter, Jesus and Judas . . . . Who is to represent us all? Is it Jesus the betrayed, the crucified, or is it Judas the betrayer and his own hangman? Or is it the binary entity of Jesus/Judas alternating and inseparable? How the thunder rolls when certain mysteries are named! Not to be understood, not to be attempted even! . . . This road is the treadmill on which we walk day into night and night into day, eden into gehinnom into eden, Jesus into Judas into Jesus.

Allusively fascinating, *Pilgermann* presents its history with the combined forces of theology, visual art (stone again as well as patterned tile), errant human suffering, and its inevitable contract with death. In a religious context, this novel appears to be connected to some sort of Gnostic doctrine (I am here thinking specifically of Valentinus's account, where Sophia appears in the thirtieth aeon. Her attempts to penetrate the abyss with knowledge caused chaos in the pleroma; as a result of her passion, she was banished and became a formless existence outside of the pleroma where the present wise being of Pilgermann appears to reside.). I am much more inclined, however, to read it under the aegis of fictional theory, and to see Hoban as a writer working without the benefit of formal philosophy toward the use of fiction as a device to present images of the narratable as opposed to the analyzable in human experience.

Hoban's road from *The Lion of Boaz-Jachin and Jachin-Boaz* to *Pilgermann* is long and arduous, marked throughout by hard thought and ingeniously experimental fictionalizing. In the process the existential self is lost for higher aims than self-expression, and indeed language and form are constantly on the verge of tumbling into a primordial creative maelstrom. As Hoban keeps turning the possibility of his style and experimenting with the nature of fiction in the frequently punning forms of his new novel, *The Medusa Frequency*, it is increasingly clear that one of his primary drives is away from the subjective center of the self that dominates Modern and Postmodern fiction. Instead, he, like Calvino, uses fiction to project another realm of intersubjectivity where every human idea is part of a narratable whole that may and doubtless should help his readers in the task of becoming human perceivers in the present place where they live, called Time.

As he progresses, Hoban indirectly exhorts his readers, but he claims complete indifference to their acquiescence or acceptance. In an interview with John Haffenden (1985), he explained something of the exalted mysticism or Romantic passion behind his subject matter:

The material requires of me that I make it manifest as clearly and as beautifully as I can. There my responsibility ends, and whether you or I understand it is secondary.... I never use the word "creative" in connection with writing. I feel as if we are all particles of a single consciousness, and that the vital force which moves the universe requires of us to be its organ of perception .... It involves a god, but it isn't a god as He, it's a god as It, a force that has no comforting personification of any kind.

Fiction has not directly claimed such a powerful urgency behind the task of the writer and hence of the reader for a long time. Hoban is unusual in his use of present, past, and future in a sublimely undifferentiated way, and his reliance on sources as diverse as sacred texts and computers leads to a brave new world that he joyfully invites us to enter. The open sense of holiness that permeates his books is a reminder of what literature, especially poetry, used to take as its province. In Hoban, the old literary world is reopened, and fictions that deeply reflect the most interesting theories of our time once again remind us that the present world may not be the cybernetic nightmare we make of it.

PART IV

Continuation and tradition

9

Iris Murdoch and
the fiction of utterance

There have always been readers who hate Iris Murdoch's novels. And in spite of her notable development from the crisp, satirical comedy of *Under the Net* (1954) to her recent expansive style since *The Sea, The Sea* (1978), readers who only reluctantly admire her novels have persistently expressed dislocated complaints. In *The Sense of an Ending* (1967), Frank Kermode argued that her polemical essays correctly locate the problem of contemporary fiction in narcissism and existentialism, but that she herself up to that point had failed to write a novel equal to the eloquence she urged on all novelists in her essays, especially "Against Dryness." Almost twenty years later, Harold Bloom, in a review article of *The Good Apprentice* in *The New York Times*, grumbled about the conventionality of Murdoch's style, her refusal of the radically experimental, her bold and *passé* use of the authorial voice to philosophize without the magisterial impact that George Eliot had more than a hundred years ago. Adhering to Henry James's dictum, Bloom claimed that Murdoch also fails to *show us* rather than *tell us*. Yet he praises her for her capacities as a spiritual writer, and concludes:

> Like nearly all of her 22 novels, Miss Murdoch's *Good Apprentice* has a surface that constitutes a brilliant entertainment, a social comedy of and for the highly literate. Beneath that surface an astringent post-Christian Platonism has evolved into a negative theology that pragmatically offers only the dialectical alternations of either total libertinism or total puritanism in the moral life. The esthetic puzzle is whether the comic story and the spiritual kernel can be held together by Miss Murdoch's archaic stance as an authorial will. And yet no other contemporary British novelist seems to me of her eminence.

The "archaic stance" identified by Bloom in this review constitutes an indirect attack on the British novel, which since Mallarmé has been steadily criticized by French experimentalist critics – including Michel Foucault – as hopelessly superseded and socially narrow in a "Bloomsburian" way. Bloom's comments represent the American urge toward a metafictional aesthetic, and re-emphasize current polemical struggles between traditional and experimental modes in American criticism. Bloom's lip service to the experimental is cancelled out in this review, however, by his sheer interest in this novel and its subject matter, as well as by his buoyant statement that Murdoch with *The Good Apprentice* is now entering a towering phase in which her formidable powers will finally triumph. I doubt this, and not only because I think her novels have been successful in a troubling, anxious way ever since *The Nice and the Good* (1968).

Murdoch's fiction is passionately dedicated to utterance – that is, to a committed presentation and advocacy of a "world" that echoes her best and most committed thinking about human fictionalizing and its ontological function. Reading her recent books – *The Philosopher's Pupil* (1983) and *The Good Apprentice* (1985) – gives the reader a full demonstration of her particular kind of creative originality and also summarizes the themes and ideas she has soldiered on with through the more than three decades of her prolific career. Both books illustrate the malaise in terms of both narratological form and ethical solution that Murdoch's writing life has been devoted to displaying. In manifold and pointed ways Iris Murdoch's novels have been studies in the impossibility of their own ambitions, and in the struggle toward and lack of coherence within the contemporary bourgeois lives they are committed to portraying.

In her slight 1957 novel, *The Sandcastle*, one of the characters, a religiously committed schoolmaster named Bledyard, queries, "Who can look reverently enough upon another human face?" The placement of the human *vis-à-vis* the divine is one of Murdoch's major thematics from the beginning, connecting her particular mode of ethical literary thought to the Dostoevskyan frame outlined in Mikhail Bakhtin's now famous essay, *Problems of Dostoevsky's Poetics* (1986). Although I use Bakhtin's terminology elsewhere in this book, it is particularly appropriate in discussing Murdoch whose derivation from the great nineteenth-century Russian novelists is of long standing.

Bakhtin saw the semantic function of literature as primary and more important than its formalist dedication to language. The ethical impetus behind Bakhtin's thought derives from his study of the relation between Christ and man, and between man and man; both are seen as an anti-solipsistic communication in which Martin Buber's "I-thou" recognition of the other is essential. When Murdoch's Bledyard asks who can look reverently enough upon another human face, he reflects an idea that Bakhtin would have recognized. In Bakhtin's reading, Dostoevsky's disciplined attempt to realize his characters fully and objectively, even when they represent principles or ideas he wishes to expunge, produces what Bakhtin calls a polyphonic fiction of the most desirable kind. The holy looking, the perceptivity of mind and spirit required not only by characters in the novel but *a fortiori* by the novelist himself, constitutes the breadth of polyphony in the full functioning of Dostoevsky's novels.

Caryl Emerson mentions that the one problem Bakhtin's work on Dostoevsky fails to confront is that of the larger unity of the fiction within the prescribed necessity of the polyphonic mode. Dostoevsky was, after all, a proselytizer driven by his Slavism and Christianity into a highly ideological fiction that sought a directed synthesis that his dialogic style could not easily deliver. The very idea of the dialogic – an idea that encompasses the capacity of the author to envisage the fully individuated being of the characters as well as the ability of the characters to perceive and respond to each other's precise nature and spirituality – withholds the power of clear statement from the fiction. This dialogic notion may, in fact, be an anti-formal signal as well as an anti-statemental one, and although Bakhtin argues that form and semantics are interwoven, he himself found it difficult to describe the workable inter-penetration of the two. It is evident that the dialogic or polyphonic novel, by the very demands of its ambition, defies unification, and is therefore always formally troubled.

Murdoch's impulse is dialogic, and like Bakhtin's Dostoevsky she feels a religious urge to reflect generously on her characters. But whereas one senses in Bakhtin a struggle to have the dialogic serve a larger formal and ideological function, the reader of Murdoch's most recent novels who tries to force them strongly into pattern will find him/herself transgressing the allowed boundaries of the text. Murdoch has always expressed her uneasiness at the tyranny of form, and criticized her own formal powers of artifice, particularly in her early novels where the tightness of contrived pattern often cost the work freedom and flexibility. As her style developed, the novels learned to sprawl in their own jealously guarded imperfection and indeterminacy. The ethical impulse has not decreased, but the patterning has become less rigid, and indeed her dialogic mode has made critical statements involving meaning increasingly difficult. Moreover, it would be fair to say that Harold Bloom's criticism of Murdoch's authorial voice is incorrect; unlike George Eliot, she enters the minds of her characters not to impose her monologic voice, but in order to allow them to speak and exist as freely as possible. But when the reader tries to unify interpretation or to get a handle on the novels, serious damage to their polyphonic structure often ensues.

Yet one of the best ways of describing Murdoch as a writer is in terms of her proselytizing about the nature of the novel: by example as well as in essays and interviews she stresses its persistence, its perhaps tacky but necessary allegiance to realism, and its duty to present the social, ethical, and philosophical lives of the unabashedly bourgeois characters who inhabit her pages and read her books. This essay will briefly examine *The Philosopher's Pupil* and *The Good Apprentice* – two of her most recent books – in order to watch how she both obliquely and directly engages large subjects within quasi-conventional plot lines. These plotted novels eloquently demonstrate her semantic ambition: *The Philosopher's Pupil* is a study of the impossibility of philosophical intrusion into the ethical life, and *The Good Apprentice* scrutinizes the very nature of human consciousness.

In *The Philosopher's Pupil*, the reader is addressed with fussy intimacy by an elderly male Jewish narrator who coyly withholds his identity, revealing himself only as N (for Nemo [no one] or Narrator). An inhabitant of the town he creates and formalizes in the novel, this friendly, ironically conceived narrator playfully identifies the spot as his own - N's Town, spelled out for authorial and fictional convenience as Ennistone. It is a marvelous place replete with extended realistic detail, but clearly a place that never was on land or sea. To counter its stylized resonance and add realism, many pages are spent - happily for traditional novel readers - in building up its geography, social customs, architecture, religious allegiances present and past, its local heroes and villains, priests and prostitutes, and its delicious gossip, in a pictorially phenomenological *pièce de résistance*. N's Town is a spa or bath town amusingly updated but ironically reminiscent of what Bath must have been to the Romans in ancient days; a town of bathers and swimmers who are almost mystically attached to the baths, it is also a contemporary place that is mythically and symbolically resonant.

It is certainly not new for Murdoch to create places. Here in *The Philosopher's Pupil*, as is usual in all her imagined places, the actual geographical world interacts with the fictional town; from Ennistone, London is an easy trip, America a place to be visited and even lived in, Belgium and Japan not inaccessible. But the novel is about N's Town itself, the place inhabited mentally and absolutely by the narrator whose sense of his job gives us a pointed definition of how Murdoch views the problems of narration and the task of the story-teller. The fact that the reader forgets all about N for long stretches of the text and is indeed surprised at sudden narratorial intrusions attests to Murdoch's carrying out in her practice of fiction a strong impulse toward that transparent, spellbinding style simply and - from the point of view of contemporary narratological theories - naively called realism in the nineteenth and early twentieth centuries. But like Trollope's narrator, N is constantly and ironically aware that realism itself is a fiction, and that the luring of the reader is a magic he must perform, usually unobtrusively, sometimes self-reflectively.

Murdoch's allegiance to the Russian tradition, as pointed out by Peter Conradi in his excellent book, *Iris Murdoch: The Artist and the Saint* (1986), has frequently led her to subtle shifts in narrative form, and a high degree of self-reflexivity is evident in most of the novels. Too easily left unread by fans of Postmodernism because of the realist texture of the fictions, Murdoch has experimented extensively, but within boundaries set by her self-consciously late-born commitment to retaining the strength of the novel as established in the nineteenth century - the century of the polemics of realism, the century that opened the way for the theory and practice of Henry James to whom she is obviously indebted, the century that produced her predecessors, Tolstoy, Dickens, Dostoevsky, Balzac, Austen, and Scott. Most current metafictional adherents reject nineteenth-century novelists (with the notable exceptions of Flaubert and Dickens) except for intertextual or parodic reference. In such a time and atmosphere, Murdoch is bound to appear recalcitrant, old-fashioned, and even stubborn.

The metafictional argument that character or plot must be rejected is alien to Murdoch's longstanding allegiances, and she remains one of the best plot-spinners in the business. Because of her dialogic style, her characters incite rage, anxiety, or acquiescence to an intense degree. This hot response is the very thing that the cool forms of metafiction eschew. Yet Murdoch's novels continue an unruffled demonstration of what fiction can actually do now as opposed to how it functioned in the past, how it can be said to operate, and what its limitations and necessary ironies are. This quiet self-consciousness works at odds with her stress on external matters like plot and character, and must not be underestimated as one of the primary sources of the reader's anxieties. Because of the novels' surface compliances with older, more comfortable, and established forms, readers feel that texts should be less unnerving and alienating than recent Murdoch novels in fact are.

The Philosopher's Pupil is an ideal example of the strong mixture of traditional and experimental that characterizes Murdoch's work and makes it dense and difficult of access even after the plot line itself has been mastered. It can justly be claimed that because her plots are instantly accessible and emotionally overwhelming, most readers stop there and fail to consider the further reaches of what each novel in differing ways demonstrates to be her fictional task. Murdoch apparently takes this problem of partial reception for granted by now, and assumes that what Borges in his "Pierre Menard, Author of the Quixote" calls "the halting and rudimentary act of reading" will be poorly done. Although most of Murdoch's novels focus little attention on the tyranny and carelessness of readers, *The Philosopher's Pupil* is concerned with accuracy in reading – texts, circumstances, and appearances. As a novelist whose work has long been under attack, perhaps Murdoch finds here a quiet occasion for a minor bit of revenge.

Twice in the middle of *The Philosopher's Pupil*, the narrator reports on events indicating not only that all literary texts are generally perceived as indeterminate, but that readers and students of literature find no particular reason to attempt accuracy or indeed to pay much exacting attention to the enterprise of reading. On the first occasion, young Hattie Meynell is asked by Father Bernard Jacoby to construe a poem by Stéphane Mallarmé, the first of the *Petits Airs* which begins, "Quelconque une solitude." A grammatically apt pupil capable of real literary excitement, Hattie takes her task seriously, and leads Father Bernard (and the reader) to consider a vivid set of new possibilities within the poem through the earnestness of her attempt to impose determinate meaning on a resistant text. The freshness of the girl's mind, with its sharp grammatical focus, forces the priest to realize that his own hazy, self-indulgently aesthetic reading of the poem, with its commitment to private identification, may be both closed and limited, despite the pleasure he takes in it. But unlike Hattie in her ardent quest for the precise evocations of the poem, Father Bernard does not pursue any possibilities beyond his privately established fantasy-interpretation. Instead, he argues fuzzily: " 'Never mind, you must get the sense of the whole'," whereupon he lapses into daydream.

The second occasion of textual misreading parallels and emphasizes this one. Again young Hattie insists on meaning and the need for comprehension in the face of a vague and inaccurate interpretation of another poem, this time Blake's *Jerusalem*, "And did those feet in ancient time/ Walk upon England's mountains green?" Hattie, again literal-minded and firmly grammatical, says she doesn't understand the question or the poem, only to be told curtly and dismissively by Tom McCaffrey (who is reading English at one of the colleges of the University of London where he has been shoddily taught), " 'It's a poem .... It doesn't have to mean anything exact. It's a sort of rhetorical question. He's just imagining Christ here.' " Obviously untutored in history, folklore, or the theories of the British Israelites, Tom is corrected by his historian friend Emma who tells him about the legendary trip of Jesus to Britain with his uncle Joseph of Arimathea. The mental and physical euphoria this piece of concrete knowledge produces in the erstwhile ignorant Tom brilliantly illustrates the difference between reading carelessly in a way that bars a text from both its literal and symbolic significance, and having initial ammunition for the reading of a poem (historical background, the intertextual references of the poet himself, a sense that the right questions to begin with in thinking about a text might be more precise and less vague than the ordinary reader is willing to deal with).

In neither case does Murdoch advocate narrow determinacy or interpretative closing off of texts, however; on the contrary, the two examples indict both the closed system illustrated by the reader who has made up his mind what the text means and is too lazy or preoccupied to reconsider it, and the hazy idleness of another sort of reader who dismisses a poem as just a poem, with which the mind cannot be actually or fruitfully engaged.

The use of the narrator as a character in this novel expands the reader's need to think consciously about the formal structure of the book as well as its semantics. As *The Philosopher's Pupil* draws to its close, the artificially created narrator, N, becomes compulsively and, from the point of view of the history of the novel, naively preoccupied with closure. He is hopelessly garrulous, officiously tying up ends, giving us thumbnail sketches of the putative future, judging the quality of intention and action, and displaying a too interested desire to consolidate and finally control certain characters, like George McCaffrey or John Robert Rozanov. To his dismay, these characters have in crucial ways slipped from his creative grasp into that realm of independence or freedom celebrated by serious novelists, from George Eliot to John Fowles, in defiance of the restrictive boundaries automatically imposed by the formal creative act. The reader whose love of closed endings has not yet been jettisoned might find an atavistic charm in seeing the novel bundled up so nicely for delivery between the covers of the book, but Murdoch obviously knows that the majority of contemporary readers long ago learned distrust of the artist–narrator and his task. Moreover, she finds it useful, in keeping the artificial nature of the N character consistent, to remind us pointedly of the slippery nature of the fictional act. Here is her last paragraph:

> The end of any tale is arbitrarily determined. As I now end this one, somebody may say: but how on earth do you know all these things about all these people? Well, where does one person end and another person begin? It is my role in life to listen to stories. I also had the assistance of a certain lady.

The Chinese box (or mirroring, or *mise-en-abyme*) effect central to contemporary fiction is evoked here to assert the human and technical curiosities attendant on both the reading and writing experiences. "Where does one person end and another person begin?" is a crucial question that can be ignored only at the expense of losing track of the central nature of fiction. Not only are human beings endlessly intertwined, but characters in fiction are also creations of the narrator who is in turn the creation of the author, and it is indeed difficult to see where one of these personae ends and another begins; the reader is also an active persona who enters the scene as (s)he both tries to conform to the created text and to withdraw skeptically from its dominant power. Murdoch's narrator defines his activity in producing this text in straightforward realist terms as quite simply the ability to listen to and write down stories. But the above quotation conveys a sense of obscurity and the Bakhtinian overlapping of roles, stressed here as part of the mysterious order of literature reflected in this complex many-directed allegory of magicians.

Indeed one of Murdoch's major themes centers on the perplexities of personae – that is, on the wide range of functioning human intelligences that make up the conceiving and receiving process of literature, and the above passage indicates some of the problems inherent in this interest. At the furthest extreme of potential unreality in the process of fiction are the characters, the dramatis personae of the tale that is told; at the opposite extreme of palpable reality is the reader in the time-bound act of reading the text and then pronouncing his/her own narrative account of it.

Characters for Murdoch are not linguistic artifacts as they have become for many contemporary novelists, but objects of study within a firm range of verisimilitude. Hence the elaborate concreteness of detail as to their precise physical appearance, dress, and possessions, as well as extended descriptions of the rooms and houses the characters inhabit – not to mention their animals, parents, and beloved dead. The central purely conventional task of the narrator is therefore the production of these characters in the fullness of their being. A flawed or corrupt narrator (like one of her many first-person male narrators – for example, Charles Arrowby in *The Sea, The Sea*) will be too preoccupied with self to nurture the reality of any other being; as Murdoch explained in her essays in the late 1950s and early 1960s such solipsists, like most contemporary novelists, are not capable of the loving attention that the narrator must turn on his/her characters in order to grant them the luminosity achieved by great realist nineteenth-century writers like Dostoevsky or Tolstoy – or indeed by Shakespeare, whose work constantly reverberates through Murdoch's.

But between the characters and the perceiving reader are the narrative persona and the author, the latter sitting at her desk with (in Murdoch's case) pen and ink, blank pages, and an ethical concept of the discipline required in the practice of art. One way in which Murdoch's practice differs from theories involving radical skepticism about the knowledgeable participation of the artist is in her old-fashioned belief in authorial narrative control and authority. The "certain lady" who gives assistance to N – the narrator who is a Nemo, a no one, or an artificially created golem – argues firmly that she knows what she is doing, that the texts she constructs reflect a meticulous and multi-faceted design. Again, this argument of design does not indicate a closed text subject to one correct reading, for in the same way that Murdoch sees people, and hence her characters, as endlessly unknowable, so she would allow significant freedom to the readers of her novels in terms of their own methodology. In this respect she is in close agreement with some of the semiotic theories of Umberto Eco who claims authorial prescience but insists upon the open text and the model reader whose freedom to move with considerable interest and accuracy within the narrative has been foreseen by the author.

N, the narrator and therefore the ostensible creative force behind the fiction, is firmly distanced from the author. Inasmuch as all narrators are created by rather than clearly identifiable with the authorial force behind the fiction, it is odd that so many readers tend to forget this central issue. As in the relation of all narrators to their text, moreover, N is absolutely particular to this novel; he has no existence outside of Ennistone, and springs to life there, as do his characters, every time a new reader or a rereader opens the novel and begins to read. Like the other characters in the book, he is not meant to mirror Murdoch, and to read him as an alter ego is to deny his integrity and that of the entire fiction. But if Murdoch claims to be in charge, she is careful to point out that N is not, and his vagaries and errors portray the inability of any work of art fully to understand or realize itself and its substance.

Voyeuristic, male, Jewish, N is so interested in his characters that he irritates them with the symbiotic relationships he sets up; fictional himself, he is allowed an *amitié intime* with the other "shadows" of the fiction's world. Hence he intrudes not only as a narrative voice but as a character who interacts with his so-called creations at a personal, quasi-realistic level. As narrator he believes himself to be in control, but given the fact that other characters in the book also wish to effect the action – like Stella McCaffrey and John Robert Rozanov, for example – his interaction with them is puzzling and even competitive. Compulsively the controller and judge – he modestly says he allows himself "the discreet luxury of moralising" – N is nevertheless shown as a limited being, not always capable of sustaining his role as puppeteer; the reader is carefully led to realize that because N is dealing with the vast complexity of human character and motivation, there are of necessity areas too perplexing for his mastery. Murdoch has always argued that the mystery of human transcendence makes characters exist beyond the capabilities of a narrator, and indeed would define art as the indefinable way in which a few godlike artists have managed to travel beyond this barrier.

N's curiosity about the marriage of George and Stella McCaffrey is a dominant case pointing to his limitations, for both characters quickly escape the strictures of his controlling hand. As he conceives them, they fail to conform to conventional characterological standards allowing straightforward narrative and narratorial analysis. As a fictional creation, Stella is the more innovative and interesting of the two, whereas George is played off, for what appear to be theoretical reasons, perhaps too extensively against various Dostoevskyan precedents.

Among the characters in the novel who are in competition with the narrator to force their will on the action and to try to gain manipulative control, Stella McCaffrey is major, almost outdoing N in her passionate desire to create and control the character of her husband. Like a narrator observing human nature and recording it while working out a dénouement, Stella watches her husband George while she awaits the moment when he will have completely enacted his own private fiction. She sees George's self-imposed tale as a violently dramatic life pattern demanding formal closure through someone's murder or his own reformation, after which he will return to her "to be saved." As George tells his mistress Diane, "Stella would like me in a wheelchair and her pushing it." She calls her husband's violent behavior "imagery, symbols – like a rehearsal for something he'll do one day that will satisfy him at last – and then he'll stop – he'll be satisfied . . . he'll have destroyed something in himself, he'll be exhausted, weak and pale like a grub in an apple." Despite her compulsion for narrative control, Stella spends a long period in hiding, during which she is absent from the novel. This peculiar absence is ultimately inexplicable to both her and N, who is willing to admit that he has somehow failed in the presentation and working out of her character.

An invented character, Stella exits from the action like a character from Pirandello or a Woody Allen film, running to her creator for safety, and is placed by N in some convenient pocket of the fiction until her reappearance can be manipulatively worked out by the two of them. She and N have thoughtful chats in which they report, in details particular to the novel that they are enacting, the struggles of any narrator dealing with resistant characters and interpreting the impending action. In fact, although N enjoys talking to the reader, he is more interested in talking to Stella, and pointedly highlights her dreadful image of personal power: "Sometimes I feel as if George were a fish I'd hooked ... on a long long line ... and I let him run ... and run ... and run .... What a terrible image." This "terrible image" of playing a fish, an image of cruel manipulation and false freedom, records precisely the power all narrators/power mages have over their subjects and characters. The demonism of power is connected to the ubiquitous background image of Prospero in this novel, and doubtless explains why he abjured his rough magic and returned powerless to Milan.

George, on the other hand, is a character who does not chat with N, and N admits that as narrator he quickly loses George as a straightforward object of explanation. At the end of the novel and after George's violent "conversion," N's obsessive curiosity about him remains unresolved. He is still talking to Stella about what might be going on in George's mind and is avidly interested in finding out more in the future; in a conversation with Stella in her hiding-place earlier in the novel, N had admitted, "I'm sorry I lost George. I hate to lose anybody."

Yet on the surface it seems that George as a character should not be all that difficult to unravel, and certainly not for an experienced, observant narrator. His apparent genesis is in Dostoevsky, and he appears in both ideology and action to be parodically compounded of several of Dostoevsky's characters, from *The Underground Man, Crime and Punishment, The Brothers Karamazov*, and *The Double*, to mention only the most obvious. From the alienation and resentment of the underground man, he goes through doubling experiences, carries a hammer, argues extensively from both Schopenhauer and the Nihilists, and is struck down by God – or rather by a twentieth-century equivalent embodied in a flying saucer that bestows a Pauline blinding. Dostoevskyan demonism does not, however, entirely fill the bill in explaining George, partly because N is not Dostoevsky's narrator, and pointedly because George (and through him, symbolically, all contemporary people?) is somehow not politically or religiously capable of being an avatar of such gripping and absolute characters. Indeed, the peculiarly pointless qualities of George's manifold failures form the major puzzle and make him spiritually unlike his Dostoevskyan ancestors. As John Robert Rozanov says of him:

"You're a fake, a *faux mauvais*, pretending to be wicked because you're unhappy. You're not mad or satanic, you're just a fool suffering from hurt vanity. You lack imagination. What made you bad at philosophy makes you bad at being bad. It's a game. You're a dull dog, George, an ordinary dull mediocre egoist, you will never be anything else .... You never tried to kill your wife, you dropped the Roman glass because you were drunk, you're just a clown."

Even this, however, does not feel lastingly useful as a description of George's character, because he brings out strong feelings of love and hatred in the other characters. His ethical attraction for the reader is minimal, however, even while both narrator characters, N and Stella, are and remain totally interested in him. N's early ruminations on character are useful, as he makes points strongly reminiscent of those that Murdoch has made throughout her entire writing career:

> I confess that I cannot offer any illuminating explanation. Every human being is different, more *absolutely* different and peculiar than we can goad ourselves into conceiving; and our persistent desire to depict human lives as dramas leads us to see "in the same light" events which may have multiple interpretations and causes. Of course a man may be "cured" (consoled, encouraged, improved, shaken, returned to effective activity, and so forth and so on) by a concocted story of his own life, but that is another matter. (And such stories may be on offer from doctors, priests, teachers, influential friends and relations, or may be self-invented or derived from literature.) We are in fact far more randomly made, more full of rough contingent rubble, than art or vulgar psycho-analysis lead us to imagine .... There was some deep (so deep that one wants to call it "original", whatever that means) wound in George's soul into which every tiniest slight or setback poured its gall. Pride and vanity and venomous hurt feelings obscured his sun. He saw the world as a conspiracy against him, and himself as a victim of cosmic injustice.

Murdoch stresses the existence of a mysterious density in people that makes their fictional representation as tenuous and incomplete as our real apprehension of each other. Thus, each of her novels presents magicians and near-demons whose opacity is almost complete. In keeping with this theory, N's self-analytical stance allows him to go on in his examination of the illusiveness of a character like George. One of his last comments as he tries to work out why George's real and not imaginary violence actually surfaced shows why a responsible narrator who honestly observes his characters must be perpetually puzzled by human activity, even as he tries to grab the elegant formal explanation. It also demonstrates why N sees his (and George's, and the reader's, since the latter is always an allusion-catcher) Dostoevskyan fiction about George's personality as only the literary, lying, quasi-explanatory exercise that it is:

> What it was that "moved" George from liberated euphoria to effective murderous hate must however remain a missing link .... The motivation of terrible deeds tends to be extremely complex, full of apparent contradictions, and often in fact bottomlessly mysterious, although for legal, scientific and moral reasons we "have to" theorize about it .... It would be a sad irony if [Stella's] inopportune mention of the philosopher's name should have prompted the violence which ended this tale as well as that which began it. Was the final "provocation" hers after all, and not John Robert's? Such are the chance "triggers" which may determine our most fateful actions and yet remain opaque particulars with which science can do little.

In spite of stress on the mysterious and slithering nature of human character, Murdoch's fiction is obsessed by form, and however arbitrary N's closure might seem, it is in effect controlled by the narrator's desire for the elegance of circularity. Thus *The Philosopher's Pupil* opens with a "brainstorm" on George's part, and aside from the fussy narratorial tidying up in the final section entitled "What Happened Afterwards," it ends with his final "brainstorm." The narrator's cycle is closed to perfection, and the tale that Stella wishes to see enacted is tidily presented to her by N. Ironically, this structure leads inevitably to misreading, and no serious student of this ambitious novel can fail to see that the quasi-Dostoevskyan George is not the center of the novel, or its hero, or the vehicle of its intention – whatever that might mean, to quote N. In other words, the literary habit of following the dictates of form is a chimerical exercise discouraged by the ironies and ambiguities of this book. To put it still another way, N has been created by "a certain lady" as a parodic figure to help obscure the way.

How, then, is the reader to react to the large effects of this novel? Certainly not by simplistically carrying this last point too far, because although N through his insistence on the formal tasks of narrator may be muddying the waters, he is after all only performing the narrow, necessary, workmanlike jobs that fiction has always had to impose on itself. Like the ambitious novelists of the nineteenth century, N must force the baggy structure of his material into a contained book, and in doing so he arbitrarily imposes what devices he can find. His task is made more difficult because this novel is an examination of fiction and creative activity to a significant degree, whatever other subjects it takes on. As a result, we have accounts not only of readers and narrators, but also of the genesis of thematics and composition, as Tom, for example, also decides he will become an artist and write the lyrics of a pop song whose music Emma will produce. From 8-year-old Adam he receives the Peter Pan line, "It's only me," and from there he opens out a space in which the lyrics (not bad ones at that) can take place.

The Philosopher's Pupil is also a novel about the dangers of teaching and learning, as the title informs us; pedagogical ideas have, indeed, always been closely involved with the traditional ethical impulse of the novel as a genre. In the case both of this novel and of *The Good Apprentice*, however, the title is ambiguous and easily misassigned. About the philosopher – John Robert Rozanov – there is no doubt (although Murdoch herself, as both philosopher and novelist, also has many pupils, including the reader), but his pupils are many, as are the functions and resonances of the novel. The obvious choice for titular pupil is George McCaffrey, but equally strong as a candidate is Father Bernard Jacoby; then there is Stella McCaffrey, Hattie, and, in a small tag-on way, Steve Glatz who appears at the end of the novel to edit John Robert's papers and carry off the rich and beautiful Anthea Eastcote. Each potential pupil (with the exception of Glatz) carries enormous plot and ideological weight, as does Rozanov himself.

John Robert Rozanov, the philosopher in question, satisfies the many Murdoch readers who have always seen her novels as philosophical *jeux d'esprit* played under the veil of allegory. Certainly this character embodies a principle she has long held - that philosophy is a God-game intolerably difficult for human beings to perform. In the single most important dialogue in the novel, between Rozanov and Father Bernard Jacoby, Rozanov confesses to horror at the limitations of metaphysics: "You see - the suspicion that one is not only not telling the truth, but *cannot* tell it - that is - damnation. A case for the millstone." His suicide at the end of the book probably results as much from despair at the impossibility of philosophy as from his ethical fears for his own behavior. His career is in self-parodic ways parallel to Murdoch's own as a philosopher, but with a stronger stress on history and mathematics, and this parodic resemblance will no doubt interest her philosophically inclined critics; his final stance has to do, however, with his will to go beyond good and evil to an unthinkable metaphysical realm that Father Bernard shudders at, and that Murdoch clearly wishes the reader to question.

As a manipulative magician - a sort of artist in his own right - Rozanov is both aware of and impatient with his power. Driven by the need to clarify his thinking through conversational discourse, he nevertheless has no pedagogical instinct. George McCaffrey, told years ago by the philosopher that he lacked a true philosophical mind, keeps reminding Rozanov of his responsibilities as a teacher, and pushily asserts himself as his perpetual student. In the service of this relationship, George culls references Rozanov made in past lectures to Dostoevsky, Nietzsche, Schopenhauer, Shakespeare - and in an inauthentic, role-playing way creates his own character as a congeries of ideas and qualities taken from these writers. Dramatically and demonically playing a Dostoevskyan role, George also sees himself as a kind of Caliban, and his enslavement to and rebellion against the powerful Prospero figure is part of the teacher–pupil relationship this novel explores.

George's inability to force Rozanov's attention by intellectual means is finally resolved by the anger he elicits from the philosopher over the affair of the Slipper House party, where he breaks in on Rozanov's granddaughter, Hattie, and is hounded away by the drunken singers in the garden. To have made a sharp impression through tawdry behavior is humiliating in itself; that it evokes such damaging rage makes George almost mad with grief and despair. The source of his desire to kill Rozanov is obscure: no doubt this episode and Rozanov's subsequent intemperate letter contribute to it, as does Stella's reference to the philosopher. But it is clear that Rozanov misunderstands the extensions of pedagogical responsibility and misperceives both pedagogy and ethical behavior.

By negative example, Rozanov's behavior illuminates the humane element that *The Philosopher's Pupil* asserts. When Father Bernard Jacoby interrupts an abortive conversation between George and Rozanov, the philosopher evokes a painful passage from the third canto of Dante's *Inferno: Guarda e passa* – look at him and pass on – in order to underline George's worthlessness. Father Bernard's response is immediately negative: "No. *No.*" As in other significant conversations with Rozanov, Father Bernard spontaneously fights against an element of ethical monstrosity expressed by the philosopher. The idea that George should be ignored is harsh in itself; placed in the context of the *Inferno*, Rozanov's prescription is horrible.

This context is made clear during one of Father Bernard's tutoring sessions with Hattie, the character who, in her innocence and youthfulness, is often made the vehicle of literary insight. Checking her knowledge of foreign languages, the priest gives Hattie the third canto to read and translate: it is the canto where the words from Rozanov's quotation occur, and Murdoch carefully sets up the context:

> Dante and Virgil have passed the gate to hell but have not yet crossed Acheron. In this no man's land, rejected both by heaven and hell, Dante gets his first glimpse of tormented people, and is duly horrified. (He was to see worse. Did he get used to it?) "Who are these people so overcome by pain?" Virgil replies that "this is the miserable condition of wretched souls who lived without disgrace and without praise. Mixed with them are the vile angels who are neither rebels nor loyal to God, but were for themselves." "Master, what makes them cry out so terribly?" "They have no hope of death, and their blind life is so abject that they envy every other lot. Mercy and justice alike despise them. *Non ragioniam di lor, ma guarda e passa.* Do not let us speak of them; just look and pass by." How terrible, Father Bernard thought, that this ferocious judgment and those words should have come spontaneously into John Robert's mind when Father Bernard wanted to talk about George; and the priest felt a sudden rage, almost a hatred, rising in him against the philosopher, and mingling with the lurid and exalted emotions aroused by the fierce words of the great poet.

It is wrong to identify George too strongly with the tormented souls in this passage, although he is certainly in a hellish no man's land; the important thing is Father Bernard's moral horror at Rozanov's judgment. George keeps arguing that he could be changed from demonism into a morally wholesome person through the simple agency of Rozanov's kindness. This is of course doubtful – his actual conversion occurs through an inner–outer vision of a much more peculiar and powerful sort – but Father Bernard's denial of Rozanov's behavior is crucial here as elsewhere.

In spite of his disagreements with the philosopher, the atheistical priest claims, in his significant letter to the narrator from an anchorite cave in Greece, "I was his last pupil and I failed the test." In many ways Father Jacoby is the most paradoxical achievement of Murdoch's novel. A mannered and silly man, he is wonderfully comic with his irrepressible curiosity about people's behavior, his bizarrely cultivated high-church antics and dress, and his chaste homosexuality. He adores the aesthetics if not the beliefs of his church, meditates to the music of Scott Joplin under the watchful eye of a statue of the

Buddha, and has a playful allegiance to Christ. Comic though he is and careless though he may be of his parish duties, Father Jacoby is also remarkably attentive to the moral atmosphere in the town.

Indeed, his ethical use of knowledge frames the novel: he is the only person to witness the indecisive act that opens the book - George's violent attempt to kill his wife, followed instantly by his remorseful jumping into the canal to save her and then kicking her as she lies gasping on the rain-spattered road. Father Bernard also, near the end of the book, sees a euphoric George leave Rozanov's room at the Bath after he has "drowned" the philosopher, and he is the one to discover and conceal the suicide note Rozanov leaves indicating his irreversible overdose. In both cases, the priest makes a moral decision to withhold information, and to use it for what he instinctively feels to be the best possible ends. In other words, he too is a power broker of major dimensions in the sequence of events; he is also, by contrast, a humble performer of small, decent actions - in his kind attachment to Diane Sedleigh, and his compassionate curiosity about the quotidian behavior of all people he comes in contact with.

What Father Bernard learns after leaving Ennistone illuminates the nature of the test that he "failed" under the tutelage of John Robert Rozanov. In his crackpot way, he becomes a spokesman for Murdochian ideas of the sort the novels have long sought to express, and as he explains that he failed because he should have spoken more decisively against the lessons Rozanov was giving, he voices the theme of ethical concentration on the details of the present that Murdoch espouses:

> If I had known what I know now I could have saved both him and George. John Robert asked me not to speak of George *and I agreed* because I was afraid of him and because I was flattered by his attention. When I spoke of pastoral duty he said, "You don't believe it", and I bowed my head, and the cock crew thrice. So it is that I have witnessed three murders, two by George and one by that philosopher (perhaps there is a teaching in this). John Robert died because he saw at last, with horrified wide-open eyes, the futility of philosophy. Metaphysics and the human sciences are made possible by the *penetration of morality into the moment to moment conduct of ordinary life*: the understanding of this fact is *religion*. This is what Rozanov distantly glimpsed when he was picking away at questions of good and evil, and he knew that it made nonsense of all his sophisms.
>
> There is no beyond, there is only here, the infinitely small, infinitely great and utterly demanding present.

In a more indirect and even oblique way, Hattie Meynell, John Robert Rozanov's granddaughter, is also the philosopher's pupil, and her little drama of sexual arousal and fairy-tale mythology is played out under the aegis of his tyrannical will. On his command a Prospero–Miranda–Ferdinand triangle is set up, with Tom McCaffrey chosen as the Ferdinand figure. Murdoch's novels rub against rather than echo their sources, however, and the dramatics of *The Tempest* are ironically perverted rather than enjoined. Tom bungles his task and shows no servitude to Rozanov; indeed his story is shaped by the strange vagaries of other archetypal sources: the questing prince and the *princesse lointaine*, the princess and the dragon, the descent to the underworld, etc. This Prospero is perverted by an incestuous lust for his granddaughter that precipitates his philosophical moral crisis and contributes to his decision to commit suicide. In long conversations with her grandfather, however, Hattie is initiated into the idea and fact of love as an overwhelming passion, and sees how his passion and barely controlled self-discipline shake his entire and complex being. This rite of passage opens her to the possibility of a normal sexual relationship with Tom, who has also paid his dues to the cavernous underworld of the subconscious. These two initiated children, like the young in Shakespeare's late romances, then go off tenuously into a mythic world of idyllic marriage.

But Stella McCaffrey is the only student we meet, aside from the almost non-existent Steve Glatz, whom Rozanov has in the past considered worthy. Because of Murdoch's greater interest in her as a vehicle for narratological demonstration, however, she is the most fragilely conceived of all of the important characters in *The Philosopher's Pupil*. As a result, Rozanov's expectations and methods as a teacher are not given extended analysis. Frustrated and despairing though he may be about human beings doing philosophy, John Robert is nevertheless perceived by these characters as the best – certainly as the most idealized – possible representative of his profession. It is clear that a philosopher in order to be good need only be good at his job; Rozanov's faltering and culpable behavior in quotidian life does not really touch the issue of what he can teach and what a good student like Stella might learn. The final obscurity of this novel is that we leave it not knowing what practical ideal of pupilhood might exist for Rozanov, if any.

*

The Philosopher's Pupil is a crowded novel that raises many subjects. Aside from its imaginative fecundity in the creation of place and an enormous set of characters reflecting the whole range of town types, the book also comments on the nature of fiction, the problems of philosophy, the relationship between teacher and student, and the power of ethical imperatives. It is also deeply committed to an ambiguous study of the incursion of magic into human life, and in this it and *The Good Apprentice* not only continue Murdoch's past querying of the uses of magic but show an intensified examination of human consciousness and illusion. If Murdoch were merely a didactic writer, the dangers of human evocations of magic would be treated in a consistently negative way. It is certainly true that in the novels her few characters of the good eschew magic and stalwartly force themselves to perceive as much reality as possible. But in *The Philosopher's Pupil* the possibilities of a magic mysticism are mysterious and pervasive, and even the philosopher John Robert Rozanov sees the ancient stones of the Ennistone Ring as spiritually endowed, describing them as being as close to gods as we can get.

Outside is inside, as many of the characters tell us, but there is considerable ambiguity about the outsideness of certain manifestations. The catalog of quasi-mysticism is long. Everyone in Ennistone agrees that the town goes through "funny times" when people act strangely and nature erupts like Lud's Rill fountain for no explicably scientific reason; the one saintly being in the book, William (Bill the Lizard) Eastcote sees a flying saucer above the Common, and George believes himself after his "murder" of Rozanov to have been blinded not by an inside force – an hysterical reaction to his own overwhelming violence – but by the outside malignity of another flying saucer. Both Alex and her gypsy servant Ruby interpret the foxes in the garden as magical manifestations, and Gabriel McCaffrey is haunted by the uncanny as she tries to save a fish caught and tortured by callow youths. Her 8-year-old son Adam is an animist who sees doubles of his uncle George, as does the priest Father Jacoby, and George himself is not only haunted by his double, but by an apparently external numerology that stresses the number 44 (his age during the action of the book) at every turn. George is also plagued by the language of the birds, a phenomenon of seventeenth-century language theory that contended that in a shamanist universe the original tongue of the original Adam is still heard as birds converse.

Added to this list is Murdoch's own mystical adherence to the efficacy of the eloquent religious Word. Her tool is Father Bernard as an agent of the incredible power of ancient incantations. Not only does he delight almost but not quite to the point of belief in the gorgeous words of Cranmer's Book of Common Prayer, but at one point he pins a troubled George down on the sofa, forcing him to recite the Lord's Prayer as an aspect of healing magic. This impressive but partial list of ambiguous inner–outer occurrences stresses the degree to which Murdoch strives to keep human experience in a vexed, undetermined area where certitude is alien. She has always seen human action as muddled and our comprehension as so limited that we will never get to the bottom of things. Here, by presenting a multitude of circumstances where objective perception is questionable, she reminds us, as she does even more dramatically in *The Good Apprentice*, that the borderline between reality and illusion cannot be discerned by the mere will to be rationally accurate.

In both *The Philosopher's Pupil* and *The Good Apprentice*, illusionist magic and redemptive theology as a branch of that magic share an important if ambiguous proselytizing function. For Murdoch as an advocate of the blank face of the Platonic Good, human incapacities are foremost, and in both of these novels she demonstrates how the perception of her characters is clouded by religious fantasies and magic redemptive devices. This does not lead to simple fictions: *The Good Apprentice* is dominated by the problems of illusion, and uses ingenious means to estimate the ubiquity of misperception and the impossibility of an accurate reading of the text of the world and human experience in it. In *The Philosopher's Pupil* Murdoch shows how laziness and a want of knowledge impede the reading of literary texts. Here in *The Good Apprentice* she evokes a deeper uneasiness that comes of the fact that no amount of human energy directed toward an accurate interpretation of experience can lead to a penetration of truth. The two good apprentices of the ambiguous title, the step-brothers Stuart Cuno and Edward Baltram, in opposite ways try to see the truth; both learn the compromises that are necessary.

Very early in *The Good Apprentice* most of the major characters engage in a dinner conversation on virtue and language, subjects dear to Murdoch's heart. Their victim is Stuart Cuno who has dropped out of graduate school in mathematics in order to study virtue and lead a good, useful life. The conversation is heated and intelligent, with Stuart's quest for virtue and his denial of certain aspects of science and technology, particularly computers, central. As the novel develops, the striving Stuart is seen by the other characters as a man in error and a death-bringer; here he presents good, subtle arguments about the crucial ethical differences between human and artificial intelligence – but fails to make an impact:

> "A machine doesn't think –" said Stuart. "A machine can't even simulate the human mind . . . because we are always involved in distinguishing between good and evil. . . . Human minds are possessed by individual persons, they are soaked in values, even perception is evaluation. . . . But it [mathematics] can't be a model for the mind, it's not a super-mind, computer logic can't be a model for the mind, there's no ideal model and there can't be because minds are persons, they're moral and spiritual all the way through, the idea of a machine isn't in place, artificial intelligence is a misnomer –"

Although Stuart is worried about human ethical and spiritual intelligence as opposed to "objective" artificial intelligence, he is even more afraid of the loss of a significant human language:

> "I'm afraid that we could lose our language, and so lose our souls, our sense of truth, and ordinary reality, our sense of direction, our knowledge of right and wrong . . . lose our value language, lose our central human language which is spoken by individuals and refers to the real world. . . . We could lose our ordinary sense of an order of the world as ultimate, our self-being, our responsible consciousness –"

The fear that a cultural and spiritual Logos might be removed from the world lies behind much of Murdoch's fiction, and here she applies it specifically to the dehumanized threat of computer intelligence. At the same time her novels insist on another sort of dehumanization – that of the very idea of God. The world she advocates thus threads its way between the Scylla of technology and the Carybdis of the theological tradition of the west. Murdoch insists in novels and interviews that although there is no God, religion must persist on this planet in order for ethical thought to remain part of our human baggage. And for her, ethical thought is entirely dependent on the survival of subtle and complex language.

202

Eric Voegelin, in volume 5 of *Order and History*, claims the gods are not something one speaks of in language, but are themselves the language one uses to speak of certain kinds of experience, and I believe that Murdoch wishes to see the language of godhood primarily in this light – as a means of expressing the existence of sovereign spiritual states. In the novels she counters her atheism by arguing for the reality of Christ, whose mythology or Christology each human being must build up for her/himself. This paradoxical system of denying the reality of God and embracing the mythology of Christ as "real" puts her and her illustrative characters into a strange position, but at the heart of her thought is the idea that Christ is an ethical model who must not be lost through the incompetence of the church and the secularism of the people.

Meanwhile, the perpetual struggle to be virtuous has not yet been lost in an apparently irreligious world. Nothing in Stuart Cuno's upbringing or cultural experience stressed a rigorous virtue as opposed to ordinary civilized decency, yet he comes up with the concept and determines to devote his life to it. His psychoanalyst uncle, Thomas McCaskerville, is fascinated by the quality and range of Stuart's mind, but warns him that he will be jeered at – as he is at that first dinner table and throughout the book. Whenever Murdoch chooses to depict a character with a commitment to the rigors of the good during her novelistic career, she presents him/her as an outsider whose participation in life is marginal and often unhappy, and Stuart Cuno is no exception. To the celebrants of life's pleasures, his abnegations and seriousness appear as a life-denying insult – as the senile, half-crazed Jesse Baltram intuits when he sees him sitting at the table at Seegard: "That man's dead, take him away, I curse him. Take that white thing away, it's dead. The white thing, take it away from here."

Vilified Stuart indeed is at every turn: his ideas are considered comic, his brother Edward refuses to listen to his good advice and throws the Bible he had recommended at him, Midge screams against him as a bringer of death because he witnessed the guilt of her affair with his father, his attempt to assuage the anger and grief of the dead Mark Wilsden's mother leads to both her and Elspeth Macran's raging against him, and his father hits him, kicks him out, and hurls a paperweight after him. This is hardly a catalog of success, but Stuart basically does nothing except watch, practice his various disciplines, and meditate. He also retains integrity right up to the end of the fiction, where he describes his decision to train as a schoolmaster of the very young as the only means of effecting change in society from its roots: "Computers, OK, but that's just mechanical. You can teach language and literature and how to use words so as to *think*. And you can teach moral values, you can teach meditation, what used to be called prayer, and give them an idea of what goodness is, and how to love it –"

Compared to his brother, Edward Baltram, who participates absolutely and wretchedly in human life, Stuart's apprenticeship is straitened, narrow, and comprehensible. Edward, crushed and blackened by his guilt in the drug-death of his schoolfriend Mark Wilsden, is the more suitable candidate as the eponymous good apprentice. Difficult though it is for Stuart to fix his eye on virtue, define it, and discipline himself to live according to it, Edward lives in a world where virtue is a lost irrelevancy and forgiveness impossible to attain. Behind both of these characters hovers the figure of the psychotherapist, Thomas McCaskerville, their elderly step-uncle, who is a kind of puppeteer, making sure that everything and everyone connects tightly in a complicated, almost Dickensian mesh of coincidence and causality. Thomas can be perceived negatively as a quasi-philosophical practitioner believing, in the R.D. Laing style, that suffering aids in spiritual development. His power over the two young men is certainly suspect, and it is evident that several of the characters fear his involvement in and interpretation of their lives. Nevertheless, although Murdoch usually satirizes psychoanalysis in her novels, Thomas comes across as an equivocal character whose drive for power is mediated by his desire to interpret validly and effect amelioration.

In an interview with John Haffenden (1985) that took place while Murdoch was working on *The Good Apprentice*, she addresses the issue of psychotherapy:

> I think people who are good – it sounds romantic, but I think I've met one or two – make a sort of space around them, and you feel you are safe with them. And there are certainly people who are menacing, who breathe up all the air so that you can't breathe, and who diminish you. This is why a good analyst would have to have this quality of making a large space – someone who is reassuring without bolstering up in an illegitimate way, because the good person also comes to one as a judge.

Thomas appears to be this sort of therapist, in that even the troubled, withdrawn Edward trusts him and obeys him, thus being manipulated in ultimately efficacious ways. Thomas's power over the action is enormous – Edward finds out near the end of the novel from his half-sister, Bettina, for example, that he had been summoned to Seegard not by the needs of his father or Mother May, but because Thomas wrote the Baltrams to suggest the visit – but he is a magically manipulative artist whose opening out of space for action allows the fiction to take place. As a version of the white magician, the novel questions but does not much blame him.

The real magic that works on Edward, however, comes from the emanations of Seegard, another of Murdoch's enchanted gothic places, rather than from his puppeteer uncle. Like the focal houses in *The Unicorn* and *The Sea, The Sea*, Seegard is a self-contained world and the semantic as well as symbolic center of the novel. The pastoral alternative world or secondary landscape of Seegard is a convincing but appalling structure used by Murdoch as an ambiguous parody of the pastoral tradition. Not only is it a place created for the proper functioning of an ambiguous fiction, a place to which Edward is called (as he superstitiously thinks to be healed), it is also a self-conscious psycho-sociological artifact designed and built by the painter Jesse Baltram, Edward's natural father. As an architectural curiosity it, like Murdoch's novel, lacks an easy formal coherence: as one of the women inhabitants remarks, the perceiver has to learn its logic and beauty. This difficulty of access also characterizes the violent styles of Jesse's painting; Edward, looking at them casually, finds them ominous and is able to make nothing much of them. Near the end of the book as Edward leaves Seegard for the last time in the novel, he negatively identifies the place as the dead enchanter's castle, and this ambiguity between death and power describes how it dominantly exists.

Although Edward has been loved and nurtured throughout his life by his step-father, Harry Cuno, Harry is impotent to cure his son's obsessive guilt through his kindness or the rational argument that Edward is having a nervous breakdown and will recover. The novel begins biblically with the guilty words from the parable of the prodigal son: "I will arise and go to my father, and will say unto him, Father I have sinned against heaven and before thee, and am no more worthy to be called thy son." Haunted by misery and deeply depressed, Edward, who can find no comfort in Harry or his alternate father figure, Thomas McCaskerville, eagerly starts out on a mystical quest in which he imagines that his real father, the famous painter Jesse Baltram who had ignored his illegitimate son up to this point, will consolingly accept his confession and absolve him of his terrible sin. The parable of the prodigal son is deeply applicable to the events of the fiction, not only in Edward's simple hope for an outside agent of forgiveness but also in the identification of Stuart with the prodigal's brother, who stayed home. In comparison with Edward's adventures from the moment of Mark Wilsden's drug-death to the end of the book, Stuart does nothing. While his brother is on a dark and hazardous spiritual journey, Stuart meditates; but as he points out to Harry, he is unlike the prodigal's brother in that the latter was resentful, whereas Stuart tries hard and wishes for the best. Stuart's quiet stance is useful in a contradictory manner: it not only serves the applicability of the beautiful parable but gives the reader her/his first indication that systematic symbolic centers supply false readings of the circumstances.

Edward's deification of Jesse and vision of himself as the prodigal son (not to mention Cain, the slayer of his brother) are illusions of the most ambiguous sort. Ultimately a product of his inventive and self-protective imagination, Edward's vision of Jesse has nebulous origins in a seance, and the combination of determinacy and chance that lead to its confirmation is questioned but unanswered in the plot process of *The Good Apprentice*. In the midst of his unassuageable wretchedness, Edward finds a card in his jacket pocket advertising seances conducted by a Mrs Quaid. Although many of the connexions in this novel spring from the careful manipulations of Thomas McCaskerville, there is also a fateful cosmic aspect manipulating the plot from the beginning.

The seance itself is more mysterious than Murdoch's art, and finally obscure beyond conjecture. Edward is unknown to the vague Mrs Quaid, and is therefore amazed when he hears an accented male voice (we learn later that Jesse has a provincial accent) saying that someone in the room with two fathers must go to his real father. This strange genesis of Edward's quest is never explained in rational terms. Its occult power is underlined in a later, desperate visit to a now dying Mrs Quaid during which Edward in a sort of stupor sees on her television screen the missing Jesse guiding him to the place on the river's estuary where his son will find his body. Edward can impose no reasonable explanation on these occurrences, and their ambiguity within the realm of magic participates in the overall sense both *The Philosopher's Pupil* and *The Good Apprentice* deliver of a world significantly haunted by the uncanny.

At Seegard, Edward's eventual discovery of the all too present Jesse offers somewhat more realistic fare. The house itself is complexly illusionistic, in that its architectural meanderings are hard to follow, and it appears to represent an idyllic fairy-tale abode of active high-thinking vitalism. The three women who inhabit it are like figures from medieval romance – the three queens of the Arthurian legend, perhaps, who guard the once and future king who in this case is Jesse, the weird enchanter who created this magical castle. The illusion wears thin quickly enough: Edward discovers that the homespun medieval garments of the women are thoroughly darned and mended and their once-active loom heavy with dust, that the house is dirty and the women for all their industry sloppy and careless in their housekeeping, and that the enchanter himself is kept locked in his tower because of illness and erratic senile dementia. But even when the illusions are destroyed, there is an abiding sense of magic at Seegard that combines eerily with the natural: strange cries fill the night (Edward who believes that it could be Jesse calling is told that it is owls or is denied explanation), poltergeists crash about and whiz past him in the hallways, the homemade fruit and dandelion wines seem to be drugged, and the herbal teas may all be dangerous potions.

Edward's perception of the weirdness of the house is increased when Harry and his aunt Midge are almost mystically drawn to it, and it is in its creepy confines that their affair becomes public knowledge through Mother May's perfidy. The scene of their arrival is extremely well handled, the characters superbly engineered and marshaled in Murdoch's distinctive, wildly hilarious style. The tawdriness of Midge and Harry's ordinary adultery stands in dramatic contrast to the silence of the "white" Stuart, who is also present, and the mad desperation of Jesse Redivivus. The success of this scene also calls into question the roles of Harry and Midge in the novel. *The Good Apprentice* is crowded with sympathetically imagined characters who add a verisimilitude to the created world; Harry and Midge are important here for the roles they play in terms of the more central characters and for the basic selfish deception of their affair. But as she often does in depicting egoistic, idle, middle-aged women, Murdoch gives too many pages to Midge's repetitive ruminations on her "sufferings," and in general the affair is one that the reader wishes to see end much sooner and more economically than it does. I suppose one could argue that Murdoch is dialogically interested in the ordinary person and Midge is certainly ordinary – but neither she nor Harry suffer interestingly, and the burden of the pages devoted to them is distracting.

The contrast between these dull lovers and Jesse is great, and can be seen as the distance separating the quotidian from the magical. Although Edward can react to the affair and Midge's confusions in a straightforward, helpful way, he cannot break the almost supernatural hold that his natural father retains over him in both life and death. The sick Jesse is unreliable in terms of consciousness, and Edward's perceptions of him are at best slippery. Mother May and Bettina keep referring to him as senile and untrustworthy, but his apparently conscious response to Edward as his long-lost son causes an allegiance that remains unbroken.

Jesse is not only a painter of great stature, although his reputation is temporarily in eclipse, but he has also been the mastermind at Seegard of a vitalist mode of life that stands in stark contrast to the crowded bourgeois world of London. In his appearances to Edward there is something fascinat-ingly monstrous and even miraculous – at one point he walks Christ-like on water toward his son who stares in amazement, only to find that it is another illusion. When his mental instability combines with his passionate sorrow for the passing of his life and his goatish love of women, the image of Jesse is one of pathos and vitality in the midst of death; his apparent communication of his death to his son through the seance–television scene gives the reader's apprehension of him still another twist. A man of self-aggrandizing, tyrannous control over the women he once commanded, he obviously also enjoys his new power over Edward; at the same time he has loved and thought about him enough (and despised the women enough too) to write and have witnessed a will before Edward's visit to Seegard, leaving his son all his possessions.

The characters agree that Jesse is a powerful enchanter and an ambiguous figure – the painter of obscurely ominous pictures, the architect of a bizarre house, and a magician who creates and manipulates the lives of those around him. As an illusionist, he may or may not be responsible for the single impossible scene Edward sees at Seegard. In an early walk in the woods, Edward comes upon a ceremonially cleared space that he labels the dromos with a column and stone plinth at one end (later he finds that it is called the Lingam Stone – the place of killing). Flowers have been placed on the stone as on an altar. On a later visit he hides in surprise at the arrival of his half-sister, Ilona, who ritualistically girds herself for a strange dance in which her feet completely leave the ground and she is swept by an alien force gracefully over and above the cleared "sacred" space. When the dance is over and she returns to the ground, she re-enters the normal world in tears: later, when she has been transformed into a Soho stripper, Edward discovers to his horror that she is totally, awkwardly unable to dance. The mystical grace of this illusion, like the seance, remains unexplained and is clearly meant to be part of the alien power exuded by Jesse's complexity.

Whatever "real" magic there might be surrounding the person of Jesse, *The Good Apprentice* focuses on more useful illusions – the inner images and outer signs through which the individual subjective mind creates its self-preserving interpretations. The inner images come from imaginative power or dreams, such as Midge's dream image of a white accusatory horseman of death as well as the pictures Edward blurts out to Thomas in order to describe his dark state of soul – a stalling airplane, a dying chrysalis, a dead butterfly. The spiders of Seegard become resonant for Jesse of Shakespeare's Leontes in *The Winter's Tale* who has "drunk and seen the spider" of human betrayal. These inner manifestations are echoed by outer signs – like the plaits of girls' hair at Auschwitz that become symbols for Stuart of all the terrible suffering the concentration camp implied, or the vitality of a mouse that actually lives and thrives by the tracks of the London Underground. Perhaps the most positively instrumental of outer signs is the robin who flutters into the room as Harry and Thomas are having it out over Midge: its fragility redirects their attention from themselves to another object, with the result that the scene loses its tension and falls into resolution.

Novel readers are signs readers, and the most compelling pattern of imposed signs in this novel is the contrast between black and white – the unremitting blackness of Edward's guilty misery and the whiteness of Stuart's meditative urge toward virtue. Mad Jesse curses Stuart as a white, dead thing, and even Thomas sees him as a figurative albino, while Midge makes him into the living presentation of her dream image of the white horseman of death. Because Stuart keeps asserting that "religion is about good and evil and the distance between them," it is tempting to arrange the complex images and patterns of *The Good Apprentice* into an appealingly comfortable dichotomy of morally simplistic black and white. But that is not what Murdoch is after – indeed as she works this novel out, it is clear that neither color evokes a single cohesive interpretation. Edward's black and Stuart's white are both troubled moral areas that mesh in the body of the novel into a complex, fused vision of a world of compromise, illusion, ambiguity, and the failure of all modes of salvation.

Behind all the image patterns, the alternative landscape of Seegard, the ambiguous character of Jesse, the bourgeois quotidian, and the good apprentices, hovers a larger theme whose exploration is central to this novel. Murdoch begins with the prodigal son's statement of guilt and sin, and from it – following the examples of such anti-original-sin thinkers as Kierkegaard and Bernard Lonergan – draws the reader into a full examination of human consciousness. Lonergan describes sin as a contraction of consciousness, and it is within a contracted consciousness that Edward Baltram unintentionally kills his friend. This terrible act leads him on his apprentice's path, as his consciousness through guilt, grief, and remorse progressively follows a path toward inward and outward awareness. Not only is his consciousness awakened, but all of the other characters are placed on a spectrum of awareness – from the clouded sporadic consciousness of the magical Jesse to the ethical thought of Stuart. Thomas McCaskerville sits in awe over the powers of the mind to create conversations, to spawn images that show self-conscious awareness, and to think metaphorically. The thrust of the entire novel is to teach the reader the wonder, the value, and the fragility of consciousness.

Yet this novel demonstrates sadness and endurance rather than despair, and this is where Murdoch would leave her reader at this point in her career. Less narratological in intent than *The Philosopher's Pupil*, *The Good Apprentice* strives for an ambiguous spiritual statement, quietly taking for granted the splendid machinery and the "archaic stance" of the living and continuing novel form. The use of fiction for such complexly resolute utterance is Murdoch's real achievement.

10

Saul Bellow and Cynthia Ozick's "corona of moral purpose"

In reviewing Bellow's collection of five story-novellas entitled *Him With His Foot In His Mouth* in 1984 in the *New York Times Book Review*, Cynthia Ozick, one of the most accomplished of contemporary American fictionists, claims that in this work Bellow newly and openly decodes himself. She finds him suddenly telling the reader that he is driven by a divine apprehension, by a placing of his work – and indeed American civilization, which is his subject – under "the Eye of God." Ozick stands to be corrected, however, because there is no suddenness here. Bellow's novels since *Mr Sammler's Planet* (1970) have prayed for and to the transcendent, and even before that, in *Henderson the Rain King* and *Herzog*, the struggle of the mind for the beyond was clear. Some critics have studied this transcendental tendency on Bellow's part and many have accused him of false apocalyptic conclusions to his novels, but most of the issues raised in discussions of his work have to do with either stylistics or American sociopolitics. In both areas he is ill used, because of his anti-university stance and his aggressively overbearing political analyses.

It is commonplace now to point out that Bellow as a writer is too conventional – like Iris Murdoch, or Michel Tournier, or many of the best writers of our period. Ozick's defense of him is therefore significant:

> No preciousness, of the ventriloquist kind or any other; no carelessness either (formidably the opposite); no romantic aping of archaisms or nostalgias; no restraints born out of theories of form or faddish tenets of experimentalism or ideological crypticness; no Neanderthal flatness in the name of cleanliness of prose; no gods of nihilism; no gods of subjectivity; no philosophy of parody. As a consequence of these and other salubrious omissions and insouciant dismissals, Bellow's detractors have accused him of being "old-fashioned," "conventional," of continuing to write a last-gasp American version of the 19th century European novel; his omnivorous "Russianness" is held against him, and at the same time he is suspecting of expressing the deadly middle class.

Even the generous English critic, Malcolm Bradbury, who has written articles, essays, and a very good monograph on Bellow, says that he finds the novels formally too conventional. And Bellow's ardent enemy, Richard Poirier, who champions Thomas Pynchon as the greatest novelist in America (or wherever he is), claims that it is time the literati stopped treating the publication of each new Bellow novel as a major literary event.

Not least among Bellow's reputed faults is his early desertion of the American Jewish writers' camp – although it is also possible to argue that the talented male Jews who came close to dominating American writing in the 1950s and on into the 1960s – Norman Mailer, Philip Roth, Bernard Malamud, Delmore Schwartz, Joseph Heller, and Bellow, to name only the major figures – did not really form a private club, and that under any circumstances it self-destructed. In interviews, Bellow expresses bewilderment at the current debased, confessional mode of Roth and the sexual, media self-projection of Mailer, and one can go far back through the decades of Bellow's fame as a novelist to see how early his revulsion against being classified as a Jewish writer occurred.

From the beginning, Bellow wished above all to be a good *American* writer, which, given the nature of the American literary and political tradition, means a writer who uses the forms of fiction to firm effect in the elucidation and amelioration of the culture in which it is set. Bellow admires Melville and Emerson, but claims the naturalism of Theodore Dreiser as his background, seeing in Dreiser's blunt exposition of the horrors of Chicago urban life a partial but real antecedent to his own historically differentiated novels. He knows that Dreiser is a poor stylist and in many ways a *naïf*, but Bellow often appears to be using writers like Dreiser in order to diminish critical notation of the effect of the European style on his fiction – to divert attention from his interest in Dostoevsky and his resemblance to certain aspects of Conrad, Joyce, or Mann, in order to stress his American lineage and the difference between American literary tradition and that of Europe. He is no Henry James.

At the same time his work bears the constant pressure of what he calls the old European culture game, and the intellectual infusion of European ideas and ideologies into American culture is for him a major conundrum and theme. It is interesting to note, too, that there is a transatlantic reciprocity here in that the English novelist, Martin Amis, admires Bellow's work and sees his descriptions of the US as model. In his 1986 collection of essays about the States, Amis took his title, *The Moronic Inferno*, from *Humboldt's Gift*, and his acute and hard-hitting critiques of American excess sound the same shocking and brittle note as Bellow's more resonant, more American prose.

Bellow's first two novels are interesting, but he actively created a distinctive style for himself with the writing of *The Adventures of Augie March* (1953), where his genius for comedy with distinct Yiddish overtones had an ebullient and hard-hitting impact. In his two earlier novels he had already established his primary strategic mode of centering the fiction's structure in the consciousness of the male protagonist – a hero with strong antiheroic tendencies, and a victim–loser in the game of life. In spite of his originality as a key figure, however, the energized comic persona of Augie March is narrow, idealistic, and too self-satisfied to carry the burden that Bellow increasingly put on his male protagonists. Solipsists like Wilhelm in *Seize the Day* and Henderson in *Henderson the Rain King* learn a lot, but it was not until *Herzog* that Bellow made his greatest stride forward in the difficult creation of an extended consciousness supple enough to express the range of ideas crucial to his sense of the proper use of the American novel.

In the debates surrounding Bellow's work, many naive readers look back wistfully to the relative ease of dealing with *Augie March, Seize the Day*, and *Henderson the Rain King*, but with *Herzog* (1964) Bellow first really challenged the reader in the way that has become his hallmark. In the more than two decades since the thunderous applause accorded *Herzog*, Bellow has published four more novels – *Mr Sammler's Planet* (1970), *Humboldt's Gift* (1975), *The Dean's December* (1982), and *More Die of Heartbreak* (1987) – and two collections of stories. Each is a distinctive contribution to an *oeuvre* that remains ideologically stable, but increasingly dense and difficult of access. In spite of his fame, the Nobel award, three National Book Awards, the Pulitzer Prize, his clear cultural presence on the American scene, and his much admired comic talents, Bellow has not chosen to welcome the reader as a partner and, in his own way, his attitude toward his audience is as mandarin as that of a trickster like Nabokov.

The reader delivers him/herself into the magisterial hands of the narrator; another way of putting it is that if you read the novel, you take the seminar. The point of the novels since *Herzog* is the transmission of passionately felt ideas. Bellow perceives these as hard-won, and as ideas that can be achieved only by filtering the steady intellectual accumulation of the last 200 years (the effects of Romanticism and post-Romanticism) through the mind of the observer of the historical present. Each of the five late books concentrates on the same set of subjects, but their clearest defining indicator is *Mr Sammler's Planet*, where Bellow has an elderly Polish *émigré*, survivor of the Holocaust, as his key character and intelligence. But it was *Herzog* that led the way.

Herzog hit the American reading public hard in 1964, and Bellow was instantly heralded as a *nonpareil*; one critic, Roger Sale, typified the enthusiasm when he claimed *Herzog* as the Great American Novel (finally!) and then compared it favorably with the epical largeness of *Moby-Dick*. It seemed then to have every ingredient the decade required – brilliant comedy, a vital American voice in language both supple and accurate, black humor, vaulting intellectual ambition, and a sense of human idealist possibilities. It was also perceived by many, to a notable degree, as a *roman à clef* that set gossips buzzing about Bellow's former marriage. The emotional vigor of the attack on the ex-buddy and wife-stealer, Valentine Gersbach/Jack Ludwig, is both convincing and salacious, but on the whole there is little profit in pursuing Bellow's habit of re-dressing his acquaintances in fictional garb. The point is that the comic brilliance of Bellow's characterization of the central person, Moses Herzog (the name is taken from a minor character in Joyce's *Ulysses*), is without parallel in American fiction. Although Bellow has created interesting protagonists since Herzog, he has not again achieved quite this degree of success – although Charlie Citrine in *Humboldt's Gift* is in close competition.

Bellow's success with the character of Herzog comes from an ingenious twisting of the old epistolary novelistic device – the writing of letters as a main part of the text. Herzog composes letters to everyone – friends, enemies, professors, government officials, Eisenhower, Heidegger, Nietzsche, the Ancients, anyone whose thought has been crucial to his education – in a manic attempt to sort out the colossal world-historical mess that is somehow symbolized in his divorce and his inability to rationalize his life. Many critics have seen Herzog as the typical Jewish *schlemiel* or blunderer, but in an interview in *TriQuarterly* in 1984 Bellow carefully distinguished between the *schlemiel*, who blunders but is not an intellectual, and the fool, who theorizes constantly to no significant avail. Herzog is clearly in the last category, and like other Bellovian heroes is in a way related to Gimpel the Fool in Isaac Bashevis Singer's story of that title.

In spite of its huge popularity, *Herzog* is the first of Bellow's books to alienate part of his audience because of its intellectual content. From this novel on in his work, Bellows pays more attention to the sifting and re-sorting of ideas than to any of the other conventional demands of the novel form, and it is in this respect that his novels become something quite unlike the reformulations of nineteenth-century realism that he has been accused of. One of his antecedents in this matter is Thomas Mann, whose novels, particularly *The Magic Mountain* and *Doktor Faustus*, are composed of extended philosophical conversations with historical and religious intention. But although there are intellectual conversations everywhere in Bellow's novels, his primary technique is to concentrate more specifically on the central consciousness in impassioned conversation with itself. In other words, Bellow is much more interested in internal monologue than other-directed dialogue, and many of his dialogues occur only to highlight the ideas of the central protagonist. Herzog does not compose his letters so that dialogue can take place, but so that he has the illusion of dialogue while he attempts to clear his own mind.

This singular quest for clarity by the thinking male is at the heart of the recent novels, but whereas Herzog, Charlie Citrine (in *Humboldt's Gift*), and Kenneth Trachtenberg (in *More Die of Heartbreak*) have alleviating comic propensities, Mr Sammler and Albert Corde (in *The Dean's December*) do not. Although Bellow opted for high comedy from the time of *The Adventures of Augie March*, his work often indicates that, aside from witty one-liners, he almost has to remind himself of his comic commitment. But his commitment to ideas remains absolute, and takes over from the other novelistic possibilities he demonstrated earlier in his career. Although most readers were exhilarated by the intellectual co-ordinates of *Herzog*, some were intimidated by the density of the book, and by its need to sort through ideologies at a rapid and highly judgmental rate.

This concentration on ideas that circle endlessly in the minds of his central male protagonists is like a protracted series of Shakespearean soliloquies, with the other characters and the limited action providing only emotional or intellectual occasions for further cogitation. On this basis, I would argue that Bellow is, in practice, not particularly reflective of the traditional novelist, but that he uses the novel form in peculiar ways for his own ends. He sticks to the broad tenets of realism without wasting his time questioning their linguistic or ontological basis, and he shapes his fiction in sturdy Aristotelian fashion toward a pointed and often apocalyptic conclusion. But his tendency toward extremely limited action, his brief, undeveloped characterization except in the case of the central male, and his lapses in courtship to the reader all indicate a redirection of energy away from the centers of traditional realism.

At one point in John Fowles's *The French Lieutenant's Woman*, the interfering narrator asks rhetorically why, since he wishes to shape the response of the reader to his own negative point of view about the Victorian period, he did not simply write a series of social essays with philosophical overtones. The answer is that as novelist he can do more because his area of persuasion is larger, and Bellow too shapes his novels so that this wide-ranging form can serve his uses. On one level, those uses have precisely to do with an examination of American culture, a politicized late-twentieth-century *The Way We Live Now* replete with criticism and subtly implied answers that may or may not be capable of realization. Bellow describes his angry attack on Chicago in *The Dean's December* as a *cri de coeur* addressed to the inability of Chicagoans to see the truth and state it. By extension, his embittered clamor is directed at the American urban situation, where Chicago's demonic corruption is the best example. As he presents his Chicago characters – many of them lawyers, some of them political fringe figures – Bellow shows how their tough American amorality springs from a culture that no longer invites accurate observation or uses language to present precise analytical observation. In such a world, integrity is lost and amelioration impossible.

The need to see and to use fiction as a communicative bridge is important to Bellow; it is equally major that the reader participate only as an invited guest, a looker-on at a splendid display of words and hard thought. The resulting novel of ideas, hung loosely on a plot situation, is Bellow's distinctive American creation. Its dominant characteristic is the clarity and personality of the voice – strong, precise, moving easily among broken sentences of acerbic assertion, eloquent paragraphs, cutting witty one-liners, and occasional brilliant dialogue. Bellow's complaint against the conventional British novel is that it lacks a distinct and individual voice, and that the decorous norms of writing in that culture create a diminishing blandness that he as American novelist must avoid in order for effective communication to occur.

The creation of an American voice is a major subject in the late twentieth century, when Americans have come to doubt the ascendancy of their culture and its "moronic inferno." Martin Amis is no doubt right in seeing Bellow as the touchstone critic of a country that is not much more bewildering to foreigners than to its own bemused inhabitants. Richard Poirier is right, too, in pointing to the rival prose of Thomas Pynchon, whose three novels also stress the shifting of American stylistics between the conventional, the poetic, and the canny slang of the American wiseacre. Both Pynchon (who has faded from center stage since *Gravity's Rainbow*, published in 1973 when he was 36) and Bellow share a seriousness in the observation of the American scene and an ethical dimension that haunts the absurdities they comically and satirically describe.

But Pynchon is much more prone to the mysteriously allegorical and the symbolically cybernetic; his novels satisfy the linguistic skepticism and theoretical bent of academic literary critics whose traditional political liberalism makes them unwilling to listen to Bellow's impatience with theory. In *Four Postwar American Novelists* (1977), Frank McConnell shows parallels between these two writers, and connects them with John Barth and Norman Mailer as producers of an American persona in the mid- to late twentieth century. Whereas Bellow hammers home what he perceives as the facts, Pynchon makes metaphoric conjectures about the almost supernatural muddle at the centers of power.

In many ways it is hard to see Bellow as a humanist literary figure in the old-fashioned sense, as a defender of aesthetic standards burnished by political concern – the ideal associated in American culture with Lionel Trilling and the less elegant Edmund Wilson. Until the publication in 1970 of *Mr Sammler's Planet*, with its outraged attack on prevailing Romanticism and the political ignorance of the 1960s generation, Bellow seemed, with his hard, comic voice, to satisfy the prevailing liberalism of the academy. His fairly early decision to limit the novelistic impact of his books in order to stress their ideological content was not unusual in a genre that has a long history of journalistic, documentary, and political intrusion.

In the American tradition, Melville, Dreiser, Sinclair Lewis, and even Scott Fitzgerald used the novel and the benefits of realism to serve some pedagogical version of the "truth"; and Bellow's European antecedents – Dickens, Balzac, Dostoevsky, Conrad, Mann – at least partly saw the novel as a vehicle of authorial thought. Although sticking to the potentialities of realism, Bellow magisterially puts aside many of the factors that traditionally led to readerly sympathy – elaborate plots, the Jamesian dilation of character, suspense, the mythic powers of extended symbolism, etc. – and opts instead for the establishment of a situation and a group of characters over which the critical mind of the narrator can hover thoughtfully throughout the course of the book.

Although most of Bellow's novels have a clangingly trustworthy third-person omniscient narrator (*Humboldt's Gift* and *More Die of Heartbreak* are the exceptions), Bellow's style has a quintessentially first-person impact. The distinctive aspects of the Bellovian voice guarantee this first-person mode, which is generally connected to the primacy of thought and diminution of widespread character development. When comedy is dominant in the novels – as in *Herzog, Humboldt's Gift*, and *More Die of Heartbreak* – the persuasive hilarity of the central character overshadows the ideology to a degree, but there is never an indication that the novelistic can overtake the ideological. There are strong reasons to argue that Bellow is at his best when narrative interests like comedy and character struggle with the intellectual content for supremacy. When this struggle fails to occur, as in *The Dean's December*, the aggressive voice is unmediated in its shrill didacticism and many readers wince at the attack's authorial violence.

The line between assaulting invective and welcome ideological illumination in Bellow's work is thin in even the most disarming of his novels. The resulting vexation for his committed readers – and they are legion – raises issues about Bellow's fiction that, when looked at directly, nevertheless expand rather than diminish one's admiration for this courageous and dedicated writer. Bellow's voice always sounds like first-person narrative because of its tonal consistency and obligation to analytical norms that do not change greatly from book to book. Questing, unceasing, often querulous, this voice can countermand the myriad failures of the central character in question (Bellow says that because of his commitment to realism he has never created a morally "good" character) and spur him on to a limited ethical clarity that could not be achieved without narratorial help. When Bellow allows his protagonist to write in the first person, moreover, he pushes him along with such aids as a secondary protagonist, intellectual dialogue that intrudes Bellow's own voice, and reminiscences of books Bellow approves of ideologically and/or spiritually.

Because the ethical and political data of each book after *Herzog* are generally equivalent, with some difference in significant emphases, the question of dilation of form can be fruitfully raised. Put simply, the reader can well ask what drives Bellow, with his steady thematics and strong statemental instinct, to create new situations productive of new novels instead of remaining with the statements of his previous fictions. In other words, why does he keep moving on, trying again and again for an arresting restatement that will enlarge and clarify his already expressed convictions? Having taken Herzog painfully and hilariously through the history of his intellectual life, Bellow could have rested on that novel's success in spreading out the central rudiments of his thought. Because of the stability and consistency of his ideas and the predominance of ideology over character or plot, the question of Bellow's strong compulsion to keep writing and getting it right emerges as major.

Read carefully, *Herzog* can indeed supply the key to Bellow's fiction – but only to a degree. Although each of Bellow's statemental novels is admirably cogent, he feels a constant need for developmental plenitude – a need to try it again, to see whether another formal situation will produce a better explanation, a clarification, an elaboration, a deepening, a theological or cosmic broadening. The restlessness of Bellow's novels in their attempt to absorb the shifting American scene and to align themselves more accurately with their historical setting energizes his style and rivets his readers. Whether he chooses to laugh or howl, Bellow keeps abreast of the mood of America's advancement through history in all its wildness and Postmodern decadence.

In this most content-oriented of authors, the demand for clarification of his message is unceasing, and each novel presents us with another example of how thinking can – indeed, must – occur in a thoroughly fucked-up civilization. The miasmic madness of American culture, its endless, pointless narcissism, and its commitment to accommodating itself blandly to appalling violence and death are not, for Bellow, subject to ingenious metaphorical turning and oblique commentary in the Pynchon style. Instead, they are issues that scream out for thought, for creativity, and for remedy. And Bellow makes it everywhere apparent that remedy is impossible without radical re-evaluation of the cultural modes and patterns of thought that characterize the American mind. As he expresses it, the ameliorative mythology bought by comfort-seeking Americans is centered on cultivated blindness, a Romanticism of the self, and the devastating demands of role-playing. At the root of his social ideology is a manic exposure of the fragilities of sexuality as expressed in an unstable society. Bellow's men are all enslaved by *machismo* and compulsive womanizing; his women – even those most admired like Corde's wife Minna and her mother in *The Dean's December* – are uncontrollably treated with contempt and condescension. Bellow's anti-feminism is famous, unremitting, and unforgivable.

Mr Sammler's Planet (1970) presents Bellow's most precise analysis of the American situation, because in it he allows Mr Sammler – a carefully chosen character – to soliloquize mentally and lengthily about his uneasiness with American thought and behavior. Of all Bellow's protagonists, Mr Sammler is the least corrupt, and the one most representative of Bellow's ideas. Although European – a Polish survivor of the concentration camp, as well as a late Bloomsburian hanger-on and follower of H.G. Wells in the 1930s – Mr Sammler dwells among the wildest vagaries of New York in the late 1960s. He is slightly older than the century and in every way reflective of it: his life spans its best and worst historical phases. Elderly, frail, with only one eye that is as observant as the lens at Palomar that will figure in the metaphysics of *The Dean's December*, Mr Sammler is indeed a telescope through whom modern history is seen. In spite of the deep Americanness of the book, Bellow

217

concentrates also through Mr Sammler and his relations on the European *émigré* roots of New Yorkers, as well as on the ameliorative thought and destructive terror inherited from Europe's infamous century.

Stylistically abrupt, *Mr Sammler's Planet* is focused entirely through Mr Sammler's observant eye as he deals with his familial relationships in a New York plagued by violent crime, uninformed student rebellion, solipsistic sexual promiscuity, general wackiness, and pitiable suffering. As in the later novel, *The Dean's December*, Bellow organizes his sociocultural co-ordinates so that this novel of ideas has a human basis for its intended illustrations. He does this by keeping the action sporadically but adequately centered on Mr Sammler's nephew, Dr Elya Gruner, who brought Mr Sammler and his silly daughter Shula to America from the transit camp in Austria after World War II, and who is now bravely, stoically dying of an aneurism. The novel begins in the quotidian of Mr Sammler's mind, and moves point by careful point toward his final prayer – a kind of Kaddish spoken over Gruner's dead body – in the last paragraph. It is important to note that essentially, from this point on in Bellow's career, death is his main underlying subject, and each of his works is a kind of Kaddish or prayer for the dead.

Although *Herzog* presents Bellow's insistent juxtaposition of the desperation in the outward lives of Americans and the inability of their education to inform their inward lives, *Mr Sammler's Planet* is more insistent, clearer, and directly analytical. Whereas Herzog wrote to and manically re-evaluated the thinkers who clogged his mind with potential world explanations until he managed to free himself from the manacles of theory, Mr Sammler has already gone far beyond Herzog's narrow world and academic limits. His mind is informed, not by the university, but by deep reading and, above all, by a close experience of the century. While remaining the most scholarly and intellectual of American authors, Bellow, like Gore Vidal, has considerable contempt for university intellectuals. As he frequently explains, the real thinker must find his way backward from an overload of ideas to the intelligent instincts that he is born with and that are obscured by the heavy accumulation of theory in our period. In Bellow's interview with *TriQuarterly* in 1984, he explained that *Herzog* is a *Bildungsroman* in reverse, in which its protagonist has to unlearn great quantities of useless stuff before he can free himself to real thought.

Mr Sammler, on the other hand, begins in this novel with a complete openness to experience – an ideal state in Bellow's work – which was gained by his forced removal from the still idyllic world of Bloomsbury to the Nazi concentration camps. There he desperately clawed his way out from a mass pit of executed Jews; thereafter he killed to stay alive, lived in solitary hiding on the reluctant kindness of a Polish farmer, and learned the ultimate shallowness of idealistic thought and intellectual theories. The reality of suffering Mr Sammler then experienced transcends anything America offers, but he knows that in terms of quite another order the wild men and women rushing around him in New York are full of pain instilled in them by an impossible milieu. This sad realization draws both extended analytical thought and pity from him. The novel takes its tone from the double necessity of living under the aegis of the past and compassionately perceiving the insane present. As a result, Mr Sammler's eye focuses relentlessly on the mad weaknesses of all members of his group, at the same time as it yearns prayerfully toward them.

Bellow pours his capacities for an American version of Dostoyevskyan Russian expressiveness into the mind of Mr Sammler in this eloquent novel. Although some of its critics see it as a conservative capitulation, its purpose is more in keeping with Bellow's courageous attempt to recover the religious concept of the soul within a culture that has almost entirely lost it. *Mr Sammler's Planet* is Bellow's first clear statement of his largest task as a novelist. The New York of this novel is consumed by external money-oriented greed, hilariously typified when Wallace Gruner tears apart and floods his dead father's New Rochelle house trying to find the illegal abortion fortune stashed away somewhere. Yet all its characters are physically comfortable enough from a material point of view, ranging from very wealthy indeed to only moderately poor. Their real poverty is inward and spiritual, as Mr Sammler explains to Govinda Lal:

> But also [man] has something in him which he feels it important to continue. Something that deserves to go on. It is something that has to go on, and we all know it. The spirit feels cheated, outraged, defiled, corrupted, fragmented, injured. Still it knows what it knows, and the knowledge cannot be gotten rid of. The spirit knows that its growth is the real aim of existence. So it seems to me.... The best, I have found, is to be disinterested. Not as misanthropes dissociate themselves, by judging, but by not judging. By willing as God wills.

Mr Sammler sees piercingly, but out of scrupulous generosity does not judge, and this entire novel – which is his prolonged meditation during the few New York days while Elya Gruner lies dying – is an attempt to be faithful to the will of God. In a spectacularly secular world, the will of God is not an easy concept, and Mr Sammler calls forward whatever possibilities he can to try to explain it. Needless to say, the religious arsenal is pathetically small when compared to the tremendous weaponry of secular thought that swamps contemporary American society. The only way that Bellow can stress it adequately is through the structure of the novel itself, and through a few sharp vignettes that must compete with the outrageously interesting and often demonic antics of the other characters.

Although Mr Sammler's mind is full of the mixed cultural images of his Bloomsburian and Holocaust past as well as his American present, he relies on memory and no longer reads much. His mind rakes over the ideas of the past, but he declines the endless verbiage of current explanatory theories. When the kind Margotte tries to defend what he sees as Hannah Arendt's naive formula about Nazism and the banality of evil at the beginning of the book, he effectively talks her down and cuts her short. Although Mr Sammler's one usable eye resists print, he still reads the few texts he considers significant – the Bible and medieval German Christian mystics like Meister Eckhardt and Tauler. This paring down of his intellectual life into direct spiritual statements contrasts deeply with the extended noise of the many theories that have shaped, and now plague and confuse, the other characters in the book.

So pervasive is American confusion and so powerful the sexual outward culture that even a mature man like Walter Bruch – a Polish *émigré* nephew who also survived the concentration camps – transforms his real experience of suffering into the self-indulgence of sexual fantasy and masturbation. Overly confessional like all the American and immigrant characters in this novel, Bruch unwelcomely insists on elaborating his humiliating arm fetish in detail in one of the book's telling vignettes. Mr Sammler's response is striking, but his effort is also clearly a lost cause:

> "Walter, I'm sorry – sorry to see you suffer . . . . I'll pray for you, Walter."
> Bruch stopped crying, clearly startled.
> "What do you mean, Uncle Sammler? You pray?"
> The baritone music left his voice, and it was gruff again, and he gruffly gobbled his words.
> "Uncle Sammler, I have my arms. You have prayers?" He gave a belly laugh. He laughed and snorted, swinging his trunk comically back and forth, holding both his sides, blindly showing both his nostrils. He was not, however, mocking Sammler. Not really. One had to learn to distinguish. . . . But distinguishing? A higher activity.
> "I will pray for you," said Sammler.

In another striking scene that prepares for the novel's end, Angela Gruner sits outside her father's hospital room in a solipsistic funk. It is evident that her father is either dead or dying at that very moment, but she is thoroughly angry because he chided her for the sexually promiscuous behavior that led to her break-up with a potential fiancé, Wharton Horricker. Mr Sammler, knowing that the one thing that might comfort Elya as he dies would be a generous, loving gesture on Angela's part, tries to persuade her to it, even though he knows he is arousing her fury and perhaps in doing so cutting off his own pension, which will henceforth be in her hands as one of Elya's heirs:

> "You've got to do something for him. He has a need."
> "What something am I supposed to do?"
> "That's up to you. If you love him, you can make some sign. He's grieving. He's in a rage. He's disappointed. And I don't really think it is the sex. At this moment that might well be a trivial consideration. Don't you see, Angela? You wouldn't need to do much. It would give the man a last opportunity to collect himself."
> "As far as I can see, if there is anything at all in what you say, you want an old-time deathbed scene."
> "What difference does it make what you call it?"
> "I should ask him to forgive me? Are you serious?"

"I am perfectly serious."

"But how could I — It goes against everything. You're talking to the wrong person. Even for my father it would be too hokey. I can't see it."

"He's been a good man. And he's being swept out. Can't you think of something to say to him?"

"What is there to say? And can't you think of anything but death?"

"But that's what we have before us."

Angela's selfishness is total here, and her ego combined with her trivial, unthought-out behavior locks her away from the spiritual and ethical possibilities that Mr Sammler begs her to consider.

And so Elya Gruner dies uncomforted, having lived a curiously admirable life. One of the most interesting things about *Mr Sammler's Planet* is the generosity of conception allotted to this character. A gynecologist who performed illegal abortions to plump up an already high income, Elya becomes, against all odds, a quirky exemplar of Kierkegaard's Knight of Faith. Mr Sammler says of this Kierkegaardian ideal:

"That real prodigy, having set its relations with the infinite, was entirely at home in the finite. Able to carry the jewel of faith, making the motions of the infinite, and as a result needing nothing but the finite and the usual. Whereas others sought the extraordinary in the world. Or wished to be what was gaped at."

Obviously some paring down of the theoretical ideal is necessary here as everywhere in Bellow's practice. Elya is not ideally Kierkegaard's Knight, nor is he a person consciously carrying "the jewel of faith, making the motions of the infinite."

The mystical image is reduced, Americanized, and retailored. Elya is an unillusioned man of enormous generosity, who works dutifully at a profession he doesn't much like in order to lavish money on his wife, his essentially worthless children (he accurately describes his daughter as "a dirty cunt" and his son Wallace as "a high-IQ idiot"), and all other relatives – like Mr Sammler himself who lives off Elya's bounty – who need his financial help. He never shirks his duty, never indulges in self-aggrandizement, and always internalizes his suffering, right up to the moment of death. To the degree that he has a religious life, it is Jewish in the communal sense – but it is an admirable example of Jewish faith in community closeness and responsibility. It is obviously important to Bellow that Elya fulfill the ideal fitfully, because in fact his own concept of the Knight of Faith is deeply reworked from Kierkegaard's formulation of it. The Bellovian restatement comes in the inspired prayer-Kaddish Mr Sammler speaks over Elya's body:

"Remember, God, the soul of Elya Gruner, who, as willingly as possible and as well as he was able, and even to an intolerable point, and even in suffocation and even as death was coming was eager, even childishly perhaps (may I be forgiven for this), even with a certain servility, to do what was required of him. At his best this man was much kinder than at my very best I have ever been or could ever be.

He was aware that he must meet, and he did meet - through all the confusion and degraded clowning of this life through which we are speeding - he did meet the terms of his contract. The terms which, in his inmost heart, each man knows. As I know mine. As all know. For that is the truth of it - that we all know, God, that we know, that we know, we know, we know."

These words are the key to Bellow's spiritual commitment within his fiction, and an expression of the aegis under which his work functions. Many readers believe that Bellow, like Mr Sammler, *should* in fact pray for forgiveness for the unremitting harsh realism through which he sees most of his characters. At the same time, Bellow, like Gruner but much more so, is self-consciously aware of his contract and the heavy duties involved. For Elya the contract was difficult but simpler - bound by duty, kindness, and humility; for Bellow, it is a spiritual activity that encompasses a moral imperative that moves relentlessly through the work. More generously than at any other comparably dramatic point in his fiction, Bellow here also opens the boundaries of the contract to embrace humankind, in that as readers and actors in the social drama, "we all know . . . we know, we know."

Because the novel is structured to allow this prayer to have maximum impact, *Mr Sammler's Planet* is a model of cohesion. Its second major subsidiary character, the Indian scientist, Govinda Lal, however, is able to focus Mr Sammler's mind on analytical statements that unite the social and scientific problems of the late twentieth century with the spiritual aspirations that are so compulsively necessary in this novel. Govinda Lal enters the fiction as the author of scientific notebooks outlining a reasonable program for human immigration to the moon as a solution to hopeless demographics. Mr Sammler's unstable daughter, Shula, steals the notebooks to give to her father, assuming that he is still interested in writing a biography of H.G. Wells, and that he shares the scientific ameliorative ideals of the early Wells. In her ignorance, she is unaware that the weight of the century crushed Wells in the 1940s before his death, as seen in the relentless pessimism of his last book, *The Mind at the End of its Tether*. Bellow says in the *TriQuarterly* interview that Mr Sammler has read this book; it is, under any circumstances, evident that Mr Sammler can no longer see social or philosophical–scientific solutions to the morass of contemporary problems.

He is, nevertheless, interested in the idea of moon travel - any former fan of Wells would be - and it is Govinda Lal who opens out the ultimate possibilities in conversation with Mr Sammler. This conversation occurs in Elya Gruner's New Rochelle house, while Margotte cooks dinner, Shula dresses up flirtatiously like a Hindu woman, and Wallace wrecks the place as he tries to find the abortion money. This context is important, because it presents a vignette of the madly mixed social background against which thought and spirit must converge if they can at all. Govinda Lal's scientific discourse is welcome to Mr Sammler, who like Bellow has a lively interest in science and its possibilities. But for Bellow science, like all discourse, remains minor unless it somehow learns also how to draw out and serve the spiritual longing that this novel insists all people have:

> So then, Dr Lal, if the moon were advantageous for us metaphysically, I would be completely for it. . . . Of course the drive, the will to organize this scientific expedition must be one of those irrational necessities that make up life - this life we think we can understand. So I suppose we must jump off, because it is our human fate to do so. If it were a rational matter, then it would be rational to have justice on this planet first. Then, when we had an earth of saints, and our hearts were set on the moon, we could get in our machines and rise up.

The justice that would produce a world of saints is part of an ethico-spiritual imperative that contemporary people do not have access to; like the will of God invoked earlier by Mr Sammler, it is difficult to recover because of the noisy surfaces cn which we live. As Bellow indicates in this conversation and elsewhere in his ruminations, there are three major barriers impeding us - a joint decision to live in a state of blindness, the Romantic concepts of the self over the last 200 years, and the devastating demands of role-playing in western civilization as the result of these self-concepts. Ubiquitous blindness is nurtured by theory - by the tendency of any *a priori* system to stretch the world on a Procrustean bed that makes the mind overlook the often chaotic complexity of the real state of things. Romanticism of the self and subsequent role-playing are seen as the sources of the loss of authenticity and, more importantly, of the soul itself as an inner possession. Because the post-Romantic self always believes it is on center stage, the impulse to play roles - to present an adequate image - has made people into creatures of the external gesture rather than allowing them to develop the "paradise within," the very concept of which was lost through the strenuous demands of Romanticism.

With these three strikes against us, we are out - and it is therefore easy to account for the extremities of Bellow's voice, his outrage at the impotence of contemporary people, and his fury at the intellectual milieux of the university that produces only theories used to rationalize the miasma of continued secular madness. Writing *Mr Sammler's Planet* in the "revolutionary" anti-Vietnam aura of the late 1960s, Bellow's case against the follies of the intelligentsia was even stronger than it might appear to readers since then - but new errors take over, and when Bellow examines a specifically university milieu as he does in *The Dean's December* in the early 1980s, a retention of liberal theory joins the administrative politics of the novel to keep that milieu again at a low level of potentiality.

At the end of *Mr Sammler's Planet*, we are left with a sense of the desperate need to remind ourselves of the spiritual and metaphysical, to recover our souls, to renew our contract. If the characters in the book are at all reflective of their New York counterparts - and they hit hard as mimetic examples - the task is difficult almost to impossibility. If any recovery of the inner spiritual life can occur, the problem of retrieval is largely methodological. How, precisely, can one move from the demanding and frightening surfaces of urban secular life in America to the state of grace that Bellow believes our souls call out for? In the next two novels, he tries two possible answers – the one manic, the other quiet. In *Humboldt's Gift* he half-playfully evokes Rudolf Steiner's anthroposophism, and in *The Dean's December* he less passionately tries the force of the poetic. For various reasons, neither speaks as clearly for him as his working of the problem in *Mr Sammler* – although *Humboldt's Gift* is probably the best book of the three.

*

For someone whose point of view is as clear as Bellow's, he has an uncommonly hard time cutting through to an audience obsessed with theory and increasingly convinced that the simplicities of extremist politics will save the world. In an infamous scene at the 1986 International PEN writers' conference in New York, Bellow tried to address the group with an outline of his ameliorative program, arguing that with material issues more or less looked after in western society, the time has come to turn inward to other concerns. His agenda of spiritualization was cut into by the German (and hardly poverty-stricken) novelist Günther Grass, who attacked the United States (which is always Bellow's usually antagonistic touchstone), sneering at its wealth and imperialist indifference to poverty in the Third World – not to mention its callousness to the poor at home. Grass's inability to listen was indicative of the general tone of the conference, whose political subject overshadowed all else; only the sensible Mario Vargas Llosa was allowed any moral authority. Cynthia Ozick subsequently wrote a biting article for *The New York Times* on the PEN conference, reflecting on the predominance of a political discourse that defended all leftist outrages and attacked any other subject. Meanwhile, Bellow's agenda went unheard.

Politically powerful as his works are, Bellow simply cannot be accurately seen within a purely political discourse. Even on the subject of politics, his opinion echoes that of Owen Barfield, the English literary critic and anthroposophist, who says contemporary people live in a world of outsides without insides. Although Bellow claims in *The Dean's December* that his beat is terra firma and persistently keeps the corrupt Realpolitik of the world before him, his fiction is spiritual in emphasis and gathers the sociopolitical universe into an ethico-spiritual focus. The implication is that the outside world of the quotidian must somehow reflect the inside world of the spirit in order for change to occur. Put another way, this means that the inner self must be freed from Romantic existentialism and role-playing so that some hope for the transformation of the social realm can be raised. This agenda bristles with moral intention, and as such is a serious reflection of Cynthia Ozick's definition of an ideal literature.

Although relatively unknown abroad – probably because of her absolute

Jewish commitment – Ozick's reputation as an essayist and commentator is well established in American literary circles. As a writer of densely resonant short stories (there are three volumes so far), her only American equal is Peter Taylor. She has also published three novels, *Trust* (1966), *The Cannibal Galaxy* (1983), and *The Messiah of Stockholm* (1987). Distinguished by a gnarled and resistant prose that is on occasion almost anachronistic, Ozick's work is felicitously marked by her capacity to incorporate great lexicons of intercultural experience and learning into tales that range from the psychosociological to the mystically religious. There is a touch of the scholarly, almost cabbalistically rabbinical in the stories, many of which require specialized knowledge in their decoding. So compelling is the work, however, that no good reader could possibly refuse to undergo the exercise of finding out what is necessary for fuller comprehension. As a result, one exits from any of her books as a re-educated person.

As an essayist, Ozick is outspoken on the side of a literary tradition that readers recognize as retaining the absolutes that guided the inception of the humanities into university curricula. This old humanism, which is now widely discounted and frequently described as illusionistic and irrational, is placed again into an old context that now, paradoxically, seems new and revolutionary once again. In an essay entitled "Innovation and redemption: what literature means" in her collection *Art and Ardor* (1983), Ozick states her literary manifesto. In her opinion, the truly "innovative" is not expressed through experimentalism but

> sets out to educate its readers in its views about what it means to be a human being
> – though it too can fiddle with this and that if it pleases, and is not averse to
> unexpected seizures and tricks, or to the jarring gifts of vitality and cunning.
> Innovation cannot be defined through mere *method*; the experimental can be
> defined in no other way. And innovation has a hidden subject: coherence.

She begins this same paragraph by claiming that "Fiction will not be interesting or lasting unless it is again conceived in the art of the didactic. (Emphasis, however, on *art*.)"

The ideas of literature having a meaning, being didactic (even artfully didactic), and insisting on coherence as its hidden subject are *de rigueur* for Ozick, and she is militant in their defense. Those readers or writers who put aside the moral sense in art, equating it only with the sociologically real or theologically ideal, are simply wrong. She clarifies her position thus, and I necessarily quote at length:

> For me, with certain rapturous exceptions, literature *is* the moral life. The
> exceptions occur in lyric poetry, which bursts shadowless like flowers at noon,
> with the eloquent bliss almost of nature itself, when nature is both benevolent
> and beautiful. For the rest – well, one discounts stories and novels that are really
> journalism; but of the stories and novels that mean to be literature, one expects *a
> certain corona of moral purpose: not outright in the grain of the fiction itself, but in the*

225

form of a faintly incandescent envelope around it. The tales we care for lastingly are the ones that touch on the redemptive – not, it should be understood, on the guaranteed promise of redemption, and not on goodness, kindness, decency, all the usual virtues. Redemption has nothing to do with virtue, especially when the call to virtue is prescriptive or coercive; rather it is the singular idea that is the opposite of the Greek belief in fate: the idea that insists on the freedom to change one's life.

Redemption means fluidity; the notion that people and things are subject to willed alteration; the sense of possibility; of turning away from, or turning toward; of deliverance; the sense that we act for ourselves rather than are acted upon; the sense that we are responsible, that there is no *deus ex machina* other than the character we have ourselves fashioned; above all, that we can surprise ourselves. Implicit in redemption is amazement, marveling, suspense. . . . Implicit in redemption is everything against the fated or the static: everything that hates death and harm and elevates the life-giving – if only through terror at its absence.

(italics added)

To put this into the Bellovian terms of *Mr Sammler's Planet*, redemptive literature with its corona of moral purpose reminds the reader of his/her responsibility to change, and through the presentation of characters in a troubled New York, Bellow's sonorous art directly urges an understanding of the divine contract that has been subverted by error and by the obscuring effects of the predominant culture. Ozick is anxious not to be misunderstood, however, and goes on to deny simple-minded "affirmative" literature, which

belongs either to journalism or to piety or to "uplift." It is the enemy of literature and the friend of coercion. It is, above all, a hater of the freedom inherent in storytelling and in the poetry side of life. But I mean something else: I mean the corona, the luminous envelope – perhaps what Henry James meant when he said "Art is nothing more than the shadow of humanity." I think, for instance of the literature of *midrash*, of parable, where there is no visible principle or moral imperative. The principle does not enter into, or appear in, the tale; it *is* the tale; it realizes the tale. To put it another way: the tale is its own interpretation. It is a world that decodes itself.

And that is what the "corona" is: interpretation, implicitness, the nimbus of *meaning* that envelops story.

Ozick's own realization of this corona of moral purpose can be seen through brief analytical reference to her novel, *The Cannibal Galaxy*. In this spare, tightly constructed book, there is indeed "no visible principle or moral imperative" that can be tidily and tritely encapsulated. The novel appears more straightforward than it is; it advances unashamedly through realistic and conventional means, and as such is a work that methodologically could have been written in any period from the eighteenth century on. Its subjects, however, are ambitious, complex, and connotative in the extreme, and include pedagogy, the decoding of metaphor, the strictures of the intellectual life, mediocrity, parental agony, cowardice, and idolatry.

As in Bellow's fictions but with notable differences, Ozick structures her work on a central male figure, Joseph Brill, who like Mr Sammler emerged from the Nazi Holocaust, but managed to avoid the concentration camps. The third-person narrator is dispassionate, a disinterested Jamesian reporter free of authorial intrusion. Judgments are made or received by Brill through thought or conversations with others: the narrator is merely a vehicle, a transparent device for the presentation of the text. In no way a *Bildungsroman*, the plot nevertheless entails an account of Brill's anxious, mediocre life from childhood to a defeated, exhausted old age. Shaped by Europe – particularly Paris – Brill from childhood had high humanistic aspirations expressed through his reading and love of museums, but he too quickly recognized his limitations in this field and bowed under pressure to train in astronomy. Here, as in all his other ambitions, his mediocrity and failure of nerve bound him to failure. After the war, he emigrated to the United States, carrying with him the *Ta'anit* given to him by his rabbi who immediately thereafter died in the Holocaust, and *The Beast* by the French Jewish literary enthusiast Edmond Fleg, whose work Brill read excitedly while confined for months by Catholic nuns who saved his life.

He came to America with these two books, and with a fruitful and even exciting pedagogical idea – the Dual Curriculum, on the basis of which he founded a private grade school. In theory, this curriculum presents at a high level the culture of Europe and of the Jewish tradition; the motto for his school comes from his astronomical studies – *Ad Astra*. The novel opens with him in middle age, reveling still in his modest success as Principal of the Edmond Fleg Primary School whose original vaulting ambition is presumably intact. But Brill is afflicted with high intelligence on which a wilful and insuperable mediocrity has been stamped from youth, when his literary blossomings were withered by a condescending friend, Claude, who identified him as a Dreyfus. Like Dreyfus, Brill is unjustly doomed to imprisonment – although his prison is metaphorical and comes from his own cowardice and, as Hester Lilt who is the chief enactor of the book says, from the fact that he has always stopped too soon, that he has lacked the persevering patience necessary for achieving the stars.

His self-irony from the beginning of the account of his principalship asserts his mediocrity, as he puns with the idea of this school that is "of the middle and in the middle" and notes the verbal similarity between Fleg and phlegmatic. Situated by an anonymous lake in the Midwest – i.e. somewhere in the dull middle of the country – the school is averse to extremes, fringes, and risk. Having stopped too soon in thinking about this pedagogical project as in everything else, Brill has long since given up reading, relying on his memory of French *haute culture*, literary quotations, and his partial training as a scientist. The school is architecturally poor, his living quarters above the old stable are tawdry, the students are middling middle-class children pushed by their mothers. The teachers are mediocre. Brill is aging. Two big events intrude into this mediocre circumstance: a brilliant academic woman, Hester Lilt, who is an imagistic linguistic logician (?!) enrolls her daughter, Beulah, in the school and Brill decides, after being intellectually crushed by this woman, to marry a pert school secretary, thus exposing himself to the possibly humiliating risks of having a child. A male child arrives, is apparently brilliant, but ends up in mediocrity, studying Business Administration at Miami University and setting out for a dull American life.

Hester Lilt's presence on the scene – although she seldom appears at the school and seems indifferent to the unscholastic obtuseness of her shy daughter, Beulah – exalts Brill and temporarily awakens his intellect from its long slumber. The dialogues between these two characters formulate the corona of moral purpose within *The Cannibal Galaxy*. The subject matter of their conversation subtly projects a profound aura of cultural usage and individual courage or cowardice. Whereas Brill has stopped thinking and rests in the arts and sciences of his long-past education, Hester Lilt projects new images, using cultural material not unlike that available to Brill if he would only call it up. Her creativity produced her professorship, her scholarly reputation, her articles, her books.

Hester Lilt's peculiar academic field leads her to write books such as *Metaphor as Exegesis, Divining Meaning*, and *Interpretation as an End in Itself* which suggest enlargements of the exploration she performs in the one lecture Brill hears. In that lecture she connects the "hoax of pedagogy" which typically (like Brill) stops too soon, failing to educate creatively through, for example, Jewish Midrashes of the fox and the bee, the laughter of Akiva, and the idea of cannibal galaxies. This last image of the cannibal galaxy from which the title is taken emerges fruitfully from Brill's own subject, astronomy, and its resonances enfold the major themes of the novel. As she first uses it, however, it is connected with the cannibalizing of children within an educational system. In astronomy, a cannibal galaxy is one that completely consumes other galaxies, although the cannibalized galaxy continues to agitate and cause motion, while its consumer is still. As a metaphor for education – and particularly for the miseducation of Hester's own child, Beulah, at Brill's faculty's hands – it is indeed effective. Beulah is devoured by the school system, but its phlegmatic rigidity knows nothing of the inward motion of this child's steady development from a shy misfit into a great painter.

Throughout the book, Hester keeps pointing out to Brill that it is necessary to be patient, not to stop too quickly, to keep going onward, to think and revise. In spite of his stale repetition of the motto *Ad Astra*, however, Brill is capable of none of this, celebrating as he does the safe and ordinary rather than the extraordinary. In certain ways, he has been swallowed by the galaxy of his system – the Dual Curriculum – whose outlines remain unaltered even though his faculty can only mediocritize them. Still, his mind becomes active enough through Hester's needling that he is capable of real interpretation. But Ozick implies that the image of the cannibal galaxy goes much further in its potentiality, including the swallowing up of Jewish civilization first by the culture and violence of Europe, and then by the conventionalism of America. Although Jewish culture threatens to become undifferentiated within the ordinary modes of the United States instead of retaining its extraordinary scope, it remains active although cannibalized, and Brill's absorption in his own cowardice and mediocrity serves as a warning, an object lesson in what to avoid.

Hester's creativity within metaphor illustrates the mind at work rather than passively slumbering. Consumed by his system and a dull striving for ordinariness, Brill is also devoured by his expectations of Hester. Under his belief in her brilliance, he moves temporarily to his own interpretative work. Using the art of analogue and connexion that characterizes Hester, he associates her metaphorically with his boyhood interest in Mme de Sévigné, the brilliant seventeenth-century French letter-writer whose Paris home became the Musée Carnavalet. In keeping with the metaphor of the cannibal galaxy, Mme de Sévigné was cannibalized by her love of her daughter, and as a result became one of the greatest letter-writers in western history. Brill suddenly realizes that Hester's work and the metaphors she chooses do not come from her intrinsic brilliance, but from her love for Beulah, the apparently mediocre child. But he gets it wrong, assuming that Hester has cannibalized her daughter, and not realizing that she has herself been cannibalized by the vast love that exists between them; it is this love within which she agitates as she produces her best work.

From this titular metaphor, Ozick builds a wide-ranging set of resonant associations and ideas that lend coherence, of the sort she advocates in her essays, to the tale of Joseph Brill. The obsessions his life illustrates and his failure to turn them creatively into the kind of work Hester Lilt performs at both the scholarly and parental level touch a core of ethical, cultural, creative, and national meaning that demonstrates how narrow and difficult the path to a worthy life is. This novel glows with meaning, as it obliquely guides the reader to a re-education in the evaluation of human potentiality. Its presentation of the "faintly incandescent envelope" that constitutes the "corona of moral purpose" is well and subtly achieved. Ozick avoids didactic statement and direct moral prescription, giving us instead a surprising literary metaphor around which all the ideas of the book delicately hover.

In spite of her own creative achievement, Ozick is nevertheless theologically afraid of the possible demonic dangers of the imagination, even though her most recent novel, *The Messiah of Stockholm*, shows signs of dissolving this fear. She has frequently written on the subject of idolatry, and indicates in her essays and her fiction that the temptation to idolatry – to worship of the thing rather than of God – is an adjunct of the imagination at work. In the essay on the corona of moral purpose, Ozick associates the negative aspects of the imagination with the current urge among both metafictionists and critics to smash the idea of achievable interpretation and to substitute an idolatrous adoration of language itself for the essential moral aura of meaning which exists to serve mankind:

> Imagination owns above all the facility of becoming: the writer can enter the leg of a mosquito, a sex not her own, a horizon he has never visited, a mind smaller or larger. But also the imagination seeks out the unsayable and the undoable, and says and does them. And still more dangerous: the imagination always has the lust to tear down meaning, to smash interpretation, to wear out the rational, to mock the surprise of redemption, to replace the fluid force of suspense with an image of stasis; to transfix and stun rather than to urge; to spill out, with so much quicksilver wonder, idol after idol. An idol serves no one; it is served. The imagination, like Moloch, can take you nowhere except back to its own maw. And the writers who insist that literature is "about" the language it is made of are offering an idol: literature for its own sake, for its own maw: not for the sake of humanity.

Her denial of self-reflexive literature by this association with demonism and idolatry is both powerful and brave, and when self-reflexive literature does not look beyond itself – as it does with the best writers – Ozick's theological accusation against it is entirely justified. If literature is only self-referential and does not exist for the sake of humanity (although what this might mean is a dangerous question), it should fold up its tent and steal away.

*

In writing about Bellow, Ozick argues that his comedy wells from his metaphysical commitment, while his eloquence springs from the clamorous thrashings of the soul. Bellow's work undoubtedly exudes meaning – his analyses and damnation of contemporary intellectual sociopolitical corruption is bludgeoningly statemental. But although he insists on the possible rehabilitation of the soul, it is in this realm that he is most tactful, experimental, and tentative. This is also the domain of his largest moral thought, and from his desire to restore soul to a lost society comes his participation in what Ozick calls the corona of moral purpose. It would be wrong-headed to argue that Bellow's heavy-handed but scrupulously honest attacks on American and western culture are other than extreme and statemental; it is equally wrong to denigrate his work on the assumption that his categorical political stance is his only point of view.

Everything that Bellow offers – including his attacks on Romantic theories of personality, blind corruption in politics, vain intellectual theorizing, and sexual indirection – is centered on experimental suggestions of spiritual possibility. The sense of experiment in this area in novel after novel implies his conviction that walking into a religious apprehension of the world is an act that contemporary people can manage only awkwardly and perhaps only experimentally. Bellow's tentativeness here strikes the right chord, and demonstrates how difficult in practice he finds the thematic task of presenting a neutral but dynamic interaction between literature and the religious. In relation to this, Ozick says that the corona of moral purpose pervading serious literature invites interpretations that open a redemptive possibility: through the literary work the reader learns her/his freedom to change and to become more freely human. This necessary corona also displays an "implicitness, the nimbus of *meaning* that envelops story."

Bellow's recent novelistic experiments in finding a suitable referent in his presentation of meaning to his readers' souls – whose primacy he hopes to establish – are interestingly diverse. In *Humboldt's Gift* (1975), his return to the high comic style after *Mr Sammler's Planet* gives him irony enough – and courage – to call forth an eccentric spiritual system that, *sub rosa comoediae*, he invests with enormous potentiality for belief. The neo-Platonic, semi-Gnostic, occult anthroposophical system of Rudolf Steiner with its allegiance to mystical Christianity, Rosicrucianism and certain versions of spiritualism is hardly the route that any reader of Bellow would have expected him to take even temporarily. But his defense of that world in *TriQuarterly* shows how committed he is to the possibilities of a system that opens up a locked spirituality through extraordinary means:

> Steiner was a very great man indeed. . . . Hostile critics who attacked *Humboldt* were not qualified . . . . They had not found it necessary to read Steiner to try to learn why he had made so great an impression on Charlie Citrine. They might have discovered that he was a great visionary – they might even have been moved by his books. This, however, is not the proper place for a defense of Steiner. I can only try to explain what it was that drew Charlie Citrine to him. It was, in a word, the recognition that everything which Charlie had taken to be commonsensical, realistic, prudent, normal – his ambitions, marriage, love affairs, possessions, business relations – was a mass of idiocies. "A serious human life? This! You've got to be kidding!" And from demonic absorption in the things of this world, he turns to an invisible world in which he thinks his Being may be founded. Is there, in fact, any basis for religion other than the persistence of the supersensible? "Science" with the air of modern philosophy – what we call the positive outlook – has driven "the invisible" into the dark night where enlightenment says it belongs. Together with it, in our simplemindedness we drive away revelation as well, and with revelation we drive out art, also we drive out dreaming.

In another interview, in *The New York Times Magazine* (1984), Bellow traces his spirituality in ways that make him look very like the spiritual adventurer he presents in the character of Charlie Citrine. Like Charlie, he is compelled to live within his craft as a writer, and to present and endure the empirical world while his inner life struggles for expression:

> the religious feeling was very strong in me when I was young and it has persisted. I would *never* describe myself as an atheist or agnostic; I always thought those were terms for a pathological state and that people who don't believe in God have something wrong with them. Just say I am a religious man in a retarded condition

and the only way I can square myself is to write.... The mind of a novelist has an empirical character ... and whatever he asserts he has to demonstrate from lived experience. I always think of Tolstoy's marvelous short novels.... He wants to reach a religious conclusion, but the steps of his art are all in this world and in the end he has to barge in with improper rudeness.... It is certainly hard to see how modern man could survive on what he gets from his conscious life.

Bellow's open appeal to spirit in the midst of an all too real world in *Humboldt's Gift* is so undisguised and absolute that it can be made secularly palatable only through comic tone. In this amazingly funny novel the central male protagonist is always having his nose rubbed in the filth of the Chicago quotidian, but he escapes into the bizarrely thoughtful mazes of anthroposophical meditation.

The text of *Humboldt's Gift* is laced with Charlie's attempts to understand the supersensible worlds and the various auras, spirit bodies, and levels of being described by Rudolf Steiner. Bellow is a good explainer, and through the automatically ambiguous openness of his comic structure, the spiritual radiance – as well as the oddity – of anthroposophy necessarily gives the reader pause. The contempt and puzzlement many reviewers of the novel expressed for this spiritual system indicate its unnerving impact in the novel (as well as their ignorance, as Bellow points out in the interview quoted above – but then he rather unpleasantly likes to stress the ignorance of others). Bellow says that even anthroposophists wrongly thought that he was being flippant about their beliefs, and this misjudgment also indicates that the comic tone lends a tentativeness to the novel that reflects both on Bellow and his audience.

The troublesome issue of the potentially serious dominance of anthroposophy is handled with consummate tact, however, although this word is not generally associated with a writer as fierce as Bellow. Charlie Citrine is a Herzogian character who is always being exploited and dumped on by tougher con-artists, and as his life, and especially his money, is besieged madly from every side, he expresses an inner heroism by studying things of the soul. Bellow's comic genius in juxtaposing the crazy events of the novel with Steineresque ruminations colors the credibility of both to a degree. But it is nevertheless the case that Charlie must seriously endure the empirical outside world even as he attempts to readjust his soul outside of the narcissism of post-Romantic existentialism. As Bellow works the problem in *Humboldt's Gift*, he balances dexterously, amuses profoundly, and keeps the novel away from moral prescription and artistically detrimental religious statement that would proselytize rather than suggest.

This novel is also, however, about Von Humboldt Fleisher, his death, and his strange gift. Never in Bellow's work has there been such an interesting and compelling secondary protagonist, and one more reflective of inner potentiality. A once successful American Jewish poet (it is generally agreed that the original for this portrait is Delmore Schwartz), Humboldt dies in alcoholic poverty and isolation. In his last days, he is ignored by his erstwhile friend and now prosperously successful protégé, Charlie, who dodges shamefully behind a car in New York to avoid talking to the shambling, destroyed hulk. In his heyday, Humboldt combined brilliant poetry and cultural aspiration with world-devouring neurosis. Later, having fallen upon hard times, he is paranoid but still voracious in his dreams of power. He has always agreed with Shelley that poets should be the legislators of the world, and wishes to take over government, the universities, English departments – all the while proclaiming

> the perennial human feeling that there was an original world, a home-world, which was lost. Sometimes he spoke of Poetry as the merciful Ellis Island where a host of aliens began their naturalization and of this planet as a thrilling but insufficiently humanized imitation of that home-world.

Aside from some genuinely good poems, Humboldt turns everything into a shambles – his failures range from his depressing "country" house, his marital jealousies, and his physical collapses to his inability to maneuver himself into an academic chair in the English department at Princeton. His death – which is the real subject of this book – is pointless and inevitable. Yet, as Charlie says, "Humboldt wanted to drape the world in radiance, but he didn't have enough material." His feeling that there is a spiritual elsewhere bears only limited resemblance to Charlie's metaphysical fumblings but, at the end of the letter that he leaves for Charlie with his "gift," Humboldt signals something his protégé has long thought – as indeed Bellow thinks we must all think: "Last of all – remember: we are not natural beings but supernatural ones."

Humboldt believes poetic literature reflects our spiritual home. For him, "Prospero is a Hamlet who gets his revenge through art," and he urges that we touch base artistically through participation in the high and even mystically or madly poetic: before Charlie writes the screenplay from the scenario Humboldt leaves to him, he is urged to "play a few sides of *The Magic Flute* on the phonograph, or read *The Tempest*. Or E.T.A. Hoffman." At the same time, Humboldt sees any serious poet in the late twentieth century as being able to renew his Orphic possibility only through routinely inevitable degradation in a corrupt society:

> To the high types of Martyrdom the twentieth century has added the farcical martyr. This, you see, is the artist. By wishing to play a great role in the fate of mankind he becomes a bum and a joke. A double punishment is inflicted on him as the would-be representative of meaning and beauty. When the artist–agonist has learned to be sunk and shipwrecked, to embrace defeat and assert nothing, to subdue his will and accept his assignment to the hell of modern truth perhaps his Orphic powers will be restored, the stones will dance again when he plays. Then heaven and earth will be reunited. After long divorce. With what joy on both sides, Charlie! What joy!

Impelled by Steiner and newly inspired by Humboldt's last letter, Charlie argues to his expensive mistress Renata and the falsely intellectual Thaxter that even contemporary life is of the doubtful poetic substance that Goethe called "the living garment of God"; he also points to the idea that "people of powerful intellect never are quite sure whether or not it's all a dream." The oneiric connexion in this novel is one of the few areas where Bellow is aligned with fictional ontologies of the sort displayed by major fictionists of our time – Kafka, Borges, Murdoch, Hoban, Eco.

Bellow, however, is not about to allow his novel to fall into the sentimentalities implied by the distance between contemporary America and the splendors of poetic Orphism. As he comically deflects *Humboldt's Gift* from a too dogged seriousness, he keeps us amused with a revised task for the artist in the maniacal dream-world of the late twentieth century: not to write poetry, not to have a chair at Princeton, but to make a wad by writing lousy filmscripts and amusing the panting masses. Humboldt's last gift to Charlie Citrine is the outline for a screenplay which he believes will pack them all into the movie houses of the world.

Years ago at Princeton, Charlie and Humboldt wrote another screenplay they entitled *Caldofreddo*, about the polar explorer, Amundsen, Umberto Nobile, and a fictive Sicilian they named Caldofreddo. In his attempt to survive after a plane crash, Caldofreddo (hot–cold) cannibalizes another crew member, but returns to live a quiet homely life in Sicily. When revealed as a cannibal late in his life, Caldofreddo expects humiliation and blame, but receives the friendship and understanding of his community. This peripeteia in the plot is explained by Charlie in an interesting way:

> And we saw the movie as a vaudeville and farce but with elements of *Oedipus at Colonus* in it. Violent spectacular sinners in old age acquire magical properties, and when they come to die they have the power to curse and to bless.

The movie script not only contains a socially redemptive peripeteia in the life of the fictional Caldofreddo, but creates one for Charlie Citrine too, when the script is pirated and made into a huge box-office success. Charlie's increasingly tangled financial troubles are assuaged by the $60,000 he receives, and he is, at the end of the book, able to bargain also for an advance and contractual rights on the new film idea he and Kathleen have inherited from Humboldt.

But the real interest this episode lends to *Humboldt's Gift* is in its connexion with the tale of Humboldt. Like Caldofreddo, Humboldt in his failure is dreadfully translated from one sort of being to another, and through Humboldt's last letter to him Charlie knows that the dying Humboldt indeed acquired magical properties. When he came to die he had and used the power to curse and to bless. Humboldt is not transfigured into a happy man like the fictive cannibal Caldofreddo; his story is an opposite peripeteia in which he descends to death outside of the community that rejects the ebullient Orphic poet figure. With his final scenario, the "gift" he leaves behind him connects significantly to the thematics of the first script, and also helps Charlie identify him justly as a failed American writer and a spiritual being:

> I have dreamed up another story and I believe it is worth a fortune. This small work has been important to me. Among other things it has given me hours of sane enjoyment on certain nights and brought relief from thoughts of doom. The fitting together of the parts gave me the pleasure of a good intricacy. The therapy of delight. I tell you as a writer – we have had some queer American bodies to fit into art's garments. Enchantment didn't have enough veiling material for this monstrous mammoth flesh, for such crude arms and legs.

Humboldt's new idea involves false and failed repetition, in a plot in which a man illicitly goes on a spectacularly happy desert island trip with a beloved mistress and writes a realistic novel about it; in order to save his bourgeois marriage before publishing this ecstatic fiction (which he believes rightly will make a lot of money), he repeats the trip with his wife. The mistress feels betrayed, the wife knows that the joys he described did not occur with her, and the man loses both women. The impossibility of trying to repeat experiences of human happiness is central, and it of course also reflects on the literary problems of realism in which a text selectively echoes reality. Again, there are implications for Bellow's novel as a whole, in that Humboldt's entire life as a poet is connected to the sustenance and repetition of the great literature of the past, and his most ardent desire is to repeat in the mediocre present the poetic glories that still existed as recently as in High Modernism when T.S. Eliot held such firm sway. But these repetitions are impossible at present, and the directions open to the contemporary American artist are indeed bleak. Charlie Citrine says after Humboldt's death:

> Is it true that as big-time knowledge advances poetry must drop behind, that the imaginative mode of thought belongs to the childhood of the race? A boy like Humboldt, full of heart and imagination, going to the public library and finding books, leading a charmed life bounded by lovely horizons, reading old masterpieces in which human life has its full value, filling himself with Shakespeare, where there is plenty of significant space around each human being, where words mean what they say, and looks and gestures also are entirely meaningful. Ah, that harmony and sweetness, that art! But there it ends. The significant space dwindles and disappears. The boy enters the world and learns its filthy cut-throat tricks, the enchantment stops.

In his next novel, *The Dean's December*, Bellow continues with this question. In that novel – as opposed to *Humboldt's Gift* – he suppresses the breadth of his appeal to spirituality, and tries to stick with poetry specifically as a small answer to the question of big-time knowledge's harmful overlordship. Albert Corde does not win any more than Humboldt or Charlie Citrine do, but he does prevail as a moral being, and the firmness of his approach to political justice and poetic expressiveness outdoes the slick opportunism of the journalist, Dewey Spangler.

In both these novels, Bellow is much preoccupied with death – the death of the friends and relatives that must be undergone, and the implied death of what is good and potentially salvageable in American sociopolitics. The reinterment of Humboldt at the end of that novel implies a holy act in which the old man, Menasha Klinger, tunelessly sings an unconventional Kaddish consisting of the aria "In questa tomba oscura" from *Aïda* and the American spiritual, "Goin' home." This touching reburial constitutes a restoration, a regathering of Humboldt's remains to the community of his relatives and to the Jewish and American milieux from which he had been alienated and discarded.

In *The Dean's December*, Bellow significantly leaves the United States for half of the action, and goes to the bleakness of Bucharest, where his hero's mother-in-law lies dying. This reversion to eastern bloc countries has been frequent in recent Anglo-American fiction (one thinks particularly of Malcolm Bradbury's *Rates of Exchange*, as well as Stoppard and Updike) and in Bellow's case is specifically connected to the anti-American invective of this novel. Bellow's task is also comparative in intention, and he demonstrates here that the wretched pain of affluent, sociologized American society is even more harrowing than the deprivations caused by eastern bloc politics. Although most of the action takes place in Romania and examines a confrontation with death, the energy of *The Dean's December* comes from Chicago and the protagonist's rage at the terminal refusal of its inhabitants to see the truth and speak it in any form at all. Albert Corde, the hero, has published two articles in *Harper's* – honest but frontal attacks on the corruption, blindness, and lies in a city that is annually further removed from amelioration. In defending these articles to Dewey Spangler who thinks he has impractically gone over the top, Corde summarizes his position, and in doing so presents us with Bellow's reiterated point of view throughout his last five novels:

> The increase of theories and discourse, itself a cause of new strange forms of blindness, the false representations of "communication," led to horrible distortions of public consciousness. Therefore the first act of morality was to disinter the reality, retrieve reality, dig it out from the trash, represent it anew as art would represent it. So when Dewey talked about the "poetry," pouring scorn on it, he was right insofar as Corde only made "poetic" gestures or passes, but not insofar as Corde was genuinely inspired. Insofar as he was inspired he had genuine political significance.

Corde argues specifically that he "was speaking up for the noble ideas of the West in their American form." The infusion of the poetic and indeed the spiritual into whatever form required – politics, ethics, journalism, drama, novels – is Corde's task as it is the job of all of Bellow's recent major protagonists. Although he believes and frequently repeats that we are in a state of ideological bankruptcy, having worn out the ideas of the last 200 years, Bellow constantly returns to his humanistic themes. He ardently demonstrates the essential American belief that community and human relationships are central although ill practiced, and he argues again and again that the ethico-spiritual aura of humanity must be sought for through the miasma of the present, so that, if at all possible, it can be restored and redeemed. This is the corona of moral purpose that surrounds his work and drives him on.

11

Doris Lessing, ideologue

Doris Lessing's name was Doris Wisdom during the brief period of her first marriage, and many of her ardent readers might wish that the name, if not the marriage, had stuck. Although critics have found some of her phases as a writer unacceptable, Lessing has built up a reputation as a wise and trustworthy writer with a following that puts her in the forefront among women writers in reputation if not in absolute value. Like many serious novelists who happen to be women, she prefers not to be stuck in the feminist mode and has recently fought hard against it. Her relatively rare public appearances are well advertised and well attended, and she is still seen particularly, although inaccurately, as an advocate of feminism and of a literature that helps to liberate the frustrated, trapped, intelligent woman into a fuller realization of herself. This theme has been important to Lessing as a writer early and late, but her stance in the last fifteen or so years has been much broader, and her criticisms of the narrow and egocentric focuses of the feminist movement harsh indeed.

Added to her demurrals against the current directions of feminism is Lessing's abandonment of party or ideological politics as a subject worthy of serious commitment. Now when political subjects are central, as they are in the fifth book of her Canopus series, *The Sentimental Agents in the Volyen Empire* (1983) or *The Good Terrorist* (1985), the position taken is heavily satiric and dismissive of women or men who give their lives to the falsity of political rhetoric when there are other things to preoccupy a forward-looking mind. Her rebellion against both feminism and politics as pre-eminent subjects is regarded with a strange combination of glee and despair by critics and readers. On the whole, though, despair is predominant, in that a writer firmly and tidily established as a feminist and political leftist has broken from a set norm and changed her mind. However, the central issue in considering Lessing must, in fairness, be her constantly changing aspect as a writer, and the panic many readers feel at the formal and contentual instability of the Lessing *oeuvre*.

Within the self-imposed demands of constant shifts in direction, the primary thing about Lessing as a novelist is her ability to write against the grain of fashion and out of total commitment. Never does the reader feel the impression of falsity, of the writer as *poseur* or trickster employing games, irony, parody – in short, all the machinery of metafiction or experimentalism – to tease or titillate the intellect at an aesthetic level. A studied, self-conscious writer like John Barth, for example, looks and is frivolous by contrast, as are his American experimentalist colleagues and the French *nouveaux romanciers*.

As a constant revisionist in her thinking, and as a writer who reverts to her own older, already used themes only when they persist through thoughtful re-examinations of them, Lessing represents a stringent moral striving of the sort that has recently had many advocates. An atmosphere has been established, particularly in the United States, in which the "moral" attacks of Solzhenitsyn and the late John Gardner (author of "theoretical" studies on moral fiction as well as such ethical fables as *Nickel Mountain*) against the narrow concerns of contemporary writers have moved many readers to embittered polarization. It seems inevitable that in such a circumstance a writer like Doris Lessing, who perfectly satisfies the norms of ethical intention, should have a strong critical following through the whole of her career. This has not been the case, and most commentators reviewing the entire *oeuvre* have been dissatisfied.

Lessing herself is impatient with her readers' impatience. The palpable result of her attitude is a tendency to write introductions to her own novels, either explaining her intentions or complaining contemptuously of the inadequacies in public response to the work that has already been published and reviewed. As a reader, I am reminded of Umberto Eco's (bossy but generous) or Nabokov's (condescending and even misleading) interference in readerly reception of *The Name of the Rose* and *Lolita*. Lessing's habit of publishing her prefatory remarks in editions subsequent to their being reviewed also increases the didactic content of the novels where her introductions occur, and does so at an irritating level. On the other hand, it is easy to understand her impatience, and she is only one of many contemporary authors driven to rebellion by the ancient quarrel between creative artist and obtuse critic.

Although I wish to emphasize Lessing's recent work, it is helpful to review her long and daring career briefly, summarizing how the shifts in thinking and creativity occur. In estimating her *oeuvre*, it is paradoxically useful to call up some features in Jean-Paul Sartre's ideology. Unlike Iris Murdoch, who actively rebelled against Sartre's brand of existentialism and its strong influence over European thought after World War II, Lessing never seemed conscious of being in its grip. The obvious philosophical content of her work is irregular and achieved through autodidactic experimental means. She has apparently pored over a wide range of narrative forms, but over no purely philosophical narrative beyond her probable study of the Marxist masters who fueled her early Communist thought. Nevertheless, the word "totalization" which characterizes Sartre's philosophical gropings, together with his sense of biography as the ideal exponent of existentialism, goes far in describing some of the anomalies in Lessing's work.

Sartre's novels all participate in the idea of biography, and indeed his fictional hero Roquentin in *La Nausée* is a biographer; Sartre himself also felt that through his interpretative biographies – of Baudelaire, Genet, and Flaubert – and his own self-interested autobiography he could depict the totality of individuals which directly reflects the totality of society itself. In his unceasing quest to find a language for the self and a narrative to contain it, Sartre saw the infusion of all details of the whole *ensemble* of himself into his work as part of the totalizing process. In spite of the length and weight of his last works, notably the two-volume *Critique de la raison dialectique*, Sartre's quest for totalization was never adequately realized, nor did his longing for integration within his own consciousness and in society as a whole fulfill itself. Lessing's quest has been parallel, combining as Sartre's did the sexual, social, existential, and political, but in her case an anti-existential mystical solution is found, and her work finally lacks the frustration and the personal futility that haunt Sartre's.

Lessing may have picked up her early existential concentration on the freedom of the self partly out of temperament, and partly from the *Zeitgeist* of the Sartrean 1950s and 1960s. She began her novelistic career impressively with *The Grass is Singing*, where she is significantly outward-directed and concerned with African life and the color bar (racism). Having lived in Africa for twenty-five years before her flight to London in 1949 at the age of 30, Lessing's first materials for her novels and short stories were an interesting amalgam of racism as the predominant African social issue, her subsequent activities in rebellious Communist groups through many years in Southern Rhodesia and England, and the unhappiness she experienced as a slave to her own sexuality and to bourgeois marriage. In spite of the proselytizingly analytical social and political African material of her first novel and short stories, she quickly settled down to a series of novels whose outline is autobiographical in the extreme, rather in the line of Charlotte Brontë's *Villette* or the rebellious stories of another colonial, Katherine Mansfield. This five-novel series, bearing the overall title *Children of Violence*, was published between 1952 and 1969, beginning with *Martha Quest* and ending with *The Four-Gated City*. Sandwiched between these autobiographical novels with a few other minor works is *The Golden Notebook* (1962), Lessing's most famous book and for feminist readers the cornerstone of her achievement.

Martha Quest's name is totally symbolic, and indicates that there is more at stake for Lessing's women than sexual fulfillment. Nevertheless the parallels between Martha's quest and Lessing's searching enquiries into the nature of personal and political being in the five novels put the reader into a voyeuristic stance. Because they are based so precisely on Lessing's marriages, sexuality, and politics, Martha Quest's continuing self-experiential investigations are essentially open-ended, and in theory there is no particular point of completion of the series as long as Lessing remains alive and working. In order to achieve their potential totality, as Sartre would see it, these narratives should follow *all* the mental and ethical struggles of their creator, of which art is the best conveyor and depictor. To the degree that closure is possible in such fiction, it is parallel to the art of biography, rounded out through interpretative means by the totalizing imagination of the biographer whose natural stopping point occurs only with the death of the subject. Like Sartre, Lessing obviously, during the decades of the 1950s and 1960s, saw her own being as the primary subject that she as writer and representative of the constituency of liberal readers in the mid-twentieth century could explore.

As the *Children of Violence* series developed, so did the texture and technical presentation of the novels. Lorna Sage (1983) argues that through these two decades Lessing was questioning the nature of literary realism and its intrinsic limitations, and that the shifting style comes from this. Most feminist critics who have taken these novels as primary texts for the new movement have seen them as pursuing Lessing's changing perception of her life as a woman who suffers and learns painfully. Under any circumstances, it must be recognized that these five novels, plus *The Golden Notebook*, do not in any way present a static body of material. Although all take the misery and confusions of women as their starting point and are autobiographical, they are also multi-directed, using women to represent all of humankind in a way that Lessing feels should have been obvious at once to all readers.

In criticizing the current feminist movement she condemns its attitude toward men, and especially its failure to make the movement into a cool, organized commitment engaging men's interest and support to achieve an amelioration of society at large. It should, of course, not go unnoted that Martha Quest and Anna Wulf of *The Golden Notebook* are both attracted to macho men who at their best are also ideologues with a more limited capacity for development than that of women. In spite of Lessing's wisdom and honesty, she is unable in any of her early realistic novels about women to break the simple tyranny of biological sexual taste. Her heroines nevertheless contradictorily refuse the cliché that biology is destiny, even while their sexual needs impede the practice of ideologies they ardently wish to follow.

Lessing accurately and movingly describes the compulsive sexual traps into which women fall and which are more enslaving than they are for the sort of men to whom Lessing's women are generally attracted. These novels thus deliver an ideology that feminists found a vital factor in their basic self-definition during the 1960s when feminism as a pronounced social movement was forged. What Lessing most laments is that too many of her readers stop here, and fail to see that this is only, even early in her career, partial and no more important than other subjects – notably politics, mysticism, and the alienating effects of the quest for freedom. Her basic point is that each person must think and behave independently within the social framework of the world, and she resents that this necessity be seen as a requirement for women alone. As she said in New York at the 92nd Street Y Poetry Center in April 1984, when asked whether her writing is specifically related to women:

> Not at all. I naturally wrote *The Golden Notebook* from the viewpoint of a woman because I am one. I tried to write a book that was a kind of map of the human mind. We tend to label and pigeonhole things. If men write books – I'm now going to strike a feminist and plaintive note – nobody dreams of saying that they've written from a male perspective or are antiwoman. But if a woman writes a book about the despair of human relationships, she is regarded as a kind of Mrs Pankhurst the Fourth.

The despair of human relationships, whether personal or political, is very much the theme of these novels, but the thematics become denser when the pressure of such thought finds a necessary objective correlative in style and form. In *Landlocked* (1965), the fourth of the *Children of Violence* series, the primary theme is the necessity of leaving the Communist party as part of Martha's quest, but it is handled as a driving urge toward the future – a systematic theme in Lessing's subsequent novels. Her work up to this point has been in many ways a plaintive examination of her experience of the past in order to see whether anything could be made of it. The answer is a resounding no, even though the qualities of honesty she brings to her past responses lend an ambivalent and humanly appealing aura to the perception of the reader.

During the period of the Martha Quest Children of Violence novels, Lessing's active creativity led her to the knowledge that the wretchedness of contemporary people springs from the fact that they spontaneously compartmentalize their ideologies, feelings, and world visions. This compulsive fragmentation is the subject of *The Golden Notebook*. Published in 1962, this novel has been received for either feminist or experimental reasons as the major work in Lessing's *oeuvre*. Its fragmentation mirrors the disquiet of a questing heroine, but its no doubt intentional uneasiness tends to arouse boredom rather than intensity. In many ways it compares with the self-consciously overdone narratological extremes of John Fowles's un-self-monitored *Daniel Martin*, which goes on too tediously in a morass of excessively indulgent confession.

As in the primary Sartrean formula used earlier in this chapter, Lessing's desire – expressed through Anna Wulf – is for wholeness, for a totalization of experience that can unify the world and the self. Whereas the Martha Quest novels at least have the totality of continuing "biography," *The Golden Notebook* sadly acknowledges that human life is confused. In it, many disjunctive narratives, instead of a single unified one, coexist for Lessing's heroine Anna of the many notebooks and the many subjects – as they do for all of us.

The desire for unity has many faces for Lessing, and one of them certainly involves the requirements of the so-called conventional novel. Lessing attacks traditional thematics in an early work called *Retreat to Innocence* (1956), where conventions are identified as being specifically English and stupidly bourgeois. Here she trots out standard themes and forms in order to parody and correct them by an incursion of middle European mess and complexity. Certainly the mid- to late twentieth century has been no place for simple, well-made structures in art, and perhaps the persistent taste of the English for conventional Bloomsburian fiction reflects a political conservatism, as Lessing indirectly argues at this point. Under any circumstances, the interwoven five-part quincunx of Anna Wulf's notebooks in the later, more sophisticated novel that has the golden notebook at its center illustrates Lessing's conviction that the novel form must be broken up to reflect the multiformity and chaos of any lived life.

The five deconstructive notebooks demonstrate the compartments that have fought for attention so far in Lessing's fiction, but the golden notebook is the one that leads Anna forward. A review of the subject matter of the notebooks is in order: black – a depiction of Anna's African years; red – her experiences as a Communist; blue – quotidian and political news and her sex life; yellow – her novel-in-progress with a heroine Ella who is a shadow of Anna who is a shadow of Lessing; golden – the central one, describing Anna's necessary mental breakdown in the midst of chaos, her curiously symbiotic, creative, but negative relationship with the neurotic American, Saul Green, and her Laingian reintegration through deconstruction, breakdown, and mental chaos into a lonely but spiritually realizable world.

Up to this point in 1962, Lessing's novels had tried in vain to integrate the themes of Anna's first four notebooks, to make them cohere in a world where she increasingly understands that coherence cannot exist. *The Golden Notebook* partially abandons coherence, but only insofar as a deep recognition of chaos is a way of dealing fruitfully with the world as we experience it. The final quasi-spiritual conclusion that allows Anna to face a world into which she has been painfully integrated as part of the whole reasserts Lessing's compulsory unitive view. The conclusion of the later novel, *The Four-Gated City* (1969), immerses its author further in mysticism, as do *Briefing for a Descent into Hell* (1971) which actually has a male hero, *The Summer Before the Dark* (1973), and *The Memoirs of a Survivor* (1975). These novels are prefatory to Lessing's next and central series, the science-fiction fantasy with the overall title *Canopus in Argos: Archives*, and it is useful to see that she was led to this series by the frenetic productivity of the 1960s and 1970s, which gradually slanted into a mystical or galactic world view. It should be kept in mind that Lessing likes series or sequences. She is an extremely prolific novelist who can write more in a single year than any other novelist in this study, and in spite of individual novels not attached to a sequence, her instinct is to continue with a series once the themes and characters of an initial novel take over her imagination. This tendency is also, of course, part of her totalizing imagination, and connected to her drive to create an extended phenomenologist construction of an elaborately conceived cosmos.

Lessing's first series starred Martha Quest, who is a version of herself; her second emphasizes the new idea of unselfing as a necessary spiritual and ethical step. As one watches her gradually explore the possibility of other worlds and states of consciousness in the novels of the 1970s, her ideological history can be clearly outlined. It helps to know the steps of her progress – from race to concentration on the suffering female self which made her an inadvertent pioneer of feminism; through Communism from which she reluctantly tore herself when Stalin's reputation became completely indefensible, to a pro-longed study of R.D. Laing's radical psychotherapeutic theories of breakdown and schizophrenia; and from there to a discipleship of Sufism – the mystical branch of Islam – which she studied under the direction of Idries Shah, who considers himself a chosen western proselytizer. This rapid survey of ideological shifts and influences makes Lessing look both fickle and easily influenced, but such a judgment could be accurate only if she totally discarded one ideological system as she moved into the next. The progression from intense existential self-orientation, to Communism, to psychotherapy, to mysticism can be roughly compared to the Renaissance Neoplatonic ladder by which the soul is led from things of this world to the divine, and Sufism would certainly encourage such an analogue.

The rising of the soul from one stage to the next in Lessing's case has not been classically Platonic (i.e. an ascent away from the world by moving from beauty to love), however, but specifically Sufic. Thus Lessing does not choose to leave the physical reality of the world, which she interprets as the setting for positive and necessary evolutionary change. The result, in novelistic terms, is that although she appears to see her life's quest as radically progressive, Lessing retains an interest in the various ideologies she has passed through, even as she refines, revises, and attempts to objectify them. At no point, therefore, does she abandon her interest in the operation of the self, although she now perceives that self as existing in another arena of more stringent ethical conditions; similarly she sees the suffering of women as an error imposed by society and biological enslavement. Both feminism and Communism are now seen as religion-substitutes, and part of a faulty world view that contemporary people must transcend. Her admiration for R.D. Laing has abated, although he appears as the psychotherapist Dr Hebert in *Shikasta*, where his work is presented as part of a larger service required during the destructive and terminal point in history. In the last several years, the real issue in Lessing's work has been a study of how radical mysticism, relayed in the great religious books, subverts all these ideas as it works quietly and perpetually to alter the human mind.

*

Although Lessing leaves nothing behind in progressively designing her totalizing fictions, her grandest stage is set when the mysticism that has long attracted her becomes major. Because of her increasing commitment to its unitive power, it is the center from which a consideration of her work can ideally proceed. As I describe her cosmic perceptions, however, I should also remind the reader that her 1985 novel, *The Good Terrorist*, returns directly to realism; this novel is not set in the galaxy, but in a "squat," in a London so seedy that it partially resembles the scenario of the decline and fall of civilization envisaged earlier in *The Memoirs of a Survivor*. Dislodged though she significantly seems from straightforward realistic perception of the world in the five-volume (to date) Canopus series, Lessing does not believe that humankind is detachable from a necessary evolutionary process within the real world itself. Lessing's study of Alice Mellings, the "good" terrorist, is not a total departure from the style of her space fantasy sequence, therefore, but is like an objective, much enlarged case study made by her inter-galactic hero, Johor, in *Shikasta*, the first of her Canopus novels.

At the end of *The Memoirs of a Survivor* (1974), the aging woman protagonist who has been given a suffering girl child with a bizarre dog-cat by some One, finally follows that One through dissolving walls into an unknown redemptive world. London has completely fallen apart, most of its inhabitants have left in roving bands, and the only way out for the woman, the child, the dog-cat, and the gang of children who follow is into another dimension or subconscious psychic "room" that has been ambiguously but deftly explored at various moments in the novel. The movement into another presumably better psychic realm in this novel gives a basis for the fiction of an overworld or Canopus that comprehends the cosmos of which we and the world we experience are only a small segment. Lessing, in the 1984 New York question-and-answer session quoted above, indicates that she considers such fantasy as *Memoirs*, her other near-fantasy novels, and the whole Canopus series as part of a continuing tradition in the realistic novel:

> There have been dreams and fantastic ventures even in realistic fiction, as in *Jane Eyre*, where there are apparitions and she hears voices. In Thomas Mann's *The Magic Mountain*, the hero has dreams and even tries to pull his brother back from the other side of the grave. Mann himself was a realistic novelist and he seemed uncomfortable writing these scenes. To-day, because of the emphasis on realism, the novel has suffered severe impoverishment. I think that one writer can contain two worlds – the realistic and the fantastic – sometimes in the same story.

Like many modern and contemporary writers as unlike as Kafka or Borges and Graham Greene, Lessing sees dreams as important source material for fiction, and uses oneiric perception as an important aspect of her mixed fantastic–realistic works. Her dissatisfaction with the limits of realism is evident, and even a complexly structured novel like *The Golden Notebook* fails to satisfy her desire that realism somehow realize itself beyond its normal boundaries.

This desire for paradoxically non-realistic realization in fiction parallels

Lessing's boundless desire to transcend earthbound twentieth-century experience, and to interpret it in a Postmodern version of the medieval *sub specie aeternitatis* – under the eye of the eternal. A logical glance at her developing ideology indicates that such an ambition makes sense: nothing in the lives of her two major heroines – Martha Quest and Anna Wulf – has cohered, and their attempts to place their faith and allegiance on Communism as a completely totalizing system for life in the real world failed miserably and irremediably in the 1950s. By contrast, the Sufic belief in the world as an arena for evolutionary/spiritual change, and its stress on life as a mystical preparation for humanity's slow development from its fallen state to reunion with higher forms, fill Lessing's so far insatiable need to comprehend the world in its totality. She is careful, however, to separate her late interest in the mysticism of the Sufi with a conventional religious drive. Reviewing her life and beliefs in an interview with Lesley Hazelton in 1982, she claimed that feminism and particularly Communism are limited religious urges, and ultimately wrong-headed.

> There are certain types of people who are political out of a kind of religious reason. I think it's fairly common among socialists: they are, in fact, God-seekers, looking for the kingdom of God on earth. A lot of religious reformers have been like that, too. It's the same psychological set, trying to abolish the present in favor of some better future – always taking it for granted that there *is* a better future. If you don't believe in heaven, then you believe in socialism. When I was in my real Communist phase, I and the people around me really believed – but, of course, this makes us certifiable – that something like 10 years after World War II, the world would be Communist and perfect.... I was once an idealistic and utopian Communist and no, I am not proud of it. The real politicos are a very different animal, and I'm angry that I didn't notice that very evident fact. I had an inclination toward mysticism – not religion – even then.

The "real politicos" are represented by the ruthless IRA and more precisely by a character like Andrew in *The Good Terrorist* – cold, practical, remorseless professionals whose commitment lacks both idealism and rhetoric. In this novel, the difference between the utopian and the real terrorist is shown clearly, and the emotional neuroses of most of the Communist squatters demonstrate their longing for some larger system, beyond practical politics. More precisely, the unspoken assumption is that Alice, as a confused representative of the contemporary idealistic western European political left, really requires the broad mysticism of continuous Sufic striving, rather than the doctrinaire religious commitment of the limited, illusion-ridden Communist ideologue.

Lessing's progressive dissatisfaction with all the ideologies she once tried in her quest to find a way of undoing the world's recalcitrance makes her movement upward to a large mystical system inevitable. Her African and European experiences shaped her awareness of global necessities, and something as humble as her father's awe beneath the blazing stars of

Rhodesian nights early nudged her toward the galaxy. She dedicates the first volume of the Canopus series, *Shikasta*, to her father with these words: "For my father, who used to sit, hour after hour, night after night, outside our house in Africa, watching the stars. 'Well,' he would say, 'if we blow ourselves up, there's plenty more where we came from!' "

The creation of the intergalactic system of Canopus–Sirius–Puttiora is undoubtedly the most ambitious piece of work in Lessing's career, and the first novel of the series, *Shikasta*, is ultimately the central document in her extraordinary ideological development. The fervor and speed with which she published the five novels in the series, between 1979 and 1983, indicate the energizing excitement that the new subject matter gave her. Of the five, however, *Shikasta* imposes the greatest demands on her as a writer, in that she must compose a universe into which to fit a mammoth cosmic interpretation. Her prefatory essay to that book speaks of the freedom from realism and from the impoverishment of conventional fiction that she feels. It also asserts her own Canopean overlordship in which she can exhibit

> the exhilaration that comes from being set free into a larger scope, with more capacious possibilities and themes. It was clear I had made – or found – a new world for myself, a realm where the petty fates of planets, let alone individuals, are only aspects of cosmic evolution expressed in the rivalries and interactions of great galactic Empires: Canopus, Sirius, and their enemy, the Empire Puttiora, with its criminal planet Shammat. I feel as if I have been set free both to be as experimental as I like, and as traditional.

With *Shikasta*, Lessing enters the troubled realms of science fiction, and in interviews indicates that in this field H.G. Wells is of course one of her masters. She wishes to make it clear, however, that for her this genre is anchored in the literature of the far past – and here and elsewhere she names her sources. Her first claim is that the major background to the book is the Old Testament, although she includes among the ancient holy source books of the Near East everything from the Bible with its midrashes to the Koran. She also mentions elsewhere that she is tapping other sources from the past 12,000 years – the epic, folk and fairy tales, and all narratives that dedicate themselves directly to the art of story-telling. For Lessing, there is complete continuity between these sources from the past and the predictive contemporary science-fiction genre.

What I as reader most miss, however, is a list of authors and titles of the great books within science fiction that have produced her unbounded enthusiasm. In her foreword to *Shikasta*, she shows tremendous and intemperate admiration for the genre:

> What a phenomenon it has been – science fiction, space fiction – exploding out of nowhere, unexpectedly of course, as always happens when the human mind is being forced to expand: this time starwards, galaxy-wise, and who knows where next. These dazzlers have mapped our world, or worlds, for us, have told us what is going on and in ways no one else has done, have described our nasty present

long ago, when it was still the future and the official scientific spokesmen were saying that all manner of things now happening were impossible - who have played the indispensable and (at least at the start) thankless role of the despised illegitimate son who can afford to tell truths the respectable siblings either do not dare, or, more likely, do not notice because of their respectability. They have also explored the sacred literature of the world in the same bold way they take scientific and social possibilities to their logical conclusions so that we may examine them. How very much do we all owe them!

These illegitimate "dazzlers" are difficult to locate: no one denies the interest of Wells or Jules Verne, and such original writers as Ursula LeGuin, Stanislaw Lem, Isaac Asimov, or even Frank Herbert with his abominably written *Dune* series. But the genre has attracted few scientists (because the fictional science is too often bad) and fewer literarily inclined readers (because of the naive level of narrative and poor writing). Although many American universities have large lecture courses in science-fantasy fiction, they are condescended to as "micks" (after Mickey Mouse). This low evaluation of the genre does not come from what Lessing calls its illegitimacy when it is put into competition with its "respectable siblings," but from its literary and scientific poverty. This does not, of course, mean that the genre is incapable of greatness - H.G. Wells proved the contrary - or that it or any other genre can automatically be disqualified from the canons of "serious" literature.

It is equally difficult to understand Lessing's assumption that predictive science fiction is the current major mode of experimentation amid an excessive conventional fiction. The growing primacy of science since the seventeenth century allowed for the development of utopian literature and scientific special effects in narrative: I am not the first to point to myths of demonism as a partial source, and to Milton's Satan and Death, whose "petrific mace" and the rebellious angelic invention of gunpowder in *Paradise Lost* are among the earliest manifestations of science fictional elements. It is universally recognized, however, that H.G. Wells was the first to crystallize the combination of science, prediction of the future, and imaginative melding power that constitute the genre. This combination is experimental only in terms of ideology or subject matter, and it competes with traditional fiction only if one believes that conventional fiction's working materials are singularly dependent on purely realistic depictions of individuals, families, and societies.

When a formal experimentalist like Calvino briefly takes on the convention of science fiction as he does in *Cosmicomics* and *t-zero*, he makes tentative and puckish statements about the past and particularly the present world where our relationship with science remains interesting and connotative in the extreme. The science fiction that Lessing calls on, on the other hand, deals with a moral replacement of our present perceptions and has a didactic earnestness that allows no room for formal games or contentual play. Although much science fiction includes often haphazard ethical and religious content, Lessing's unacknowledged forerunner is an ideological proselytizer like C.S. Lewis, whose trilogy from the 1950s – *Out of the Silent Planet, Perelandra*, and *That Hideous Strength* – used the genre as a means of resurrecting Arthurian myth, material from *The Golden Bough*, and strong Christian polemics. Both Lewis and Lessing have bizarre attitudes toward science: Lewis uses it haphazardly to attack itself and to substitute older values; Lessing takes its potentialities completely for granted and is calmly indifferent to it, using its positive and negative powers only when they serve her cosmic morality.

The most acute critic of the genre is one of its best practitioners – the Polish Stanislaw Lem, whose writings on science and popular knowledge of it have set him beyond his competitors. His theoretical work is now translated into English, and in quoting his critiques of science fiction, I am using essays from his *Writings on Science Fiction and Fantasy* (1985). He claims that "For me, the scientific ignorance of most American science fiction writers was as inexplicable as the abominable literary quality of their output." Like Lessing, Lem began to write science fiction because it "deals with human beings as a species (or, rather, with all possible species of intelligent being, one of which happens to be the human species)"; like her, he was interested in its conjectural quality and its need to be internally consistent – although his standards are scientific rather than ethical.

Ideally, Lem feels the genre should be used to study science problems by putting them into hypothetical fictional contexts, and is angry at the predominance of romantic claptrap and special effects. He is particularly interested in the tough and precise project of fictionalizing science, but he regrets that most writers in their scientific ignorance cannot do it, and do not even understand the fruitful seriousness of the project. Lem thinks that the task of science fiction is to dramatize the adventures of the scrupulously scientific human spirit in search of knowledge, and the word knowledge must be the key to the whole enterprise. Lessing too searches for knowledge but of a different sort – hers is mystically controlled and anthropomorphically ethical. As such, it is more dependent on understanding a hypothetical far past symbolically and suggestively encoded in sacred books, and reinterpreting it to shape a future than it is on facing the inscrutable paradoxes of advanced contemporary science and our excited but still dim comprehension of it. Basically, Lem is more critical of science fiction and less hopeful than Lessing, but he does see significant possibilities for its practitioners. No doubt he, too, would like to have a bibliography of the dazzlers Lessing so casually mentions.

Shikasta is several cuts above most science fiction, in spite of its relative indifference to science and its failure to conform to Lem's strict principles. A complex, many-layered fiction presenting a variety of styles, it frees Lessing from realism and from the constraints of traditional ideas of narratology and fictional possibilities. In spite of her contempt for the bourgeois novel in earlier works, her formal style so far generally participates in conventionally accepted norms. Although an ideologue and a considerable preacher from her earliest published work, Lessing up to this point had narrowly managed to keep within the boundaries of the literary discourse established by and after Henry James. And in *The Good Terrorist* (1985), published after the five Canopus novels, she returns to the Jamesian norm of showing rather than telling, which is an almost biblical dictum since his time. The questing characters in Lessing's earlier books, of course, automatically limited her urge to preach and tell, because she took care to have the autobiographical central character rather than the author speak eloquently of her feelings and discoveries.

In *Shikasta* all that is changed through the book's documentary format. The cumbersome full title, *Canopus in Argos: Archives. Re: Colonised Planet 6, Shikasta. Personal, Psychological, Historical Documents Relating to Visit by Johor (George Sherban) Emissary (Grade 9). 87th of the Period of the Last Days* is redeemed only by the editorial decision to present *Shikasta* in bold print, thus encouraging much needed abbreviation. In another writer, one might assume comic intention in a title that thus parodies the official jargon afflicting most establishments and information filing systems, but Lessing is so enamored of the systematic organization of her beliefs that parodic self-consciousness has no place. The lack of comedy combines with the documentary pretensions of *Shikasta* to give the novel an auspicious tone of quasi-objective presentation. The intrusion of specious propaganda and journalistic fact-finding that make up the tradition of the documentary novel is strong here (see Barbara Foley's superb account of this genre from a Leninist point of view, *Telling the Truth: The Theory and Practice of Documentary Fiction* (1986)). In addition, Lessing's reader must busily absorb both a strongly presented ethical view and an intergalactic system that interprets the large problems of hierarchy, good and evil, origins of life, etc. that make up every overarching religious system.

Lessing's positive achievement can be measured to some degree by considering the problems encountered even by an infinitely more skillful fictionist, John Milton, who, together with William Blake, was the greatest proponent in English of the idea of wedding cosmic and astronomic ideas to the metaphoric demands of literature. Readers of *Paradise Lost* are confronted by a text that self-confidently asserts its ability to justify the ways of God to man by the powers intrinsic to the divine poet and the vatic potentialities of poetry. Milton imagines a cosmos riddled with theological ideas (many of them heretical), deeply pondered not only in the process of his intensive study of the Bible and its Rabbinical and Christian commentaries, but through a lengthy spelling out of his own manifold system in his theological manifesto, *De Doctrina Christiana*. The amount of ideological energy systematically informing *Paradise Lost* is awesome and its truth-claims shrill. This poem brought about the parodic demonism of Romanticism because it demonstrates at every turn the ironic impossibility of its task and its necessary fragmentation of metaphor.

It also shows the failure of an overarching theological argument, which is broken tonally almost instantly by the characterization of a God whose voice is defensive and whose theology is illogical.

Readers dedicated to the canon of English literary history will no doubt find Lessing's rough prose ill-suited to comparison with such a master, but the ambitions of Milton and Blake with their ideological, systematic presentations are her two strong antecedents in English. The task of the artist projecting a moral system through cosmic metaphor appears doomed from the beginning, and can retain its interest only to the degree that the system can convince – and even convert – the reader to an acquiescence to the congeries of metaphors it presents. Milton's mammoth success through the annals of English poetry rests on his prosodic genius and heretical glories, but also on the fact that *Paradise Lost* participates in establishment Christianity – although it is certainly not an orthodox statement of that culturally unifying religion. In Lessing's case, the questionable and unorthodox underlying issue of truth-telling and attempted conversion to a new system is no doubt the basis for most of the demurrals critics have expressed against the Canopus series – not the mystification that some of them have claimed.

In fact, Lessing's doctrine is clear and simple. The cosmos of these novels is one in which good (Canopus) is dominant and will prevail against its evil but weaker Puttiora–Shammat opposite. Scientific–biological data are the basis on which moral as well as physical evolution within the universe can and does progress. So strong is Lessing's insistence on biology that there is a third planetary force between good and evil, Sirius, whose development is entirely based on biological experimentation and control. At an early point, this planet fought against but was defeated by Canopus, and now its amoral scientism is aligned to the good as it slowly absorbs ethical Canopean influence.

Of the great number of planets and systems under Canopean lordship, Rohanda (the earth) – meaning fruitful and thriving – was the fairest, but through cosmic physical accident and the evil influence of Shammat, the planet's link and imposed "lock" with Canopus were weakened and it is now called Shikasta – the broken one. Paternalistic Canopus is unwilling that this misalignment – in every way parallel to ancient myths of the Fall, just as Rohanda was once parallel to Eden – should mean the loss of the formerly blessed planet, and therefore sends emissaries into Shikastan incarnations in an effort to guide the planet slowly back to its ethical and almost perfect original state. The people of the planet (who at the time of the main action are those of the late twentieth century going through events that we know both from our history books and from our quotidian lives) are ruined and misguided in every way, but nevertheless retain a remote sense of the Signature and SOWF. These two "sacred" metaphors in Lessing's system refer to the bonds that continue to link, however weakly, the good in humankind to the absolute wisdom of Canopus. The Signature is some sort of gleaming amulet that even benighted minds recognize as symbolically authoritative and capable of calling forth the power of goodness in those who recognize it; SOWF is the selfless Substance-Of-We-Feeling that underlies the entire Canopean ethical system.

Lessing's thought at this point turns from the extreme solipsistic existentialism of her earlier books, where her heroines seek to know themselves so that they can make sense out of the suffering they undergo. Like many contemporary writers – Nabokov, Murdoch, Hoban, Bellow, Calvino – Lessing now begins in this Canopus series to raise the issue of unselfing, of trying to illustrate the destructive effects of Romantic individualism and to turn the duty (a negative term for existentialists like Sartre or John Fowles) of the reader towards all sorts of objective and ameliorative concerns. *Shikasta*, which lays the foundation of the Canopean system, argues that the besetting ills of the world lie primarily in selfishness and are opposed to what Johor (the main Canopean spokesman and undoubted hero of the novel) identifies on the first page of his account as love. In order to separate this love from self-interest, Lessing coins the acronymic term SOWF, which stresses the necessity of seeing each living being as part of a corporate body with ethical interresponsibility. In Lessing's system, every human misery is attributable to the want of love or SOWF, including our blameworthy separation from and misuse of animals, the harmful generation gap, and old age (called the Degenerative Disease) – which comes to us so quickly, although human beings should be like Adam and Methuselah, who lived long beyond our narrow span. In Lessing's system, biology must be accepted to a degree, but she has no doubt that the interrelationship of evolution and ethics is central in causing both the strength of the species and its degeneration.

Shikasta, like the symbolic medieval system, has its spiritual nimbuses, and the world is surrounded by six zones that figure to some degree in each of the Canopus novels. The sixth zone is the one closest to the earth, the one to which Shikastans are translated after their death, and from which they re-enter through reincarnation. Here the majority show their spiritual inadequacies; they sing hymns that express their longing to be delivered by some divine being rather than learning to accept their own responsibility through painful lives on Shikasta, where they can slowly evolve to higher spiritual states. Whereas Shikasta emphasizes the need for development within the Shikastan world, Lessing's second Canopean novel concentrates on the next three zones, and is called *The Marriages Between Zones Three, Four and Five*. At the end of this romantic sexual fantasy, which Lessing puzzlingly describes as "more realistic" than *Shikasta*, the heroine–queen goes on to the spiritual reaches of a more ethereal zone as part of the forging of her mystical being. The other Canopus novels explore Shikasta and other troubled and dying planets, as Lessing dodges around the peripheries of the myth set out strongly and coherently in the first novel.

The series is uneven, but if *Shikasta* succeeds – in spite or because of its fresh cosmic vision and deployment of a belief-oriented system – the other novels should follow in value and popularity. The Canopean structure subsumes the curious biblical accounts of giants, angels, agrarian patriarchs, divine chariots, etc., and refers to a folkloric time in the world when the aerial fairies, elves, and earthy dwarves were not driven out by the coarsening sensibilities of the human race. The idea of a planet visited by friendly aliens who come repeatedly to heal the fatal rifts of earth is old in science fictional or even mystically redemptive terms. In constructing *Shikasta*, Lessing deliberately presents as rational the kinds of material that the scientific mind sees as merely fanciful, and this evocation can charm or alienate, according to the reader's will to accept a reshaping of the cosmos or deny it. Lessing does not choose to accept the opposition between scientism and mysticism in the late twentieth century, and therefore the possibilities of her success are not as large as her own fervor and conviction will them to be.

Formally, *Shikasta* is a welter of techniques and modes, from putative documentary reports, objective journals, sociological or scientific information sheets, and quasi-historical descriptions, to personal diaries that convey standard first-person narratives of the sort novels have long employed. The multiple points of view thus received by the reader dramatically stress the difference between the benighted state of human perception in Shikasta and the ameliorative effects of the wise Canopean agents. The latter strive to effect the survival of the human race in spite of the destructive nuclear holocaust which comes inexorably, leaving only a few well-trained survivors from whom new harmonious civilizations are expected. Lessing forcefully intends the reader to side with the compassionate realism of the Canopean overview, and to pity and abhor the frailty of individual Shikastans who become characters in the plot.

Because many readers of fiction are not in any way given to systematic thought, however, and prefer the tormented twistings and blind turnings of suffering characters, the effects Lessing appears to have planned are not entirely foolproof. In other words, the perfected Canopean hero Johor – incarnated for the duration of the action of the novel under the name of George Sherban – is not, for many readers, as sympathetic or interesting as his touching, confused, wrong-headed sister Rachel, whose diaries appeal to the sort of receptor who enjoyed Anna Wulf in *The Golden Notebook*. In other words, the jolting diversity of style employed by Lessing does not alter the response of readers whose taste ineluctably veers to the old stand-bys of fiction – character and action within a romantic framework. Moreover, for such readers (and they are many) the Canopean material is a distraction and even a drag on a flimsy plot.

If it is assumed that the cosmic or Canopean quasi-historical material is background only, and not part of a viable fictional plot or action, Lessing's novel is greatly reduced in impact. As soon as the Canopean material is focused in *Shikasta*, we are ready for the plot to unfold, and there can be no doubt that it is decidedly limited. The Canopean agent, Johor, having been sent several times to Rohanda/Shikasta through the millennia, is required to undergo another reincarnation because his fellow agent, Taufiq, has fallen into the negative moral miasma of the planet. As a now elderly English lawyer named John Brent-Oxford, Taufiq has become a confused political leftist with no sense of overview or purpose. He is therefore unable to effect the various tasks of amelioration, particularly among terrorists and schizophrenics (there are several case histories of both types, including one that looks suspiciously like an exaggeration of Lessing's own case during her first fifteen years in Britain), that he ought to have undertaken in preparation for larger, crucial tasks as yet unknown. Johor drags two old Shikastan friends, Ben and Rilla, who have failed in previous lives, from Zone Six into reincarnation with him. Ben becomes his fraternal twin and moral inferior; Rilla his confused and suffering sister who is killed fairly early in the action.

Meanwhile, the late-twentieth-century world declines desperately as it did in earlier Lessing fictions. Race conflict is absolute, the planet is overcrowded, youth armies lawlessly roam through the world, and nuclear holocaust is inevitable. George Sherban reaches young manhood and labors tirelessly to bring about what good he can; Ben and Rachel are marshaled to help him with the youth armies after the death of their selfless, weary parents. Finally, there is an international mock "trial" among the young, presided over by George, in which all other races of Shikasta attack the history of white ascendancy and racism. The spokesman for the non-whites is George, who had an Indian grandparent, and the defendant of the whites is a revived John Brent-Oxford. Riots miraculously do not occur (presumably because of the Canopeans, Johor, and the reawakened Taufiq), and little is decided except that violence is wrong and the guilt of the current human races real. As a climax to the fictional plot, the "trial" is an absolute fizzle, but global nuclear holocaust occurs rather uneventfully (!!) and vaguely, and those trained in survivalism by George–Johor begin new geometrically harmonious societies reminiscent of those of the original Rohanda. Johor–George is allowed to disincarnate and go home to Canopus, and presumably all will be well enough after this new start.

Putting aside Lessing's Sufic doctrines and her related belief that contemporary people must learn the technical elements of survivalism in order to live out the evolutionary change that constitutes the next step forward, this is a less than fascinating plot, not least because its focus – the "trial" – lacks dramatic impact and convincing dénouement. To put it more cruelly, the trial fails to make a point and it is quite unable to command the plot in a dominant way – through ideology, character, or the further action through which Lessing wishes to persuade the reader of a possible idyllic post-nuclear future. Lessing's novels to this point have consistently shown characters unable to move beyond the blind wretchedness of the present, and although a character

254

like Anna Wulf in *The Golden Notebook* learns her independence and responsible unity with the world, the future is not clearly envisaged. Here in *Shikasta*, Lessing achieves that future too simply by wiping out the world, and starting anew. Her hero Johor-George does not achieve much in his human incarnation, and the large claims of his and Taufiq's Canopean tasks are not well realized. The plot action fails to sustain the weight Lessing puts upon it, and as real people in a real world, George, Ben, Rachel, and their friends are at best only momentarily engaging.

The double intention of *Shikasta* – to present a mystical overview and to envisage some action in the world that might lead to a brave new world of harmony and ethical concern – is impossibly difficult, and there is no doubt that Lessing's fiction breaks under the strain. But this novel is interesting from many points of view, not least that of the imaginative presentation of a system that brings into clever alignment mythologies from the serious fantasies of the past – from religious books to epic to folklore – with an admirably determined will to use science fiction to urge the reader to see and think more clearly. The enormous ambitions of *Shikasta* are not as evident in the remaining novels in the Canopus series, however. None of them is ultimately as interesting – or for that matter as fragmented and failed – as this first one, and both their intention and their success are smaller. Lessing seizes on smaller flawed fragments of human personality and experience in the next two, and on larger political and personal error in the last two. The five taken together, although not necessarily read in order, are nevertheless an eloquent testament to their author's large, generous, and infinite wishes for the betterment of a world undoubtedly floundering in the cosmic sea.

*

Unlike a writer like J.R.R. Tolkien who can be considered analogous to Lessing in the creation of a continuous fantasy, Lessing does not allow herself to be completely possessed by the charms of her created world. Whereas Tolkien could not stop himself from endlessly enlarging his one fiction right up to his death, Lessing busied herself with other sorts of work even as she turned out the Canopean volumes at an amazingly fast rate. Although the Canopus series is her central ideological breakthrough, she continues to show that it is not a stumbling block to her literary growth, and that she is not limited to a single genre. In her fecundity, Lessing has given us three recent novels (up to 1987), aside from this science-fiction group. In keeping with her consistent diversity, they are of two distinct types: two of them fall to some degree into the Barbara Pymite sort of novel, the other is a clearly perceived satiric, Conradian depiction of one kind of modern terrorist. For readers who might wonder where Lessing could go after the science-fiction foray, these three novels give a suggestive reply.

Critics who identify the two-novel mini-series now published under the title *The Diaries of Jane Somers* as Pymite are right, but these books are informed with ethical intention beyond Pym's gentle depictions of lonely women. Lessing's new heroine Janna is busy with re-education, with learning about unselfing, and with slowly assuming a humanly felt sense of what Lessing called SOWF (Substance-Of-We-Feeling) in *Shikasta*. In her earlier novels, the selfish, rebellious freedom of her women and their longing for independent happiness were major themes; now in both *The Diary of a Good Neighbour* (1983) and *If the Old Could*... (1984) the heroine is taught to turn attention from herself and to share and understand the suffering of other people who are not, on the social or selfish surface of things, interesting or important. The didacticism of the two novels and the effect of the ethical system presented through the metaphors of the Canopus work are undeniable.

Basically, however, these two competent novels are not extraordinary. They lack the distinctive strength of statement typical of Lessing's fictions in other manifestations, and indeed they were written as a trick played against publishers and critics alike. They were submitted a year apart under the pseudonymous authorship of a putative journalist named "Jane Somers." The first, *The Diary of a Good Neighbour*, was turned down by several British publishers, including Lessing's usual firm, Jonathan Cape; only Robert Gottlieb of Knopf in the United States is credited with having recognized her authorship. When the novels were finally published they received few reviews, and sold few copies. Lessing then confessed her authorship, arguing that she was simply demonstrating the uphill struggle of the beginning novelist in a profession dominated by established names and undiscriminating critical response. The efficacy of the experiment is unconvincing, if only because these novels display Lessing at her most pallid. Although entirely professional books, they are easily lost in the wilderness of contemporary novels about and by women in ordinary circumstances, and unless one is addicted to the specious genre of the suffering contemporary woman, they are not noteworthy.

When Lessing reissued them jointly as *The Diaries of Jane Somers* in 1984, she added one of her explanatory prefaces which is not only an attack on publishers but a curious defense of her own multiformity as a writer:

> *The Diary of a Good Neighbour* got written when it did for several reasons. One: I wanted to be reviewed on merit, as a new writer, without the benefit of a "name"; to get free of that cage of associations and labels that every established writer has to learn to live inside. It is easy to predict what reviews will say. Mind you, the labels change. Mine have been – starting with *The Grass is Singing*: she is a writer about the colour bar ... – about communism – feminism – mysticism; she writes space fiction, science fiction. Each label has served for a few years.
>
> Two: I wanted to cheer up young writers. ...
>
> Another reason, frankly if faintly malicious: some reviewers complained they hated my Canopus series, why didn't I write realistically, the way I used to do before; preferably *The Golden Notebook* over again? These were sent *The Diary of a Good Neighbour* but not one recognized me. Some people think it is reasonable

that an avowed devotee of a writer's work should only be able to recognize it when packaged and signed.

It's hard to understand why those who admired the passionate selfishness of the heroine of *The Golden Notebook* would recognize the creator of the unselfish Janna in the two later novels; indeed it's not clear what sort of statement Lessing is actually making in this preface. She says that the Canopus series set her "free to write in ways I had not used before. I wondered if there would be a similar liberation if I were to write in the first person as a different character." Lessing goes on triumphantly to say that "as Jane Somers I wrote in ways that Doris Lessing cannot. . . . Jane Somers knew nothing about a kind of dryness, like a conscience that monitors Doris Lessing *whatever she writes and in whatever style*." I have added the italics in this quotation because of the sheer illogicality of the argument, where Lessing is both herself as a writer and not herself. Before the end of this preface, she also claims that she is *au fond* recognizable in the Jane Somers novels as she is in every other work. Her astonishment that she should fail to be seen as unique, and that her work might even temporarily be identified with Barbara Pym, is amusing and a bit surprising. Even more so is her childish, shamelessly egoistic feeling of vindication as the result of her little trick.

The 1985 novel, *The Good Terrorist*, on the other hand, demonstrates both her strengths and her ability to write unexpectedly and well in a mode that has not been characteristic of her past forms and experiments. There are certain necessary kinds of fiction that are dreary to read for good reasons, and *The Good Terrorist* is one of them. Lessing, who spent a good part of her adult life enamored of the Communist Party and leftist modes of rebellious behavior, is not an innocent reporter of the psychological sets that create the character of revolutionaries. This novel abounds in honest and fascinating accounts of a whole spectrum of personalities within political radicalism. Although in many ways reminiscent of Conrad's *The Secret Agent*, this fiction with its unremitting objectivity forges its own iron chains of political stupidity. This is not to say that Lessing advocates an alternative political possibility – she is certainly not a Conservative convert like Ronald Reagan or Paul Johnson. Her achievement in this novel is admirable within the social-realist mode: it is a direct, unflinching demonstration of the self-deceiving actions and thoughts of a realistically presented woman in contemporary Britain who, as a political radical, lives out her neuroses and the demands of her chosen situation.

The age of this anti-heroine, Alice Mellings, is carefully calculated – at 36 she is not an innocent girl, so the off-beat life she chooses to live cannot be simply attributed to juvenile intoxication with radical politics or a rebellion against her bourgeois parents. Lessing's long study of psychotherapy, however, gives her access to the kind of sympathy required for a just characterization of Alice. It is clear that this woman suffers from hysteria of various origins, including the two mentioned above – the hysteria of the blindly committed and that of anti-parental trauma. Her neurotic repression of her sexuality is stressed throughout the action of the novel. Hovering in the background is a strong suggestion that she falls into mental fits that border on the epileptic, but are more likely to be hysterically than physically induced.

Alice is not the only psychological aberrant among the characters assembled in the squatters' house she works hard to rehabilitate to minimal domesticity. Her non-lover, Jasper, is neurotic and untouchable, except by men during his sprees of homosexual cruising; Faye is irreversibly damaged by childhood battering and cannot be helped by either radical politics or a comforting lesbian relationship with maternal Roberta; Philip is victimized by his physical limitations and his inability to establish himself as a reliable contractor; Jim, the only apolitical person in the squat, has been in serious, unspecified legal trouble and cannot believe that he will ever be able to re-enter society as a trusted worker. In comparison with these walking wounded, Alice is a picture of still-too-bourgeois health. Behind these neurotics hover the more serious, non-idealistic ideologues and professionals, who live next door in another abandoned house and are apparently connected to the KGB through their major contact, Andrew.

The two central squats or houses of the novel are thus symbolic: Alice's house, on which she lavishes so much domestic care, contrasts personal neurosis with the crisp professionalism of the house next door. By the last part of the novel, the professional house empties as its inhabitants go purposively off, but a few of them remain to join Alice's company of radical neurotics – the so-called CCU (Communist Centre Union). Instantly the atmosphere is hardened – revolutionary *matériel* begins to arrive at the house, anonymous international agents threaten, and bomb-building manuals lie around to be mastered and put into practice. The novel's dénouement is hardly a surprise; the group almost serendipitously decides to plant a car bomb in front of a noted international London hotel. In spite of their bungling, they manage to kill a lot of people, plus the manic Faye – to whom the reader bids a relieved farewell. As the group afterward draws toward a purposeless dissolution and drifts piecemeal out of the house, Alice is left alone in her now cosy quarters, awaiting a meeting with an obviously and dangerously professional agent, Peter Cecil.

As she waits for the scheduled meeting at the book's end, Alice is allowed to meditate upon the contradictory blend of domesticity and radicalism that composes her personality. The cool narrator directly and ironically associates her heroine with her literary pre-type, the innocent Alice of Lewis Carroll's Wonderland, whose incalculable distance from the contemporary world has fascinated so many Postmodernist writers:

> Smiling gently, a mug of very strong sweet tea in her hand, looking this morning like a nine-year-old girl who has had, perhaps, a bad dream, the poor baby sat waiting for it to be time to go out and meet the professionals.

Alice Mellings's rabbit-hole wonderland is a world in which the fantastic political world is entirely a product of her own drifting, imagining mind. She has fallen into adult life without attaining the maturity required to cope with it, and remains to the end a "poor baby" whose quasi-ideological commitment is at odds with the hard realism of political professionals. Her strong, vestigial commitment to domesticity is her only tie with "reality," and she is in fact very good at sustaining this tie. But housekeeping and homemaking are bourgeois qualities, as Jasper and the others keep telling unappreciated Alice. They are also a way of ordering the world, and one of Lessing's strongest messages in this novel is that systematic organization of the psyche or the world lies at the heart of all power and imagination. As we read page after tedious page of Alice's attempts to get money by any means, to persuade the local Council to permit them to squat, to help Philip make the premises minimally habitable, to cook the stew, to keep peace, etc., etc., it is overwhelmingly evident that this is a psyche held together only by a careful unitive act. Sexually repressed and politically inept, Alice creates a house that is a coherent but skewed metaphor for definable and even systematic happiness of the sort required for human life to continue.

Lessing's presentation of the professional radicals like Andrew of the KGB and the cool new agents that become dangerously present in Alice's life is a model of proficiency, giving us a plausibly realistic picture of how the recruitment of undercover "moles" might in fact take place. In this respect, Lessing is in the line of Conrad, Graham Greene, and John Le Carré, and chillingly capable of projecting an aura of the darker reaches of political commitment. When the fictional material of *The Good Terrorist* is related to a thematic interpretation of Lessing's fiction, the primary contrasts present throughout her work remain intact. On the one hand there is the confused seeking mind of the quasi-heroine (in Alice's case handled with something close to contempt, as opposed to the sympathy given to earlier heroines) who fumbles toward a coherent overview with little success; on the other hand, and coexisting with the heroine's bewilderment, is a system firmly and awesomely in place. Alice and her mates are neurotically incapable of doing other than spouting the clichés of Communism, and are therefore often unintentionally comical. The reality of the matter and its systematic presentation are seen through Andrew, the IRA, and the other professional agents, who have nothing but contempt for these childish incompetents. Alice and her friends are like the befuddled inhabitants of Shikasta, whereas the systematic professionals are like a limited, perverted version of the controlling Canopeans in the science-fiction series.

Lessing's stand on the delicate and contradictory contrast between fantasy and realism – the co-ordinates of all her fiction – is intricate and shifting. But at base it involves a conviction that literature functions well when it contrasts the two through her particular and often contradictory definitions of fantasy. For

Lessing, fantasy is often seen as false convention, or illusionistic inability to perceive the objective truth. It is useful at this point to allow the overly connotative word imagination to intrude, for Lessing has obviously felt that the imaginative creation of a "fantastic" cosmos like Canopus serves her purposes well. It demonstrates the higher realism of a rigorously imagined rational order, as opposed to the lower realism that occurs when she depicts people in our world who are afflicted by the degenerative fantasy of solipsism and therefore incapable of seeing the truth. The important issue here is that Lessing believes absolutely in truth. This adamant belief shapes all of her work into ideological documents, and makes her an extraordinarily didactic writer. Moreover, like many novelists – and indeed all satirists – Lessing also consistently expresses the need to valorize and justify the fictional act by tacitly showing its ameliorative intention.

The most negative criticism one can level against Lessing is that her didacticism, ideological bent, and downright preaching, which are everywhere intrusive in her work, are encroachments on the Modernist traditions of ambiguity and multiple meaning. The reader is given little freedom in her work, and indeed her fans are disciples to an extraordinary degree. But this ambitious and committed writer and thinker never flags in her need to demonstrate the consistent human imperative to grope toward truth and the good. Regardless of how intensely the reader might disagree with her, Lessing's skill, her commitment, and her bizarrely commanding accomplishment cannot be denied.

CONCLUSION

12

Roads not taken

A study of contemporary fiction can go in any direction, and my attempts to avoid univocalism are vivid reminders of many other possible directions. Because distinctions are difficult and necessarily quirky in studying the present, a rationale of sorts is in order. I chose a handful of writers among a plethora of peers, in order to show by individual studies how full and interesting the current fictional situation is. Most of the writers fall within the Anglo-American range, because my audience is presumably Anglophonic rather than totally international. Another factor is linguistic, in that I feel it incorrect to write about texts not readable in the original language – and am thus barred from eastern European and oriental writers. The fictionists finally chosen are all deeply interesting to me, and although I originally considered a few rather negative studies of writers like John Barth, Peter Handke, and John Hawkes, I rejected this as a mean-spirited exercise not in keeping with the aim of this book, which is to persuade readers of the fortunate choices that lie before us as textual receptors.

I am, however, full of regrets at the many roads not taken, and would like to mention a few that I find particularly unfortunate. In some ultimate world I would like to write an extended essay on John Fowles, John Barth, and Michel Tournier, all of whom I find tremendously talented and, in varying ways, on the puzzlingly unsuccessful edge of things for reasons that range from failures of nerve or ideology to stylistic risks that are received badly by either general readers or those in academic power. Of the three, Tournier strikes me as the most important novelist as well as the most profound thinker on the subject of narratology. I considered substituting him for Russell Hoban – a seriously underestimated writer who forms a less intellectual analogue to Tournier. Both translate an obsession with childhood into an adult phenomenology; both express an uneasy combination of the ordinariness and strangeness of the world. Tournier's view, expressed in the autobiographical essays of *Le vent Paraclet*, sees the novelist as a sort of polymorph, whose life as artistic or literary creator comprises a fabulous overcompensation for the series of characterological fiascos that are somehow expressed in the fictional act.

Tournier's interest in the psychic malformations or obsessions of individuals creates what he describes as cosmic comedy. He explains that "the more I laugh, the less I joke," and in this respect he is reminiscent of John Barth at his most successful. All of Tournier's work evokes a Paideiac Sophia, and his ability to cover the didactic through his rethinking of such mythic themes as the Robinson Crusoe story in *Vendredi*, or the St Christopher-cum-erl-king myth in *Ogre (Le Roi des Aulnes)* is part of his radical refocusing of attention on the extraordinary. In this he is like John Fowles, whose style is always too peremptory and narrowly masculine, but whose attempts at forcing his audience to rethink both the literary past and the humanely informed present are various. Fowles is capable of really bad books – like *Daniel Martin* (1977) and *Mantissa* (1982), but he is also the author of the superbly effective and serious novel, *The French Lieutenant's Woman* (1969), and, most recently, *A Maggot* (1985).

Whereas Tournier's problems seem to come entirely from the fact that he has stylistically, narratologically, and thematically opposed the academically based *nouveaux romanciers* (the French public, however, loves him), Fowles pleases most general readers and academics, but only some of the time. No one, alas, thinks that he is really a great writer, or that he is quite worthy of the attention his strong didactic intelligence pulls from his audience. John Barth is like these two in his attempts to refocus his readers on major fictional issues. He says that his themes are regression, re-enactment, and reorientation, and there is no doubt that he urges these on his serious readers. His real problem is that in spite of stylistic strengths, he does not have the individual voice that both Tournier and Fowles exert – and his courage is so impersonally directed that his cold texts fail to engage his readers. His is a real but barren talent, and unlike that of Tournier or Fowles, illustrative of how reorientation and reperception of the fictional, mythical, and historical past can be used to alienate the reader.

These three taken together are useful in seeing how problematic the role of the contemporary writer is in terms of audience response at the level of both academic critic and general reader. A strong positive case can be made for each of them – and a negative one as easily. The same thing can be said of all writers, of course, since fame is fragile and judgments unstable. But Barth, Fowles, and Tournier come better equipped than most, and are more manifoldly ambitious than many of their contemporaries. A study of their careers is tempting, but unfortunately outside the arbitrary boundaries of this book.

Another issue beyond my intention is the study of particular political subjects like feminism and the fascism of right or left. In this I am not so much asserting a political point of view as an aestheticism that dislikes the confining of a text to theoretical, narrowly conceived *a priori* subject matters. There are magnificent political writers, particularly those in or from Latin American and eastern bloc countries. The middle European most known in the west at present is Milan Kundera, whose thematics range far beyond the political and whose literary power is impressive. I reluctantly admit that I know no purely feminist writer who has not limited her books to the point of dismissing a large part of a potentially sympathetic audience. At the same time, I have included a study of Saul Bellow, a serious but rebarbative writer whose political stances are dominant and whose anti-feminism is appalling. His mixture of cultural thought and moral purpose nevertheless joins his distinctive American voice to make him one of the great writers of our period.

I would particularly note the health of the British novel as opposed to the doldrums of the American at this historical point. The English are always being hammered by their experimental French counterparts, and suffer terrifically from a francophiliac conviction of inferiority. With the *nouveau romancier* faltering, and names like Robbe-Grillet and Philippe Sollers no longer in the vanguard, the only real success story in France is that of Michel Tournier, who is loved by his readers and ignored by the academy. The British situation is unlike this, in that there the reading public is crankily faithful to its writers. The loyalty of British readers may come from the power of media preoccupation with things like the annual Booker McConnell prize. A stronger case can be made, however, for the persistence of a novel tradition that has never been experimental in the American, Italian, or Latin American way, but that has retained a standard that has never been seriously challenged. English critics are a nervous lot: on the one hand they cleave to their native products, but on the other they are pettish whenever a writer like Angela Carter or John Fowles imposes other standards. I have used only a few English novelists here, but feel strongly that the English novel, both in its older practitioners and in a younger generation including Martin Amis, Julian Barnes, Angela Carter, and A.N. Wilson, is a subject ripe for study.

As is the Latin American novel. In dealing only with Borges and García Márquez, this study is remiss, as it is in many other respects. The fecundity of imagined forms and subjects in Spanish American fiction, the literary potentiality in language and generic styles, and the range of subject matters cannot easily be summed up. Every novel by Manuel Puig, for example, is a surprise, and Latin American women are working at a level of originality not equaled in North America.

All in all, I intend this book of mine to be largely introductory and persuasive of the fact that we live in a period of great fictional ferment. As readers, we have large tasks – at first glimpse they may seem almost too daunting. The best of contemporary fiction is not an easy read, and in certain ways the bourgeois history of the novel has been dangerous to the contemporary artistic enterprise. The ease with which one reads a novel by Jane Austen or Trollope or Dickens or Tolstoy is no longer available. The genre has indeed changed, and will continue to do so, as contemporary writers riskily try to pull a placid audience after them in their serious enterprise. The great glory of fiction is that it perversely slips away from us into new directions and slithering forms; all the works of every period are transitory and succumb to the next decade of creativity. It behooves us to float freely with the genre, and, like Benvenuto Cellini, to go on our way rejoicing.

Critical bibliography

Allain, Marie-Françoise (1983) *The Other Man: Conversations with Graham Greene*, London: Bodley Head.

Alter, Robert (1975) *Partial Magic: The Novel as a Self-Conscious Genre*, Berkeley: University of California Press.

Alvarez, A. Alfred (1978) *Beckett*, Glasgow: Fontana/Collins.

Amis, Martin (1986) *The Moronic Inferno: And Other Visits to America*, London: Jonathan Cape.

Bakhtin, Mikhail (1986) *Problems of Dostoevsky's Poetics*, ed. and trans. Caryl Emerson, Minneapolis: University of Minnesota Press.

Barth, John (1967) "The literature of exhaustion," *Atlantic Monthly*, 220 (2), August.

Bayley, John (1979) "Under cover of decadence: Nabokov as evangelist and guide to the Russian classics," in Peter Quennell (ed.) *Vladimir Nabokov: His Life, His Work, His World: A Tribute*, London: Weidenfeld & Nicolson.

Bellow, Saul (1984) "A candid talk with Saul Bellow," interview in *New York Times Magazine* by D.J.R. Bruckner, 15 April.

Bellow, Saul (1984) "Interview with Saul Bellow," interview in *TriQuarterly* by Rockwell Gray, Harry White, and Gerald Nemanic, Spring/Summer (60), Evanston, Ill.: Northwestern University Press.

Bloom, Harold (1986) "A comedy of worldly salvation," review article on *The Good Apprentice*, *The New York Times*, 12 January.

Borges, Jorge Luis (1964) *Other Inquisitions, 1937-1952*, trans. Ruth L.C. Sims, Austin: University of Texas Press.

Borges, Jorge Luis (1972) *A Universal History of Infamy*, trans. Norman Thomas di Giovanni, New York: Dutton.

Burke, Kenneth (1970) *The Rhetoric of Religion: Studies in Logology*, Berkeley: University of California Press.

Butler, Lance St John (1984) *Samuel Beckett and the Meaning of Being: A Study in Ontological Parable*, New York: St Martin's Press.

Calvino, Italo (1986) "The written and the unwritten word," in *The Uses of Literature: Essays*, trans. Patrick Creagh, San Diego: Harcourt Brace Jovanovich.

Cannon, Jo Ann (1981) *Italo Calvino: Writer and Critic*, Ravenna: Longo Editore.

Conradi, Peter (1986) *Iris Murdoch: The Artist and the Saint*, London: Macmillan.

Cortázar, Julio (1986) *Around the Day in Eighty Worlds*, trans. Thomas Christensen, San Francisco, CA: North Point Press.

Driver, Tom E. (1961) "Beckett by the Madeleine," *Columbia University Forum*, 4(3), Summer.

Eco, Umberto (1962) *Opera Aperta: Forma e indeterminazione nelle poetiche contemporanee*, Milan: Bompiani.

Eco, Umberto (1966) *Aesthetics of Chaosmos: The Middle Ages of James Joyce*, trans. Ellen Esrock (1982), Tulsa, Okla.: University of Tulsa.

Eco, Umberto (1979) *The Role of the Reader: Explorations in the Semiotics of Texts*, Bloomington: Indiana University Press.

Eco, Umberto (1984) *Semiotics and the Philosophy of Language*, Bloomington: Indiana University Press.

Eco, Umberto (1984) *Postscript to The Name of the Rose*, trans. William Weaver, San Diego: Harcourt Brace Jovanovich.

Federman, Raymond (1975) *Surfiction: Fiction Now and Tomorrow*, Chicago: Swallow Press.

Foley, Barbara (1986) *Telling the Truth: The Theory and Practice of Documentary Fiction*, Ithaca: Cornell University Press.

Frazer, James George (1922) *The Golden Bough*, London: Macmillan.

Freccero, John (1975) "The fig tree and the laurel: Petrarch's poetico," *Diacritics* Spring, 34-40.

García Márquez, Gabriel (1983) *The Fragrance of Guava* (Plinio Apuleyo Mendoza in conversation with Gabriel García Márquez), London: Verso.

Gardner, James (1985) "Italo Calvino 1923-1985," *The New Criterion*, December, 4 (4), 6-13.

Genette, Gérard (1980) *Narrative Discourse: An Essay in Method*, trans. J.E. Levin, Ithaca: Cornell University Press.

Graff, Gerald (1979) *Literature Against Itself: Literary Ideas in Modern Society*, Chicago: University of Chicago Press.

Greene, Graham (1936) "Henry James: the private universe," in *Collected Essays* (1969), London: Bodley Head.

Greene, Graham (1971) *A Sort of Life*, New York: Simon & Schuster. Also (1971) London: Bodley Head.

Greene, Graham (1980) *Ways of Escape*, London: Bodley Head.

Haffenden, John (1985) *Novelists in Interview*, London: Methuen.

Hassan, Ihab (1986) *The Postmodern Turn: Essays in Postmodern Theory and Culture*, Columbus: Ohio State University Press.

Hazelton, Lesley (1982) "Doris Lessing on feminism, communism and 'space fiction'," interview with Doris Lessing, *The New York Times Magazine*, 25 July.

Hoggart, Richard (1970) "The force of character," in *Speaking to Each Other*, Oxford: Oxford University Press.

Hutcheon, Linda (1984) *Narcissistic Narrative: The Metafictional Paradox*, London: Methuen.

Hyde, G.M. (1977) *Vladimir Nabokov: America's Russian Novelist*, London: Marion Boyars.

Jameson, Fredric (1981) *The Political Unconscious: Narrative as a Socially Symbolic Act*, Ithaca: Cornell University Press.

Kenner, Hugh (1987) *The Mechanic Muse*, New York: Oxford University Press.

Kermode, Frank (1967) *The Sense of an Ending: Studies in the Theory of Fiction*, New York: Oxford University Press.

Kermode, Frank (1984) "Old Testament capers," *London Review of Books*, 20 September – 3 October.

Lem, Stanislaw (1985) *Writing on Science Fiction and Fantasy*, ed. Franz Rottensteiner, New York: Harcourt Brace Jovanovich.

Lukàcs, Georg (1983) *The Historical Novel*, trans. Hannah and Stanley Mitchell, Lincoln: University of Nebraska Press.

Lyotard, Jean-François (1979) *The Postmodern Condition: A Report on Knowledge*, trans. (1984) Geoff Bennington and Brian Massumi, Minneapolis: University of Minnesota Press.

McConnell, Frank (1977) *Four Postwar American Novelists*, Chicago: University of Chicago Press.

Mitgang, Herbert (1985) "Italo Calvino, the novelist, dead at 61," *New York Times*, 20 September.

Monegal, Fmir Rodriguez (1972) "Prose for Borges," in Mary Kinzie (ed.) *Borges: the Reader as Writer*, *TriQuarterly*, 25, Fall.

Nabokov, Vladimir (1970) *The Annotated Lolita*, ed. and annotated by Alfred Appel Jr, New York: McGraw-Hill.

Nabokov, Vladimir (1980) *Lectures on Literature*, ed. Fredson Bowers, New York: Harcourt Brace Jovanovich.

Nabokov, Vladimir (1984) "The tragedy of tragedy," *Harper's Atlantic Monthly*, 26 October, 79–85.

Newman, Charles (1985) *The Postmodern Aura: Fiction in an Age of Inflation*, Evanston, Ill.: Northwestern University Press.

Ozick, Cynthia (1983) *Art and Ardor: Essays*, New York: Knopf.

Ozick, Cynthia (1984) "Farcical combat in a busy world," review in *New York Times Book Review*, 20 May.

Paz, Octavio (1950) *The Labyrinth of Solitude: Life and Thought in Mexico*, trans. Lysander Kemp (1962), New York: Grove Press.

Propp, Vladimir (1968) *Morphology of the Folktale*, trans. Laurence Scott, Austin: University of Texas Press.

Ricoeur, Paul (1985) *Time and Narrative*, 2 vols, trans. Kathleen McLaughlin and David Pellauer, Chicago: University of Chicago Press.

Rowe, W. W. (1981) *Nabokov's Spectral Dimension*, Ann Arbor, MI: Ardis Publishers.

Sage, Lorna (1983) *Doris Lessing*, London: Methuen.

Sartre, Jean-Paul (1985) *Critique de la raison dialectique*, Paris: Gallimard.

Scholes, Robert (1979) *Fabulation and Metafiction*, Urbana: University of Illinois Press.

Shenker, Israel (1956) "Moody man of letters," *New York Times*, 55, 6 May.

Sorrentino, Fernando (1982) *Seven Conversations with Jorge Luis Borges*, trans. Clark M. Zlotchew, Troy, New York: Whitston Publishing Co.

Spurling, John (1983) *Graham Greene*, London: Methuen.

Steiner, George (1985) "Viewpoint: a new meaning of meanings," *The Times Literary Supplement*, 8 November.

Stephens, Walter E. (1983) "Echo in Fabula," *Diacritics*, Summer, 13 (2).

Symons, Julian (1982) "The strength of uncertainty," review article on *Monsignor Quixote*, *The Times Literary Supplement*, 8 October.

Tanner, Tony (1971) *City of Words: American Fiction 1950-1970*, London: Jonathan Cape.

Tournier, Michel (1977) *Le vent Paraclet: essai*, Paris: Gallimard.

Vargas Llosa, Mario (1971) *García Márquez: Historia de un Deicido*, Barcelona: Barral Editores.

Vargas Llosa, Mario (1975) *The Perpetual Orgy: Flaubert and Madame Bovery*, trans. (1986) Helen Lane, New York: Farrar Straus Giroux.

Voegelin, Eric (1974) *Order and History*, Baton Rouge: Louisiana State University Press, 4 vols (1956–74).

Webb, Eugene (1970) *Samuel Beckett: A Study of His Novels*, London: Peter Owen.

Wilde, Alan (1981) *Horizons of Assent: Modernism, Postmodernism and the Ironic Imagination*, Baltimore: Johns Hopkins University Press.

Name index

Adler, Renata 141
Alter, Robert 5
Alvarez, A. 92
Ambler, Eric 16
Amis, Martin 211, 215, 265
Appel, Alfred, Jr 76, 80
Apuleyo Mendoza, Plineo 17, 18, 23, 25
Aquinas, St Thomas 122, 125
Aristotle 137–8
Asimov, Isaac 248
Austen, Jane 149, 189, 265

Bacon, Francis 63
Bacon, Roger 131, 138
Bakhtin, Mikhail 6, 63, 151–2, 186–7
Balzac, Honoré de 189, 215
Barfield, Owen 224
Barnes, Julian 25, 265
Barth, John 7, 8, 11, 46, 48, 63, 70, 96, 99, 160, 161, 165, 215, 239, 263, 264
Barthelme, Donald 9, 48, 99, 141, 160
Barthelme, Frederick 11
Barthes, Roland 9, 92, 98, 118
Baudelaire, Charles 129
Bayley, John 70
Beattie, Anne 11
Beckett, Samuel 5, 14, 16, 45–6, 91–114, 140, 161, 162, 163
Bellow, Saul 4, 19, 35, 117, 140, 154, 165, 170, 210–37, 252, 265
Benjamin, Walter 78, 143

Benvéniste, Emile 98
Berkeley, Bishop George 54, 62, 63
Blake, William 62, 250, 251
Bloom, Harold 75, 185–6, 187
Bloy, Leon 62, 63
Borges, Jorge Luis 45–66, 103, 132, 177, 189, 234, 265
Bosch, Hieronymus 131
Bradbury, Malcolm 210–11, 236
Brontë, Charlotte 240, 245
Brontë, Emily 127
Browne, Sir Thomas 57, 63
Browning, Robert 18
Buber, Martin 186
Buchan, John 17
Burgess, Anthony 3
Burke, Kenneth 153
Burroughs, Edgar Rice 18
Butler, Lance St John 92

Cabrera Infante 24
Calvino, Italo 3, 10, 12, 27, 46, 67, 70, 91–114, 118, 130, 147, 152, 155, 161, 162, 165, 170, 180, 248, 252
Cannon, Jo Ann 99
Carlyle, Thomas 63
Carpentier, Alejo 18, 24
Carroll, Lewis (Charles Dodgson) 22, 66, 77–8, 147, 177, 258
Carter, Angela 265
Cartland, Barbara 75
Carver, Raymond 11
Catullus 77